(continued from front flap)

Section three considers the important social and economic factors. A detailed class analysis is carried out, and refinements of class models of political movements are presented and tested against data from movements in other countries. The resistance of the poor to rising movements, the problems of mobilization of a mass following, and the particularly high susceptibility of youth to new movements, are also considered.

The fourth section starts with a critique and reformulation of the popular theory of mass society that demonstrates the inability of mass analysis to adequately substitute for class analysis.

The final section of the book explores the role of psychological forces. It challenges theories concerning personality factors and examines the mediation hypothesis concerning political alienation.

The book concludes with a final consideration of the Social Credit Party in Quebec that summarizes the findings of the study and projects the prospects of the party for the future.

MAURICE PINARD, Ph.D., The Johns Hopkins University, is Associate Professor of Sociology at McGill University in Montreal, Canada.

THE RISE
OF A THIRD PARTY
A Study
in Crisis Politics

THE RISE
OF A THIRD PARTY

A Study
in Crisis Politics

by

Maurice Pinard

McGILL UNIVERSITY

42752

PRENTICE-HALL, INC., *Englewood Cliffs, New Jersey*

General Sociology Series, Neil J. Smelser, Editor

To Minola

© 1971 by Prentice-Hall, Inc.,
Englewood Cliffs, N. J.

P–13–781278–7
C–13–781286–8

Library of Congress Catalog Card Number: 72–130375
Printed in the United States of America

Current printing (last number):

10 9 8 7 6 5 4 3 2 1

PRENTICE-HALL INTERNATIONAL, INC., *London*
PRENTICE-HALL OF AUSTRALIA, PTY. LTD., *Sydney*
PRENTICE-HALL OF CANADA, LTD., *Toronto*
PRENTICE-HALL OF INDIA PRIVATE LIMITED, *New Delhi*
PRENTICE-HALL OF JAPAN, INC., *Tokyo*

Foreword

In this remarkable monograph, Professor Pinard's initial objective is clear and simple enough: to give a sociological account of why the Social Credit party—an extreme right-wing political party in Canada—which had gained less than one percent of the votes in Quebec's 1958 election, demonstrated an unexpected and unprecedented show of strength by capturing more than one fourth of its electorate in 1962. In pursuing this objective, Professor Pinard refers to standard sociological variables of economic and political strain, the existing avenues of political expression, rural-urban status, age, and the like. The execution of the study, however, reveals a number of features of Professor Pinard's style that make this book a model of sociological research.

In the first place, while the problem selected by Professor Pinard is an empirical and historically specific one, his analysis throughout is *theoretically relevant*. His propositions are traced explicitly to the formulations of Marxist theory, mass society theory, theories of collective behavior, recent theory and research in political sociology, diffusionist theory, and other important branches of thought in sociology.

Second, his analysis is *eclectic* in the best sense of the word. Refusing to rest content with the weak eclectic position that each of these traditions of thought have some general contribution to make to his explanation, Professor Pinard attempts systematically to combine the diversity of variables he brings to bear on third party movements, and to show where received explanations do and do not contribute. Furthermore, when his empirical data so demand, he does not hesitate to reformulate existing explanations of social movements into alternative statements of his own which seem to offer better accounts of his material—for example, his model of the political conditions that are structurally conducive to third party movements in Chapter 4, and his promising attempt to revise mass society theorists' formulations of the role of primary and secondary groups in social movements in Chapter 11.

Third, Professor Pinard is able to make his theoretical positions *empirically relevant*. He is correct in his assertion that the modern techniques of survey research have rarely been brought to bear on the study of various kinds of collective behavior. What is unusual about his research is that he is able to represent a diversity of types of variables ingeniously by reference to the electoral and attitude survey materials available to him. In some places his methods are not beyond criticism—for example, his effort to operationalize the variable of "mobilization" by reference to the social status of the Social Credit candidates in Chapter 7. But in all cases Professor Pinard bravely takes the step that so many are unwilling or unable to take: he attempts to make the qualities of his data correspond to the logic of his general theoretical categories.

Finally, his work displays what might be called *empirical imaginativeness*. Far from limiting his research to a single case study, Professor Pinard moves deftly from one empirical situation to another, examining other, related data that throw light both on the Social Credit movement and on the general propositions he is considering. Note, for example, his examination of the relations between one-party dominance and the rise of a third party at the federal and provincial levels in Chapter 3, and his analysis of political unrest and the third party at the provincial and individual levels in Chapter 5. In the other cases he compares his findings with research on other movements in Canada, the United States, and Europe.

Needless to say, a study which blends so many facets of sociological research cannot fail to provoke. I found myself thinking a lot as I read Professor Pinard's study; and this cannot be said of too many books one reads. In considering his hypotheses that one-party dominance in a two-party system encourages the formation of third parties, for example, I could not help speculating about the recent party history of the United States. Beginning in 1932, the Republican Party suffered twenty years in the role of political opposition at the national level during the Roosevelt and Truman administrations, and was able to come to power in 1952 with Dwight Eisenhower, who was a trans-political figure in many respects, who despite his own popularity, enjoyed Republican Congressional control during only one of the four Congressional terms in his administration. Attempting to run a moderate candidate and failing barely in 1960, and attempting to run an extremist candidate and failing miserably in 1964, the Republican Party seemed to have been starved for a sufficiently long period to drive at least a portion of its adherents toward a third-party mentality. This reasoning is not meant, of course, to account for the whole of the Wallace movement in 1968; it probably also gained much support from traditional

Democrats who felt threatened by various social, political, and racial changes that had been pressed by the Democrats in the 1960's. But Professor Pinard's hypothesis does shed some possible light on why right-wing sentiment took expression in third-party form in 1968.

Another provocative hypothesis concerns the role of the poor in the Social Credit protest in particular, and in social protest in general. What Professor Pinard uncovers is an interesting curvilinear relationship by virtue of which the very poor and the very rich are unlikely to be drawn into protest in the early stages of a movement. He examines a number of psychological and other factors that might account for the observed political apathy of the poor—factors such as lack of hopefulness, worry, low exposure to propaganda, and political alienation. Professor Pinard's data do not permit him to present definitive results on the independent significance of these variables, but his analysis does raise the intriguing question of whether poverty as such or other factors associated with poverty might better account for the apparent political apathy. As better data become available, it will be most fruitful to press this investigation further, looking especially at the level of education and the character of social organization among the poor as possibly key variables that might account for their apparently low level of participation.

I was fascinated by Professor Pinard's discussion of psychological variables in Chapter 12. I suspect that in this chapter he was driven to assume what I consider to be an unduly negative view of the importance of personality variables for two reasons. First, he takes as his main starting points several quite naïve versions of psychological explanation—namely, that psychological variables such as authoritarianism are, in some simple sense, the causal motors of extremist movements. And second, the measures of his psychological variables admittedly left something to be desired, as is often the case with administered survey instruments. I share his skepticism about psychological theories that posit that some personality disposition (usually a psychopathological one) accounts for recruitment into movements. The alternative is not, however, to shun psychological variables, but rather to frame propositions about their role in more subtle ways. In his own exploratory analyses of the poor (Chapter 8) and the young (Chapter 9), Professor Pinard indicates a possible explanatory role of certain psychological variables, though his data do not permit him to discover what kind of independent contribution they might make. I suspect also that psychological variables are determinants of whether or not an individual will conform to, ignore, or react against the perceived pressures from primary groups, occupational associations, and other groups. For example, variables like retreatist alienation and rebellious alienation—suggested by Professor Pinard—may be helpful in accounting not only for an individual's reactions to the symbols of a movement's ideology, but also to the ways he will react to the political behavior of others in his meaningful social *milieux*.

These are only a few of the observations provoked by reading the monograph. If I were to follow my temptation to record the other lines of thought that were stimulated, this foreword would surely run on to objectionable lengths. My temptation does signal to me, however, that Professor Pinard deserves commendation for producing a work that simultaneously throws light on an important case, develops reformulations of several major theoretical traditions, provides methodological leads to the student of collective political behavior, and stimulates so many questions and suggestions in the mind of the reader.

NEIL J. SMELSER
University of California at Berkeley

Preface

The sudden upsurge of a new political movement usually raises many perplexing questions in the mind of the political analyst. I experienced this situation when faced with the unanticipated rise of the Social Credit party in Quebec, in the 1962 federal election.

I was about to begin a study of a forthcoming provincial election, when the party had its remarkable success at the polls. Subsequently, I decided not to miss an excellent opportunity to apply modern techniques of survey research to the study of this sudden success of a new political movement—something which has rarely been done before.

This book thus presents an analysis, based primarily on survey data, but also on other sources, of the political, economic, social, and psychological forces which accounted for the emergence of Social Credit in Quebec. But its main purposes are neither descriptive nor historical. The analysis is primarily concerned with the rise of Social Credit to the extent that it permits the development and testing of general hypotheses concerning the rise of new political movements.

Thus, after a brief introduction which presents some background information on Social Credit, the study moves immediately in its second section to an exploration of the political factors underlying voters' change to a new party. The findings lead to the development of a theoretical model which takes into consideration the prior state of the party system, and the model is then tested against data on other third party movements in Canada since the beginning of this century. The third section considers the most important social and economic factors. A detailed class analysis is carried out, and refinements of class models of political movements are presented and tested, often against data from other movements which have appeared on this continent or abroad. This is particularly true in the analysis of the resistance of the poor to rising movements. General problems of mobilization of a mass following and the particularly high susceptibility of youth to new movements are also considered in the light of general explanatory schemes.

The fourth section starts with a critique and a reformulation of the popular theory of mass society, and then proceeds to a test of the new model. It will become clear that mass analysis is no substitute for class analysis. The role of psychological forces constitutes the focus of a fifth section. In particular, we challenge some theories concerning personality factors and empirically examine the so-called mediation hypothesis concerning political alienation.

It is my hope that such a theoretical approach will carry us closer toward a better understanding of crisis politics in general and of protest movements in particular.

I have relied heavily on the understanding collaboration of a large number of people, to whom I would like to convey my deep sentiments of sincere appreciation:

My most immediate debt is to James Coleman, Arthur Stinchcombe, and Donald Von Eschen, who have encouraged me throughout and who have inspired many of the themes of this study, the first two through lectures and all three through discussions at The Johns Hopkins University; their extensive comments and insightful suggestions on earlier drafts have made possible substantial improvements of the present text.

Without however, the existence of the Social Research Group in Montreal, this study would probably never have been even started. And without the support of some of its members, it would certainly not be what it is. Albert Breton, Raymond Breton, and the late Howard Roseborough deserve a special mention: all three of them freely took added duties to permit me to spend more time on this study. But I am also grateful to those who were then full-time members of the Social Research Group, in particular, Jean-Pierre Alix, Rodrigue Johnson, Pierre Laporte, Guy Lecavalier, and Serge Rousseau. The latter, in particular, assisted me in all the data gathering phases of the project and wrote the preliminary draft of a report of this study.

Many of the ideas developed here were first elaborated in a study of the sit-in movement in Maryland, which was conducted jointly by Jerome Kirk, Donald Von Eschen and myself. Each of them contributed a great deal to these ideas and though it is often no longer possible to differentiate between what were their, and what were my insights, it is certain that they deserve a large part of the credits for some of the original points of this study.

I am also indebted to Claude Ducharme and Maurice Sauvé, both of whom were at the time with the Quebec Liberal party organization, which sponsored the original study. As laymen, they showed a great understanding of the concerns and interests of academic social scientists. Needless to say, if they had so wished they could have prevented me from giving to the original project the scope which permitted me to engage in the present study.

Many people have at one point or another commented on at least parts of earlier drafts. In particular, the encouragements and support of Neil Smelser during the last phase of the study were most stimulating. I am also pleased to mention particularly Albert Breton, Raymond Breton, Terry Copp, Frank Jones, Jerome Kirk, Pierre Laporte, Vincent Lemieux, John Porter, Peter Regenstreif, the late Howard Roseborough, Mildred Schwartz, Sanford Silverstein, Michael Stein, Charles Tilly, and Dennis Wrong.

To the central organizer of the Progressive Conservative party, who answered a short questionnaire on his party, but had been promised anonymity, I express my gratitude. To Jean-Paul Schuller, who acted as my research assistant during one summer and, in particular, collected and tabulated the data on the candidates analysed in Chapter 7, I also acknowledge my indebtedness.

The Department of Social Relations at the Johns Hopkins University, as well as the Department of Sociology and the Faculty of Graduate Studies and Research at McGill University were most helpful in providing me with some assistance, financial and otherwise, for certain parts of the study. Many members of the personnel at the Computing Centres of both universities were also most helpful for the analysis of the data.

While at The Johns Hopkins University, I was awarded Canada Council Fellowships in both the academic years 1960–61 and 1961–62; moreover, in 1962–63, I obtained a Hopkins Woodrow Wilson Fellowship which permitted me to concentrate on this project.

A very special debt is owed to the anonymous respondents who provided us with our most precious material and to the many interviewers who collected these data.

To the many secretaries who worked hard to decipher my tortuous drafts, I am greatly indebted: in particular, Denise Dionne, Lily Liquornik, Evelyn Weinreb, Jeanette Wilson and Doris Brosllury; all showed great patience in typing and retyping the many drafts of the manuscript.

Acknowledgements also go to Professor Carl J. Couch for permission to use unpublished data, and to The University of Toronto Press, The Society for the Study of Social Problems and The University of Chicago Press for rights to reprint materials from *The Canadian Journal of Economics and Political Science*, *Social Problems*, and *The American Journal of Sociology*.

This book has been published with the help of a grant from the Social Science Research Council of Canada, using funds provided by the Canada Council, and we are grateful to them.

I offer my thanks and appreciation to the editorial staff of Prentice-Hall and in particular, to Mrs Helen S. Harris, Production Editor. Her enthusiastic dedication to this task was most rewarding.

Finally, I created a debt of gratitude of a very special kind toward the one person who shared more than anyone the tribulations accompanying the production of such a piece of work. To Minola, my wife, my affectionate thankfulness.

MAURICE PINARD

Montreal,
June 1970.

Contents

Tables

THE RISE
OF A THIRD PARTY

A Study
in Crisis Politics

I

INTRODUCTION

The
Background
of the
Movement

CHAPTER ONE

Election results in democratic nations often create no surprises at all or only mild ones. True, every now and then one witnesses the unforeseen upset of an incumbent party. But such a surprise is scarcely comparable to the astonishment created when a new political movement, which almost no observer was taking seriously, suddenly erupts as a political force to be reckoned with. This is what happened in 1930 in Germany, with the success of the Nazi movement at the polls, "to the surprise of everybody, including the party leaders."[1] This is what happened in France in 1956, with the sudden success of *L'Union de Défense des Commerçants et Artisans* (UDCA) or Poujadist movement, which was "a surprise for most observers."[2] This is also what happened in one province of Canada, Quebec, in the 1962 Canadian federal election, with the unforeseen success of Réal Caouette's *Ralliement des Créditistes*, the federal branch of the Social Credit party in that province.

In the last instance, again to the surprise of most political observers,[3] the So-

---

[1] The party, which obtained 18.3 percent of the votes in 1930, had drawn only 2.6 percent of the votes in the 1928 election; on these data and the element of surprise, see Theodore Abel, *The Nazi Movement: Why Hitler Came to Power* (New York: Atheling Book, Atherton Press, 1966), pp. 91–93.

[2] The party, which was running for the first time, got 11.7 percent of the votes; computed from François Goguel, "Géographie des élections du 2 janvier," in Maurice Duverger *et al.*, eds., *Les élections du 2 janvier 1956* (Paris: Librairie A. Colin, 1957), p. 470; on the element of surprise, see Maurice Duverger, *ibid.*, p. xv.

[3] Peter Regenstreif, who had polled the province, was a rare exception. For his pre-election forecast, which gave at least 20 seats to Social Credit, see his *The Diefenbaker Interlude: Parties and Voting in Canada* (Toronto: Longmans Canada Ltd., 1965), p. xi. On the element of surprise and the reactions of the candidates and the mass media to the results of the election, see Léon Dion, "The Election in the Province of Quebec," in John Meisel, ed., *Papers on the 1962 Election* (Toronto: University of Toronto Press, 1964), pp. 109–128, esp. pp. 121ff.

cial Credit party[4] obtained 25.9 percent of the votes in the province of Quebec, as against 39.2 and 29.6 percent for the two traditional parties, the Liberals and the Progressive Conservatives respectively, and took 26 of the 75 Quebec seats in the federal Parliament. If one considers that this party had obtained no seat and less than 1 percent of the votes in Quebec in the preceding election,[5] the feat was indeed astonishing. In fact, the 1962 federal election marked the first time that a genuine third party had met with such a success in Quebec; never before had a third party obtained more than 15 percent of the vote and 5 percent of the seats in a federal or provincial election.[6]

The sudden rise of the Social Credit movement is the main concern of this study. Before presenting the theoretical orientations adopted in the study, it may be useful to describe briefly the context within which the Social Credit party arose and some historical background of this movement.

THE SOCIAL
AND
POLITICAL CONTEXT

The Social Credit upsurge of 1962 took place in a context of political instability and widespread social unrest. First, particularly long and stable administrations had recently come to an end in both Ottawa and Quebec. A few years earlier, in 1957, the country had broken loose from twenty-two years of Liberal administration in Ottawa by electing Diefenbaker's Progressive Conservatives, though short of Quebec's support. The Conservatives[7] came to power as a minority government and forced the electorate to return to the polls a year later to obtain a more decisive mandate, which was unambiguously given (in fact, it was the most decisive mandate given by the Canadian electorate since Canada's Confederation). The 1962 election marked the end of the first full term of the Conservatives in office since their 1930–1935 term, and they were then returned to power, but again only as a minority government.

In Quebec, the provincial Liberals had put an end in 1960 to sixteen years of *Union Nationale* (Quebec's alternative to the Conservative party) provincial administration. Under the strong conservative leadership of Maurice Duplessis, the *Union Nationale* had totally dominated Quebec politics for nineteen of the previous twenty-four years. The relative stagnation of Duplessis' reign was

[4] This is the name that was commonly used to refer even to the Quebec wing of the party prior to the 1963 schism and that we shall use throughout. (On the schism, see Chap. 13.)

[5] See Table 1.1.

[6] See Michael B. Stein, *The Dynamics of Political Protest: Social Credit in Quebec* (Toronto: University of Toronto Press, 1971), Chap. 1.

[7] At the 1942 convention, the name of the Conservative party was changed to that of the Progressive Conservative party. Henceforth, following traditional usage, the first name will generally be used. For a brief and recent introduction to Canada's parliamentary and party systems, see Allan Kornberg, *Canadian Legislative Behavior: A Study of the 25th Parliament* (New York: Holt, Rinehart & Winston, Inc., 1967), Chap. 2.

being followed by politically induced modernization at an unusually rapid pace. Engaged in these changes (which a "new" *Union Nationale* had in part initiated after Duplessis' death in 1959), the Liberals were to ask for a new electoral mandate a few months after the 1962 federal election and two years ahead of time, in order to obtain a sanction of their policy of nationalization of electric companies.

These changes—Quebec's so-called "Quiet Revolution"—were accompanied by widespread social unrest. A rejuvenation of nationalist forces in French Canada had led to particularly strong recriminations against English Canada and to the re-emergence of French-Canadian separatist movements. Often linked to the latter as well as between themselves, there were other movements in Quebec, especially among the well-educated youth and the students. More important among them were the movement to obtain a neutral school system, socialist groups of different tendencies, and pacifist groups.

The sources of this unrest laid at least in part in the economic situation. Since the late fifties, Canada like the rest of North America had been in the throes of a serious economic recession, and Quebec was particularly hard hit by its effects. The effects of the recession will be detailed later, but as a first indication of its seriousness, unemployment in that period affected as many as fifty percent of the family heads in some small communities during the course of one year.

In short, the long post World War II period of social and political stability and of economic progress had at least temporarily subsided in Canada and particularly in Quebec. The times were propitious for the appearance of a protest movement on the political scene.

SOCIAL CREDIT
IN CANADA

The Social Credit movement was never much of a political success in England, the country in which the doctrine was formulated in the early twenties by a mechanical engineer, Major C. H. Douglas. The reasons for this will not be considered here, though immediate factors seem to have been Douglas's lack of interest and talent for political action and the rudimentary means he developed when he finally decided to engage in it.[8]

But if the Social Credit movement failed to flourish in England, it soon took firm root in the Canadian soil.[9] Its success was especially rapid in one Canadian province, Alberta.[10] The Douglas doctrine was first propagated in that province

[8] For a short history, see C. B. Macpherson, *Democracy in Alberta: Social Credit and the Party System*, 2nd ed. (Toronto: University of Toronto Press, 1962), Chap. 5.

[9] The movement has also had some measure of success in other countries; as recently as 1966, it ran a full slate of candidates in the New Zealand general election and obtained 15 percent of the votes and one seat.

[10] For a detailed account of the growth of the Social Credit movement in Alberta, see John A. Irving, *The Social Credit Movement in Alberta* (Toronto: University of Toronto Press, 1959). For short notes, see Macpherson, *Democracy in Alberta*, Chap. 6. The present account follows both.

through the United Farmers of Alberta, who were the party in power at the provincial level from 1922 to 1935. Yet despite many efforts, the U.F.A. finally refused to make it a part of their platform.

Douglas's ideas, however, had already found in William Aberhart the man who was to become their first great propagator in Canada. A high school teacher and a lay preacher, Aberhart had developed a very large religious following in Alberta and Saskatchewan. Literally converted to the doctrine overnight, in the early summer of 1932, by reading a book presenting Douglas's ideas, Aberhart immediately started to disseminate his new beliefs through his Calgary Prophetic Bible Institute and his weekly Sunday radio broadcasts, which had begun in 1926. Like their leader, his religious following quickly found in social credit a solution to the great economic problems of the Depression.

Though at first Aberhart was opposed to political action, the many social credit study groups that he created were mushrooming throughout Alberta. They soon became restive, and the developing movement rapidly engaged in action; so fast, in fact, that in the provincial election of 1935, the movement found itself with candidates in all constituencies of the province. By election night, still without a party leader because Aberhart had refused to run, the group had been mandated by 54 percent of the voters and held 56 of the 63 seats in the provincial legislature. The incumbent U.F.A. party was actually left without a single seat, though it had presented 45 candidates. This is indeed another example of the astonishing upsurge—in this instance, directly into power—of a recently born movement.

Social Credit soon became a political force in federal politics and in some other provinces of Canada as well. The movement sent 17 deputies to the federal Parliament—15 from Alberta and 2 from Saskatchewan—two months after its success in Alberta. Provincial branches developed in many provinces, and it gradually gained ground in western Canada, particularly in British Columbia, where it came to power in 1952.[11]

SOCIAL CREDIT
IN QUEBEC

Quebec was not long to follow suit.[12] Spurred by the disastrous conditions of the Depression, as well as by the success of the movement in Alberta, three discoverers of the doctrine in Quebec, Louis Even, Armand Turpin, and Louis

11 The characteristics of the Social Credit party in British Columbia are well described in Martin Robin, "The Social Basis of Party Politics in British Columbia," in H. G. Thorburn, ed., *Party Politics in Canada*, 2nd ed. (Scarborough, Ont.: Prentice-Hall of Canada, Ltd., 1967), pp. 201-211.

12 The only detailed historical accounts of the Social Credit movement in Quebec are Michael B. Stein, *The Dynamics of Political Protest: Social Credit in Quebec*, and "The Structure and Function of the Finance of the Ralliemert des Créditistes," in Committee on Election Expenses, *Studies in Canadian Party Finance* (Ottawa: Queen's Printer, 1966), pp. 405-457; our presentation closely follows Stein's.

Dugal, started an organization in Quebec. In May 1936, they founded *La Ligue du Crédit Social de la Province de Québec*, and Louis Even initiated the publication of *Cahiers du Crédit Social* the same year, on an irregular basis. The *Cahiers* were to provide a link to the local study groups which, following the Alberta pattern, were being created throughout the province. The movement grew fast enough for the *Ligue* to hold its first provincial convention in 1938. In fact, according to Stein, "the years 1937 and 1938 marked the period of greatest success in the *Ligue's* history," particularly among farmers and workers.

Gilberte Côté (now Mrs. Côté-Mercier) who with Louis Even, was to become one of the movement's two most influential leaders, joined the *Ligue* at that time. Together, they created a bimonthly newspaper, *Vers Demain*, in the fall of 1939. This newspaper became the movement's primary source of mass propaganda for years to come, and with the support of an Institute of Political Action acting as the political arm of the journal, the latter soon reached a very large number of people. Indeed, in 1942, the paper allegedly reached 35,000 subscribers, and at its height in 1948, Stein reports it had a circulation of 65,000.

However, this early enthusiasm was not sufficient to engender a successful political movement. The Ligue ran two candidates in the 1940 federal election, and both lost the election. After this setback, the editors of *Vers Demain* turned primarily to political education and severed their association with the *Ligue*, which thereafter almost disintegrated. But they did not give up political action altogether. In 1944, they declared the subscribers of *Vers Demain* united into a *Union of Social Credit Electors*. True to social credit doctrine, which was opposed to the creation of a political party, the Union was supposed to be some kind of political pressure group working toward social credit objectives, but in ways different from those of ordinary political parties. In particular, its elected representatives were supposed to take their directives from the people, not from a party leadership.

In the same year, the Union joined with other provincial Social Credit groups in the formation of the Social Credit Association of Canada, and in the 1945 and 1949 federal elections, it participated heavily by presenting 43 and 50 candidates, respectively. The Union refused to present a program in the first election, since this was identified with traditional parties; they simply asked the voters to approve a few basic principles of the social credit doctrine and promised that elected representatives would come back to the people for important decisions.[13] Both efforts met with dismal failure; the party obtained no seats and only 4.5 and 5.1 percent of the votes in each election, respectively.[14] No other serious

---

[13] Shortly after the 1945 defeat, the movement shifted its political action and decided that it would work toward the election of a "parliament of electors," composed of "mandators"; the group changed its name to the *Union des Electeurs*.

[14] The Quebec branch of the movement had only once gained a seat in federal Parliament, when Réal Caouette was elected in a by-election for the district of Pontiac in 1946.

Table 1.1

Social Credit Efforts in Quebec Federal Politics
1940–1958*

	ELECTIONS					
	1940	1945	1949	1953	1957	1958
Number of Candidates**	2	43	50	—	4	15
Seats Won	—	—	—	—	—	—
Votes Obtained (%)	0.9	4.5	5.1	—	0.2	0.6

*Data from Howard A. Scarrow, *Canada Votes.*
**The total number of candidates possible runs from 65 in 1945, 73 in 1949 to 75 for the rest of the period.

efforts were to be made in' subsequent federal elections until 1962 (see Table 1.1). In fact, the Union decided to withdraw completely from electoral politics, and the few candidates who ran in 1957 and 1958 did so under the sponsorship of the national movement, and against the will of the Union.

But during the forties, the Union of Electors had also tried to make some inroads in provincial politics. After a modest and fruitless effort in the 1944 provincial election, in which it presented only twelve candidates, the movement presented a full slate of candidates in the provincial election of 1948. The results were slightly better than at the federal level, since the group obtained 9.3 percent of the votes (though with a complete slate this time). But again, it could not secure a single seat;[15] all its major candidates lost their deposits.

As we have just mentioned, the failure of the movement in the federal election of the following year, 1949, really ended its active involvement in electoral politics until the creation of the *Ralliement des Créditistes.* Indeed, the period of the fifties saw a decline of the Union of Electors, which henceforth limited its action to educational and pressure group activities, in line with the movement's doctrine. The movement is still in existence today, although it is reduced to only a few hundred members.[16]

These meagre electoral results, however, should not be taken too lightly. The movement continued publishing its newspaper, *Vers Demain,* and it had many groups of very dedicated militants who were making every effort to spread its ideas and to act as pressure groups. Moreover, during the forties, the party obtained relatively large proportions of the votes in some constituencies, and these turned out to be areas of Social Credit strength in 1962.[17] It seems, therefore, that the early proselytism of the Social Credit movement laid the base for its later victories.

15 Data from Howard A. Scarrow, *Canada Votes: A Handbook of Federal and Provincial Election Data* (New Orleans: The Hauser Press, 1962), pp. 208–210.
16 Stein, "The Structure and Function," pp. 422–423. The religious activities of the movement are now their major concern.
17 See Vincent Lemieux, "Les dimensions sociologiques du vote créditiste au Québec," *Recherches Sociographiques,* VI (1965), pp. 181–182; see also Chap. 7 below.

LE RALLIEMENT
DES CRÉDITISTES

The Social Credit success story of 1962 really began in 1957, when a group of alienated members of the Union of Electors, who disagreed with the increasingly religious orientation of the movement and its lack of involvement in electoral politics, formed a parallel organization. After a series of meetings during the summer of 1957, they decided to create a group which would organize for electoral politics but still maintain some link to the older organization. However, it proved impossible to achieve such an arrangement, and the new group soon broke completely with the Union and established an independent organization, the *Ralliement des Créditistes du Québec*. Its formation was officially announced on June 4, 1958, a few days after the federal election.[18]

The main founders of the movement were all old *Créditistes*, and the three most important figures were Réal Caouette, who was to become the strong man and charismatic leader of the new party, Laurent Legault, the prime organizer of the movement during the forties and again in 1962, and Gilles Grégoire, who was to be the secondary leader until he broke from the party in 1966 to engage in provincial politics. *The Ralliement* met no great difficulty in enlisting the support of many other prominent former *Créditistes* and soon succeeded in attracting a number of more prestigious new recruits.

The break from the old movement, however, meant that the new party was left without a formal organization and a large membership, and without the very influential mean of communications provided by *Vers Demain*. On the other hand, it could now readily rely on the large pool of sympathetic followers of the movement throughout the province. And, of course, it was easier to create a new organization to mobilize this potential membership than to have to recruit a completely new following.

From the start, the new party's main propaganda medium was television. Due to the very high cost of television, its use was first limited to a few areas, but it met with such success that coverage was gradually extended to wider and wider areas. As will be seen later,[19] the use of television proved eminently effective. The movement backed this activity by the creation of its own monthly newspaper, *Regards*, and the formal recruitment of members, whose one-dollar-a-month subscriptions were supposed to defray the cost of television. Meanwhile, the main leaders of the party were touring the province to help organize the movement locally.

At the local level they established "cells" on the basis of the following of the former movement. The cells in turn were charged with the responsibility of

---

18 The historical details of this and subsequent paragraphs closely follow from Stein, *The Dynamics of Political Protest*, and from Richard Daigneault, "Un portrait politique: Réal Caouette," *La Presse* (Montreal), August 25, 1962.

19 See Chap. 7.

local recruitment and the sale of membership cards to finance the TV appear-
ances of the leaders (particularly Caouette) in their region.

The new Quebec group allied itself with the National Social Credit League
in 1960, and the actual organizational work for the 1962 federal campaign
began after the national leadership convention of 1961, at which Robert Thompson closely defeated Caouette as national leader of the party. This convention
was followed by a provincial convention in Hull, where the strategy for the
Quebec campaign was defined.

The television programs, which already reached the Rouyn-Noranda,
Saguenay-Lake St. John, Quebec, and Sherbrooke areas, were now extended
to cover the Lower St. Lawrence region. At the constituency level, the typical
cadres of the party were supposed to consist of an organizer-in-chief, section
organizers for at least every ten polls, and an organizer for every hundred votes
necessary to win, that is, about one by poll, and, finally, assistants to the poll
organizer. A first meeting of the organizer-in-chief and the section organizers
was to lay the ground for the recruitment of the poll organizers within a month.
The organizers were then to meet together, subscribe membership cards, and
prepare for a third meeting for the choice of the constituency's candidate.[20]

This organizational preparation seems to have run rather smoothly since, on
election day, the Quebec electorate was presented with a full slate of Social
Credit candidates. They had appealed to the discontented with simple promises
that their party could solve the problems they were facing. As we have seen
before, the results were astounding. Many voters had indeed agreed with the
party's simplistic slogan: "You have nothing to lose."

THE PHILOSOPHY
OF SOCIAL CREDIT

As mentioned, the social credit doctrine originated in England in the early
twenties, with a mechanical engineer, Major C. H. Douglas.[21] Succinctly
stated, "the gist of the social credit theory was that modern technology had
made possible an era of great plenty and leisure both of which could and should
be distributed throughout the community as unearned income, and that this
could be done by some comparatively simple monetary devices which would
not interfere with the structure of ownership and private enterprise."[22] Proposals
for monetary reforms were therefore a fundamental part of the doctrine.

However, the doctrine rested on a basic fallacy stemming from the ambig-

[20] From *Le Ralliement des Créditistes*, "Plan d'organisation pour l'année 1961–1962", (dittoed,
n.d., n.p.)

[21] For a detailed account of the Social Credit doctrine, the reader is referred to Macpherson,
Democracy in Alberta. For the ideology of the movement in Quebec, see Stein, *The Dynamics of Political Protest*.

[22] Macpherson, *Democracy in Alberta*, p. 94. What follows here is based on Macpherson's detailed
presentation and discussion.

uous statement that total money incomes were not sufficient to buy all that was produced. This was stated in the well-known and simplistic "A plus B theorem," which can be briefly summarized: Since "all payments made to individuals (wages, salaries, and dividends)" (A) and "all payments made to other organizations (raw materials, bank charges, and other external costs)" (B) "go into prices, the rate of flow of prices cannot be less than A plus B." But "the rate of flow of purchasing-power to individuals is represented by A" only, and obviously, "A will not purchase A plus B."[23] Hence the necessity to create money to distribute as social credit dividends to consumers to cover B, or as subsidies to producers to permit them to fix prices at A.

These simple ideas, which we shall not try to disprove here,[24] are the basis for the monetary reforms proposed by the party in Canada since the thirties, reforms which seem to have had so much success with the voters in times of crisis, particularly in the lower classes. As Guindon puts it, "to set off the printing presses is an alarming idea for those who have money because of its inflationary effect, for those who do not have money, it becomes a pleasant dream. . . . And when believed in, it becomes a political force."[25]

The promise to distribute dividends to people had long been part of the Social Credit platform in Quebec, though Caouette seems to have been cautious on the subject during the 1962 campaign. Most often in his speeches,[26] he cut short of this specific proposal; he stressed only the need for the creation of more money, and the need for increasing every consumer's purchasing power.[27] However, given the previous propaganda of the party on dividends to consumers, it was certainly natural for the voters to expect some such distribution. Indeed, they would have been right in so doing, since a post-election article for a Montreal newspaper, written by Caouette and Gilles Grégoire, attests that the idea of dividends to consumers was still part of the party's platform.[28]

But social credit is not merely a system of monetary reform. It also provides the ideological adherent with a well-developed conservative social and political philosophy. Many aspects of this philosophy will be dealt with later,[29] but an overall description may be helpful at this point.[30] The core of the philosophy, which places the Social Credit party on the extreme right of the political spec-

23 C. H. Douglas, *Credit-Power and Democracy*, quoted from Macpherson, *Democracy in Alberta*, p. 108.

24 On this, see Macpherson, *Democracy in Alberta*, pp. 109ff.

25 Hubert Guindon, "Social Unrest, Social Class and Quebec's Bureaucratic Revolution," *Queen's Quarterly*, 71 (1964), p. 161.

26 Those we know of at least; it may have been different in his other speeches, or in those of the secondary leaders and candidates.

27 One of the means often proposed was the reduction of taxes; see *Réal Caouette Vous Parle* (Montréal: Les Editions du Carrousel, n.d.), *passim*. (This book is a collection of some of Caouette's speeches during the 1962 campaign, and it also includes a post-election interview and a post-election newspaper article.)

28 *Ibid.*, p. 93. See also the post-election interview, p. 82.

29 See in particular Chap. 12.

30 For a detailed study of this aspect of the doctrine, see again Macpherson's excellent presentation and discussion, *Democrocy in Alberta*. For Quebec, see Stein, *The Dynamics of Political Protest*.

trum, consists in a strong opposition to many of the basic trends of modern industrial societies. The doctrine is opposed to the growing centralization and bureaucratization of society, and to the concentration of power, whether in government, business, or labor organizations. All such concentration is seen as a basic threat to individual freedom, liberty, and democracy.

Restoration of these values is the movement's ultimate objective. The whole monetary reform is but one element, though a crucial one, in this effort. Since the institutions of private property and of private management of industry and agriculture are essential to the preservation of liberty and democracy, the movement is strongly opposed to socialism and to any form of public ownership. The ills of capitalist society, according to the doctrine, cannot be traced to the system of private ownership, but to the control of the financiers over the economic system, and to their restriction of credit and production. The financiers—and then the Jews—could, therefore, easily become the scapegoats of the movement.

Finally, the original doctrine claimed that the democratic system had also been corrupted: the real will of the people was denied its true expression and political parties, far from promoting the expression of this true will, were contributing to its diversion. The solution proposed was to abandon the party system altogether, and to return to a true democracy, where "the electorate would be consulted only as to ultimate objectives, while the choice of methods and the power to put methods into effect would be left to experts, subject to the people's right to have the experts removed if they failed to produce the desired results."[31]

The Canadian Social Credit movement was deeply influenced by these ideas of Major Douglas, in spite of its failure to implement the political reforms he propounded. Although at the beginning great stress was placed on the proposals for economic reform, so that in the thirties the Alberta movement looked very much like a radical reform movement, Social Credit has become in that province, as well as in British Columbia, one of Canada's most conservative parties. In Quebec, from its origin, the movement exhibited a very conservative orientation. At least until Caouette created his party, the movement adopted a purist stance toward Douglas's doctrine and manifested orthodoxy in its social and political ideas as well as in economic doctrine.[32]

The social ideas of the early Quebec movement stressed the development of the human person and to that end, it espoused the program of corporatism. It was equally opposed to communism and collectivism, and to the present system of capitalism, and generally claimed to be inspired by the teachings of the Catholic Church. Politically, the movement adopted the general lines of the

[31] Macpherson, *Democracy in Alberta*, p. 135.
[32] See Stein, *The Dynamics of Political Protest*, Chap. 2. The following paragraph also follows from this source. On the ideological orientations of MP's elected in 1962, and in particular Social Credit MP's, see Kornberg, *Canadian Legislative Behavior*, pp. 121–126.

doctrine, that is, opposition to party politics and restoration of a true democracy under the guidance of experts. The only genuine proposals added were the corporatist idea of an upper chamber organized along occupational lines, and a general emphasis on nationalism, which brought the Quebec movement to clash with the movement elsewhere in Canada.

A reading of Caouette's speeches during the 1962 campaign clearly establishes that he was also a most orthodox follower of the general philosophy of the movement, if not of its specific political proposals. Although he was ready to form a political party and accept the existing political system, he was a faithful disciple in the social and economic realms. Time and again in his orations, he emphasized the values of individual liberty and free enterprise. This was often accompanied by strong condemnations of the arch enemies, socialism and communism (or, as he put it, "communistic socialism"), and by disapproval of government control and planning, and of economic concentration.[33]

Yet somewhat like the successful Albertan movement of the thirties, the core of Caouette's appeals tended to focus on the need for economic reform, with the blanket assertion that his movement's platform for monetary reform could solve the serious economic ills affecting so many Quebecers. Unemployment, high taxes, inflations and recessions, and a weak purchasing power generally were presented as the natural ills of the present system, which could easily be eliminated if only the Social Credit platform were implemented. To accomplish this, the people had also to give up the traditional parties, whose traditional solutions had failed to work. Caouette's basic appeals were always simple and ran like this:

> You have nothing to lose, try Social Credit. You have tried the Liberals for years, you have already given the Conservatives four years, the results are the same. If you take the two organizations, the two political parties, put them in the same pocket, the first which emerges from the pocket is exactly the same as the one which remains in the bottom of the pocket.... Try Social Credit once to see what results you can get from it.... Social Credit will do harm to no one....[34]

The movement was thus characteristically appealing to the protest dispositions of large segments of the electorate, in a truly populistic tradition; like Poujadism,[35] it constituted a right-wing protest movement offering an outlet for the resentment of those who were affected by economic adversity.

33 See *Réal Caouette Vous Parle*, passim. On the basis of written evidence, it seems that the anti-Semitic streaks of the movement were not apparent during the 1962 campaign, though during the 1965 campaign, Caouette was infuriated by Peter Regenstreif's forecasts and referred to him as "this good French Canadian, probably born in Jerusalem...." See *La Presse* (Montreal), Oct. 19, 1965.

34 *Réal Caouette Vous Parle*, p. 35. The English translation follows Ronald I. Cohen, *Quebec Votes: The How and Why of Quebec Voting in Every Federal Election Since Confederation* (Montreal: Saje Publications, 1965), p. 98.

35 See Donald V. Smiley, "Canada's Poujadists: A New Look at Social Credit," *Canadian Forum*, 42 (Sept., 1962), pp. 121–123.

THE STUDY
AND ITS METHODS

As mentioned above, we are interested both in uncovering the set of forces which accounted for the sudden upsurge of this political movement, and in developing, at a more analytical level, a set of hypotheses about the rise of political movements in general. To this end, we will frequently embark into analyses of other political movements, insofar as these appear useful to better establish some general propositions.

It should be pointed out that this study is not a descriptive account of an electoral campaign and its aftermath, in the tradition of the Nuffield studies in England.[36] Our research methods are basically different. The bulk of our data stems from a sample survey carried out during the autumn of 1962, a few months after the June 18 federal election. Conducted by the Social Research Group, it took place just prior to the November 14 provincial election, in anticipation of which it was sponsored. But given our interest in the previous federal election, a subset of questions pertaining to that election were added to the rest of the questionnaire. From this survey, 998 structured interviews of slightly more than an hour were obtained from a multi-stage stratified cluster sample.[37] The multivariate analysis of these data constitutes the core of this study, though it is often complemented by the analysis of electoral statistics and census data, and at one point, by the analysis of the candidates' social background and the impact it had on the election.

This study marks the first time in Canada that sample survey tools were used to analyze a federal election at the level of at least a province. Moreover, though similar studies have been conducted in other countries for many years, particularly in the United States and England, these have always been deficient in respect to the analysis of political change in detail, since the samples obtained always yielded too few party changers to permit such an analysis. In the present instance, the entire study can be considered as a detailed analysis of political change, since, for all practical purposes, all those who voted Social Credit in the 1962 election had not been supporters of this party in the previous election.[38] To be sure, the study is not a perfect substitute in this regard, because the "political movement" type of upsurge we shall examine requires a different kind of analysis than political change between traditional parties. Nevertheless, it is hoped that it will prove useful as the first study of its kind.

---

[36] A first Canadian study in this tradition is John Meisel, *The Canadian General Election of 1957* (Toronto: University of Toronto Press, 1962).

[37] The sample design is described in detail in Appendix A and the relevant parts of the questionnaire are presented in Appendix B.

[38] Recall that the party had obtained less than 1 percent of the votes in 1958.

THE FRAME
OF REFERENCE

The study lies at the crossroads of two major fields in sociology, the field of collective behavior and social movements and the field of political sociology.

The study owes much to the techniques used and the insights gained in voting behavior research in the United States as well as abroad. As stated above, both the techniques of survey research and those of ecological analysis, so intensively used in this field, are major tools in our study. Substantively, much of our questionnaire was inspired by researchers in voting behavior, and as will be seen throughout, the analysis often follows paths first opened through their studies.

But if this study is formally very similar to previous voting studies, it should be stressed that it draws much more heavily on past studies and theories in the field of collective behavior and, in particular, social movements.[39]

The basic theoretical perspective which appeared increasingly useful in our analysis is that of Smelser.[40] In particular, we think that his value-added scheme, with its unique combination of determinants, constitutes a very important contribution to the field. Smelser argues that there are six important determinants for any episode of collective behavior, and that their unique combination is a necessary and sufficient condition for a specific type of collective behavior. Briefly, these determinants are: *structural conduciveness*, i.e., the set of conditions which permit or encourage an episode of collective behavior; *structural strain*, i.e., the impairments in social conditions which lead to social unrest; a *generalized belief*, which identifies the sources of strain and proposes certain responses; *precipitating factors; mobilization of the participants for action*, and especially the behavior of the leaders; and finally, the operation of *social control*, which arches over the other determinants and constitutes the counter-determinant aspect of any episode of collective behavior.[41] Our analysis is largely organized around this set of determinants, as the table of contents already suggests. In Chapter 13, we shall return to this theoretical scheme for a more general appraisal.

It should be added that the study also derived many of its specific hypotheses from the work of Lipset, particularly from his study of the rise of the C.C.F. party in Saskatchewan and from *Political Man*.[42] This is especially true of Chapter 8, which deals with the response of the poor.

[39] Though the methodology we used has rarely been employed in the study of political movements.

[40] Neil J. Smelser, *Theory of Collective Behavior* (New York: The Free Press of Glencoe, Inc., 1963).

[41] Smelser, *Theory of Collective Behavior*, pp. 12–21.

[42] S. M. Lipset, *Agrarian Socialism: The Cooperative Commonwealth Federation in Saskatchewan* (Berkeley, Calif.: University of California Press, 1950), and *Political Man: The Social Bases of Politics* (Garden City, N.Y.: Doubleday & Company, Inc. 1960).

Before proceeding to the analysis, a few additional comments are in order. First, some remarks are necessary about the basic dependent variable of the study, that is, whether or not people voted Social Credit in the 1962 federal election. The data were obtained from the following questions:

At the last federal election, last June, in which Mr. Diefenbaker's government was reelected, did you vote or not?

(If yes) Did you vote for the Progressive Conservative candidate, the Liberal candidate, the Social Credit candidate, or the New Democratic Party (CCF) candidate?[43]

The distribution of the answers to these questions is presented in Table 1.2.

Table 1.2

The Survey and Actual Distribution of Party Preferences, 1962

	% OF TOTAL SAMPLE	% OF THOSE REVEALING PREFERENCE	% OF ACTUAL VOTE IN QUEBEC*
Social Credit	14	22	25.9
Progressive Conservative	19	30	29.6
Liberal	29	46	39.2
New Democratic Party**	1	2	4.4
Others	—	—	0.9
N		(630)	100.0
Don't know	2		
Won't answer	19		
Did not vote	14		22.4**
No answer	1		
N	(998)		

*Source: see Table 13.1, p. 251.
**Formerly the C. C. F. (Socialist) party.
***Source: computed from the *Report of the Chief Electoral Officer,* 1962 Election (Ottawa: Queen's Printer, 1963).

From these data, it can be seen that the survey underestimated the proportion of nonvoters by some 8 percent; this is a pattern which has generally been found in voting studies, and is usually explained by the reluctance of many people to admit that they did not vote. It must be stressed, however, that all others did not answer they had voted: in fact, only 83 percent of our sample did; some others (3 percent) refused to answer, said they did not know, or simply did not answer (they are now included in these respective categories). The 83 percent who said they voted is, therefore, only 5 percent above the ac-

[43] The Canadian electoral system, like that of Great Britain, allows a voter to cast a ballot for a candidate in a district, rather than for a party or a premier.

tual turnout of 78 percent. The survey also yielded a relatively large proportion of people who, though they said they had voted, refused to say whom they had voted for (19 percent). This pattern of answers, which seems to be peculiar not only to Quebec, but also to Canada in general, has not yet received serious attention from Canadian social scientists. Actually, in most tabulations, we shall consider only the 630 respondents who revealed their party preferences. This could appear as a serious weakness of the survey data, but it is counterbalanced by other considerations. For instance, as will be seen, the results based on survey data were often replicated with results obtained from the analysis of electoral statistics, and in *no instance* did these two types of data yield conflicting results. Moreover, our results were often themselves replications of results obtained in other studies.

Finally, our confidence is further strengthened if we consider the party distribution of those who revealed their preference. As shown in Table 1.2, despite the number of non-responses, the sample distribution is very close to the actual distribution. Our crucial estimate, the Social Credit support, is only about 4 percent below the actual proportion; on the other hand, the New Democratic Party vote is underestimated by about 2 percent only, and the vote for the Conservatives is correctly estimated. Our worst mark is with the Liberal party vote, which is overestimated by some 7 percent. In short, the sample distribution and, particularly, the proportion of respondents who voted Social Credit are close enough to the actual distribution to make us feel basically confident in the survey data.

The way in which the results are presented also requires some comment. In the most important zero-order tabulations (i.e., those introducing only two variables), we have generally presented the proportions of the votes for each of the four parties in the election, so that the reader who is interested in the supporters of any one party may have some indications of their distributions according to a given factor. But since we are almost exclusively concerned with the Social Credit vote, all higher-order tabulations present only the proportions who voted Social Credit in various subgroups. In these instances, the total number of cases (N) on which each of these proportions were computed is presented in parentheses, and 100 percent minus the percent Social Credit gives the proportion who voted for the three other parties together.

Finally, statistical tests of significance were generally computed whenever there could be some doubt about the significance of a relationship. Since no single level of significance is sacred, we have simply indicated the actual level the test yielded, though the text usually includes appropriate comments on the significance of the results obtained. In general, we have simply relied on Coleman's test,[44] since it is an appropriate and easily computed one. (In the instances when

44 James S. Coleman, *Introduction to Mathematical Sociology* (New York: The Free Press of Glencoe, Inc., 1964), Chap. 6.

the independent variable was broken into a trichotomy, we have generally compared extremes, even if it meant losing some cases.) Whenever no significance tests were computed, this was because the relationships stated were either obviously significant or obviously non-significant at the standard levels or, in some cases, because the point made was only secondary to the major thread of the argument. It should be kept in mind, however, that we believe statistical tests of significance are of limited value in survey studies like this one, for various reasons that shall not be dealt with here.[45] This is reflected in the weight we have given to the tests computed.

With these few notes and comments, the stage is now set for the detailed analysis of the Social Credit support. An examination of the political factors involved will be our first task.

---

[45] The interested reader is referred to the discussion of this problem in S. M. Lipset, M. A. Trow, and J. S. Coleman, *Union Democracy* (New York: The Free Press of Glencoe, Inc., 1956), pp. 427–432.

II

THE

POLITICAL

CONDITIONS

The Conduciveness of the Party System*

CHAPTER TWO

The rise of Social Credit in Quebec was not the result of a single overriding factor. As our analysis will reveal, many facets of reality—social, economic, and political—were involved. But apart from the condition of *strain*, to be dealt with later, no other factor seems to have been as important as the peculiarities of the Quebec party system at the federal level.

The purpose of this chapter is to show in what ways the political situation at the federal level in Quebec was particularly conducive to the rise of a third party. In the next chapter, to obtain a better test of the hypothesis derived, the rise of third parties during other periods and elsewhere in Canada will be considered in the same light. Finally, in Chapter 4, an attempt at generalization will be made and a model regarding the condition of *conduciveness* for the rise of third parties will be proposed.

The following analysis strongly supports Smelser's contention that if strain is an important condition for the appearance of any type of collective behavior (including political movements), other determinants—in particular, structural conduciveness—must also be present. That is, the structural characteristics of the social system must be such as to permit or encourage an episode of collective behavior, given, among other things, the existence of strain.[1] In this instance, as will be shown, the element of conduciveness existed in the political system, and more specifically in the characteristics of the federal party system in Quebec.

---

*The material of Chap. 2 and Chap. 4 has been presented in a slightly different form in "One-Party Dominance and Third Parties," *The Canadian Journal of Economics and Political Science*, 33 (August 1967), pp. 358-373.
[1] Smelser, *Theory of Collective Behavior*, pp. 14 ff. and *passim*.

At the federal level, the province of Quebec has long been an area of one-party dominance[2] by the Liberals. From the outset of Confederation in 1867 until 1891, the Conservatives dominated the province. But from 1891 on, the Liberals replaced them until at least the late fifties. From the election of 1896 to that of 1958, the Conservatives never obtained a majority of Quebec votes at the federal level. And though they remained a strong opposition in Quebec from 1896 to 1911, their percentage of the votes dropped sharply in 1917, and from that time until 1958 it hovered around a low average of 27.1 percent. More strikingly, the Conservatives never won a majority of Quebec seats in Parliament between 1891 and 1958, and from 1917 to 1958 they won the surprisingly low average of 7.8 percent of the seats.[3] In fact, in some districts, the local organization of the Conservative party was so weak that the only activity that would take place during the electoral campaign would be the official nomination of a candidate—who often came from Montreal and was completely unknown in the district—and the sticking of posters and the like; not a single popular meeting or other appearance of the "mysterious" candidate would take place. Meisel writes that in 1957 the party's "organization in many Quebec constituencies was almost non-existent" and that "some of the Conservative standard-bearers were largely token candidates without effective organizations to back them."[4]

The reasons for the Liberal ascendency in Quebec and their subsequent dominance are well-known: the Conservatives allegedly alienated the French Canadians by a series of inimical stands at the end of the nineteenth and at the beginning of the present century, in the Riel Rebellions, during the South African War, and with regard to the Naval Bill of 1911, the conscription issue of 1917, and the Ontario school controversy. Coupled with this alienation and at least as important, was the accession of Laurier, a French Canadian, to the leadership of the Liberal party in 1887.[5]

Considering that the Conservatives remained the major opposition party in Quebec throughout this long period—with the possible exception of 1945, when a nationalist party, the *Bloc Populaire Canadien*, appeared for one election and obtained more votes than the Conservatives—the opposition was very weak indeed, and did not offer much of an alternative to the Liberals. Given the presence of grievances in the population, such a system of one-party dominance

[2] As a working definition, one-party dominance in a two-party system (or a system approaching it) will be temporarily defined as a situation in which the party in power cannot be seriously challenged by the opposition party; the latter is too weak to replace the former. Later, on the basis of the findings, this definition will be further refined.

[3] The source of these data is Scarrow, *Canada Votes*. On the weakness of the Conservatives in Quebec, as well as in some other provinces during that period, see John R. Williams, *The Conservative Party of Canada: 1920–1949* (Durham N. Car.: Duke University Press, 1956), Chaps. 4 and 6.

[4] *The Canadian General Election of 1957*, pp. 133, 174.

[5] On this see, for instance, Walter O. Filley, "Social Structure and Canadian Political Parties: The Quebec Case," *Western Political Quarterly*, 9 (1956), pp. 900–914.

meant that the Quebec electorate could not perceive the Conservatives as a likely substitute for the Liberals. They did not possess completely open avenues of political protest, as would have been the case with a healthy two-party system. This, as Smelser suggests, is, given other conditions, highly conducive to the rise of a norm-oriented movement, such as the Social Credit party.[6] Let us then try to test empirically the hypothesis that a long period of one-party dominance in Quebec was largely responsible for the rise of a third party.

THE RISE
OF SOCIAL CREDIT IN QUEBEC

If the system of one-party dominance in Quebec federal politics—that is, the lack of a Conservative alternative to the Liberals—has in fact been a factor leading to the rise of the Social Credit party, one should observe a negative relationship at the district level between the strength of the Progressive Conservative party and the successes of Social Credit.

The overall weakness of the federal Conservatives in Quebec during this century has been described. But this general weakness was not, of course, the same in all electoral districts in the years preceding the 1962 election. First, in previous elections, the party had kept a few strongholds in the province. Moreover, following the Conservative tide in the 1957 election in the rest of Canada, which brought Diefenbaker to power and which Quebec resisted, the Conservatives had given some signs of resurgence in many districts of Quebec. The following year, in the 1958 election,[7] they made their first serious inroad in Quebec in this century by winning 50 of its 75 seats.[8] *But this sudden revival did not imply a complete and overall reinforcement of the Conservative party. In particular,* and this is crucial for our argument, *it remained weak in many districts,* especially in those which still voted Liberal in 1958.[9]

Thus on the basis of the 1957 and 1958 election results, the federal districts of Quebec can be classified in terms of Conservative strength or weakness in the following way. A few districts which were won in 1958 by the Conservatives had already been held by them since at least 1957; these can be assumed to be their few strongholds in Quebec. In the majority of cases, however, the seats won in 1958 were captured from the Liberals; these districts can be considered as districts of medium Conservative strength. Finally, some districts remained

6 *Theory of Collective Behavior,* pp. 278ff., esp. p. 284.

7 The reader will recall that the Progressive Conservatives were elected as a minority government in 1957 and provoked a new general election in 1958, in which they won the greatest majority of seats (208 out of 275) in Canadian history; See Chap. 1.

8 For the first time since 1891, they also obtained a plurality of the total vote: they got 49.6 percent of the votes as opposed to 45.7 percent to the Liberals. See Scarrow, *Canada Votes,* p. 176.

9 For an account of this period in Canadian electoral politics, and, in particular, in Quebec, see Meisel, *The Canadian General Election of 1957,* and Regenstreif, *The Diefenbaker Interlude.*

in the Liberal fold in 1958 despite the Conservative sweep; these can be assumed to be the districts where the Conservatives were at their weakest.[10] If the thesis advanced above is correct, one should observe that the stronger the Conservatives were in 1957 and 1958, the weaker the Social Credit party should have been in 1962.

This is strongly borne out, for the districts outside of Montreal,[11] by the data of Table 2.1. At one extreme, none of the presumably strongest Conservative districts—that is, those districts which had been Conservative in both 1957 and 1958—went Social Credit. At the other extreme, two-thirds of the weakest Conservative districts, those which had remained Liberal, were won by Social Credit. The other group of districts of medium Conservative strength held an intermediate position.[12]

Table 2.1

*Actual Electoral Strength of the Progressive Conservative Party in 1957–58
and Successes of the Various Parties in the 1962 Election
(Montreal districts excluded)*

FEDERAL DISTRICT WON IN 1957 BY:	PROG. CONS.	LIBERAL*	LIBERAL
FEDERAL DISTRICT WON IN 1958 BY:	PROG. CONS.	PROG. CONS.	LIBERAL
(PROG. CONS. STRENGTH:	STRONG	MEDIUM	WEAK)
	%	%	%
Outcome 1962:			
Social Credit**	0	50	69
Progressive Conservative	57	24	0
Liberal	43	26	31
N (districts) =	(7)	(34)	(13)

*The Liberal-Prog. Conservative column includes one district which elected an Independent in 1957 and a Conservative in 1958; the Liberal-Liberal column includes one district which elected an Independent in 1957 and a Liberal in 1958. There are no districts which changed the other way around, from Prog. Conservative in 1957 to Liberal in 1958.

**a_1 (effect of 1957–58 outcomes, i.e., P.C. weakness, on Social Credit outcome in 1962, comparing extremes) $= .69$; p $(a_1^* \leq 0) < .0001$. (This measure of effects and this test of significance follows James S. Coleman, *Introduction to Mathematical Sociology* (New York: The Free Press of Glencoe, Inc., 1964), Chap. 6.

[10] Reflecting the general trend, no district changed from Conservative in 1957 to Liberal in 1958.

[11] If we exclude not only the Montreal districts, but also the Montreal region districts, the relationship of Table 2.1 becomes even stronger: the proportions of districts electing Social Credit candidates become 0, 63, and 82 percent respectively, as we move from strong to weak P.C. districts (N's equal to 7, 27, and 11 respectively). (The nine Montreal region districts, mostly suburbs of Montreal, are in this study: Argenteuil-Deux-Montagnes, Beauharnois-Salaberry, Chambly-Rouville, Châteauguay-Huntingdon-Laprairie, Longueuil, Richelieu-Verchères, St. Jean-Iberville-Napierville, Terrebonne and Vaudreuil-Soulanges.)

[12] In a different and at first sight more refined analysis, one could consider the percentage increase in the Conservative vote from 1957 to 1958 as an indication of the strength of that party: the larger the increase, the stronger the party. But this creates problems since the percentage increase is dependent on the level previously obtained. If we take out the 7 seats already in the Conservative camp in 1957, we obtain results similar to those of Table 2.1: the larger the increase in the Conservative vote in previous elections, the weaker the Social Credit success in 1962 (The data are presented in my "One-Party Dominance and Third Parties," p. 362, fn. 14).

Notice furthermore that together with the strong *negative* relationship between the independent variable and Social Credit victories in 1962, there is a strong *positive* relationship between the former and Conservative victories in the same election, while the independent factor bears no clear relationship to Liberal victories. What is most likely the case is that the dominant Liberals were strong more or less equally in all districts. That is, there were no districts characterized by Conservative one-party dominance. This finding supports our argument that it was the weakness of the Conservative party which was conducive to the Social Credit success.[13]

In order to test the preceding ideas in a more direct fashion, a main organizer of the central organization of the Progressive Conservative party for the Province of Quebec was interviewed and asked to rank "the strength of the Progressive Conservative organization in each federal district during the 1957–58 period, on the basis not of the electoral results obtained, but of the number of important citizens participating in it, the dynamism of the organization, the degree of activities displayed during these elections." To do this, my informant wrote that he "consulted most of (his) colleagues in the Commons from 1958 to 1962."[14]

The results obtained on the basis of these ratings are in all respects similar to those of Table 2.1. Among the districts my informant rated as "very strong," only 15 percent elected a Social Credit M.P.; among those he rated as "fairly strong," 56 percent did so; among those he rated as "fairly weak" or "very weak," 71 percent did so.[15] This substantiates more directly the hypothesis that the weakness of the Conservative party and the ensuing Liberal one-party dominance created a situation conducive to the rise of the Social Credit Party.[16] It is worth quoting my informant at this point. He wrote: "One must take into consideration that since 1887 the Progressive Conservative party succeeded only once, namely in 1958, in getting a majority of the Deputies elected in the province of Quebec. Because of these disconcerting results, it was necessary at nearly every election to start from scratch as far as the organization was concerned."

13 These results can be considered from a different angle, which is particularly revealing on the areas of weakness of the Conservatives: We find that two-thirds of the time, the Conservative candidates lost their deposits in 1962 in the districts which were presumed weak, while this never happened in their few presumed strongholds. The relationship runs the other way for the Social Credit candidates. Only rarely did the Liberal candidates lose their deposits in any type of district. (The data are presented in "One-Party Dominance and Third Parties," p. 363, fn. 16.)

14 In a private communication (my translation).

15 N's equal to 13, 34, and 7 respectively, with an a_1 (effect of Prog. Cons. organization strength on Social Credit outcome, comparing extremes) of .56; p $(a_1^* \leq 0) = .002$.

16 It is interesting in this respect to consider the ecological distribution of the Social Credit victories: the districts won by the Social Credit candidates form a solid block within which only one seat escaped them (in Quebec city) and outside of which they did not win a single district. But it is interesting to note that the Social Credit tide was literally stopped by districts where the Conservatives tended to be stronger. For instance, five of the seven districts where the Conservatives were the strongest are contiguous to the Social Credit block of districts.

Given such a situation, the Quebec Conservatives were not much of an alternative to the Liberals. When the rest of Canada rejected the Liberals in 1957, very few districts in Quebec did the same. Many more went on the Conservative bandwagon in 1958, but still some did not. Therefore, when the Social Credit presented itself, with a strong populist leader—charismatic in many ways —the electorate which had not turned against the Liberals went with that new party.[17]

Some readers may object that we cannot argue that the Conservatives were not a viable alternative to the Liberals, since in 1958—though for the first time in this century—they had in fact replaced the Liberals in Quebec. To be sure, this constitutes a deviation from our model if you consider the province as a whole. However, our point, we repeat, is that it is *particularly* in those districts where the Conservatives had continued to fail even in 1958, but also where they had been weak before, that Social Credit emerged most strongly.

On the other hand, to take the Conservatives' overall resurgence into account, our argument could be made slightly more complex. It seems that in some instances, as will be seen in the next chapter, the passage from one-party dominance to a third party is a two-step process. After a long period of dominance by a strong party, a dissatisfied electorate turns *in part* to the traditional opposition party. But if this party is *soon* considered to have failed, as the Conservatives were in 1962, then the electorate is not ready to return so rapidly to the dominant party it just repelled; they shift instead to a third party. In short, in some circumstances, the one-party dominance model becomes a two-step process based, so to speak, on a double frustration: first, a half-hearted move to the weak opposition party in some quarters; second, a shift to an altogether new party, particularly where the first move was weak.

SOCIAL CREDIT IN MONTREAL

Thus far, I have omitted from the tabulations the twenty-one Montreal federal districts. What about them? The Social Credit party turned out to be

[17] Though claiming that the thesis presented above is "unimpugnable," Lemieux wrote that our demonstration at the district level is debatable and, choosing the results of the 1953 and 1957 elections rather than those of the 1957 and 1958 election to characterize the Progressive Conservative party's strength, he claimed to find a positive rather than negative relationship between that party's strength and the Social Credit party's successes; see Vincent Lemieux, "Les dimensions sociologiques du vote créditiste au Québec," *Recherches Sociographiques*, VI (1965), pp. 181–195, esp. pp. 185–190. In our comment on this paper, we have shown that there is no such positive relationship in Lemieux's data when the latter are subjected to a refined analysis; see Maurice Pinard, "La faiblesse des Conservateurs et la montée du Crédit Social en 1962," *Recherches Sociographiques*, VII (1966), pp. 360–363; see also Lemieux' reply, *ibid.*, pp. 363–365. The remaining "ambiguity" between our two positions lies in the fact that Lemieux fails to realize that there can be more than one operational definition of a nominal concept. The present test of the hypothesis, that is, in terms of the 1957–58 outcomes in rural *districts*, is as valid as the test to be used in the next Chapter, that is, whether the main opposition party has kept in a *province* an average of 33 per cent of the votes in a few preceding elections.

extremely weak in Montreal. It won no seats, and in only two districts did it get more than ten percent of the votes. On the average, Social Credit obtained only 6.1 percent of the votes in Montreal compared to 35.8 percent in the fifty-four other districts of the province.

When one looks at the effect of the past Conservative strength in these districts on the percentage obtained by Social Credit in 1962, the results obtained, though not statistically significant at standard levels, are nevertheless the same as in the rest of the province. As shown in Table 2.2, the weaker the Conservatives in the 1957–58 period, the stronger the Social Credit vote in 1962. Moreover, though most of these districts have been rated by my informant in the same category—fifteen out of twenty-one were rated as "fairly strong"—the relationship obtained with these ratings again confirms the results of Table 2.2: 33 percent of the "very strong" Progressive Conservative districts gave more than 5 percent of their vote to Social Credit, as opposed to 40 percent and 67 percent of the "fairly strong" and of the "fairly weak" districts, respectively (N's equal to 3, 15, and 3, respectively).

Table 2.2

Actual Electoral Strength of the Progressive Conservatives in 1957–58
and Success of the Social Credit Party in 1962
(Montreal districts)

FED. DISTRICT WON IN 1957 BY:	PROG. CONSERVATIVE OR LIBERAL	LIBERAL
FED. DISTRICT WON IN 1958 BY: (PROG. CONSERVATIVE STRENGTH	PROG. CONSERVATIVE STRONG OR MEDIUM %	LIBERAL WEAK) %
Percentage Social Credit Vote in 1962:		
Greater than 5 percent*	44	67
Less than 5 percent	56	33
N (districts) =	(9)	(12)

*a_1 (effect of 1957–58 outcomes, i.e., P.C. weakness, on Social Credit vote in 1962) = .23; $p(a_1^* \leq 0) = .15$.

But this does not explain the relative weakness of the Social Credit party in Montreal, which is all the more surprising at first sight, if one considers that the federal Conservatives were weaker in Montreal than in the rest of the province.[18]

The explanation certainly lies in large part in the lower amount of strain in Montreal as revealed by, among other sources, our survey data;[19] and the presence of strains, as will be seen, is also a necessary condition for the rise of a third party. Part of the explanation also lies in the fact that the party concentrated its

[18] For instance, in 1957, the Conservatives had less than 30 percent of the votes in 67 percent of the Montreal districts, as compared to only 18 percent in the rest of the province (N's equal to 21 and 54 respectively). In 1958, the Conservatives had less than 45 percent of the votes in 43 percent of the Montreal districts and in only 13 percent of the others.

[19] See Chap. 6.

mobilization in the rural areas.[20] But it seems that it may also be due to a structural effect of the party system.

I would contend that in Montreal the voters perceive the strength or weakness of a party on the basis of its organization, not at the district level, but at the national level; the contrary is true for rural districts. Thus the rural voter can quite easily weigh the strength of a party in his own district according to the composition and the activities of its organization, the success of its electoral meetings, and other things of that sort. But he pays very little attention during an electoral campaign to what goes on outside of his own district. The metropolitan voter, on the other hand, is perforce much more cosmopolitan in his outlook. He sees very little of a party's organization at the district level;[21] he often will not even know in which electoral district he lives.

That such differences exist between the two types of voters is supported by the survey data. They indicate that 38 percent of the respondents in the most rural districts personally knew one or more organizers of the provincial parties, while in the least rural districts and in Montreal, 26 and 11 percent, respectively, had the same personal knowledge.[22] In short, the rural voter sees a national electoral campaign through his district campaign, while the metropolitan voter sees his district campaign through the national one.

Since Social Credit was still a weak party at the national level, the Montreal voters could not perceive it as a viable alternative and turn to it; their rural counterparts, on the other hand, could easily perceive the Social Credit wave in their own districts, and did not consider its national weakness. It is worth noting in this regard that in the early thirties, Berlin resisted the Nazi party longer than the rest of Germany[23] and also that the Social Credit party in Alberta, according to Irving, spread much faster in rural villages than in urban areas.[24] The C.C.F. party was also more successful in rural areas in Saskatchewan.[25] Similarly, third parties in the American South have fared better in rural than in

---

20 See Chap. 7.

21 As a matter of fact, organizations are probably much weaker in the Montreal districts than in the rural districts. Contrary to the U.S.A., there is no such thing in Quebec as big city political machines. It is interesting to note in this regard—contrary again to what happens in the U.S.A.—that the turnout is much lower in the Montreal districts than elsewhere in Quebec: 93 percent of the rural districts had turnouts of 80 percent or more in the 1958 federal election, while the corresponding figure for Montreal is 5 percent (N's equal to 54 and 21 respectively). See also Howard A. Scarrow, "Patterns of Voter Turnout in Canada," in John C. Courtney, *Voting in Canada* (Scarborough, Ont.: Prentice-Hall of Canada, Ltd., 1967), pp. 104–114.

22 N's equal to 320, 238, and 332 respectively. The most rural districts of the sample are the provincial electoral districts of Argenteuil, Chicoutimi, Mégantic, Montmorency, Rivière-du-Loup. The least rural are Chambly, Trois-Rivières and those of Quebec City. On this, see also Regenstreif, *The Diefenbaker Interlude*, p. 95.

23 See William L. Shirer, *The Rise and Fall of the Third Reich* (New York: Crest Books, Fawcett Publications, 1962), and Lipset, *Political Man*, p. 146. To be sure, the strength of the Communists and the Socialists in Berlin were probably more important factors here.

24 *The Social Credit Movement in Alberta.*

25 Lipset, *Agrarian Socialism*, Chaps. 6 and 8.

urban areas.[26] Though the strain might have been more severe in rural then in urban areas in these instances, we suggest that the factors just discussed are also involved here.

THE PROCESS
AT THE INDIVIDUAL LEVEL

Finally, the survey data permit one to verify the basic hypothesis at the individual level. Unfortunately, I have no data on the respondents' 1957 vote at the federal level; but I have data on their vote at the 1958 federal election. If the foregoing analysis is correct, one should find that in those districts in which the Progressive Conservatives were weak in 1957 and 1958, the Social Credit should have recruited more votes among former Conservatives than among former Liberals. Conversely, where they were strong, no such relationship should exist, since in these districts both major parties were presumably strong.

The data are presented in Table 2.3. First, it is evident that the weaker the Conservatives in a district, the larger the number of voters Social Credit recruited. But what is of more interest here is that in the five districts of weak and intermediate Conservative strength, the Social Credit recruited more voters among former Conservative voters than among former Liberals, while there is no such difference in the two districts where the Conservatives were strong.[27]

Table 2.3 also reveals that in the districts of weak strength, former Conservative voters were more likely to turn toward the Liberals than were former Liberals to turn toward the Conservatives; but this difference gradually disappears as we move towards the districts where the Conservatives were strong. Moreover, the reader should notice the strong contextual effect which is exerted

---

26 V. O. Key, Jr., *Southern Politics* (New York: Vintage Books, Random House, Inc., 1949) pp. 117, 162, 177, 190. On the other hand, the C.C.F. or New Democratic Party (as it is now called) has more recently fared better in urban rather than in rural areas and generally the same thing holds for Communist and Socialist parties in different countries (see Leo Zakuta, *A Protest Movement Becalmed, A Study of Change in the C.C.F.* (Toronto: University of Toronto Press, 1964), p. 159, and Lipset, *Political Man*, p. 231, pp. 249 ff.) This is undoubtedly due to greater organizational efforts in urban areas and to ideological differences between cities and country; but we suspect that it does not challenge the above structural argument. We suggest that, everything else constant, these parties would succeed more easily and faster in rural areas than in urban areas because of these structural differences. (The conduciveness of rural areas and small communities generally is further discussed in Chap. 11).

27 This means paradoxically that, in districts of Conservative weakness, the chances of Social Credit were better where the proportion of former Conservatives was larger. This apparent paradox accounts, we suggest, for Lemieux' finding that in a district where the Conservatives were very weak (Lévis), the stronger the Conservatives in 1958 in a *community*, the stronger Social Credit was in 1962 (an ecological finding within a district contrary to all those reported above when comparing districts). On that basis, he indeed suggested "that the Social Credit party recruited its support more from the Conservatives than from the Liberals"; see Vincent Lemieux, "Election in the Constituency of Lévis," in Meisel, *Papers on the 1962 Election*, pp. 46–50. Regenstreif also found that former Conservatives were more likely to vote Social Credit than former Liberals; he adds that former Conservatives were also more likely to be *early* recruits; see his *The Diefenbaker Interlude*, pp. 119–120.

Table 2.3

The Social Credit Was Stronger among Former Conservative Voters in Weak,
but Not in Strong Conservative Districts

FEDERAL VOTE IN 1958:	FEDERAL VOTE IN 1962				
	SOCIAL CREDIT %	P.C. %	LIBERAL %	N.D.P. %	N
I. Weak P.C. districts*:					
Liberals**	36	6	56	2	(97)
Conservatives	46	36	14	3	(69)
Did not vote	60	27	13	0	(15)
II. Intermediate P.C. districts:					
Liberals	8	8	85	0	(39)
Conservatives	29	59	12	0	(49)
Did not vote	50	20	30	0	(10)
III. Strong P.C. districts:					
Liberals	8	8	83	0	(36)
Conservatives	4	86	10	0	(49)
Did not vote	0	75	25	0	(4)
IV. Montreal and Quebec districts:					
Liberals	7	7	85	1	(113)
Conservatives	14	59	22	4	(90)
Did not vote	4	24	60	4	(25)

*The seven rural provincial districts of the sample were classified as follows: strong P.C. districts: the two districts (Argenteuil and Trois-Rivières) corresponding to federal districts which were classified as very strong by our informant and were also among the four strongest in terms of the other indicator (1957–58 outcome); intermediate: the two districts (Montmorency and Rivière-du-Loup) which were classified as fairly strong by the informant and were also among the four strongest on the other indicator; weak: the three districts (Chambly, Chicoutimi, and Mégantic) which were classified as fairly strong by the informant and were among the three weakest on the other indicator.

**a_1 (effect in I and II of a 1958 Conservative vote compared to a Liberal one, on the 1962 Social Credit vote) $= \frac{1}{2}(.46 - .36) + \frac{1}{2}(.29 - .08) = .155; p(a_1^* \leq 0) = .002;$

a_2 (effect in I and II of not voting in 1958 compared to voting, on the 1962 Social Credit vote) $= \frac{1}{2}(.60 - .40) + \frac{1}{2}(.50 - .19) = .255; p(a_2^* \leq 0) = .008;$

a_3 (effect in I and II of a 1958 Conservative—or Liberal—vote on change to a 1962 Liberal—or Conservative—vote and a N.D.P. vote) $= \frac{1}{2}(.17 - .08) + \frac{1}{2}(.12 - .08) = .065; p(a_3^* \leq 0) = .05;$

a_4 (effect of strength of Conservative districts in leading 1958 Liberals to vote Social Credit, comparing I and III) $= .28; p(a_4^* \leq 0) < .0001.$

on former Liberals in districts where the Conservatives were weak. The Liberals in these districts were much more likely to become Social Credit than in other districts.[28]

Finally, an interesting additional finding from Table 2.3 regards previous nonvoters. The data indicate (though the N's are quite small) that the 1958 nonvoters seemed the most likely Social Credit supporters in the first five dis-

[28] All the effects reported in the last two paragraphs about weak and intermediate rural districts generally hold for the eight Montreal and Quebec districts (where the Conservatives were weak). Moreover, these results hold with economic strains constant, both the latter and one-party dominance having independent effects. Finally, the 1958 Conservative support was more likely to have come from the working-class and since, as will be seen later, this is also true of the Social Credit support, a control of class was made in the data to check whether the findings were spurious, but they were not.

tricts (groups I and II in Table 2.3), but the least likely in the other districts.[29] We shall return to this finding at the end of the chapter.

WHY A NEW PARTY?

At this point, a possible objection must be considered. Assuming a state of dissatisfaction with a dominant party, why are the people not turning to a weak opposition party, rather than to a completely new party which is obviously much weaker to start with?

This objection must be considered at two different levels: that of the leaders and that of the supporters of the new party. The potential *leaders* of a new party are in all likelihood not ready to try to take over and rejuvenate an old and weak opposition party; for one thing, the belief of some in the new movement's ideology prevents them from doing so; moreover, they realize that the chances that such efforts could be successful are probably very low. The organization of an old and weak party is highly bureaucratized, is devoid of any fighting spirit, is controlled by leaders with administrative skills rather than popular appeal and prestige. They have lost confidence of ever winning and are therefore unable to mount any new sustained drive. On the other hand, they are entrenched in their positions in the party and will resist anyone trying to challenge them.

These characteristics of the opposition party in an area of one-party dominance have been ably documented by V. O. Key in his descriptions of the Republican party in the American South.[30] Rather than try to subdue and rejuvenate such a machine, the new leaders prefer to create an altogether new organization under the charismatic enthusiasm of a popular leader. Indeed many secondary leaders could not easily be recruited to anything but such a new party, since the old party has lost any attraction for them. From there on, the new party is no longer a weaker party to start with, and its *supporters*, by turning to it, are not choosing an altogether weaker alternative.

NONVOTERS AND NEW MOVEMENTS

While comparing the political choices of former Conservatives and former Liberals, we found that former nonvoters were the most likely Social Credit

[29] Regentreif's data also indicate that, in general, former nonvoters were more likely to vote Social Credit than either former Liberals or Conservatives, among those who expressed a party preference; see his *The Diefenbaker Interlude*, pp. 117–118 (compare his tables 1 and 2, excluding the "don't know and refused" category).

[30] *Southern Politics*, Chap. 13, esp. pp. 292ff. Key writes: "Southern Republican leaders . . . are not politicians in the usual sense of the word. They might be called palace or bureaucratic politicians, since their chief preoccupation is not with voters, but with maneuvers to gain and keep control of the state party machinery. . . . They exert themselves only to keep the party weak in the South in order that there will be fewer faithful to reward"; *ibid.*, p. 292. See also Williams, *The Conservative Party of Canada*, p. 116.

recruits in districts which turned out to vote strongly for that party, and the least likely in the other districts (Table 2.3). Although not directly related to the problems raised in this chapter, this finding is of particular interest in view of the controversy regarding the contribution of previous nonvoters to the rise of new political movements. Bendix, together with others, had been arguing on the basis of his examination of electoral statistics, that the early Nazi gains (from 2.6 percent of the votes in 1928 to 18.3 percent in 1930) were in part attributable to the sudden participation of previous nonvoters.[31] Lipset, on the contrary, argued on the basis of a more detailed analysis—and actually convinced Bendix —that nonvoters had not been the early recruits of the Nazi movement, but that they came to it only at a later phase (after 1930), when it had already become a major movement.[32] The theoretical explanation advanced by Lipset was that "the most outcast and apathetic sections of the population" cannot be won to "a new and small movement" because they lack the "relatively complex, long-term view of the political process" required for such support. Only "a *mass* movement which presents a *simple* extremist view of politics" can awaken the apathetic.[33]

The controversy seemed settled until recently when O'Lessker rechallenged Lipset's analysis and methodology, and produced new evidence which sustained Bendix's observations. He concluded that it was in fact the increased turnout together with defections from the Nationalists which were the two most important factors of the 1930 Nazi surge.[34] O'Lessker's methodology was in turn challenged by Schnaiberg, but his reanalysis of O'Lessker's data only suggested that Nationalist defections were much more important to the Nazi surge than the participation of previous nonvoters. Nonvoting remained, however, one of the factors—admittedly with others—which was positively associated with the Nazi vote of 1930.[35]

In short, the more recent evidence indicates that former nonvoters made at least some contribution to the Nazis' early success—certainly more than defectors from middle-class parties, contrary to Lipset's empirical statement regarding the 1930 election. Our own data suggest that they may have been the most likely Social Credit supporters in districts where Social Credit made a major

[31] Reinhard Bendix, "Social Stratification and Political Power," in R. Bendix and S. M. Lipset, eds., *Class, Status and Power* (New York: The Free Press of Glencoe, Inc., 1953), pp. 604–605. Bendix also attributed part of the Nazi gains to defections from the nationalist parties of the right and to young voters (*ibid.*).

[32] Francois Goguel also reported that in France the hypothesis that former nonvoters were particularly prone to have supported the Poujadist movement in 1956 could not be retained; see his "Géographie des élections du 2 janvier," in Maurice Duverger et al., eds., *Les élections du 2 janvier 1956* (Paris: Librairie Armand Colin, 1957), p. 480.

[33] Lipset reported a small *negative* correlation between the percent increase in the Nazi vote and the percent increase in turnout for the 1930 election; *Political Man*, pp. 149–152. Italics in the original.

[34] Karl O'Lessker, "Who Voted for Hitler? A New Look at the Class Basis of Naziism," *The American Journal of Sociology*, 74 (1968), pp. 63–69.

[35] Allan Schnaiberg, "A Critique of Karl O'Lessker's 'Who Voted for Hitler?'," *ibid.*, 74 (1968), pp. 732–735.

advance, that is, in the two groups of weaker Conservative districts, but the least likely in the other two groups. Is there a possible reconciliation of these *data* and of Lipset's *theoretical* position? We suspect there is, and in fact, in more than one way.

Our first argument centers around the operational definitions of "major" and "minor" movements. Here, following Lipset's argument, our reasoning would be that Social Credit was already a major movement *by election day* in the first two groups of districts of Table 2.3 and thus disproportionately attracted nonvoters, while it was practically nonexistent in the other districts, and therefore failed to recruit them. In the case of the Nazi movement, the analysis has so far failed to distinguish between areas of relative Nazi strength and weakness, and one only obtains, in the last analysis (that of Schnaiberg) an overall relatively moderate positive relationship between increase in turnout and Nazi gains. Add to this that the point at which a movement becomes strong enough to reawaken nonvoters remains an unsettled empirical question. It may well be that with 18.3 percent' of the votes in 1930, the Nazi movement was *already*—not just after 1930 as claimed by Lipset—perceived as a major alternative, at least in some areas.[36]

The second argument, to which we tend to give more weight, also raises a problem of operational definition. Lipset's thesis is that the "most outcast and apathetic sections of the population" are not the early recruits of a new movement, that they come only later. We suggest that this theoretical statement is correct, but that to test it with previous nonvoters cannot be too convincing. If many nonvoters are among the most apathetic and outcast—particularly the chronic nonvoters—many others are not. Some may have been nonvoters before as a result of rebellious attitudes toward contending parties and/or the system itself, or related to that, because of the lack of an acceptable alternative;[37] others, because their interest was not strong enough in a given election, although they are not apathetic citizens or chronic nonvoters by any means. There are probably other reasons, too.[38]

I suggest that these groups, which do not constitute chronic nonvoters, were among the first to be attracted to the Nazi party in 1930 (and to other parties, particularly the Communist and Catholic center parties), as they were also among the first, overall, to be attracted to Social Credit. These nonvoters do not need that "major" a movement to be motivated to participate anew. In other words, a movement may be "major" enough at one point to reawaken nonvoters who are mildly apathetic—if at all—while not yet strong enough to reawaken the

---

36 It should be clear that this reasoning does not rest on Lipset's empirical observation of a negative relationship between increase in turnout and increase in Nazi vote. The more recent analysis has invalidated that finding.

37 This may explain, for instance, the support of previous nonvoters in weak Conservative districts.

38 See, for instance, J. A. Laponce, "Non-Voting and Non-Voters: A Typology," *The Canadian Journal of Economics and Political Science*, 33 (1967), pp. 75–87.

most outcast. On the other hand, the chronic nonvoters or "the most apathetic," probably stayed at home, possibly even after 1930. One must not forget that in Germany nonvoting decreased by only 6.4 percent between 1928 and 1930 (down to 18.0 percent), and that this rate remained relatively stable until the last free election of 1932.[39]

In short, the nonvoters who flocked into the active electorate in 1930 are not necessarily among the most outcast and apathetic citizens. On the other hand, the general theoretical position of Lipset seems sound; it has in fact been documented in a more appropriate empirical context by Lipset himself with regard to the response of the lower classes—particularly the poor—to rising movements. He found these groups to prefer the stronger of the Communist and Socialist movements in many countries,[40] and documented that the C.C.F. in Saskatchewan attracted the poor workers and farmers only when it became a strong movement (1944), but not in its early stage (1934).[41] It will be shown later that Lipset's proposition holds for many more movements, including Social Credit in Quebec, and we will try to explain this phenomenon.[42] For the moment, we would stress that while some groups of previous nonvoters flocked to Social Credit in disproportionate numbers in at least some districts, the poor did not do so in any group of districts.[43] We suggest that the poor constitute a better empirical referent for the most outcast and apathetic, and we find that when considering them, Lipset's theory holds.

To recapitulate, we think O'Lessker to be empirically correct in holding that previous nonvoters did make an overall contribution to Hitler's success as early as 1930, but whether this is generally true irrespective of the Nazis' gains in different areas is still an open question. More importantly, however, we propose that O'Lessker erred in concluding that his findings cast serious doubt on Lipset's general thesis regarding the most apathetic.[44]

CONCLUSION

The analysis presented so far indicates that the weakness of the Progressive Conservative party in Quebec was largely responsible for the rise of Social Credit. A long period of one-party dominance by the Liberals created a political structure conducive to the rise of a third party. When this combined with

[39] See the relevant data in O'Lessker, "Who Voted for Hitler?" Table 1.

[40] Lipset, *Political Man*, pp. 122–126.

[41] Lipset, *Agrarian Socialism*, pp. 163ff.

[42] See Chap. 8.

[43] Even when only the communities of our sample in which Social Credit obtained more than 30 percent of the votes are considered, we still find that the poor in that first surge of Social Credit were less likely to have voted Social Credit than the middle income group—31 percent versus 51 percent. (N's equal to 54 and 77 respectively.)

[44] See O'Lessker, "Who Voted for Hitler?" p. 69; compare, however, his counterthesis with our comments, pp. 146ff.

strains, as will be seen in Chapter 6, the time for the rise of the Social Credit party was ripe.

But before considering the role of strains, we shall enlarge on the scope of our enquiry and ask in Chapter 3 whether the ideas developed in this chapter are also relevant for the rise of other third parties. On the basis of our findings, we shall try in Chapter 4 to develop a model of the conducive factors involved in such occurrences.

One-Party Dominance and Other Third Parties[*]

CHAPTER THREE

The hypothesis that one-party dominance is conducive to the rise of third parties seems to account for instances other than the 1962 upsurge of Social Credit in Quebec. First, consider the rise of third parties in the United States. It is remarkable that these often rose in rural areas characterized by long periods of political stability and a close identification to a single party. The similarity with Social Credit in Quebec is striking, as can be seen from MacRae's remarks:

> It is not the attitude of the community on issues of the moment that is maintained by tradition; it is its identification with a party name and allegiance to its symbols. Attitudes on persistent issues may be maintained along with this allegiance, but the effect of a drought or depression on agriculture may still arouse discontent. However, the reaction of protest is more likely to take place through the traditional party in the rural community than in the urban. If these efforts to attain legitimacy within the traditional party fail, the next step is likely to be the creation of a new party. In this way the support of traditionally Republican areas could be given to some of the agrarian movements mentioned above [the Populists, the Progressive movements of 1912 and 1924, the Non-Partisan League of North Dakota, and the Farmer-Labor Party] and the support of Southern areas to the States' Rights Democrats.

> Thus, while traditional allegiance to one party does not preclude political change, it renders very unlikely the possibility that this change will take place through a switch

*This is a substantially revised and much extended version of a section of my paper "Political Factors in the Rise of Social Credit in Quebec," read at the Canadian Political Science Association meetings, Charlottetown, 1964.

to the other major party. In rural areas we may observe both pronounced political stability, relative to urban areas, and changes of entire communities from their traditional party to a third party.[1]

It seems therefore that third parties in the United States rose under similar political conditions. We strongly suspect that the same hypothesis, even if extended, can account in general for the rise of new parties in Canada.[2] Let us briefly consider these instances, first at the provincial level, then at the federal level. This examination may appear to lead us outside our subject, but since one of our purposes is to throw light upon the rise, not only of Social Credit in Quebec, but of political movements in general, it deserves some attention.

In the following pages, we will consider in a somewhat detailed fashion all Canadian provincial elections since 1900 in which the party in power was defeated, as well as those elections in which a third party emerged, in order to empirically assess the relationship between the previous state of the party system and the rise of such third parties. We will then consider some instances at the federal level, though in a much more concise way. To be sure, a more detailed analysis of the type carried out for Quebec in 1962 would be most useful, but it is beyond the scope of this study. Our analysis here will remain at the level of provinces, not of individual districts.

As shall be seen, the data strongly support the hypothesis that new parties elsewhere in Canada rose out of situations of one-party dominance, even in a multi-party system. Whether there is only one opposition party, which is too weak, as has often been the case, or whether there are more than one, but all of them weak, a system of one-party dominance is likely to be conducive to new parties. The crucial point is that these opposition parties cannot be considered as viable alternatives to the party in power.

More specifically, the indications are that whenever the opposition party (or the strongest of many opposition parties) fails to retain at least a third of the votes while in opposition, it tends to be replaced by "third" parties. In other words, a third of the votes seems to be the empirical cutting point below which a situation of one-party dominance is created. Conversely, whenever there exists a strong two-party system, third parties usually fail to make any serious inroads. Finally, there are a few instances in which the situation is marginal: the main opposition party has previously retained more than a third of the votes, but is suddenly weakened by various circumstances, which manifest themselves usually by the failure of this party to contest all seats in an election. This situation produces the same effect as that of a weak opposition party.

---

1 Duncan MacRae, Jr., "Occupations and the Congressional Vote, 1940–1950," *American Sociological Review*, 20 (1955), p. 339; see also Smelser, *Theory of Collective Behavior*, p. 283. On the surge of reform movements in American cities under one-party dominance, see also Duncan MacRae, Jr., *Parliament, Parties, and Society in France, 1946–1958* (New York: St. Martin's Press, Inc., 1967), p. 283.

2 It would be interesting to determine whether the rise of the British Labour party also took place under circumstances similar to those to be presently described.

Before we present the detailed qualitative evidence supporting these propositions, it may be worth summarizing our results immediately. The sixty-five cases (elections) we will be considering separately below constitute a sample large enough to permit some quantification. In Table 3.1, all cases have been classified on two dimensions. First, the previous state of the party system: a) the main opposition party had previously maintained, while in opposition, an average vote of less than 33 percent, a clear situation of one-party dominance; b) though a proportion superior to that was maintained, the opposition party suddenly weakened, a marginal situation; c) the main opposition party remained a strong party with more than 33 percent of the votes, a situation with a strong two-party system, or two strong parties in a multi-party system. The second dimension refers to the emergence and success of third parties, and is self-explanatory.[3]

Table 3.1

One-Party Dominance Led to the Rise of Third Parties in Canada

	PREVIOUS STRENGTH OF MAIN OPPOSITION PARTY*		
ELECTION OUTCOME:**	A. PREVIOUSLY WEAK %	B. SUDDENLY WEAK*** %	C. STRONG %
1. No Third Party (or) Third Parties' Vote Less than 10%	23	0	82
2. Third Parties' Vote Between 10% and 20%	18	10	6
3. Third Parties' Vote Greater than 20%****	59	90	12
N (elections) =	(22)	(10)	(33)

*See text for explanation of categories.

**When there was more than one third party, the votes of these third parties were added together.

***In six of these cases, the main opposition party though having maintained an average of more than 33% of the votes, had generally been out of power for a long time but above all, found itself suddenly weakened, as indicated by its failure to contest a large proportion of the seats. In the other four cases, the main opposition party had relinquished its role by entering into a coalition with the government party or (in one case) with a third party.

****a_1 (effect of strength of opposition party, comparing columns A and C) = .47; $p(a_1^* \leq 0)$ < .0001.

From Table 3.1, it is evident that a strong relationship exists between one-party dominance and the success of third parties. As column C reveals, except for a few instances (18 percent of the cases),[4] a strong opposition party constitutes a serious handicap for the success of third parties. On the other hand, a

3 In the rest of the chapter, the description of each of the cases is followed by an indication of where it has been classified in Table 3.1. Thus a code "A-1" indicates that a case has been classified in column A, row 1; B-3 in column B, row 3; etc.

4 Some of which, as will be seen, were classified in this column to make our test conservative.

situation of one-party dominance is clearly conducive to third parties, as the data of column A—and also column B—indicate. Notice that in the first column, the deviations are more numerous: this may only suggest that in some instances, the condition of conduciveness, but not the other determinants, may have been present. Indeed, the whole Table supports Smelser's contention that conduciveness is a necessary, though not a sufficient, condition for the emergence of a political movement.

It should be noted, moreover, that even if one were to argue that the cases of column B are instances of a strong opposition party and should accordingly be placed with those of column C, the results would not be seriously altered; the relationship observed would remain strong. In 63 percent of this new set of cases (N = 43), there would have been no third party or the third parties' vote would have been inferior to ten percent, while in 7 and 30 percent of the cases, respectively, the third parties' vote would have been between ten and twenty percent, or superior to that. Therefore, even such a stringent test of the hypothesis would still yield a strong relationship.

With this overall picture in mind, we may now turn to a qualitative examination of each case.[5]

THIRD PARTIES
AT THE PROVINCIAL LEVEL

BRITISH COLUMBIA

Let us start at the provincial level with British Columbia. Governments in that province professed no political affiliations until the election of 1903 in which the pattern of personal government was abandoned for the usual pattern of elections fought on party lines.[6] The Conservatives won that election and the three following ones (1907, 1909, and 1912) with increasingly strong majorities. The Liberals were a relatively solid opposition party, except for the last of these elections, in which they contested only nineteen seats out of forty-two, and obtained only 25.2 percent of the votes.[7] On the average, the latter secured 38.0 percent of the votes in the first three elections; even counting the last of these elections, their average for the four elections was still at 34.8 percent.[8]

---

[5] Some readers may want to skip this presentation of the evidence; they may immediately go to the next chapter for generalizations and then to Chap. 5 where the analysis of the Social Credit upsurge is resumed.

[6] Fred H. Goodchild, *British Columbia: Its History, People and Industry* (London: George Allen and Unwin Ltd, 1951), pp. 47–48; Margaret A. Ormsby, *British Columbia: A History* (Toronto: The MacMillan Company of Canada, Ltd., 1958), pp. 334ff.

[7] In general, the provincial election data from 1920 on are taken from H. A. Scarrow, *Canada Votes*. Prior to that date, the usual sources are the *Canadian Parliamentary Guide* and *The Canadian Annual Review*, unless otherwise indicated.

[8] Since the size of the electorate is changing rapidly, the average proportions of votes are averages of proportions; the average proportions of seats are based on absolute numbers.

As the model would predict, when the economic strains produced by the war, the resignation of a very popular Premier (McBride), and charges of corruption as well as divisions within the Cabinet seriously weakened the Conservative government,[9] the Liberals emerged as a viable alternative. In the election of 1916, they were supported by 50.0 percent of the electorate and came to power with thirty-seven seats out of forty-seven, the Conservatives obtaining only nine seats and 40.8 percent of the votes (C1).

The Socialist movement, however, gained roots in British Columbia much earlier than in other Canadian provinces precisely because, among other factors, of "a weakly developed party system"[10] and a pattern of personal government at the beginning of this century. Indeed, in the first of these elections to be fought on party lines (1903), there were already ten Socialist candidates and five Labour candidates, polling respectively 6.7 and 8.3 percent of the votes, for a total of 15.0 percent (A2). But the strength of these groups declined gradually until the 1920 election and in fact, the socialist and labor vote was never to exceed the 1903 mark until the thirties.

Elected in 1916, the Liberals formed the government until the election of 1928. But in the 1924 election, a third party, the Provincial party, made up of dissident Conservatives and backed by the United Farmers of British Columbia, polled 24 percent of the votes and won two seats. This constitutes a first deviation from our model, since the Conservatives had kept 40.8 and 31.5 percent of the votes in the two previous elections for an average of 36.1 percent (C3). It should be mentioned, however, that as an opposition party, the Conservatives had been weakened in 1924 by the dissidence over the leadership of their party, which indeed had led to the emergence of the Provincial party.[11]

With a new leader and the disappearance of the Provincial party, the Conservatives made a strong comeback in 1928; they were returned to power with 53.3 percent of the votes. Since they had kept an average of 34.0 percent of the votes in the three previous elections, they still constituted, though barely so, a viable alternative to the Liberals (C1).[12]

As was often repeated in Canadian history, the adverse economic conditions of the thirties made the Conservatives' resurgence of short duration. Indeed, in the 1933 election, in their effort to cope with a financial crisis, they decided not to run as a separate party and instead, one of their leaders headed a Non-Partisan movement.[13] Faced with only one traditional party, the Liberals, and two new political movements, the Non-Partisans and the new C.C.F. (Cooperative Com-

---

9 Ormsby, *British Columbia*, pp. 383ff.

10 Robin, "The Social Basis of Party Politics in British Columbia," p. 203.

11 Ormsby, *British Columbia*, pp. 420–421.

12 The disappearance of the Provincial party probably entailed a return of dissidents to the Conservatives, and a consequent reinforcement of their party.

13 The Non-Partisan movement was the Conservative government's answer to a financial crisis and expressed its desire to cope with it on a non-partisan basis. They elected only two members, as opposed to 34 Liberals and seven C.C.F. See Scarrow, *Canada Votes*, p. 226.

monwealth Federation) party, a plurality of the electorate opted for the Liberals, who were returned to power with 41.7 percent of the votes and thirty-four seats out of forty-seven. This should not be surprising, since the Liberals, with 40.5 percent of the votes during their term on the opposition benches, were a strong party.

Among other voters, however, many more opted for the C.C.F. party than for the Non-Partisan movement. They obtained, respectively, 31.5 and 10.3 percent of the votes. Strictly speaking, the success of the C.C.F. constitutes a deviation from the hypothesis: this success cannot be accounted for by the weakness of the opposition party, since the Liberals were strong. But the rise of the C.C.F. could be seen as linked to the new weakness of the Conservatives and the ensuing fluidity of the party system. Moreover, it is interesting to note that this situation bears some resemblance to the Quebec situation of 1958–1962, with the Conservatives here making a comeback in 1928 before leaving the scene to a third party in 1933.[14] To make our test rigorous, however, we shall consider this instance as a deviation, since the Conservatives had not been as weak in that province as in Quebec, and even though the withdrawal of an incumbent party is a rather peculiar situation (C3).

In the following elections, the Conservatives reappeared on the scene, but the C.C.F. maintained its positions or slightly improved them. In the 1941 election the C.C.F. strength was great enough to force the Liberals and the Conservatives into a coalition which lasted from 1941 to 1952, and the C.C.F. became the main opposition party; from 1933 to 1949, it kept an average of 33.2 percent of the votes and 18.8 percent of the seats. However, the coalition ceased to work prior to the 1952 election, and the Liberals, having a bare majority (26 seats out of 48), formed the government, with the Conservatives acting now as the official opposition.[15] An election soon followed, which had the worst consequences for the former partners of the coalition. The two traditional parties were left with fewer votes than the new ones; the Liberals obtained 23.5 percent of the votes and six seats; the Conservatives, 16.8 percent, and four seats. On the other hand, the Social Credit party appeared as an alternative in part to the C.C.F., which was still a weak opposition party, as just mentioned, but also as an alternative to the Conservative opposition which was also very weak, now that the coalition had ceased to work.[16]

In a way which is characteristic of the Social Credit party and of protest movements in general, the former party scored a substantial and unexpected success in a single election. Though officially leaderless, it won 27.2 percent of the votes and nineteen seats and formed the government (A3). A year later, in

14 See our comments on p. 26 on the two-step variation of our model.

15 On the 1952 election, see H. F. Angus, "The British Columbia Election, June, 1952," *Canadian Journal of Economics and Political Science*, XVIII (Nov. 1952), pp. 518–525.

16 Strictly speaking, this had become a situation not of one-party dominance, but of no-party dominance. But the model applies *a fortiori* to such a case.

1953, the Social Credit as the younger movement in the province won a majority of the seats, and came unambiguously to power. It has been victorious ever since.

<h2 style="text-align:center">ALBERTA</h2>

Since its creation in 1905, the Province of Alberta has apparently always been an area of one-party dominance.[17] The Conservatives never won an election in that province and the Liberals were in power uninterruptedly from 1905 to 1921.[18] To be sure, during that period the Conservatives kept a relatively high average proportion of the votes (38.4 percent) and of the seats (24.2 percent); they would therefore appear to have been a relatively strong opposition party.

There are, however, other indications of, and general agreement about, the Conservatives' weakness. In the first two elections (1905 and 1909), their average proportions of the votes and of the seats were low—33.3 percent and 9.1 percent respectively[19]—and their subsequent greater successes are reported to be the result of votes of opposition to the government rather than Tory votes.[20] The party's situation might have been similar to that of the Quebec Conservatives in the 1958 federal election before their collapse against Social Credit in 1962. Moreover, there is agreement that the Conservatives' machine was very weak, as compared to the "extremely powerful" machine of the Liberals.[21] Finally, the crucial point, this weakness clearly came to light in the 1921 election, *when the Conservatives practically withdrew from the scene, contesting only sixteen of the sixty-one seats*, and only three against the candidates of the new United Farmers of Alberta. Several of their prominent leaders either retired from the provincial political scene or joined the U.F.A.[22] Given the Liberal dominance, the pattern observed above thus developed. Coupled with the discontent of the people,[23] the situation was ripe for the rise of a third party; though the United Farmers of Alberta obtained only 28.8 percent of the votes, they came to power with 63.3 percent of the seats.[24] But given the strength of the Conservatives in terms of votes, we have classified this case in the middle column of Table 3.1 (B3).

17 This is contrary to Macpherson's assessment, and it is important for the points we shall make below; see Macpherson, *Democracy in Alberta*, p. 217; but see also p. 205.

18 See W. L. Morton, *The Progressive Party in Canada* (Toronto: University of Toronto Press, 1950), p. 36, p. 230, and L. G. Thomas, *The Liberal Party in Alberta: A History of Politics in the Province of Alberta: 1905–1921* (Toronto: University of Toronto Press, 1959).

19 In the 1909 election, for instance, nine liberals were elected by acclamation.

20 See Thomas, *The Liberal Party in Alberta*, pp. 171–172, p. 203.

21 See *ibid.*; also Morton, *The Progressive Party in Canada*, pp. 111ff.

22 See Thomas, *The Liberal Party in Alberta*, pp. 203–204.

23 "Behind the frenzy [of the U.F.A.] lay four years of complete or partial crop failure, uncertainty with respect to the price of wheat, and the sense of crusade arising from the farmers' entry into politics." Morton, *The Progressive Party in Canada*, p. 111.

24 "The campaign itself was distinguished in two respects, by the revolutionary zeal of the farmers' electioneering, and by the complete absorption of the Conservative party and vote by the U.F.A. . . . As had happened in Saskatchewan, the long Liberal dominance of Alberta drove the Conservatives into the U.F.A. political movement, but the result was to deliver control of the province into the hands of the U.F.A." *Ibid.*, p. 112.

The U.F.A. in turn developed into a system of one-party dominance. During its reign, it destroyed the old parties in rural Alberta;[25] the main opposition party, the Liberals, was reduced to an average of 26.2 percent of the votes and 17.9 percent of the seats. Accordingly, following the same pattern again, the U.F.A., which had become "old in the sense that it had been tried,"[26] was overthrown during the Great Depression, in 1935, not by the Liberals, but by another third party, the Social Credit party (A3).

The Social Credit party has clearly established a new era of one-party dominance. The main opposition party—which has been, according to the time periods, the Liberals, the Independents, the C.C.F., or the Conservatives—has held ever since, on the average, the low proportion of 24.8 percent of the votes and 10.3 percent of the seats.[27] This would suggest that Social Credit could only be overthrown by another political movement (or some quasi-third party of the Quebec *Union Nationale* type);[28] it also suggests a partial explanation for the exceptionally long tenure of that party. If the next election is held in 1971, Social Credit will have been in power for no less than thirty-six years.

SASKATCHEWAN

Saskatchewan presents somewhat the same pattern. To an even greater extent than Alberta, this province, from its inception in 1905 to the forties, was dominated by the Liberal party. As Morton puts it, Saskatchewan "became a bulwark of Liberalism in the West, matching the other main pillar of the party after 1896, the province of Quebec."[29] From the start, the Conservatives, so to speak, missed the boat. In the first two elections (1905 and 1908), they assembled around Haultain, the former prestigious territorial premier, who was himself a Conservative in federal politics, and they ran under the banner of a Provincial Rights party.[30] As such, they formed a relatively successful opposition party; the Provincial Rights party obtained 47.7 and 47.9 percent of the votes in these two elections, respectively.[31]

But in 1911, at a Conservative convention, the Provincial Rights party was

25 Morton, *The Progressive Party in Canada*, p. 286; see also Macpherson, *Democracy in Alberta*, p. 204.

26 Morton, *The Progressive Party in Canada*, p. 287.

27 The Social Credit party has kept an average of 52.3 percent of the votes against all others during this period.

28 It is noteworthy in this regard that the only serious challenge to Social Credit came in 1940 when a slate of Independents ran against them (the two old parties did not participate), and obtained the highest proportion of opposition votes in that period (42.5 percent).

29 *The Progressive Party in Canada*, p. 6; see also p. 34, p. 262.

30 See Thomas, *The Liberal Party in Alberta*, pp. 3ff., esp. p. 24; Morton, *The Progressive Party in Canada*, p. 34. In a way, that province started in Confederation with a quasi-third party of the Quebec *Union Nationale* type. The party was a "combined Provincial Rights and Conservative party." See the *Canadian Annual Review*, 1907, p. 590.

31 The Liberals obtained 52.0 and 50.8 percent respectively. Computed by the author from Saskatchewan Archives Board, *Directory of Saskatchewan Ministries, Members of the Legislative Assembly, Election 1905–1953* (Regina and Saskatoon, 1954), and from various issues of the *Canadian Parliamentary Guide*.

abandoned as a distinct party. A resolution was passed declaring that success "would be most speedily effected by the union of the Conservative and Provincial Rights parties under one party"[32] and from then on the Conservative party provided the opposition to the Liberals. The Conservatives, however, apparently failed to build a strong organization. In the 1912 and 1917 elections, the party kept a high proportion of the votes but gradually lost ground. Its proportion of the votes dropped from the 48 percent of the Provincial Rights party in the previous two elections to 41.6 and 36.3 percent in 1912 and 1917 respectively. After the 1912 election, Haultain, who seems to have held the party together, resigned from its leadership. Together with the very small representation in the Legislative Assembly,[33] this seems to have been a major factor accelerating the decline of the party.

After the resignation of Haultain, a period of particularly unstable leadership prevailed. Following the 1917 election, Willoughby, who had replaced Haultain as opposition leader, resigned and MacLean became opposition leader. But MacLean resigned on the eve of the 1921 election. The party was apparently so weak at that point that the convention did not even name a leader; instead it only appointed a committee to make arrangements for the coming election and decided to concentrate on districts "where there was a chance of success, and candidates were to run as straight Conservatives."[34]

In the end, "*very few Conservatives ran as such*"[35] and "*there was no organized Conservative opposition*";[36] in fact, sixteen Liberals went to the people unopposed.[37] Therefore, given that "the provincial Conservative party had disappeared,"[38] and given the serious strains of the period, an Independent movement arose for the 1921 election; it was made of various opposition groups, the Conservatives being the basic element, but comprising as well, Non-Partisans, Labourites and others.[39] The Liberals, who had been responsive to the agrarian ferment and interests and who had the backing of the majority in the Saskatchewan Grain Growers Association,[40] were reelected with 52.2 percent of the votes and forty-six of the sixty-three seats. But the Independent party became the strongest

32 Reported in *Canadian Annual Review*, 1911, p. 577. The *Review* goes on to report that "It was felt that the present position of the Liberals as to the Provincial lands question rendered a Provincial Rights party unnecessary." *Ibid.*

33 The Conservatives retained only 8 and 7 seats, out of a total of 54 and 59, in the 1912 and 1917 elections, respectively. This is an average of 13.3 percent.

34 *Canadian Annual Review*, 1921, pp. 809ff.

35 *Canadian Annual Review*, 1921, pp. 809. (Italics are ours.) Morton reports that only three Conservatives ran (see *The Progressive Party in Canada*, p. 111), while Scarrow lists seven Conservative candidates, three of whom were Independent Conservatives (see *Canada Votes*, pp. 218–19).

36 *Canadian Annual Review*, p. 808. (Italics are ours.)

37 Scarrow, *Canada Votes*, p. 219.

38 Morton, *The Progressive Party in Canada*, p. 230; see also p. 60.

39 It was described as a "rather vague organization," functioning not as a political party, but as a Central Committee for the time of the campaign, with a well-known Conservative "acting as a sort of leader." *Canadian Annual Review*, 1921, p. 812.

40 See *Canadian Annual Review*, 1921, p. 808; also Morton, *The Progressive Party in Canada*, p. 36, pp. 231ff. Compare with Lipset, *Agrarian Socialism*, pp. 124–125.

opposition group; it obtained 25.8 percent of the votes and seven of the sixty-three seats.[41] Accordingly, this case is classified in B3.

In the following elections, a great degree of political instability was exhibited as far as the opposition parties were concerned. The weak Independent movement of 1921 was replaced by the Progressives as the main opposition group after the 1925 election; the Progressives obtained 23.0 percent of the votes and six out of sixty-three seats (A3). They in turn remained weak[42] and practically vanished in the 1929 election. This election saw a resurgence of sorts on the part of the Conservatives. Though they had obtained a lower proportion of the votes than the Liberals (36.5 compared to 46.7 percent), they obtained twenty-four seats, as compared to twenty-eight for the Liberals. They were still, however, too weak to form a government, and they had to form a coalition with the Independents[43] to come to power for the first time since 1905. As often happened with the Conservatives, this moderate resurgence did not last for long. The election of 1934 saw a defeat of their government and a return of the strong Liberals to power. But apparently as in Quebec again, in a two-step process, this election saw the emergence of the C.C.F. movement as an answer to the strain produced by the economic depression; the C.C.F. candidates obtained 24.0 percent of the votes and five of the fifty-five seats (A3).[44]

The Conservatives were completely routed: they were left without a single seat in the Legislative Assembly and only 26.7 percent of the votes. The C.C.F. had replaced them as the main opposition party and was to keep that position[45] in the following election in 1938. In that election, the Liberals were maintained in power with 45.5 percent of the votes, but the Conservatives' decline continued. They obtained only 12.1 percent of the votes and no seat again. On the other hand, the C.C.F. also lost some ground in popular support (18.8 percent of the votes), and though it gained ten seats, it was challenged by a new movement, Social Credit, which obtained 15.8 percent of the votes and two seats (A2).

In the 1944 election, the C.C.F. finally came to power in a clear sweep of the Liberals. The first party obtained 53.1 percent of the votes, as compared to 35.4 percent for the second (A3). The weak Conservatives had declined further to 10.7 percent of the votes.

---

41 Data from Scarrow, *Canada Votes*, pp. 218–19. Scarrow distinguishes the "Independent Party" from the other groups of the "vague organization" described by the *Canadian Annual Review*. The rest of the votes went to the Conservatives (7.4 percent), the Progressives (7.5 percent), the Labourites and Non-Partisans (7.1 percent together). Lipset reports that "independent farmers' candidates carried twelve of the thirteen seats for which they ran"; *Agrarian Socialism*, p. 125.

42 See Morton, *The Progressive Party in Canada*, pp. 210–211.

43 See Dean E. McHenry, *The Third Force in Canada: The Cooperative Commonwealth Federation, 1932–1948* (Berkeley, Calif.: University of California Press, 1950), p. 209.

44 An analysis at the district level would be very important here to better establish the conditions of this case.

45 In terms of seats, with five and ten respectively in these two elections; they obtained slightly less votes than the Conservatives, however, in the first of these elections (24.0 and 26.7 percent respectively).

In short, almost all the period from 1905 to 1944 could be described as one in which Saskatchewan was groping for a viable opposition to the dominant Liberals. The Conservatives and various quasi and real third parties failed to fill the gap, but the C.C.F. was finally successful.

From 1944 to 1964, the province was governed by the C.C.F. party, which was not challenged too seriously. It almost, in turn, established a system of one-party dominance: the Liberals kept an average of only 33.8 percent of the votes and 24.8 percent of the seats in the five elections between 1944 and 1960. This may actually account for the relative success of the Social Credit party in the 1956 election. The party obtained 21.5 percent of the votes as compared to 3.9 percent in the previous election (A3). Nevertheless, the Liberals, as the traditional opposition party, were able to stage a comeback in the 1964 election and defeat the C.C.F. party. Does this present a deviation from the hypothesis? Given that the Liberals had kept, on the average, one-third of the electorate, this becomes a marginal case as far as the hypothesis is concerned. To make our test conservative, however, we consider this case as a deviation (A1).

MANITOBA

For at least the first fifteen years of this century,[46] Manitoba, contrary to Saskatchewan and Alberta, maintained a well-balanced two-party system. In the five elections from 1899 to 1914, the Liberal party, in opposition, kept an average of 45.8 percent of the votes, compared to the 49.6 percent obtained by the Conservative party led by Premier R. P. Roblin.[47] In 1915, the Parliament Buildings scandal[48] deeply shook the Conservative government and though they had a majority, they felt compelled to resign. The Liberals were invited to form a new government and soon after they called an election (1915). The electorate unambiguously repudiated the Conservatives. While only a year before the Conservatives had polled 46.6 percent of the votes, they were left with a proportion of only 33.0 percent; 60.6 percent of the voters now supported the Liberals,[49] who had been a strong opposition party (C1). The repudiation of the Conservative party was pervasive, except among French Canadians in the prov-

---

[46] "Prior to 1900 political parties barely existed in Manitoba. Party politics really began about 1900 when a government Conservative in fact as well as in name took office." Before that date, the groups were nevertheless described as Liberal or Conservative. M. S. Donnelly, *The Government of Manitoba* (Toronto: University of Toronto Press, 1963), p. 46.

[47] The parties kept 34.1 and 64.9 percent of the seats respectively. Data computed from *Canadian Parliamentary Guide* and *Canadian Annual Review*.

[48] The Conservatives were accused by the Liberals of having defrauded the public purse of some $800,000 for election funds in the construction of new parliament buildings, and a Royal Commission of Enquiry found the charges proven. The Premier and three of his ministers were later sued in courts. See W. L. Morton, *Manitoba: A History* (Toronto: University of Toronto Press, 1957), pp. 344ff.

[49] The Conservatives fought the battle with an almost completely beheaded and dishonored party; the new leader, Aikins, was supported by only one of the former Conservative ministers. See *ibid.*, pp. 347ff.

ince:[50] the party was left with only five seats out of forty-seven, four of which were gained by French-Canadian Catholics from the five French districts of the province. The new leader of the party was himself defeated and one of the French-Canadian members became opposition leader. The party which had been in power for fifteen years was suddenly crushed in the short period of one year.[51]

The Conservative party was to take a long time to recuperate from this stinging defeat. It first found itself unable to provide a viable opposition to the Liberals in the following election (1920). It presented only 30 candidates for the 55 seats[52] and ran candidates in less than half of the districts outside of Winnipeg (20 candidates for 45 seats). In the districts without a Conservative candidate, the opposition to the Liberals (who ran 52 candidates) came from Independents as well as from unofficial United Farmers of Manitoba candidates[53] and Labour party candidates.[54] Therefore, once more the weakness of the Conservative party was to be at the origin of these third-party successes: the Farmers elected 12 deputies, the Labour, 11, and the Independents, 4;[55] they had received, respectively, 15.8, 20.8, and 10.6 percent of the votes (A3).

The Liberals stayed in power as a minority government until 1922, when an election brought the Farmers to power (A3). Having fought and won without a leader, they recruited John Bracken, who had not participated in politics before, to head the government. He was to dominate Manitoba politics as Premier for twenty years, first as leader of the United Farmers of Manitoba or Progressives (1922 to 1932), then of the Liberal-Progressive party[56] (1932 to 1942).

Henceforth, a multi-party system was to persist, mainly due to the strength of the Labour-C.C.F. group. It led to a series of coalition and nonpartisan

50 No doubt due to the conciliatory position of the Conservatives, as opposed to the Liberals, on the question of the Bilingual School system.

51 "It was a leaderless rump, four-fifths French, which represented the party of Macdonald and Roblin." *Ibid.*, p. 348.

52 According to Scarrow, *Canada Votes*, p. 214. The *Canadian Parliamentary Guide* (1921, pp. 435–437), however, lists only 27 Conservative candidates.

53 The United Farmers of Manitoba had refused to formally enter provincial politics and left the decision to each constituency. Some candidates were chosen by locals of the U.F.M., some by sections of the locals, and some by groups independent of the U.F.M. *Canadian Annual Review*, 1920, pp. 741ff.

54 Of the 15 districts outside of Winnipeg, in which both Liberal and Conservative candidates were running, only 5 had also third-party candidates, and only 3 were gained by the latter. This is based on the *Canadian Parliamentary Guide* data (1921, pp. 435–437).

55 The Liberals were left with 21 deputies and the Conservatives, with 7. From Scarrow, *Canada Votes*, p. 214.

56 In 1928, the waning U.F.M. withdrew from politics, and the Bracken government moved closer to the Liberals. This was to lead to a fusion of the Liberals and the Progressives, which was almost completed by 1932. See Morton, *Manitoba: A History*, p. 465; Donnelly, *The Government of Manitoba*, pp. 63–64. Over the years, "as the 'Progressive' element within the Liberal-Progressive Party became less dominant, the Liberal-Progressive Party became in effect Manitoba's provincial Liberal Party. In 1961, the word 'Progressive' was finally removed from the party's name." Scarrow, *Canada Votes*, p. 216.

governments from 1936 to 1950. The elections of 1941, 1945, and 1949 were peculiar contests, since parties in the coalitions were dividing the field,[57] and on the average 23 percent of the seats were filled by acclamation. From 1942 to 1950, the main opposition to the Conservative, Liberal-Progressive, and Social Credit Coalition was provided by the C.C.F. party.[58] It should not be surprising, therefore, to find that the C.C.F. doubled its share of the votes in the 1945 election (from 17.3 percent in 1941 to 34.1 in 1945), since it was the only serious opposition (B3).

If, however, we consider the Coalition and Anti-Coalition forces as a two-party system, it can be seen that the main opposition party, the C.C.F., remained weak, with an average of 30.1 percent of the votes in the 1945 and 1949 elections. When the coalition broke up in 1950, a return to a multi-party system took place and all opposition parties remained weak[59] until 1958 when the Liberal-Progressive party was replaced in power by a nominally old party, the Conservatives, rather than by a third party.

Strictly speaking, this constitutes an exception to the hypothesis (A1). But the reader should note that the rejuvenated Conservative party of Duff Roblin had many of the characteristics of a new political movement. When the party emerged from the coalition in 1950, "their organizational base was almost gone."[60] As one "typical" instance, Donnelly reports the case of a district in which "the Conservative organization . . . had been dead for forty years."[61] The top leadership was not much stronger, since the end of the coalition deprived the party of most of its leaders. Of their nine members in the Legislature in 1949, four were in the cabinet and when the coalition broke up, three of the latter bolted the party to become Liberal-Progressive and remained in the cabinet.[62] On the other hand, the rejuvenation took place in 1954 by the choice of a new leader, Roblin, in an unusual, non-bureaucratic fashion;[63] to rebuild the party, Roblin's rule "was to find the best man to run in each riding, get him nominated and build the organization around him."[64] Therefore, Roblin did not have much of an entrenched leadership to fight against, and he could go about re-building the party very much like the leaders of new political movements do.

The Conservatives remained in power until 1969, when the New Democratic Party (the former C.C.F. party) stunned the country—and Manitobans themselves—by an unexpected victory over the two old parties. While the C.C.F./N.D.P. percentage of the votes had hovered between 15 and 23 percent in the four previous elections (1958 to 1966) to make the party the third one, it

57 Donnelly, *The Government of Manitoba*, p. 65.
58 In 1942, the C. C. F withdrew from the coalition, which broke up in 1950. *Ibid.*, pp. 65–66.
59 The strongest opposition party to emerge from the 1953 election was the Conservative party which obtained only 21.0 percent of the votes.
60 *The Government of Manitoba*, p. 67.
61 *Ibid.*
62 *Ibid.*, p. 66.
63 The candidates to the leadership stumped the province holding public meetings.
64 Donnelly, *The Government of Manitoba*, p. 67.

emerged as the winner from the 1969 contest, with 39 percent of the votes and twenty-eight seats out of fifty-seven.[65] Once more, this otherwise surprising upset by the N.D.P. is in line with our model. In the four previous elections, the Liberals had been the main opposition party with the low average of 33.8 percent of the votes; they were clearly a relatively weak opposition party, though again at a critical point. But again, to make our test conservative, this case has been classified as an exception (C3).

ONTARIO

From the beginning of the century until 1919 the two-party system was relatively more vigorous in Ontario than in some of the other provinces so far examined, though on the whole Ontario has been and still is a Conservative stronghold. The political scene from 1905 to 1919, was dominated by the Conservatives, who were in power during the whole period; the Liberals, who had been defeated in 1905, became a somewhat weak opposition party, but nevertheless managed to keep an average of 39.5 percent of the votes in the following three elections.[66] However, in 1919, to the surprise of all observers, the United Farmers of Ontario succeeded in capturing 22.0 percent of the votes and 45 of the 111 Ontario seats and formed a government with the 11 Labour deputies.

Since the opposition party had maintained a vote average of more than 33 percent, the previous situation did not seem to be one of one-party dominance, and according to the hypothesis, a third party should not have been successful. Why was it? First, the Liberal party, which was obviously not a very vigorous party in the previous election, had apparently not yet recuperated from the divisions in the federal branch of the party which had occurred in 1911 and 1917.[67] Second, the Liberals and Conservatives had apparently reached a tacit understanding of collaboration for the period of the war, which was broken just prior to the 1919 election.[68] Third, the strength of the Liberal party in the province did not seem to be very uniformly spread; the party had areas of strength, but also apparently areas of great weakness.[69]

As in some of the other instances examined above, this uneven strength

---

65 The Conservatives' vote dropped from 39 to 35 percent and their number of seats dropped from 31 to 22; for the Liberals, the drop in votes was from 34 to 24 percent, and in seats, from 14 to 5; the N.D.P. went from 23 to 39 percent of the votes, and from 11 to 28 seats.

66 They obtained 38.9 43.2, and 36.4 percent of the votes in the 1908, 1911, and 1914 elections, respectively.

67 In 1911, eighteen Toronto big businessmen bolted the party and campaigned for the Conservatives, and in 1917, the Liberal party was split between Laurier and Unionist groups. See Morton, *The Progressive Party in Canada*, pp. 22, 51.

68 See the *Canadian Annual Review*, 1919, p. 644.

69 It is revealing that in the 1908 and 1911 elections, 6 and 17 Conservatives were elected by acclamation, respectively. In the 1914 election, only 3 Conservatives were so elected, but in 19 other districts, the opposition to the Conservatives did not come from the Liberals, but from "Temperance," Labour, or Independent candidates. (The party affiliations were obtained from the Toronto *Globe*, June 23, 1914.)

became evident in the 1919 election, *when the Liberals failed to contest 35 percent of the seats*.[70] The opposition to the Conservatives in those seats came mainly from the United Farmers of Ontario, who contested almost as many seats as the Liberals.[71] It is noteworthy that the U.F.O. won 30 of the 33 seats which they contested and in which either the Liberals (27) or the Conservatives (6) had failed to run; on the other hand, the new party won only 10 of the 20 seats also contested by both old parties.[72] Our comments indicate that pockets of weakness on the part of the Liberal party may have been the conducive factor for the rise of a new party.[73] But since this is not a situation of one-party dominance in terms of vote, this case is classified in the middle column of Table 3.1 (B3).

The U.F.O. government to be sure did not last for long. It was roundly defeated by the Conservatives in the following election (1923); the U.F.O. dropped from 45 to 17 of the province's 111 seats, even though it kept about the same proportion of the votes (22.1 percent in 1923 to 22.0 in 1919); the Conservatives, on the other hand, increased their vote from 33.4 to 49.8 percent, and gained 76 seats. This return of the Conservatives does not seem too surprising, given their previous strength in Ontario (C1). It should be noted, however, that during its short stage in the opposition, this party barely kept the minimum support which seems required (it obtained only 33.4 percent of the votes in 1919, as compared to an average of 55.2 percent in the four preceding elections), so that this could possibly be considered as a marginal case.

From then on, the Conservatives clearly became the dominant party of Ontario. They continue to be. Indeed, in the three elections of the twenties, the Liberals kept in opposition an average of only 26.3 percent of the votes. Surprisingly, however, the economic depression of the thirties did not give rise to a third party, but provoked a strong resurgence of the Liberal party, which defeated the Conservatives in the 1934 election with 49.8 percent of the votes and seventy seats out of ninety. This constitutes a clear exception to the model, if one adds that the Liberals also remained in power in the 1937 election with 51.1 percent of the votes and sixty-six seats out of ninety (A1). It should be remarked, however, that the Liberals' victories seemed to owe a great deal to the personality of their leader, Mitchell Hepburn. In fact, Wrong wrote that "like Huey Long, whom he resembled personally in many respects, Hepburn

[70] That is, 39 out of 111 seats. (The Conservatives contested all but 10 seats.) The Liberals had apparently entertained the hope of absorbing the farmers by not opposing their candidates. On this, see Morton, *The Progressive Party in Canada*, p. 215.

[71] 69 out of 111 seats.

[72] In the six other districts in which the U.F.O. ran candidates, it could not be determined whether the other candidates represented the old parties or not. (Data from *The Canadian Annual Review*, 1919, pp. 661ff.)

[73] This lack of homogeneity in the strength of the Liberal party would make a rigorous test of the hypothesis more necessary in this instance than in the previous ones. This would be all the more necessary since Morton reports observations of a "coincidence between the areas of U.F.O. activity and those of the old Grit (Liberal) party." (See *The Progressive Party in Canada*, p. 83.)

was a talented demagogue combining both leftist and rightist appeals to the electorate. The provincial Liberal party failed to become a political force independent of his personal magnetism."[74]

Hepburn's Liberal government was indeed unable to overcome the postwar unrest and was defeated in the 1943 election. But in that election, the surprising upsurge of the C.C.F. from a minor-party status to that of a second party, with 31.6 percent of the votes and thirty-four seats out of ninety, constitutes another exception to the model (C3). Given the strength of the Conservatives' opposition, which had kept 39.8 percent of the votes in each of the two previous elections, the model would have predicted a failure of the C.C.F. party. But if we consider the size and the heterogeneity of the province and its respective pockets of weakness for each of the traditional parties,[75] it may be that here the test of the hypothesis at the level of the province as a whole is too crude.[76] Clearly a more detailed analysis of the type carried out for Quebec in the preceding chapter is called for in this instance.[77]

At any rate, the C.C.F. did not keep its official opposition status very long. The Conservatives, who had formed a minority government in 1943, soon regained a majority (1945)[78] which henceforth they never lost. From 1945 on, the Liberal party reoccupied its position of second major party (in terms of popular support), but it has remained nevertheless a weak opposition: its average of the votes in the seven elections from 1945 to 1967 has been 32.3 percent. In this light, the C.C.F./N.D.P. resurgences of 1948 (A3) and 1967 (A3) (with 26 percent of the votes each time) should not look too surprising. In fact, the Liberals, with the support of only about a third of the electorate, are in a precarious situation, and the model would lead us to expect that their chances of making a comeback are not too great. Given strains, one could easily witness new upsurges of the N.D.P. and, perhaps, as in Manitoba in 1969, a victory of that party.

QUEBEC

While from 1867 to the end of the nineteenth century, the Conservatives were the strong party in Quebec provincial politics, the 1897 election marked the beginning of the ascendancy of the Liberal party. From that time on, the

74 Dennis H. Wrong, "Ontario Provincial Elections, 1934-55; A Preliminary Survey of Voting," *The Canadian Journal of Economics and Political Science*, 23 (1957), p. 400.

75 See above and Wrong, *ibid.*

76 Let us also mention that "the way for (the C. C. F.) advance had been opened by a long and bitter feud between two of the Liberals' leaders—the Prime Minister of Canada and the Premier of Ontario—which so weakened their provincial party that it has still not recovered its position"; Zakuta, *A Protest Movement Becalmed*, p. 59, fn. 3.

77 In particular, one should investigate whether the traditional weakness of the Liberal party in Ontario, particularly during the twenties, has not been an important factor; the Liberals' resurgence with Hepburn during the thirties would again have been like the federal Conservatives' resurgence in Quebec in 1958, and the two-step variation of the model would again have to be considered.

78 With 44.2 percent of the votes and 66 of the 90 seats.

Liberals won no less than eleven successive elections, and formed the government for an uninterrupted period of thirty-nine years (1897 to 1936).[79]

As they did at the federal level, the Liberals apparently created a system of one-party dominance at the provincial level even though from 1897 to 1935 the Conservative party obtained on the average 36.7 percent of the votes.[80] Our judgment is based on the fact that an astonishingly large number of seats were often not contested by the Conservatives, which revealed pockets of extreme weakness; indeed, on the average, one out of every five seats (19.2 percent) went to the Liberals by acclamation during that period. For instance, in the elections of 1900, 1904, and 1919, the Liberals won more than half the seats by acclamation, so that the contest was already decided before polling day.[81] Therefore, if in computing the average proportion of votes for the Conservatives in that period, one takes into account the elections by acclamation, the average proportion drops to 29.3 percent.[82] The true percentage of Conservative preferences in the population probably lies between these two proportions, that is, around 33 percent. But the important consideration is that the Conservatives were in all likelihood extremely weak in certain districts.

These facts, in our mind, account for the Conservatives' inability to defeat the Liberals again. The Liberals' first serious challenge came in 1935 when they competed against a new political group, the alliance Duplessis–Gouin, made up of the old Conservative party, led by Duplessis, together with the *Action Libérale Nationale*, a group of dissident Liberals led by Gouin, and independent nationalists.[83] The coalition obtained 48.4 percent of the votes and forty-two seats out of ninety. The Liberals remained in power, but were finally forced to resign a year later, and the 1936 election witnessed the success of a quasi-third party, the *Union Nationale*, born of the 1935 coalition. Under the strain of the period, Duplessis' Union Nationale swept the province with 57.5 percent of the votes and seventy-six seats out of ninety. Thus the rise of this quasi-third party seems to be related to an extremely long period of one-party dominance by the Liberals in Quebec provincial politics. Given, however, that the proportion of the

79 The resurgence of the Liberal party could probably be dated to its temporary transformation into a quasi-third party, Mercier's National Party, in the 1886 election.

80 Except for the 1935 election, this average is based on the election results presented in Jean Hamelin, Jacques Letarte, et Marcel Hamelin, "Les élections provinciales dans le Québec," *Cahiers de Géographie de Québec*, 4 (1959–60), pp. 5–207. The 1935 election results are from Scarrow, *Canada Votes*, p. 208. If the results for the three elections of 1923, 1927, and 1931 are taken from Scarrow rather than Hamelin *et al.*, the average drops from 36.7 percent to 35.9 percent.

81 See Hamelin, *et al.*, "Les élections provinciales dans le Québec," *passim*.

82 This average is computed from the proportions for each election which take acclamations into account; these proportions are presented in *ibid.*, *passim*.

83 The *Action Libérale Nationale* was formed in 1934 by a group of young nationalist dissident Liberals. On the eve of the 1935 election, they formed an alliance with Duplessis' Conservative party under the label of the *Union Nationale Duplessis–Gouin*. Following disagreements between the two leaders, Gouin quit the coalition; Duplessis was left as the sole leader, and with his followers and most of the A.L.N. followers, he formed the *Union Nationale* party which won the 1936 election; on this, see Hamelin *et al.*, "Les élections provinciales dans le Québec"; Herbert F. Quinn, *The Union Nationale: A Study in Quebec Nationalism* (Toronto: University of Toronto Press, 1963), Chap. 4.

votes obtained by the Conservatives while in opposition (if one does not consider the elections by acclamation) is above 33 percent, but that a large number
of seats were often not contested, this case has been classified in the middle
column of Table 3.1 (B3).

Elected in 1936, the Union Nationale was soon defeated, in the 1939 election, and the Liberals, as a strong opposition party,[84] could easily return to
power (C1). In 1944, a new nationalist group, the *Bloc popularie*, appeared to
compete with the Union Nationale against the incumbent Liberals; its success,
though limited,[85] was probably related to the same traditional weakness of the
old opposition party, the provincial Conservatives (A2).

In that election, the Union Nationale defeated the Liberals, though the
latter obtained more votes than the former.[86] The Union Nationale remained in
power until 1960. The only third party effort to occur during this period was
that of the Union of Electors in the 1948 election. As we have seen in Chapter
1, this party was the Quebec branch of Social Credit during the forties. Despite
great organizational efforts[87] and a full slate of candidates, the Union of Electors
could not secure more than 9.3 percent of the votes and it gained no seat. Again,
though other factors, such as the lack of strain, could have been involved, we
suggest that the strength of the Liberal opposition[88] was also a serious handicap
for the rise of this third party (C1).

The Liberals returned to power in 1960, after sixteen years in the opposition.
They were able to replace the Union Nationale because they had remained a
strong opposition party.[89] They had kept on the average, from 1944 to 1960,
41.5 percent of the votes and 23.9 percent of the seats. The Union Nationale had
failed to develop a system of one-party dominance (C1).

Even more characteristically, the return to power of the Union Nationale in
1966 and the failure of two new separatist parties, the *Rassemblement pour l'indé-
pendance nationale* (R.I.N.) and the *Ralliement National* (R.N.)[90] fit the hypothe-

---

84 The Liberals' 1936 vote, which was its lowest in this century, was still at 41.8 percent according
to Hamelin *et al.*, "Les élections provinciales dans le Québec," p. 46 (or 39.4 percent, according to
Scarrow, *Canada Votes*, p. 208).

85 The *Bloc popularie* obtained 14.4 percent of the votes and 4 seats; (computed from Scarrow,
Canada Votes, pp. 206–208. This new party however soon disintegrated; (see Quinn, *The Union Nationale*, p. 111, p. 154).

86 The Union Nationale obtained 38.0 percent of the votes and 48 seats; the Liberals, 39.3 percent
of the votes and 37 seats; from Scarrow, *Canada Votes*, pp. 206–208. (The rest of this section is based
on this source.)

87 See Stein, *The Dynamics of Political Protest*, Chap. 2.

88 In the previous election, the incumbent Liberals had been defeated with a vote of 39.3 percent,
and 37 seats out of 91.

89 See Hamelin *et al.*, "Les élections provinciales dans le Québec." The authors note that the Union
Nationale never was as omnipotent as the Liberals had been before them. It never obtained more than
55 percent of the votes, while the Liberals before had at times reached the 80 percent mark (p. 174).

90 The first was the main party calling for the separation of Quebec from Canada; it ran 73 candidates and obtained 5.6 percent of the votes. The second was a new provincial branch of Social Credit
which had made an alliance with a much weaker rightist separatist group; it ran 90 candidates and
obtained only 3.2 percent of the votes. (Data from *Le Devoir*, June 13, 1966).

sis perfectly. Since the Union Nationale had kept an average of 44.3 percent of the votes and 38.9 percent of the seats, it was able to stage a comeback (C1). Third parties on the other hand remained weak.[91]

MARITIME PROVINCES

The three old provinces of the Maritimes[92] constitute an ideal ground to test the hypothesis that a wellbalanced two-party system offers a very serious handicap for third parties. Contrary to all other provinces, no genuine or quasi-third parties ever attained power in these provinces. In fact, except for very few instances, third parties in the Maritimes have always completely failed with the electorate, being restricted generally to less than ten percent of the votes, when not to less than five percent. And characteristically, since the beginning of this century at least, all three provinces have maintained relatively strong two-party systems. In New Brunswick and Prince Edward Island, in particular, the two traditional parties—Liberal and Conservative—have alternated in power regularly since the beginning of this century, except for the period from 1935 to the mid-fifties, which were marked by stable Liberal governments in each case. Let us briefly consider each province separately, starting with a less "pure" case, that of Nova Scotia.

NOVA SCOTIA

In Nova Scotia, the Liberals remained uninterruptedly in power from the beginning of this century to 1925. Indeed "the most striking feature of the operation of the Nova Scotian party system has been that the voters elect Conservative governments merely by spasms and those spasms are of short dura-

---

91 At the time of going to press, we can report however that the model's prediction did not hold in the 1970 election. Despite the strength of the Liberal opposition (they had kept 47 percent of the votes in 1966), two new parties made serious inroads in Quebec's party system. A new party led by René Lévesque and regrouping all separatist forces, the *Parti Québécois*, and a new provincial wing of Social Credit, the *Ralliement Créditiste*, obtained 23 and 11 percent of the votes and 7 and 12 seats, respectively. The Liberals were elected with 45 percent of the votes and 72 seats, while the incumbent Union Nationale sustained a stinging defeat losing half of its previous support. It was left with 20 percent of the votes and 17 seats. This constitutes a major exception to our model which cannot be examined here. It would fall in C3 in Table 3.1. Let us mention however, among what seems to have been key factors of this departure from a general pattern, the disarray of the Union Nationale under Mr. Bertrand's poor leadership, the strong charisma of Mr. Lévesque, as well as persisting unrest despite shifts between both old parties in recent years, and these frequent political shifts themselves (that political change is conducive to further political change will be documented in Chapter 5).

92 The fourth one, Newfoundland, only lately entered Confederation, in 1949, and has had since something approaching a system of one-party dominance under the Liberals. In the first three elections (1949, 1951, and 1956), the Conservatives obtained only an average of 33.6 percent of the votes and 14.1 percent of the seats. It may be symptomatic that in the fourth election, in 1959, two new parties (the Newfoundland Democrats, with labor union backing, and the United Newfoundland, a Conservative splinter group) appeared on the scene and polled respectively 7.2 and 8.2 percent of the votes, leaving the Conservatives with only 25.3 percent. See Scarrow, *Canada Votes*, p. 201.

tion."[93] But despite this voting behavior, what is striking is that the Conservatives' proportions of the votes rarely dropped below 40 percent. They were, therefore, able to stage comebacks in 1925 and 1956.

The only serious inroad made by third parties came in 1920 when, following the general unrest of that period, the Farmer and Labour groups obtained respectively 14.0 and 16.9 percent of the votes, and seven and four seats.[94] This seems to constitute an exception to our thesis since in the four previous elections, from 1901 to 1916, the Conservatives had retained an average of 44.5 percent of the votes (though with only 19.7 percent of the seats). It must be mentioned, however, that "normally the Conservatives have possessed nothing like the same organization" as the Liberals, and they were generally registering "surprise at the size of their popular vote despite the strength of the contending forces."[95] *In fact, as in other instances above, the Conservatives had failed to contest nine of the forty-three seats*[96] *in that election* (the Liberals running for all but three seats), and five of the seven seats won by the Farmers were among the latter.[97] On the other hand, the four labour members were all from Cape Breton County, a coal-mining area which, as elsewhere, has traditionally been a marginal region exhibiting strong leftist tendencies.[98] Given the failure of the Conservatives to contest some seats, this case is entered in the middle column of Table 3.1 (B3). Moreover, these third groups disappeared rapidly: in the following election (1925), with the Conservatives presenting a full slate of candidates again,[99] these groups got only 2.8 percent of the popular vote.[100] In fact, the Conservatives were strong enough[101] to stage a comeback; they swept the province with 60.9 percent of the votes and forty of the forty-three seats (C1).

In 1933, during the Depression, the Liberals in turn defeated the Conservatives. Again, this was to be expected since they had kept an average of 41.7 percent of the votes in the two previous elections (C1).

In general, after 1920, Nova Scotia remained strongly resistant to third

93 See J. Murray Beck. *The Government of Nova Scotia* (Toronto: University of Toronto Press, 1957), p. 157. From 1867 to 1956, the Conservatives were in power for only 12 years (1878–1882 and 1925–1933); see *ibid.* They have been in power, however, since 1956.

94 The Liberals were maintained in power with 44.4 percent of the votes and 29 seats out of 43.

95 Beck, *The Government of Nova Scotia*, p. 161.

96 The difficulties the Conservatives met in finding candidates has been noted. See *The Canadian Annual Review*, 1920, p. 683. The Conservative leader attributed the defeat of his party "to the brief period at our disposal for organization, and the remarkably short notice we had that an election was pending." *Ibid.*, p. 685.

97 Established from the *Canadian Annual Review*, 1920, p. 684 and the *Canadian Parliamentary Guide*, 1922, pp. 413–414.

98 For an interpretation of these tendencies, see Beck, *The Government of Nova Scotia*, pp. 168–169, and Lipset, *Political Man*, p. 234.

99 They had had a full slate of candidates before, as for instance in 1916; see *Canadian Parliamentary Guide*, 1917, pp. 372–374.

100 Beck, *The Government of Nova Scotia*, p. 168.

101 From 1901 to 1920, they maintained an average of 40.5 percent of the votes.

parties. Despite its repeated efforts since 1941, the C.C.F. party has been most unsuccessful. Its greatest success came in 1945, when it obtained 13.6 percent of the votes;[102] but almost half of this support came again from Cape Breton County alone.[103] The weakness of the C.C.F. should not be surprising since the Conservatives, the main opposition party in the three previous elections (1933, 1937, and 1941), had polled an average of 44.1 percent of the votes and obtained 18.9 percent of the seats (C2).

In 1956, the same Conservative party was returned to power to replace a Liberal administration which had lasted since 1933. As should be expected, the Conservatives as the main opposition party had secured a relatively high proportion of the votes during the six elections of the previous period (41.4 percent), even though they had retained only 19.1 percent of the seats (C1).

NEW BRUNSWICK

The case of New Brunswick is very similar. From the beginning of this century, both the Conservative and Liberal parties have been strong, although the Conservatives have probably been stronger here than in Nova Scotia; consequently, third parties have also been unable to replace the old parties. From 1903 to 1917, the two old parties regularly alternated in power. This was made easy by the fact that in each election the opposition party kept at least an average of 42 percent of the votes.[104] The alternations were as follows: Liberals, 1903–1908; Conservatives, 1908–1917 (C1); Liberals, 1917–1925 (C1).

As in many other provinces, however, the Farmers and Labour made an inroad in the two-party system in 1920, obtaining, respectively, 21.1 and 6.2 percent of the votes. But as in Nova Scotia, the new groups were unable to gain a substantial representation[105] and the incumbent Liberals were maintained in power. When one looks at the state of the party system before that election, one finds that as in Nova Scotia—and even more so—the Conservatives had given sudden signs of weakness. They had been overthrown in the 1917 election after the Conservative Premier, Mr. Flemming, had been found guilty of political corruption by a Royal Commission in 1914 and forced to resign from the Premiership. Mr. Flemming's successor resigned in turn from the leadership of the party after the calling of the 1920 contest, and a new leader was chosen to carry the campaign.[106] At any rate, *they had contested only twenty-seven of the fourty-eight seats.* Therefore, once more the failure of the Conservatives to put

---

102 It had obtained 7.0 percent in the previous election (1941) and in all elections from 1949 to 1960, it always remained below 10 percent. During the thirties, the maximum number of candidates presented by a third party was three.

103 Beck, *The Government of Nova Scotia*, p. 169.

104 Hugh G. Thorburn, *Politics in New Brunswick* (Toronto: University of Toronto Press, 1961), Table XXI, p. 198.

105 They obtained 9 and 2 seats respectively. See Scarrow, *Canada Votes*, p. 206. However, *The Canadian Annual Review*, 1920, reports only 6 Farmers and 2 Independent-Labourites elected (p. 717).

106 See Thorburn, *Politics in New Brunswick*, p. 120; *The Canadian Annual Review*, 1914, p. 562, and 1920, p. 715.

up a full slate of candidates was directly responsible for the Farmers' and Labour's successes. Indeed the new groups were unable to obtain a single seat from the districts contested by the Conservatives.[107] Accordingly, this case is also entered in the middle column of Table 3.1 (B3).

As in Nova Scotia, these new groups lasted for only one term and disappeared in the next election (1925),[108] when the Conservatives offered a full slate of candidates and indeed came back to power. They had retained, as the main opposition party from 1917 to 1925, an average of 37.5 percent of the votes (C1).[109] Ten years later, in 1935, they were replaced in turn by the Liberals who had kept, in opposition, an average of 46.2 percent of the votes and 29.2 percent of the seats (C1).[110]

During the forties and fifties, the C.C.F. and Social Credit parties tried, but in vain, to make an inroad in this relatively healthy two-party system. They "have both been singularly unsuccessful."[111] The C.C.F. peaked in 1944 with 11.7 percent of the votes[112] and no seats. Its poor showing is probably related to the fact that the Conservative opposition in the two previous elections (1935 and 1939) had retained an average of 42.6 percent of the votes and 25.0 percent of the seats (C2). Social Credit ran a few candidates in the 1948 and 1956 elections, but with even less success (C1).[113]

Meanwhile, the alternation between the two old parties has continued regularly. The Conservatives, who had retained an average of 39.1 percent of the votes and 20.4 percent of the seats in the four previous elections (1935 to 1948), were returned to power in 1952 (C1). The Liberals replaced the Conservatives again in 1960, after they had kept an average of 47.6 percent of the votes and 29.8 percent of the seats during their two terms in opposition (1952 to 1956) (C1).

PRINCE EDWARD ISLAND

As an ideal contrasting example, one could not find better than the province of Prince Edward Island. Except for two long periods of Liberal administration (1891 to 1911, and 1935 to 1959), the parties have regularly replaced each other in power, often after only one four-year term in office.[114]

107 Established on the basis of the data presented in *The Canadian Annual Review*, 1920, pp. 716–717, and the *Canadian Parliamentary Guide*, 1922, pp. 435–436.

108 That year, the Farmers put up only three candidates and obtained only 1.9 percent of the votes. There were no Labour candidates; see Scarrow, *Canada Votes*, pp. 206–207.

109 Data from Thorburn, *Politics in New Brunswick*, Table XXI, p. 198.

110 These data as well as those below are from Scarrow, *Canada Votes*, pp. 206–207.

111 Thorburn, *Politics in New Brunswick*, p. 102. For details on the efforts of these two parties in New Brunswick, see *ibid.*, pp. 102–106.

112 Their second highest mark was attained in 1948 with only 6.0 percent of the votes.

113 Their 5 candidates in 1948 obtained less than 1.0 percent of the votes and their 18 candidates in 1956 obtained 1.6 percent of the votes; see Scarrow, *Canada Votes*, pp. 206–207.

114 From 1911 to 1935, there were three Conservative administrations, one of eight years and two of four years (1911–1919; 1923–1927; 1931–1935), separated by two Liberal administrations of four years each (1919–1923; 1927–1931); see Frank MacKinnon, *The Government of Prince Edward Island* (Toronto: University of Toronto Press, 1951), p. 365; Scarrow, *Canada Votes*, p. 202.

Again, the failure of third parties appears to be clearly related to the surprising strength of the two old parties; (as always, of course, the absence of strain could be another reason). From the beginning of this century to the present, the opposition party, while out of office, has always kept an average of more than 43 percent of the vote.[115]

Thus, the Conservatives returned to power in 1911, having kept an average vote of 47.2 percent between 1900 and 1908 (C1). The Liberals replaced them in 1919, their average vote between 1911 and 1915 having been 44.8 percent. Characteristically, the farmers organized in 1919, but not as a party, simply encouraging the nomination of farmers as candidates in rural districts,[116] and the electoral contest turned out to be a straight two-party battle between Conservatives and Liberals for every seat except two;[117] the latter party unseated the former (C1).

In the following four elections (1923, 1927, 1931, and 1935), the incumbent party was each time defeated and replaced by the opposition party. Each time the latter had maintained an average exceeding 43 percent of the votes. On the other hand, the Progressive party put up five candidates in 1923 and obtained only 3.4 percent of the votes (4 times C1).

The Liberals were in power for no less than twenty-four years after that (1935 to 1959), but despite such a long stay in office, they did not even come close to the creation of a system of one-party dominance. The Conservatives kept an average vote of 45.4 percent and defeated them in 1959 (C1). During the forties and early fifties, the C.C.F. party tried to secure a foothold in the province, but failed to elect a single candidate in three elections. In 1943 and in 1947, all C.C.F. candidates lost their deposits.[118] The party attained its high-water mark in 1947, with 4.3 percent of the votes (C1).

Finally in 1966, the Conservatives were in turn defeated by a Liberal party which had kept an average of 49.0 percent of the votes in the two previous elections (C1).

In short, it appears that third parties have been conspicuously unsuccessful in this province due to the relative strength of the two traditional parties. According to Dennis Wrong, the failure of third parties in the Maritime Provinces is a deviant case since these provinces, like the western ones, are divided from the rest of Canada by sectional interests.[119] While it might be true that such sectional interests exist, they have not given rise to sectional consciousness as in the

115 Only once, and for a single election, did one of the two traditional parties get less than 40 percent of the votes; this was in 1911 when the Liberals, as the *incumbents* after twenty years in power, received only 39.8 percent of the votes and were defeated. But as an opposition party between 1911 and 1915, the Liberals still maintained an average of 44.8 percent of the votes.

116 MacKinnon, *The Government of Prince Edward Island*, p. 248.

117 According to electoral results published in the *Canadian Parliamentary Guide*, 1922, pp. 492–493. In the two exceptions, the Liberals were opposed by Independents.

118 See MacKinnon, *The Government of Prince Edward Island*, p. 248.

119 "Parties and Voting in Canada: A Backward and Forward Glance in the Light of the Last Election," *Political Science Quarterly*, 73 (1958), pp. 397–412.

Western Provinces[120] and consequently a one-party dominance system has not developed.[121] Hence, the fact that third parties in these provinces rarely obtained any substantial success at the polls and never won an election,[122] far from being a deviant case, fits the present theory perfectly well.

THIRD PARTIES
AT THE FEDERAL LEVEL

As far as the federal level is concerned, the situation does not seem to have been much different. The hypothesis, as was shown in detail in Chapter 2, accounts for the rise of Social Credit at the federal level in Quebec in 1962. Recall that from 1917 to 1958, the Conservatives' proportion of the votes in Quebec hovered around 27.1 percent, so that they constituted a very weak opposition party (A3). Let us add a few brief comments[123] to suggest that the model probably accounts for the rise of other third parties at the federal level in Canada.

In Quebec federal politics again, we may consider the resurgence of the Conservatives in 1958 as a deviation (A1), though the reader is referred to our comments on the two-step modification of our model.[124] But the success of the Nationalists in 1911 and that of the *Bloc Populaire Canadien* in 1945 are revealing. In both cases, the Conservatives failed to contest many ridings; they made an alliance with the Nationalists in 1911 (B2),[125] and they ran in only twenty-nine districts out of sixty-five in 1945 (A2).[126]

One-party dominance was apparently also a conducive factor for the success of the Progressive party at the federal level in 1921, mainly in the Western Provinces and Ontario. The federal and provincial party organizations were far

120 See Beck, *The Government of Nova Scotia*, pp. 169–170, for the case of Nova Scotia: "The economic development of the province up to now has not been such as to evoke any pronounced feelings of class-consciousness. . . . Furthermore, there is no substantial economic group which, in the manner of the grain growers in Western Canada, is able to maintain a cohesive political existence by attributing the insecurity of its material position to dependence upon outside financial interests. For while primary producers may subsist in what Professor Macpherson describes as a state of 'quasi-colonialism,' their problems are so diffuse that combined action to improve their lot is rendered extraordinarily difficult" (p. 169).

121 The link between sectional interests and one-party dominance will be discussee in the next chapter.

122 The strength of the two-party system in these provinces may also be linked to the particularly long existence of the two old parties, since these provinces entered Confederation earlier than the Prairie Provinces; see Regenstreif, *The Diefenbaker Interlude*, pp. 163–164.

123 As mentioned before, only a few federal "cases" will be considered here. What follows should therefore not be taken as as complete an examination of the subject as was done at the provincial level.

124 See page 26.

125 About 25 seats were contested by Nationalist candidates.

126 The first of these two cases is classified in the middle column of Table 3.1 since percentagewise, the Conservatives were strong before 1911 (see page 22). But from 1917 to 1940, the Conservatives kept a low vote average of 29.2 percent. The *Bloc* gained 13.0 percent of the votes in 1945.

from independent of each other in the West until that time,[127] and the weakness of the Conservative party prevailed at the federal level as well as at the provincial level in both Saskatchewan and Alberta.[128] The federal Conservative party was said to have practically disappeared from these provinces after 1911, though it retained around 40 percent of the votes in both provinces in 1911.

But the real blow to a healthy two-party system in the Prairie Provinces was apparently to come in 1917, with the split of the Liberals into Laurier and Unionist groups.[129] The Prairie Liberal provincial organizations turned against Laurier and supported a Union Government with the Conservatives, and in the 1917 election, the Prairie Provinces returned forty-one Unionists out of forty-three seats.[130] The effect of this Unionist victory is reported to have been nothing less than the destruction in the West of the federal organizations of the two old parties, with the Conservatives losing their identity as a federal party.[131]

At the following election, in 1921, a dissatisfied Prairie electorate, who had been left with no alternative after four years of coalition between the two old parties, swept the Progressives in, giving them 54.5 percent of their votes (for the three provinces considered together) and thirty-eight of their forty-three seats (B3). Similar remarks could probably be made with regard to the success of the Progressives in Ontario in 1921, where they obtained 27.7 percent of the votes and 29.3 percent of the seats (B3).[132]

From then on, the federal party system in the Western Provinces became and was to remain a multi-party system. This renders the test of the hypothesis much less simple.[133] A few considerations are nevertheless worthwhile.

Though the Progressive party slowly disappeared during the twenties, the organization behind it[134] contributed to the formation of the C.C.F. when the depression of the thirties came. Social Credit also appeared on the national scene, after its provincial success in Alberta in 1935.[135] These new parties ran first in the 1935 federal election, which was fought against the incumbent Conservatives. The Social Credit success was greater, but was largely limited to Alberta, where the party obtained 46.8 percent of the votes and fifteen of the seventeen seats. It is noteworthy that this was the Western area where the Liberal party, as the

---

127 See Morton, *The Progressive Party in Canada*, p. 60.

128 *Ibid.*, pp. 51–52, p. 230.

129 *Ibid.*, p. 55.

130 *Ibid.*, pp. 55–59.

131 *Ibid.*, p. 60.

132 Again, the success of the Progressives in Ontario would have to be analysed in more detail. It is to be noted that the Unionists got 74 out of 82 seats in that province in 1917.

133 This difficulty is increased by the fact that the opposition party at the federal level for Canada as a whole may be the stronger party at the same level within a province.

134 Together with provincial labor parties and some Farmer candidates; see Scarrow, *Canada Votes*, p. 88.

135 A Reconstruction party was also formed, and it entered candidates in every province; but it remained weak in the West and it shall not be further considered here: See *ibid.*

weaker of the two old parties, had retained, from 1921 to 1930—in four elections—an average of only 24.1 percent of the votes (A3).[136]

In the three other Western Provinces, the C.C.F. emerged as the strongest of the new parties, though its success in these provinces was relatively weaker than that of Social Credit in Alberta. And characteristically, the weaker of the two old parties had retained in the four previous elections 26.6, 26.8, and 35.6 percent of the votes in Manitoba, Saskatchewan, and British Columbia, respectively (A3).[137] Thus it appears that weak federal opposition parties within these provinces set the stage for the Social Credit and C.C.F. parties in the thirties.

But what about the rejuvenation of the Progressive Conservative party and its return to a majority position in the Western Provinces, as in Quebec, in the 1957 and 1958 elections? If one considers that it had become one of the weakest parties in that area, its comeback constitutes a deviation from the hypothesis (A1). One could, however, explain this deviation by noting that third parties in that region largely replaced the Conservatives as the main opposition to the Liberals from 1935 to 1957, mainly in Saskatchewan and Alberta, where they were often the parties with the largest pluralities in federal elections. Therefore the comeback of the Conservatives in these provinces could be attributed to the fact that the third parties, which had become "traditional," had failed in their effort to overthrow the Liberal administration. Indeed, given the charismatic appeal of Diefenbaker, who was also a very popular local politician, one can think of the resurgence of the Progressive Conservative party in that area as akin to the rise of a new party to replace *hopeless* opposition "third" parties.[138]

To be sure, in Saskatchewan, the C.C.F. obtained an average of 35.9 percent of the votes from 1935 to 1957, and the comparable figure for Social Credit in Alberta is 39.0 percent.[139] They were not, therefore, weak opposition parties in terms of votes. But to the electorate, these parties may have appeared as having no chance of overthrowing the federal Liberal administration, given their purely regional strength. And after the first resurgence of the Conservatives in 1957

136 If instead of the weaker of the two old parties, we consider the strength of the main opposition party in each election, whether old or new, we get also a low average of 28.4 percent of the votes.

137 The parties are the Liberals in Manitoba and British Columbia, and the Conservatives in Saskatchewan. If the main opposition party is taken, rather than the main traditional opposition party, the figures we obtain are 31.6, 29.4, and 35.6 for Manitoba, Saskatchewan and British Columbia, respectively.

138 I owe this suggestion to Peter Regenstreif. Diefenbaker came from Saskatchewan and was credited for the resurgence of his party in the Western Provinces. See Regenstreif, *The Difenbaker Interlude*, Chap. 7, Clark also noted the similarity between the Conservative sweep of 1958 in Alberta and Saskatchewan, and the Social Credit success of 1935 in Alberta; S.D. Clark, "Group Interests in Canadian Politics," pp. 64–78, esp. pp. 74–75; see also John Porter, *The Vertical Mosaic* (Toronto: University of Toronto Press, 1965), pp. 377–378.

139 During the same period, the Conservatives had kept the low average of 16.8 and 17.9 percent of the votes in each province, respectively.

in the rest of Canada, these two provinces gave a clear majority to that party in 1958.[140]

In Manitoba and British Columbia, the "new" and old opposition parties were of approximately equal strength from 1935 to 1953, the Conservatives maintaining an average of 25.4 percent of the votes in both and C.C.F., an average of 24.0 and 29.9 percent of the votes in each, respectively. But again the interpretation would be the same, with this difference here that the C.C.F., being weaker and not in power at the provincial level, gave way to the Conservatives somewhat earlier, in 1957, rather than in 1958 as in the other two provinces.[141]

With this, we come to the end of a long incursion into outside territories, the results of which have already been summarized in Table 3.1. Before returning to the analysis of the Social Credit upsurge in Quebec, we shall present, in Chapter 4, a few generalizations derived from the analysis of this and the preceding chapter. These will be followed by the discussion of a more general model of the determinant of conduciveness in the rise of third parties.

[140] The party, which had obtained but 23.2 and 27.6 percent of the votes in these two provinces in 1957, obtained 51.4 and 59.9 percent of the votes in 1958. The difference with Quebec in these instances was that the resurgence lasted for more than one election.

[141] The Conservatives obtained 35.9 and 32.6 percent of the votes in these two provinces, respectively, in 1957; for 1958, the figures are, respectively, 56.7 and 49.4 percent.

One-Party
Dominance:
A Model

CHAPTER FOUR

The analysis of the previous two chapters gives clear indications that one-party dominance created conditions which were strongly conducive to the rise of third parties at both the provincial and national levels in Canada. Closer empirical verifications would of course be needed before the hypothesis could be considered substantiated.

A FEW GENERALIZATIONS

The data so far presented nevertheless suggest a few generalizations.[1] First, if a two-party system is to be maintained—or if a multi-party system is not to be further extended—the main opposition party cannot obtain less than a third of the votes.[2] The evidence which has been summarized in Table 3.1, column C, indicates that there are only very few cases indeed where a strong opposition party kept more than that proportion of the votes and was seriously challenged by a third party. The overwhelming pattern in such situations is for that opposition party to constitute a viable alternative to the incumbent party and to replace it whenever the latter is defeated. In fact, when one considers the few

---

[1] We shall not return to the two-step variation of the model; on this, see Chap. 2, p. 26, and Chap. 3, *passim.*

[2] No generalization can be made on the basis of the proportion of the seats retained by the main opposition party; this should not be surprising, given the variations in electoral systems and the distortions they introduce in terms of representation. Moreover, the proportion of the votes maintained is only an indicator of one-party dominance, though it appears to be a very good one.

instances in which a third party actually arose under these conditions (six out of
the thirty-three cases examined), it is evident that either the challenge was not
very serious or the opposition party was not very strong. In two cases (cell C2
in Table 3.1), the third party (C.C.F.) got only 13.6 and 11.7 percent of the
votes respectively.[3] The four remaining cases (cell C3 in Table 3.1) all seem to
be instances where at least one of the two traditional parties could be characterized, by indicators other than the votes maintained, as at least not overly
strong.[4]

Conversely, in a situation of one-party dominance in which the main opposition party maintains the support of less than a third of the electorate,[5] the likelihood of the emergence of a third party is quite strong (see column A of the
same Table). In the twenty-two instances examined here, a third party got at
least 20 percent of the votes about six times out of ten, and in fact came to power
about two times out of ten. In a few other instances third parties also arose,
though they were less successful; but this should not be too surprising, as mentioned before, since conduciveness is not the only determinant of success for a
new political movement. Seen differently, what is striking here is that weak
traditional opposition parties were able to return to power in only five of the
twenty-two instances examined.[6] Characteristically, therefore, one-party dominance entails very long administrations by the dominant party, with third party
outbursts of varying magnitudes and occasional third party victories.[7]

Finally, the data summarized in column B of Table 3.1 suggest the following
two generalizations. First, even if the two old parties are strong, whenever they
are driven into a coalition by a crisis, it creates conditions of conduciveness for
the subsequent rise of third parties.[8] By definition, the strength of the opposi-

3 In Nova Scotia in 1945, and in New Brunswick in 1944.

4 In one case (British Columbia, 1924), the Conservatives were divided, and some of the dissidents formed the third party which arose. In another one (British Columbia, 1933), the Conservatives,
though the incumbents, withdrew as a separate party. In the third case (Ontario, 1943), pockets of
weakness of both old parties may be involved, particularly the traditional weakness of the Liberals,
except for the Hepburn era. Finally, the fourth case (Manitoba, 1969) is really a marginal one, since
the Liberals had maintained an average of only 33.8 percent while constituting the main opposition
party. As mentioned above (p. 54, fn. 91), we should now add a fifth case (Quebec, 1970).

5 It does not seem possible to specify clearly the length of time one-party dominance must prevail
for the system to become conducive to third parties.

6 It is difficult to make any generalization about these deviations, except perhaps to mention that
charismatic, or at least strong leaders were often involved: Hepburn in Ontario in 1934; Diefenbaker
in the Western Provinces in 1957–58, and the same in Quebec in 1958; (the latter case is also a clear
instance of a strong bandwagon); Roblin's rejuvenation of the Conservatives in Manitoba in 1958;
Thatcher's victory in Saskatchewan in 1964 (but since his party had kept an average of 33.8 percent
of votes, this is a marginal case).

7 In Table 3.1, cell A3, there are four such victories: Social Credit in British Columbia in 1952–
53, and in Alberta in 1935; C. C. F. in Saskatchewan in 1944; United Farmers of Manitoba in 1922.
(There are also four other third-party victories; one is classified in C3 to make the test more conservative: NDP in Manitoba in 1969; the three others are classified in B3: the United Farmers of Alberta
in 1921, the United Farmers of Ontario in 1919, the Union Nationale in Quebec in 1936.)

8 Of course, if the opposition party was already weak, then the rise of a third party is just that
much more likely.

tion party becomes nil and the rise of a third party becomes a possibility if other conditions—mainly strains—are present.[9]

Secondly, if for one reason or another, a strong opposition party (by our 33 percent criterion) fails to contest a large number of seats, the situation becomes highly conducive to the rise of a third party.[10] This again should not be surprising, since a failure to at least present a full slate of candidates is also an indication of some areas of weakness. But we have to enter a word of caution concerning this last generalization, since here the sudden weakness of the main opposition party is simultaneous with the emergence of a third party. This weakness may not precede the latter and may not in fact be a factor of the second; both could be results of a third factor, the presence of deep-seated unrest in some segments of the population, leading to the abandonment of the old opposition party as a channel for the redress of grievances, and the adoption of a new one. This is suggested at least by the fact that five of the seven cases considered here (see last footnote) occurred around 1920, during a period of intense farmer and labor unrest. If this is correct—and it would certainly deserve greater attention than can be given here—these cases would constitute an exception to the general model to be presented in the following pages. While the general model predicts that cleavages of various sorts lead first to one-party dominance, which later leads to the emergence of third parties, here we would need a special model stating that class cleavages lead to the rejection of both old parties and their replacement by a new class party. The reader will notice that this special model bears resemblance to Macpherson's model to be discussed presently.

In short, the general observation is that one-party dominance tends to render a democratic party system unstable, whether this dominance stems from the weakness of the second party in a two-party system, or whether it stems from the weakness of each opposition party in a multi-party system.[11] To be sure, the dominant *party* can remain in power for a very long time—witness Social Credit in Alberta—but our point is that the party *system* thus created cannot easily bear party changes without an alteration of the system itself. It seems

9 This occurred in Manitoba in 1945, with the rise of the C.C.F. against a coalition of other parties; at the federal level in 1921, in the Prairie Provinces and in Ontario, following the 1917 Union government.

10 Seven of the ten cases in column B are in that category, and the proportions of seats not contested range from 19 to 89 percent. Provincially, the Conservatives failed to contest a large number of seats in Alberta and in Saskatchewan, in 1921; in Quebec, from 1897 to 1935; in Nova Scotia and in New Brunswick, in 1920; the Liberals were involved only once: in Ontario in 1919. Federally, the Conservatives did not contest about 40 percent of the seats in Quebec in 1911, given their alliance with the Nationalists. Generally, the party involved had been on the opposition benches for a relatively long period.

11 Hence the almost endless multiplication of parties which often happens once a multi-party system has emerged. Recall here that prior to the dictatorship, Italy had fifteen parties, Germany, thirty-eight, and Poland, thirty. From J.O. Hertzler, "The Causal and Contributory Factors of Dictatorship." *Sociology and Social Research*, 24 (1939-40), pp. 3-21, quoted in Smelser, *Theory of Collective Behavior* p. 333. Smelser stresses the point that such a breakdown of the party system is conducive to the emergence of *value-oriented* political movements.

that in a democracy a healthy two-party system possesses more than any other system the inherent conditions for its own stability.

TWO DIFFERENT MODELS

Let us at this point present a more general model. The inquiry will now be pushed óne step further to determine the sources of one-party dominance itself. We shall also indicate in which ways this model differs, at both the structural and individual levels, from that of Macpherson,[12] which obviously cannot account for the rise of third parties in provinces like Quebec and Ontario, and which, on the other hand, cannot account for the failure of third parties in the Maritimes.

I propose that the rise of third parties can be accounted for by the following process. Structural cleavages of various sorts or certain types of community structure or widespread and flagrant corruption in very high places—all this possibly reinforced by single-member plurality elections—lead to alienation from one major party and to one-party dominance; this in turn, assuming the presence of strain, becomes a situation conducive to the rise of a third party[13] (see Figure 4.1).[14]

Let us elaborate briefly the factors of one-party dominance. Various conditions for the appearance of such a system can be mentioned. One of these may be, aş suggested by Lipset,[15] the existence of structural cleavages of various sorts, as for instance, economiç, regional, ethnic, or religious cleavages. Note that one element of the economic cleavages referred to here is what Macpherson calls the quasi-colonial economic position of the Western Provinces, that is, their

12 Macpherson, *Democracy in Alberta*.

13 On the basis of the foregoing analysis, the causal sequence could even be extended. Once third parties have arisen and a multi-party system has emerged, the search of an alternative to the party (or coalition parties) in power will tend to lead to the further emergence of new parties, at times in a seemingly endless process.

14 Thus the political structure, I suggest, rather than presumed differences in political culture would account for the presence of third parties on the Canadian political scene. For a cultural view, see G. Horowitz, "Conservatism, Liberalism, and Socialism in Canada: An Interpretation," *Canadian Journal of Economics and Political Science*, XXXII (1966), pp. 143–171. It should be noted that Horowitz's thesis fails to account for variations within Canada in the strength of third parties, in particular, for the weakness of socialist parties in the Maritimes.

15 See S.M. Lipset, "Democracy in Alberta," *Canadian Forum*, 34 (Nov. and Dec. 1954), pp. 175–177 and 196–198. (See also C.B. Macpherson, "A Reply," *ibid.*, 34 (Jan. 1955), pp. 223–225). For a recent statement of this, see also Frederick C. Engelmann and Mildred A. Schwartz, *Political Parties and the Canadian Social Structure* (Scarborough, Ont.: Prentice-Hall of Canada, Ltd., 1967), pp. 52–55. Notice however that neither the latter, nor Lipset state that the development of one-party dominance is the intervening factor between the existence of cleavages and the rise of political movements. See also S.M. Lipset, *Political Man*, pp. 270–279; Dennis H. Wrong, "Parties and Voting in Canada: A Backward and Forward Glance in the Light of the Last Election," *Political Science Quarterly*, LXXIII (1958), pp. 397–412; S.M. Lipset, *The First New Nation: The United States in Historical and Comparative Perspective* (New York: Basic Books, Inc., 1963), Chap. 9. For an earlier view on the crucial importance of cleavages in explaining party systems, see Leslie Lipson, "The Two-Party System in British Politics," *American Political Science Review*, 47 (1953), pp. 337–358.

Figure 4.1

Models for the Rise of Third Parties

A—AT THE STRUCTURAL LEVEL

1. *Macpherson's Model*

   Quasi-colonial economy *and* Homogeneous class composition ⟶ Non-party ideology and aspirations ⟶ Rise of third parties

   ⟶ Establishment of a quasi-party system (one-party dominance system)

2. *The New Model Proposed*

   Structural cleavages (economic, ethnic, etc.) and/or Structural attachments and/or Flagrant corruption aided by Single-member plurality electoral system ⟶ (Alienation from one of the major parties) ⟶ Emergence of a one-party dominance system ⟶ (Search for alternative to party in power) ⟶ Rise of third parties

B—AT THE INDIVIDUAL LEVEL

1. *Macpherson's Model*

   Long-term dissatisfaction with party-system ⟶ Conscious rejection of the party-system ⟶ Vote for a third party

2. *The New Model Proposed*

   Short-term grievances (often economic) toward party in power ⟶ The voters perceive strong traditional alternative (strong two-party system) ⟶ Switch to the other old party

   ⟶ The voters perceive no traditional alternative (one-party dominance) ⟶ Switch to a new party

dependency on economic institutions of central Canada and on federal economic policies which are made in opposition to their interests.[16]

These cleavages can have particularly strong effects and leave residues for very long periods if they engender bitter contests, as for instance the Civil War in the United States. At any rate, such cleavages strongly alienate a group from one of the two major parties and tie it to a single party as the sole protector of its interests, hence leading to one-party dominance.[17] A one-party dominance system can also possibly arise from, or at least be reinforced by, the structure of social attachments. As argued elsewhere, it seems that small communities cannot easily afford the strains of divisions and factions within their elites, due to their close social ties[18] and thus are led to a monopolistic political organization. The social structure of the Western Provinces, made of small communities, could thus have been an important additional factor of one-party dominance.[19] Moreover, the detection of flagrant corruption among the most important leaders of a party—particularly a Premier—can also destroy a previously strong traditional party and suddenly create a system of one-party dominance lasting for a long period.[20]

Finally, on the Prairies, the situation of one-party dominance has possibly been further fostered by the electoral system—the single-member plurality vote system[21]—and the homogeneity of the various districts, which meant that by obtaining a relatively low percentage of the votes consistently in most districts a party could get a very large majority of the seats.[22]

On the other hand, Macpherson's well-know argument[23] is that political

16 Macpherson, *Democracy in Alberta*, pp. 6ff., esp. p. 9. But these economic cleavages can also be class or urban-rural cleavages.

17 Generally at the level of a province, or only of a region within a province, as apparently occurred in Ontario.

18 See Maurice Pinard, "Structural Attachments and Political Support in Urban Politics: The Case of Fluoridation Referendums," *American Journal of Sociology*, 68 (1963), pp. 513-526, and Chap. 7 below; see also James S. Coleman, *Community Conflict* (New York: The Free Press of Glencoe, Inc., 1957), p. 16, and Lipset et al., *Union Democracy*.

19 Though the Maritime Provinces, and especially Prince Edward Island, could constitute an exception here.

20 See for instance the discussion in Chap. 3 of the 1915 election in Manitoba.

21 At the provincial level, however, it has not been used uniformly throughout the periods considered in all provinces; see Scarrow, *Canada Votes*.

22 On this, see Lipset, "Democracy in Alberta"; on the effects of electoral systems on party systems generally, see Maurice Duverger, *Political Parties* (London: Methuen & Co. Ltd., 1954); Lipset, *The First New Nation*, esp. pp. 301-302. But these views have possibly been overstated: It seems that the electoral mechanics act as a buttress rather than as a foundation of the party system and some evidence would indicate that party systems determine electoral systems rather than the opposite; see Leslie Lipson, "The Two-Party System in British Politics," and mainly John G. Grumm, "Theories of Electoral Systems," *Midwest Journal of Political Science*, 2 (1958), pp. 357-376; also Maurice Duverger, *The Idea of Politics: The Uses of Power in Society* (London: Methuen & Co. Ltd., 1966), pp. 114-116. Grumm's empirical verification, though most illuminating, is often overlooked by students of this problem.

23 C. B. Macpherson, *Democracy in Alberta,* esp. Chaps. 1 and 8.

movements in Alberta and the Western Provinces are the outcome of two necessary conditions—the quasi-colonial status of these provinces and their homogeneity in class composition, that is, the predominance of small independent
producers. According to Macpherson, these two factors give rise to a quite conscious ideology of rejection of the alternate-party system among community
leaders and eventually among the electorate, who finally reject this system at the
polls and vote for a new party.[24] Out of this process emerges what Macpherson
labels a quasi-party system, which I have called a one-party dominance system
(see Figure 4.1).

As can be seen, my thesis differs from this. Certain structural conditions tend
to produce one-party dominance, but class homogeneity is not necessary to
explain the latter, as Lipset has pointed out.[25] It is doubtful whether one can
correctly describe Alberta or the Western Prairies as class homogeneous. This
homogeneity is at least not reflected in political action, as revealed by the fact
that the winning parties retain close to fifty percent of the votes. Moreover,
Macpherson's condition obviously does not account for the rise of political
movements in Ontario and Quebec, which cannot possibly be described as
class-homogeneous provinces.

My thesis also differs in that it does not consider the one-party dominance
system—or quasi-party system—as a *concomitant* or *consequent* effect of the rise
of political movements, but, on the contrary, as an *antecedent* necessary condition
for the rise of such movements. Note in this respect that for Macpherson, the
period prior to the rise of the United Farmers of Alberta in 1921 was not a period
of one-party dominance but of "alternate-party government"[26] (though he also
explicitly makes the opposite statement "that there never had been an alternate-
party system in Alberta").[27] I have described above the period prior to 1921 as
a period of one-party dominance by the Liberals, which permitted the rise of the
U.F.A. *In short, one-party dominance precedes and is a factor in the rise of new movements; it does not follow from the rise. And one-party dominance is itself produced by
structural cleavages or strong structural attachments, not by class homogeneity.* The
only qualification we would enter here is that a special model somewhat anal-

24 That the Prairies have developed a fundamental non-partisan tradition and have been consistently opposed to the old party system is challenged by the facts. As pointed out by Smith, the Liberal
party in Saskatchewan, ruling almost without interruption from 1905 to 1944, was most of the time in
open, even defiant, union with the federal Liberal party; and the Progressives in Manitoba allied
themselves with the Liberals after 1928 and from 1931 on, described themselves as a Liberal-Progressive coalition. See Denis Smith, "Prairie Revolt, Federalism and the Party System," in Hugh G. Thorburn, ed., *Party Politics in Canada* (Toronto: Prentice-Hall of Canada, Ltd., 1963), pp. 126-137. On
the other hand, there have been groups explicitly rejecting the party system even outside the
Western Provinces; see for instance the discussions on this matter among Ontario farmers in
Morton, *The Progressive Party in Canada*, p. 75.

25 "Democracy in Alberta."

26 Macpherson, *Democracy in Alberta*, p. 217.

27 *Ibid.*, p. 205; also pp. 20–27.

ogous to that of Macpherson[28] might possibly be required to account for the wave of farmer-labor movements around 1920, as mentioned in the previous section.

Macpherson's model and the general model also differ at the individual level. Macpherson's implicit model at the individual level is that for the reasons given above, the population has for a long time been strongly dissatisfied with the party system *as such* and has thus consciously rejected it, switching to a new non-partisan political movement.[29] Even though this process undoubtedly took place among certain groups of the political elites,[30] I doubt very much that such a conscious analysis is ever carried out by the mass of the electorate, let alone accepted.

I prefer to see the process as one in which the presence of short-term grievances pushes a portion of the electorate against the party in power. If there is a strong two-party system, the traditional opposition party will receive their votes. If not, a new party is likely to become the alternative to which they will turn (see Figure 4.1).

CONCLUSIONS

This analysis has interesting implications. It throws new light on some nagging questions, such as the failure of third parities in the Maritimes, as mentioned before, or the fate of third parties at the federal level in Canada.

At the federal level, inasmuch as the main opposition party remains a weak party in a region, third parties are likely to appear in a recurrent way and then to linger for some time, especially if they have also gained power at the provincial level. But inasmuch as the weakness of the traditional opposition party is not general all over the country, these parties are bound to meet major obstacles in trying to spread outside their original regional base.[31] This accounts for their bad fortune in the past at the national level and makes their future chances seem relatively slim. And since their regional limitations render them weak national parties, they are probably bound to virtually disappear each time the

---

[28] This special model would still be different from that of Macpherson, in that the former does not call for a quasicolonial economy and class homogeneity (after all, Ontario is among the cases to be explained), but simply for class cleavages; it does not call either for the rejection of the two-party system as such, but simply for the rejection of the two traditional parties as failing to represent certain class interests.

[29] See also J.R. Mallory, "The Structure of Canadian Politics," in H. G. Thorburn, ed., *Party Politics in Canada*, pp. 22–29, esp. pp. 24–25.

[30] Though there was definitely no consensus on this even among the elites, as the maintenance of the old parties clearly indicates. See Thomas, *The Liberal Party in Alberta*, pp. 3–4, on the disagreements among Albertan elites about the appropriateness of party politics.

[31] The same conclusion has also been reached by Engelmann and Schwartz, *Political Parties*, pp. 54–55.

main opposition party reaffirms itself, as they did with the Conservatives' resurgence in 1958 in the Western Provinces.[32]

To be sure, the model is no less probabilistic than other sociological models. Nevertheless, the relationship discovered in Table 3.1 is by sociological standards a very strong one. But there are exceptions, as we have seen, and as the 1970 Quebec provincial election indicates. The sources of these deviations however remain to be clearly understood.

[32] Some of these parties, however, may one day profit from the fact that over time there are more and more people who have at least once supported them and therefore may find it more easy to do it again. If they were to do it simultaneously, these parties might be more fortunate.

Political
Unrest
and
Social Credit

CHAPTER FIVE

As seen in Chapter 2, the characteristic weakness of the Progressive Conservative party at the federal level in Quebec created a situation that was highly conducive to the rise of Social Credit.[1] Many dissatisfied voters saw no alternative but to turn to a new party, particularly in the districts which had remained Liberal in 1958.

There is a second aspect of the political scene in Quebec that could have been conducive to the rise of a new political movement in 1962: this is the state of political unrest which had manifested itself in many movements in the preceding few years. The well-known moderate and extremist separatist movements in Quebec were not the only such manifestations. Less noticed but nevertheless present at the same time were the activities of the *Mouvement laïc de langue française*, a movement for the secularization of various aspects of life in Quebec, mainly education, the renewed efforts and factionalism of socialist groups, and the activities of pacifist groups. Each of these movements has typically tended to recruit followers among the same groups of people.

In a more institutionalized context, but probably not unrelated to the above, much political turnover had also taken place at the same time in Quebec. As mentioned before, at the provincial level, the Quebec electorate had broken away from the Union Nationale party in 1960 and elected the Liberals for the first

---

[1] Again, the 1958 success of the Conservative party in Quebec should not obscure the facts of its organizational weakness and its lack of a solid partisan base, particularly in some districts, as seen in Chap. 2.

time in sixteen years. At the federal level, despite the weakness of the Progressive Conservative party, Quebec severed its traditional ties to the Liberals in 1958 and in a bandwagon effect, a year later than Canada, returned a majority of Conservatives to Parliament—fifty out of seventy-five—though with only a slight plurality of votes over the Liberals—49.6 percent of the votes as compared to 45.7 percent.

More generally, a long period of conservative government had led to stagnation in the public sector, and the early sixties witnessed a series of systematic efforts to modernize Quebec society. Though there may be a tendency to overemphasize the political impact of this Quiet Revolution, it is nevertheless possible that the induced transformations may have triggered a new readiness to change.[2]

In short, it is not unlikely that such a situation of widespread unrest and political change could generate further political movements. As Smelser suggested, once social change has begun, under the impact of social unrest, the organizations that are adopted to vent grievances are often easily perceived as ineffective and obsolete, and new ones are created.[3] A turn toward the Social Credit party could therefore be interpreted as the last in a series of changes, each one making more likely the next one. In other words, this hypothesis would be predicated on the assumption that *social change is conducive to further social change.*[4]

But at first sight this hypothesis is apparently challenged by the findings of the second chapter. Recall that it was found that those districts which *changed* from Liberal to Conservative in the 1958 federal election were *less* likely to vote Social Credit than those which remained Liberal (see Table 2.1). The lack of political change in that instance, rather than its presence, was conducive to the rise of a new political movement. The solution of this paradox is that one should strictly conceptualize the latter situation as characterized, not by the *lack* of political change, but by the *impossibility* of *traditional* political change,[5] due to the weakness of the Conservatives; this is what led to a new political movement. From the above analysis, one must deduce that, had the federal Conservative party been a strong party, the group of districts which remained Liberal in both 1957 and 1958 would probably have shown the highest rate of turnover to the Conservatives; they did not change because no viable alternative was available.

---

[2] On the Quiet Revolution in Quebec, see, for instance, Edward M. Corbett, *Quebec Confronts Canada* (Baltimore: The Johns Hopkins Press, 1957).

[3] Smelser, *Theory of Collective Behavior*, pp. 298–306.

[4] Peter Regenstreif and Vincent Lemieux have also commented on the state of political instability which existed in Quebec in 1962. See Regenstreif, *The Diefenbaker Interlude*, pp. 113 ff.; Lemieux, "Les dimensions sociologiques du vote créditiste au Québec," p. 188.

[5] Where there was a possibility of traditional change—i.e., where the Conservatives were strong—stability led to the failure of Social Credit, which supports the hypothesis presently discussed.

POLITICAL CHANGE
AT THE PROVINCIAL LEVEL

The hypothesis must then be tested otherwise. Instead of the political change which took place at the federal level in 1957–1958, the political change prevailing at the provincial level between the 1956 and the 1960 elections will be considered. The reader will recall that at that level, there is a strong two-party system, and hence the possibility of traditional political change. Let us see if the actual change which had taken place at that level produced an effect on the subsequent rise of the Social Credit party at the federal level.

The data are presented in Table 5.1.[6] The left-hand panel of the Table shows

Table 5.1.

Political Change at the Provincial Level (1956–60) Is Positively Correlated with a Switch to Social Credit at the Federal Level (1962)

Provincial Districts Won in 1956 by:*	UNION NATIONALE				LIBERALS	
Provincial Districts Won in 1960 by:	UNION NATIONALE		LIBERALS		LIBERALS	
	Strong**	Weak	Weak	Strong	Strong	Weak
(Amount of Political Change:	Low			High	Low	High)
	%	%	%	%	%	%
Federal Districts 1962						
Social Credit***	9	41	41	77	0	71
N (Districts) =	(11)	(22)	(17)	(13)	(4)	(7)

*The results for 1956 are those of the general election that year or, in some seats, of the by-elections between 1956–60. No districts switched from Liberal in 1956 to Union Nationale in 1960. The federal outcomes were allocated to provincial seats; Montreal and Quebec cities are excluded; see note 6, below.

**U.N. strong in 1960; Liberal vote $\leq 46\%$; U.N. weak: Lib. vote $> 46\%$. Liberal weak in 1960: Lib. vote $< 54\%$; Lib. strong: Lib. vote $\geq 54\%$. A district which was Union Nationale in 1956 and remained a strong Union Nationale district in 1960 is considered as having exhibited the least amount of political change. At the other extreme, a district which was Union Nationale in 1956 and became a strong Liberal district in 1960 is considered as having exhibited the greatest amount of political change. Similarly among the districts which were Liberal in 1956, those which remained weak Liberal districts in 1960 are considered to have exhibited more change than those which remained Liberal but with a strong vote.

***a_1 (effect of a move away from the U.N., comparing extremes) $= .68$; $p(a_1^* \leq 0) < .0001$; a_2 (effect of a move away from the Liberals) $= .71$; $p(a_2^* \leq 0) < .0001$.

6 The federal and provincial districts do not correspond perfectly; among other things, there are fewer federal districts. Thus, on the basis of map comparisons, the federal outcome were allocated to the provincial districts. Even where there is a one-to-one correspondence, boundaries differ, but not enough to invalidate such comparisons. These calculations exclude the seats in Montreal and Quebec City for two reasons: first, it is more difficult to establish federal-provincial correspondences for those seats; second, Montreal resisted almost completely the Social Credit wave, as seen before.

a very strong tendency—from 9 percent to 77 percent—for the electoral districts which moved away from the Union Nationale at the provincial level in 1960 to similarly switch to Social Credit at the federal level in 1962; and the stronger the switch in 1960, the greater were the chances of Social Credit in 1962. A similar trend also seems apparent for the districts which moved away from the Quebec Liberal party, though a complete comparison is missing here, given that no districts switched from Liberal to Union Nationale (right-hand panel of the Table).

These data clearly support the hypothesis that the political change which had previously taken place between the old parties at the provincial level affected the rise of Social Credit at the federal level.[7] Political change does indeed seem conducive to further political change.

Furthermore, these results do not appear to be a spurious artifact. Though there is a direct relationship between political change at the provincial level and the weakness of the Progressive Conservative party at the federal level, both factors are independently related to the rise of the Social Credit party, as shown in Table 5.2. To be sure, in the districts with a strong Conservative organization, political change at the provincial level had no effect (see third row of Table 5.2);

Table 5.2

Both Political Change at the Provincial Level (1956–60) and Weakness of the Progressive Conservative Party at the Federal Level (1957–58) Are Independently Related to the Rise of Social Credit (% Social Credit Victory in 1962)

Provincial Districts Won in 1956 by:	UNION NATIONALE		LIBERALS	
Provincial Districts Won in 1960 by:	UNION NATIONALE	LIBERALS	LIB. STRONG*	LIB. WEAK
Strength of the Progressive Conservative Party:**				
Weak***	67	67	0	100
	(3)	(12)	(1)	(2)
Medium	36	53	0	75
	(22)	(17)	(2)	(4)
Strong	0	0	0	0
	(8)	(1)	(1)	(1)

*See notes of Table 5.1.
**Weak: districts which were Liberal in both 1957 and 1958; medium: districts which were Liberal in 1957 and P.C. in 1958; strong: districts which were P.C. in both 1957 and 1958.
***a_1 (average effect of political change for the first four pairs of comparisons) = $\frac{1}{4}$(.00 + 1.00 + .17 + .75) = .48; $p(a_1^* \leq 0) <$ .0001. (If weighted procedures are used [see Coleman, *Introduction to Mathematical Sociology*, pp. 203ff.] for three of these comparisons [excluding the top right-hand comparison], we obtain a weighted $a_1' = .316$ and $p(a_1'^* \leq 0) = .00.4$)

[7] Analogous findings were independently reported by Vincent Lemieux, "Les dimensions sociologiques du vote créditiste au Québec," pp. 188ff.

in fact, Social Credit failed to made any headway under these conditions, as if a strong two-party system is sufficient to prevent the rise of new parties. But in the other two rows of Table 5.2, the relationship observed in Table 5.1 is maintained in three comparisons out of four and is highly significant: the districts with most political change at the provincial level were most likely to become Social Credit in 1962 at the federal level. Similarly, when economic grievances, as indicated by net-migration movements are controlled, the relationship is also maintained (see Table 6.11).

It is worth emphasizing that these data support *a contrario* the hypothesis discussed in Chapters 2 to 4. At the provincial level, *both parties*—the Union Nationale and the Liberals—had strong organizations. A well-balanced two-party system existed at that level, giving the electorate an alternative to the party in power. Dissatisfied with the Union Nationale party, they could turn—as they largely did in 1960—to an old party, the Liberals. The districts that were to turn to Social Credit in the 1962 federal election could turn against the incumbent Union Nationale in 1960 at the provincial level.

But now, what has been shown is that this political change at the provincial level was by itself conducive to the rise of a third party at the federal level (as it might have been to the rise of the separatist and Social Credit parties in the 1970 provincial election).

THE EFFECTS
AT THE INDIVIDUAL LEVEL

The individual mechanism through which political change is conducive to further political change seemed to be that those who were able to change their allegiances from one of the old parties to the other at the provincial level in 1960, were now more readily available for a switch to a new party at the federal level in 1962. Once a political attachment has been broken, a readiness to further breaks is developed.

These ideas can be substantiated with survey data. On the basis of the foregoing analysis, one should expect that the changers at the provincial level from 1956 to 1960 were among the most likely to join the new movement.

It should be noted first that only 8 of the 103 changers reported in Table 5.3 went from Liberal to Union Nationale; all others switched the other way, to the opposition party. Moreover, the data presented in Table 5.3 clearly show that in the rural districts the *changers* at the provincial level between 1956 and 1960 were, in general, more likely than either the *stable Liberal or Union Nationale voters* to have switched to Social Credit at the federal level in 1962. Looking at the first three panels of Table 5.3, it can be seen that this pattern is true in five of the six possible comparisons. However, there are no such differences for the Montreal and Quebec districts; this may reflect the fact that Social Credit barely

Table 5.3

In Rural Districts, Changers at the Provincial Level in 1960 Were More
Likely to Vote Social Credit in 1962 Than Stable Voters

| | FEDERAL VOTE IN 1962 | | | | |
	SOCIAL CREDIT %	P.C. %	LIBERAL %	N.D.P. %	N
PROVINCIAL VOTE 1956 AND 1960*					
1. Weak P.C. rural federal districts:**					
Changers***	48	16	34	2	(44)
Stable Liberals	23	13	64	0	(53)
Stable Union Nationale	58	33	7	2	(43)
2. Intermediate P.C. rural federal districts:					
Changers	43	29	29	0	(14)
Stable Liberals	6	9	85	0	(34)
Stable Union Nationale	24	69	7	0	(29)
3. Strong P.C. rural federal districts:					
Changers	7	43	50	0	(14)
Stable Liberals	0	10	90	0	(21)
Stable Union Nationale	3	88	9	0	(34)
4. Montreal and Quebec districts:					
Changers	3	45	48	3	(31)
Stable Liberals	5	12	80	2	(96)
Stable Union Nationale	21	70	7	2	(43)

*"Changers" are those who switched between the two old parties at the provincial level in 1960.
**See note to Table 2.3.
***a_1 (comparison of changers to stable Liberal on Social Credit vote in rural districts) = $\frac{1}{3}$(.25 + .37 + .07) = .23; $p(a_1^* \le 0)$ = .0001;

a_2 (comparison of changers to stable Union Nationale on Social Credit vote in panels 2 and 3) = $\frac{1}{2}$(.19 + .04) = .115; $p(a_2^* \le 0)$ = .09;

a_3 (comparison of stable Union Nationale to stable Liberals on Social Credit vote in rural districts) = $\frac{1}{3}$(.35 + .18 + .03) = .187; $p(a_3^* \le 0)$ < .0001;

a_4 (comparison of stable Union Nationale to changers on Social Credit vote in panel 1) = .10; $p(a_4^* \le 0)$ = .17.

got started in Montreal, so that it did not appear as an additional avenue of change.

Notice moreover that the exception to the general pattern shown in rural districts is interesting: the *stable Union Nationale voters* in weak Conservative federal districts tended to be the strongest Social Credit supporters of all at the federal level.[8] But this is part of another general pattern. Indeed we find that the stable Union Nationale voters were generally more likely to have voted Social Credit than the stable Liberals, and the size of the differences increases as one moves from strong to weak Conservative federal districts. This is as should be expected. Notice how there was relatively little split-voting in these elections between the federal and provincial levels; voters were Liberals and—to

8 The difference between these U.N. voters and the changers of that category of districts is, however, not significant at standard levels.

a lesser extent—Conservative (Union Nationale) at both levels. But, precisely, for the Union Nationale supporters there tended to be no real alternative at the federal level,[9] and this was particularly true in weak Conservative districts. We therefore find in that group a very large reservoir of federal Social Credit supporters. That this was in fact due to the lack of an alternative is supported by the finding that in intermediate and strong Progressive Conservative districts, the stable Union Nationale supporters were indeed less likely than the changers to have been Social Credit voters.[10] In short, in these cases, the first generalization holds more generally: changers were more likely to have voted Social Credit than either group of stable voters.[11]

SOCIAL CREDIT
AND THE PROVINCIAL ELECTION
OF 1962

As mentioned before, a few months after the June 1962 electoral success of Social Credit in Quebec federal politics, the provincial Liberal government decided to hold an anticipated election in November 1962. Many Social Credit organizers wanted the party to run candidates in that election also, despite a previous decision to the contrary.[12] After a few days of public debate by the principal followers of Caouette, the party held a meeting to take a new decision on the issue. Caouette himself was again definitely opposed to letting his party run in Quebec provincial politics, on the official ground that Social Credit's monetary platform was impossible to implement at the provincial level—monetary politics being constitutionally in the realm of federal powers.[13] The meeting followed Caouette's wishes and decided again not to run.

In the light of the foregoing analysis, it is interesting to wonder what would have been the movement's success had the party decided to run. We have already suggested that success would not have been as easy at the provincial level as it was at the federal level, for the province already had a healthy two-party system. To be sure, the party would have had the advantage of its earlier success

9 So that, in a sense, the Social Credit party was helped by the presence of a balanced two-party system at the provincial level; given the small amount of split-voting, there was a large reservoir of provincial voters who had no strong party to turn to at the federal level. This is one source of Caouette's reticence to have his party run at the provincial level, a problem to be presently discussed.

10 In the context of this finding, it is interesting to note that many newspaper reporters in the province remarked that while the Social Credit had recruited many of its *organizers* from those of the provincial parties, a much larger proportion were from the Union Nationale party than from the Liberal party. Social Credit was also reported to have been actively opposed by many more provincial Liberal organizations than by Union Nationale ones.

11 See also fn. 64, p. 111.

12 Earlier disagreement on the subject had led the annual convention in August to formally decide to stay away from provincial politics "for the time being," Caouette opposing any involvement on the provincial scene. See *The Montreal Star*, August 27, 1962, p. 1.

13 It may also be conjectured that his complete control over the organization would have been challenged by the rise of a provincial leader.

at the federal level. But whether it could have overcome the difficulties of fighting a strong two-party system is problematic.

The survey data can throw some light on this problem. Respondents were asked their vote intention for the forthcoming provincial election. Since at the time of the construction of the questionnaire, it was still unknown whether Social Credit would run at the forthcoming provincial election, the structured question provided for a Social Credit vote intention, among others. Furthermore, a follow-up question was directed to those who did not say they intended to vote Social Credit: "If Mr. Caouette's Social Credit party were to present candidates at the *provincial level*, would you be very inclined, a little inclined, or not inclined to vote for them?" These two questions, together with the date of the interviews, enable us to consider what happened as the provincial election campaign ran its course.[14] It is first very interesting to find (Table 5.4) that during the week preceding the announcement of the provincial election and the following week (though the actual campaign had not yet started)—September

Table 5.4

As the Provincial Election Campaign Progressed, Former
Federal Social Credit Votes Moved Away from a Potential
Provincial Social Credit Party

	INTERVIEW DATE		
1962 PROVINCIAL VOTE INTENTION*	SEPT. 10 TO SEPT. 24 %	SEPT. 25 TO OCT. 4 %	AFTER OCT. 4 %
	Among Social Credit Supporters (Federal, June '62)		
Supporters of Social Credit**	50	35	12
Strong potential supporters	5	11	8
Weak potential supporters	22	14	30
Not potential supporters	15	38	20
Undecided	8	3	30
N =	(40)	(37)	(40)
	Among Other Parties' Supporters		
Supporters of Social Credit	2	5	3
Strong potential supporters	3	1	2
Weak potential supporters	11	9	6
Not potential supporters	68	77	81
Undecided	15	8	8
N =	(89)	(184)	(171)

*Supporters: gave a S.C. vote intention; strong potential supporters: said they would be very inclined to support such a party if it were to run; weak potential supporters: said they were a little inclined; not potential supporters: not inclined; undecided: did not know if they would support such a party.

**a_1 (effect of the campaign on the tendency to report oneself as a supporter of S.C. among former Crediters, comparing extremes) = .38; $p(a_1^* \leq 0) < .0001$.

[14] The field work started one week before the announcement of the provincial election and continued throughout the campaign.

10 to 24—there were already among Social Credit supporters in the previous federal election a group of 15 percent who said they would "not be inclined" to vote Social Credit if there were such a party at the provincial level. Another group of 22 percent claimed they would only be "a little inclined" to do so. Together, in these early interviews, there was already a group of 37 percent among the Social Credit voters of a few months before (June 18, 1962) who were weak or non-potential provincial supporters.

Table 5.4 also shows the change which occurred during the campaign. It is not too surprising to find that among former Social Credit supporters, the proportion who said they would vote Social Credit at the provincial level finally dropped sharply—from 50 percent to 12 percent—since the party was in fact not running. But note that the proportion of those saying they would be very inclined to back such a party if it were to run did not increase proportionately. There was rather an increase in the proportion of those saying they would "not be inclined" in the second period considered, and an increase in the group of those only "a little inclined" or "undecided" in the third period (which is the period of actual campaigning by the two old parties).[15]

Those who mentioned they had supported other parties in the June federal election offer an interesting control group. It can be seen that among them, there was much less change during the campaign. It is also worth noting that as the campaign developed, former Social Credit supporters gradually moved closer to them. This strongly suggests that the Social Credit party, if it had decided to run in that provincial election, would have started with some advantage, but that thereafter it would have been much weakened by the active campaign of the two old parties. And once more this supports *a contrario* the previous interpretation that the lack of a healthy two-party system at the federal level was largely responsible for the rise of the Social Credit party.[16]

SEPARATISM AND NATIONALISM

Changes at the political level proper are not the only ones to which the rise of Social Credit could be related. As mentioned before, Quebec has been the

15 It could be claimed that if the party had *actually* run, the picture might have been quite different; this is certainly in part correct. But this does not explain the 37 percent of weak or nonsupporters on the eve of the campaign, at a time when the decision not to run was not yet made.

16 What happened in the 1966 provincial election clearly supports the above conclusions. As mentioned before, Social Credit did run this time as the *Ralliement National*. In a survey conducted before the campaign, it was found that 13.1 percent of those who expressed a vote intention said they would vote Social Credit (N = 1665). This clearly dropped during the campaign, as the Union Nationale reasserted itself, since the party finally got only 3.2 percent of the total vote (or 3.7 percent of the vote in the 90 districts in which it ran candidates). (The survey results were personally communicated to the author; the election results are from Paul Cliche, *Le Devoir* (Montreal), June 13, 1966 p. 5.) The success of the new wing of the party in the 1970 provincial election was somewhat greater (it obtained 11 percent of the votes). It remained however inferior even to its worse showing on the federal scene (in 1968, with 16.4 percent of the votes—see Table 13.1).

seat of much social unrest and of many social movements in recent years. The separatist movement, as an extreme form of the perennial French-Canadian nationalism, is only one of the forms this has taken. On the basis of the ideas set forth above, one may wonder whether the Social Credit upsurge was also linked to separatism and, by extension, to nationalism.[17] We will consider separatism first.

In the present study, the respondents were asked if they were "for or against the separation of Quebec from the rest of Canada"; and they were asked if they would personally vote for a separatist party, if such a party were to be formed. Let us mention first that the support of the separatist movement was much weaker than that of the federal Social Credit party:[18] 71 percent of the French-Canadian[19] respondents said they were opposed to the separation of Quebec, while only 8 percent favored it.[20] And while 67 percent said they would not vote for a separatist party, only 5 percent said they would.[21]

Though the proportion of separatists is small, the data presented in Table 5.5 indicate that people favoring changes through one movement—separatism— were more likely to desire changes through the other movement—Social Credit. A similar association, which is slightly stronger and statistically significant, appears in the case of potential support of a separatist party. (Notice moreover how the support for separatism is also related to the support for the socialist New Democratic Party.)[22]

Again, social change tends to be conducive to social change. It should be mentioned, however, that even though there is a relationship, as expected, its strength is not overwhelming and, above all, it involves few people. This should not be very surprising, since in 1962 the support for the separatist movement was much weaker than that for Social Credit and since the first movement was shown to have a quite different social base than Social Credit. The separatists tend to be better educated white collars from urban areas,[23] while, as will be seen in the next chapter, Social Credit tends to recruit rural workers and farmers.

Moreover, the direction of causality is not clear. In the first part of this chap-

17 It has been shown that the various waves of separatism since World War I (during the early twenties, the thirties, and the present wave) have been accompanied by other manifestations of unrest, such as Canadianism, anti-Semitism, anti-clericalism, etc. See Raymond Breton et Albert Breton, "Le séparatisme ou le respect du statu quo," *Cité Libre*, XIIIè année, No. 46, April 1962, pp. 17-28.

18 Though in the 1966 provincial election the separatist R.I.N. got more votes than the creditist R.N. (see Chap. 3).

19 Since the few other respondents were overwhelmingly opposed to separatism and French-Canadian nationalism, as well as to Social Credit, they are excluded from the following analysis to assure a control.

20 12 percent gave a qualified answer and 8 percent said they did not know (N = 880).

21 18 percent gave a qualified answer and 10 percent said they did not know (N = 879).

22 So that the relationships between the support of separatism and the support of both new parties considered together is significant in both panels of Table 5.5.

23 Based on data from a study done in Quebec by the Social Research Group in 1963. Some of these data have been presented in *MacLean's Magazine*, Nov. 1963, pp. 13ff.

Table 5.5

There Is an Association between Social Credit and Separatism Support

VOTE IN 1962	SEPARATION OF QUEBEC		
	FOR %	QUALIFIED ANSWER %	AGAINST %
Social Credit*	31	24	23
Conservative	24	33	29
Liberal	36	43	46
N.D.P.	10	0	2
N =	(42)	(49)	(440)

VOTE IN 1962	SUPPORT OF POTENTIAL SEPARATIST PARTY		
	YES %	QUALIFIED ANSWER %	NO %
Social Credit**	45	24	23
Conservative	23	31	29
Liberal	23	44	46
N.D.P.	9	1	2
N =	(22)	(80)	(429)

*a_1 (effect of support of separation of Quebec on Social Credit support, comparing extremes) = .08; $p(a_1^* \leq 0)$ = .14;

a_2 (effect of support of separation of Quebec on joint Social Credit and N.D.P. support, comparing extremes) = .15; $p(a_2^* \leq 0)$ = .03.

**a_3 (effect of support of a potential Separatist party on Social Credit support, comparing extremes) = .22 $p(a_3^* \leq 0)$ = .02.

ter, a causal relationship was inferred: previous political changes at the provincial level were deemed to have caused (in part) the subsequent Social Credit success. Can the same causal inference be made here? It does not seem possible on the basis of these data alone since here the time sequence of the two factors is unknown.[24] It is highly possible that the two influenced each other and that the readiness to give up the old parties influenced the readiness to abandon the present Canadian constitutional arrangement altogether, and vice-versa. At any rate, even if one wanted to assume that separatism was the main causal factor, the weakness of this movement at the time as well as the relative weakness of the relationships in Table 5.5 should prevent one from asserting that the Social Credit upsurge was simply another manifestation of French-Canadian separatism. The only thing that can be said is that the two are slightly associated, as was expected, and that probably each movement created some conducive conditions for the rise of the other. And since Social Credit was a stronger move-

[24] The present wave of separatism started around 1958, but we do not know at which point in time our respondents decided to favour separatism and/or Social Credit.

ment, it is not unlikely that it influenced separatism more than the latter influenced Social Credit.

This is an important point since it has been assumed by many that Social Credit was as much a manifestation of French-Canadian nationalistic[25] protest as a manifestation of economic protest, and that the former was more important than the latter.[26] This assumption, however, was at times based on rather weak grounds. Since the available data indicated that the poorer constituencies were relatively weak in their support of Social Credit—a finding which we also obtained and which is discussed at length in Chapter 8—it was readily assumed by Irvine that economic discontent was not a crucial factor. This of course implied a first major confusion between poverty and economic grievances, an important distinction to be dealt with below. Moreover, from the rejection of economic discontent as a factor to the assumption that the crucial factor is nationalistic discontent, there is a gap that neither the data available nor logic could bridge.[27]

What do our data indicate? Is there a relationship between nationalist feelings or ethnic consciousness, and support for Social Credit? The results just presented with regard to separatism would lead one to answer positively. So does the fact that nationalism has been the main axis of French-Canadian social thought since at least the beginning of the nineteenth century,[28] and that this belief system is widely shared, though in greatly varying degrees, by many French Canadians. Since the 1962 upsurge of Social Credit took place only in French Quebec, it was natural for many observers to conclude that these sentiments had played an important role.

On the other hand, as we have just seen, the number of people in our sample who were both separatists and *créditistes* is rather small, and it could be that for a few people, both movements had become *channels* for the expression of a general mood of discontent. It would not necessarily follow that ethnic feelings were at the *source* of the options of most or even many Social Credit supporters. For one, this belief system is not as articulated and as intense in the mass as it is among certain segments of the elites, and it is not necessarily linked to political

25 While separatism is clearly a social movement which has previously come by waves, nationalism has been the constant political ideology of French Canadians.

26 See for instance W. P. Irvine, "An Analysis of Voting Shifts in Quebec," in John Meisel, ed., *Papers on the 1962 Election*, pp. 129–143, esp. pp. 129–133. See also Marcel Rioux, "Conscience ethnique et conscience de classe au Québec," *Recherches Sociographiques*, VI, 1965, pp. 23–32; Herbert F. Quinn, *The Union Nationale*, p. v; Ronald I. Cohen, *Quebec Votes*, p. 36, p. 98.

27 It is worth noting in this regard that a content analysis revealed that the Social Credit party in Quebec was the party *least* concerned during the 1962 campaign about the "Anglo-French relations" and "the questions pertaining to Confederation." For data on this, see Léon Dion, "The Election in the province of Quebec," in John Meisel, *ibid.*, pp. 112–115.

28 See Fernand Ouellet, "Le nationalisme canadien-français: de ses origines à l'insurrection de 1837," *The Canadian Historical Review*, XLV (1964), pp. 277–292, esp. pp. 284ff.; Pierre E. Trudeau, "La province de Québec au moment de la grève," in Pierre E. Trudeau, ed., *La Grève de l'Amiante*, pp. 10ff.

preferences in the mass, except under feelings of ethnic threats.[29] Moreover, ethnic consciousness being often dormant in the mass, it does not, contrary to an ongoing movement, easily become the natural set of beliefs through which grievances are expressed, unless it is mobilized to that end. Social Credit did not try to tap this consciousness in 1962, and the separatist movement had failed to do it to any great extent among the groups who were to turn to the former movement. Given these factors, we expected little relationship between ethnic consciousness and Social Credit support.

From the present study, many measures of the respondents' ethnic feelings are available. What are actually the relationships between these attitudes and the support for Social Credit? At first sight, the data seem to reveal some inconsistencies (Table 5.6). For the first three questions presented, the "nationalist" respondents (those who answered "agree" or "yes") did not give stronger support to Social Credit than the non-nationalist respondents.[30] However in the case of the last two questions, there is a positive relationship between nationalism and Social Credit (though it drops in the extreme category of question 4). But notice how only the last two questions refer explicitly to the Federal Government, to which the voters had just elected twenty-six Social Credit members from Quebec. Given the absence of relationship with the first three questions, we suggest that what the last two questions measured were general grievances and alienation from the Federal Government, rather than specific French-Canadian ethnic grievances. One must remember that during the 1962 campaign, much was said about the fact that the Diefenbacker government had done a great deal for western farmers (mainly by huge sales of Canadian wheat to Communist countries) and for the West generally, but nothing for eastern farmers, and the East generally. This was spontaneously mentioned many times by Social Credit voters to the author in the course of preliminary interviews. And indeed, our indices of the respondents' political alienation and of their economic conditions are related to the last two questions.[31]

To test our inference, we ran three-variable tables, adding the index of poli-

---

29 On this, see Maurice Pinard, "La rationalité de l'électorat: le cas de 1962," in Vincent Lemieux, ed., *Quatre élections provinciales au Québec, 1956–1966* (Ouébec: Les Presses de l'Université Laval, 1969), pp. 179–195, esp. pp. 187–190. On the general problem of the lack of constraint or interdependence of belief systems in the largest part of the population, see Philip E. Converse, "The Nature of Belief Systems in Mass Publics" in David E. Apter, ed., *Ideology and Discontent* (New York: The Free Press, 1964), Chap. 6.

30 There is however a slight tendency for those who gave a qualified answer to have been greater supporters of the new movement, though the difference is significant only for the second question. Our only interpretation of this, after many controls failed to account for the differences, is that Social Credit voters were in the process of reevaluating their nationalistic feelings as a sequel to their first expression of protest.

31 These indices are presented in Appendix C. Those who were highly alienated or whose economic conditions were bad were more likely to give a nationalist response on questions four and five than their opposites (the differences are about 18 percent in each case.) On the other hand, only political alienation is related to that extent, and this only to the first of the other three questions. (The other differences here are 8 percent or less.)

tical alienation or that of economic conditions, to see whether the last two relationships of Table 5.6 would disappear. In the case of question four, we found that the relationship disappeared among those who had a low or moderate degree of alienation or were under good or moderately good conditions, but that it was maintained or even increased among those who were highly alienated

Table 5.6

The Relationships between Ethnic Consciousness and Social Credit Support
(% *Social Credit*)

	AGREE	QUALIFIED ANSWER	DISAGREE
1. French Canadians must often keep a watch in order that English Canadians do not take advantage of them.	23 (362)	27 (41)	23 (134)

	YES	QUALIFIED ANSWER	NO
2. Do you think that there are too many companies in Quebec that are owned by English Canadians or Americans?*	22 (312)	35 (79)	20 (128)
3. (If yes to 2 above) Do you think it is the Provincial Government's role to turn these companies into the hands of the French Canadians by nationalizing them?	21 (188)	24 (41)	19 (68)

	VERY WELL	FAIRLY WELL	FAIRLY BADLY	VERY BADLY
4. In your opinion, are the rights of the French Canadians in the Federal Government, in Ottawa, very well respected, fairly well respected, fairly badly respected, or very badly respected?**	15 (46)	22 (260)	31 (172)	21 (47)

	YES, AS MUCH	QUALIFIED ANSWER	NO, NOT AS MUCH
5. In your opinion, does the Federal Government when it decides a question, take as much care of the interests of the French Canadians as of those of the English Canadians?***	18 (228)	22 (85)	31 (217)

*a_1 (difference in Social Credit support between those who gave a qualified answer and those who answered yes) $= .13$; $p(a_1^* \leq 0) = .01$.

**a_2 (effect of a nationalist attitude on Social Credit support, comparing those who answered very and fairly well to those who answered fairly and very badly, i.e. collapsing the first two and the last two columns) $= .29 - .21 = .08$; $p(a_2^* \leq 0) = .02$.

***a_3 (effect of a nationalist attitude on Social Credit support, comparing extremes) $= .13$; $p(a_3^* \leq 0) < .001$.

or under very bad economic conditions. In the case of question five, the strength of the original relationship was not affected at all by these same controls. At least the first of these two findings suggests that our interpretation may be correct: Only when people were very alienated or under very adverse economic condi- tions did their "nationalist" attitude against the Federal Government increase their tendency to vote Social Credit. Thus we suspect that the last two measures of ethnic consciousness were rather, for some people, other measures of aliena- tion and economic grievances.[32] Otherwise, it becomes difficult to interpret the absence of relationships observed in Table 5.6 with the first three questions.

It seems therefore possible to conclude that ethnic consciousness did not pro- duce the strong effects on Social Credit which some have assumed. On the basis of the foregoing data, our own conclusion is that nationalism had little, if any- thing, to do with this upsurge.[33]

CONCLUSION

In this section, political conditions of conduciveness for the rise of Social Credit and other new parties have been investigated.

In the first three chapters, it was found that a system of one-party domi- nance—assumed to arise out of various conditions, such as structural cleavages, residues of bitter contests, corruption in high places, structural attachments— creates a situation which is highly favorable, given the existence of discontents, to the rise of third parties, whether in Quebec or elsewhere in Canada. On the other hand, it was shown that when the old opposition party is strong, third parties are conspicuously absent from the political scene at either the provincial or the federal level.

In particular, the serious weakness of the federal Progressive Conservative party in the province of Quebec for some seventy-five years made the political system highly vulnerable to Social Credit, since it left the unsatisfied voters with no real alternative. It created a state of seeming stability which finally broke into a new party.

We are thus in presence of a case where political stability is obtained at a potential heavy cost for the future maintenance of the system. If, at one extreme, a party system with a great number of parties can become ineffective and give rise to political mass movements led by strong charismatic leaders—Mussolini's Fascist party in the twenties, Hitler's Nazi party in the thirties, Poujade's U.D.- C.A. in the fifties, De Gaulle's U.N.R. only recently—at the other extreme,

[32] Another way of interpreting this finding is to see both a Social Credit option and a Federal Government's rejection as effects of economic discontent and other factors to be discussed further on.

[33] Contrary to what many think, ethnic consciousness does not seem to have, and may not have had, much effect in Quebec provincial politics either; see Maurice Pinard, "La rationalité de l'élec- torat," pp. 187ff., and "Working-Class Politics: An Interpretation of the Quebec Case," *The Ca- nadian Review of Sociology and Anthropology* 7 (1970), pp. 87–109.

one-party dominance in a democratic system can also have very similar effects. Caouette's Social Credit in Quebec seems to be only one instance among many others in Canada, not to mention American movements. Thus the general proposition that pluralism is a necessary condition for the stable functioning of a democratic system seems to hold true, in the particular sense that in democratic nations, at least a two-party system seems usually necessary to insure the stability of the system itself. These findings are of the highest interest since they enable us to foresee the success or failure of political movements on the basis of our knowledge of the political system.

This last chapter substantiated the idea that political change is easily conducive to further political change. Districts which had shown a tendency to switch their allegiance to the Liberals at the provincial level in 1960 also tended to support the new party at the federal level in 1962. And individuals who changed their political allegiance between the two old parties at the provincial level (mainly from the Union Nationale to the Liberals) were more likely than stable voters to switch to Social Credit at the federal level.

Furthermore, it was shown that people favoring another form of change, separatism, were also more likely to be Social Credit supporters, though a two-way relationship was provably involved. This finding is all the more surprising since the separatist movement was quite weak and, on the whole, rested on completely different social bases than Social Credit.

On the other hand, the data did not support the idea that Social Credit was only another manifestation of French-Canadian ethnic consciousness. Basically, the source of the movement lies in economic grievances, not nationalist grievances. These economic grievances will be dealt with in the next chapter.

III

THE

SOCIAL

AND

ECONOMIC

FACTORS

The
Economic
Strains

CHAPTER SIX

One of the basic premises of this study is that structural conduciveness is not a sufficient condition for the rise of a new political movement. Indeed, if it were, Quebec—and other provinces as well—would have had more third parties than it actually has had. Another condition is necessary: strains must also be present. Without them, one-party dominance, for instance, can only lead to long tenures by the dominant party.

There were very serious strains in rural Quebec on the eve of the 1962 election. We shall now document this fact, and attempt to show the relationships between these strains and Social Credit support. To begin, however, let us first consider the social basis of Social Credit in that election. This presents two particularly striking characteristics.[1]

---

[1] What appeared at first sight to be a third surprising characteristic turned out to be spurious: we found that 25 percent of the homeowners, as opposed to only 18 percent of the renters, voted Social Credit (N's equal to 319 and 305 respectively). However, this was due to the fact that rural residents tend to be homeowners, while Montreal and Quebec City residents tend to be renters. Controlling for this, we found that in the last two cities, 10 percent of the homeowners and 9 percent of the renters voted Social Credit (N's equal to 63 and 175), that in other communities of more than 5000 voters, these figures are, respectively, 19 and 29 percent (N's equal to 78 and 75), and that in smaller communities, the figures are, respectively, 33 and 31 percent (N's equal to 178 and 55). (See also p. 172, fn. 39. Compare also with Table 8.9, second panel, and accompanying text.) We cannot, unfortunately, control for suburban areas, to see whether the important grievances of suburban homeowners has led them to be protest voters, as suggested by Clark; see his "Group Interests in Canadian Politics," in J. H. Aitchison, ed., *The Political Process in Canada* (Toronto: University of Toronto Press, 1963), pp. 70ff.; see also Porter, *The Vertical Mosaic*, pp. 377–378; Lemieux, "The Election in the Constituency of Lévis," p. 46.

THE SOCIAL BASIS
OF SOCIAL CREDIT

First, as already indicated, the support for the party was almost exclusively rural.[2] The population of Montreal,[3] which in 1961 comprised 35.6 percent of the Quebec population, was barely moved by the party (Table 6.1). We have seen above that the weakness of the Progressive Conservative party in the context of rural districts may have been in part responsible for the rural basis of the party.[4] Here, we shall ask if the economic conditions in the rural areas of the province can also account for part of this variation.[5]

Second, the class base of the party presents some apparent contradictions. As can be seen in Table 6.1, the support of the party was concentrated among small businessmen, farmers and workers.[6] That Social Credit should have disproportionately recruited small businessmen might after all be explained by an ideology stemming from their condition of a "doomed class": they might have been attracted by the party's conservative and even reactionary ideology. Since Social Credit stands in reaction against many aspects of modern society, its ideology is particularly attuned to the needs of small businessmen who strive to cling to obsolete business patterns.[7] The same could be said to a large extent with regard to farmers. Since Quebec farming is largely of the family small-holding type, which is not at all adapted to a modern economy, farmers are also a doomed class.

But the particularly strong working-class base[8] of the party is *a priori* surprising in terms of a rational analysis of political behavior; it is all the more so if one realizes that workers who had a working-class identification or who were members of labor unions were more likely to support the new party than their respective counterparts, as will be seen in Chapters 8 and 11. Indeed, what we

2 For lack of a better term, in this study "rural districts" refer to electoral districts that lie outside the Montreal and Jesus Islands. The Quebec City electoral districts, which gave a strong support to Social Credit, are included in this rural category, unless otherwise stated.

3 Specifically, the population of the electoral districts on the Montreal and Jesus Islands.

4 See pp. 26–29.

5 Other aspects will be dealt with in Chap. 11.

6 But, surprisingly enough, not among the self-employed workers (artisans, etc.). We shall return to this in the following section on small businessmen.

7 See Martin A. Trow, "Small Businessmen, Political Tolerance and Support for McCarthy," *American Journal of Sociology*, 64 (1958), pp. 270–281. The case of the small businessmen and farmers will be further discussed in pp. 113ff.

8 Farmers' reaction to economic pressures with political protest was frequent in the United States throughout the nineteenth century. But this has not been the case among the working class: the farmers' response has been seen to have "an explosive quality—great force without duration—which is unique." Angus Cambell, Philip E. Converse, Warren E. Miller, and Donald E. Stokes, *The American Voter* (New York: John Wiley & Sons, Inc., 1960), pp. 402–403.

Table 6.1

The Regional and Class Bases of the Social Credit Party

	SOCIAL CLASSES*						
	LOWER-MIDDLE			WORKING			
VOTE IN 1962	UPPER-MIDDLE %	SALA-RIED %	SMALL BUSI-NESSMEN %	SKILLED %	SEMI-SKILLED %	UNSKILLED AND SERVICE %	FARMERS %
	Rural districts						
Social Credit**	14	15	29	30	46	29	32
Conservative	31	40	29	33	26	29	32
Liberal	56	40	42	36	27	39	36
N.D.P.	0	5	0	0	1	2	0
N =	(59)	(40)	(21)	(99)	(70)	(51)	(72)
	Montreal						
Social Credit	0	8	—	8	6	7	—
Conservative	23	33	—	25	42	27	—
Liberal	71	59	—	60	50	60	—
N.D.P.	6	0	—	7	3	7	—
N =	(35)	(39)	(3)	(60)	(36)	(15)	(1)

*The social class scale used is described in Appendix C.

**a_1 (average regional effect on Social Credit support) = .21; $p(a_1^* \leq 0) < .0001$;

a_2 (social class effect, comparing all workers together to the first two groups together, in rural districts) = .21; $p(a_2^* \leq 0) < .0001$;

a_3 (social class effect, comparing farmers to the first two groups together, in rural districts) = .18; $p(a_3^* \leq 0) = .003$;

a_4 (social class effect, comparing small businessmen to the first two groups together, in rural districts) = .15; $p(a_4^* \leq 0) = .08$.

observe here is that each of the two major social strata in modern society, the "middle class" (not considering the small businessmen) and the "working class," acted as "real classes," characterized by real discontinuities in political behavior, that is, a sharp increase in Social Credit support in rural areas as one moves from the first two groups of the middle class to the working class groups. This pattern reflects at least some degree of class consciousness and certainly, by definition, a class awareness-in-behavior.[9] This in turn implies that even in a loosely stratified class system, class actualization and class politics can take place in a situation which, as we shall see, was one of crisis.

Yet, conservative political movements are expected to be more likely to have, if not a middle-class, at least a lower-middle-class base, while workers are rather

[9] On this, see Dennis H. Wrong, "Social Inequality Without Social Stratification," in Celia S. Heller, ed., *Structured Social Inequality: A Reader in Comparative Social Stratification* (New York: The Macmillan Company, 1969), pp. 513–520.

attracted to socialist, communist or at least reformist movements.[10] How then are we going to account for the working-class support of Social Credit?[11]

WHY SOCIAL CREDIT?

Put differently, why did the working class turn to the conservative Social Credit party, rather than to the socialist New Democratic Party? Many, no doubt, would argue that there is nothing in this to be surprised about, given the hold conservative and traditional values have in Catholic Quebec. Had not the C.C.F./N.D.P. forces repeatedly failed to take root in French Canada? According to this view, the French-Canadian working class is much too conservative to turn to a leftist movement.

It is our contention that such an explanation constitutes a gross oversimplification. First, Social Credit has had success before among workers of other provinces in Canada.[12] Moreover, this cultural interpretation of the working class support in Quebec is directly challenged by our data: as will be shown in Chapter 12, we find that, for all practical purposes, conservative attitudes bear no relationship to support for Social Credit. The party made as many recruits among conservative or traditionalist respondents, as among others; this is particularly true within the working class.[13]

A more elaborate view of the political process would also lead one to consider this rightist vote on the part of the working class as something which can be expected. For one thing, Social Credit may be a party the basic political tenets of which place it squarely on the right of the political spectrum, but it was also in Quebec a protest movement with strong populist orientations and a platform

---

[10] In terms of Lipset's typology, Social Credit represents an exception; this is an instance of a movement of the right with a leftist base, thus indicating that parties' ideology and support do not necessarily correspond. See "'Fascism'—Left, Right and Center," in *Political Man*, Chap. 5; see also Raymond Aron, "Les sociologues et les institutions représentatives," *European Journal of Sociology*, 1 (1960), pp. 142–57, esp. p. 151, and Lipset's view on the role of ideology in *Agrarian Socialism*, esp. pp. 121ff.

[11] A first line of inquiry was to ascertain that the disproportionate working-class base of Social Credit did not result from some of the conditions of conduciveness discussed above. That is, we found (see Table 5.3 and accompanying text) that stable Union Nationale voters, at the provincial level, were more likely to have voted Social Credit than stable Liberal voters, since the former had no real alternative at the federal level. (In fact, our data indicate that this relationship holds even when we consider all voters, stable or not.) On the other hand, we know that at the provincial level, Quebec workers are more likely to vote Union Nationale than middle-class persons (see Maurice Pinard, "Working-Class Politics: An Interpretation of the Quebec case"). But when we controlled voting behavior at the provincial level (U.N. vs. Liberal), the original relationship between social class and Social Credit support (Table 6.1) was not reduced, so that other explanations have to be looked for.

[12] In particular, Robin reports that in British Columbia "there is little ideological" in the working man who votes Social Credit; "it is essentially pragmatic. . . . Social Credit is a prosperity party and to many workers it spells employment"; Martin Robin, "The Social Basis of Party Politics in British Columbia," p. 206.

[13] This will be qualified concerning the small businessmen.

stressing immediate economic redress for the lower social classes. The party was therefore not presenting a purely conservative facade. But this is more important.

We contend that in the absence of (1) a well-developed class-consciousness, and (2) class organizations which go beyond the economic problems to encompass the social and political life of the working class, this unincorporated class is as likely to support a conservative movement as a progressive one, whichever is most available, when their conditions lead them to revolt.[14]

That is not to say, however, that the ideology of an emerging movement is completely independent of its mass base. Depending on whether the intelligentsia (in a very broad sense) of the new movement is trying to defend the interests of the working class, the middle class, or the upper class, the movement may often—but not always—tend to develop an ideology which is congruent with that base, at least on economic matters. But many other factors—historical, cultural, and social—may also affect the ideological orientations, mainly on non-economic matters, of the intelligentsia and of the new movement. In other words, one often forgets that there is an intelligentsia between the mass base and the movement's ideology; though the movement's ideology is of course well articulated among the members of its intelligentsia, there may be a gap between them and the masses. Given the fact that the masses are, by and large, neither sensitized nor interested in most facets of the movement's ideology, we claim that unincorporated masses, once faced with a crisis, will choose the movement that appears to them most likely to be successful, whether it is conservative or progressive in the eyes of the sophisticated observer. The ideology of the existing movements at that point is of little relevance to them. More particularly, this is true for peasants and farmers, who are often unorganized, but also for the workers, when their organizations are politically very weak.

On this we concur entirely with what the authors of *The American Voter* wrote about rural protest:

> Most discussions of this problem share an underlying assumption that there need be some basic congruence between the ideology proposed by the elite and the motivations of the mass base. . . . Certainly such movements must have points of strong attraction. But to presume that the mass base is endorsing the ideology as the analyst conceives it is to presume that such programs—that usually call for change in the pattern of political and economic relationships—are in some real sense comprehended

14 It is important to note in this regard that contrary to many European countries, the working class is not organized into mass parties in America. Their participation in the political process is only mediated through cadre parties, according to Duverger's distinction. See his *Political Parties*, pp. 63–71. (The distinction between these two types of parties rests on their structure, not on the size of their membership; mass parties are recruiting members to insure their political education as well as the financing of the party. Cadre parties, on the other hand, are organized around an elite of notables, who are chosen on the basis of their influence, their political skills, or their financial means; they have no members, in the sense of people signing an undertaking to the party and paying subscriptions regularly. See *ibid.*, pp. 63–64.)

by more than a handful within the mass base. . . . (T)his assumption (is called) into question even for the moderately educated and moderately involved voter. . . . (N)o commonly recognized political actor would be less likely to fulfill this assumption than the farmer.[15]

We also share Lipset's contention that "the strong appeal in the middle 'thirties of Social Credit and progressive coalition movements was clear evidence that the particular ideology of socialism was not important to farmers. If Social Credit would fight the 'interests' and give security to the (Saskatchewan) farmers, they would become Social Crediters like the farmers of Alberta."[16]

To put it in terms of the framework adopted in this study, we contend that, as far as the unincorporated masses are concerned, the support of a new movement does not entail much congruence between that movement's and its followers' ideology or belief system—if by chance the latter have any—but simply requires the development of a *generalized belief* which identifies the sources of strains in the system and envisages an overall cure.[17] Often in our culture, this simply involves identifying the government leaders and their policies as the evil, and embracing a new slate of leaders who claim to have found all-encompassing solutions, whatever the philosophy underlying these solutions.

Thus the small farmers of Germany backed the Nazi party,[18] while peasants working on backward farms support the Communist party in France.[19] Farmers in North America and the lower classes in Latin America have shown the same indifference to opposite ideologies.[20] And in France, at least in one department, which is traditionally oriented to the left politically, there was a correspondence in 1956 between the Poujadist advances and the Communist losses.[21]

Closer to us, the farmers and workers of Alberta joined the right-wing Social Credit movement during the thirties,[22] after they had been supporting the left-wing U.F.A. during the twenties, and while the same groups in the thirties and forties rallied behind the socialist C.C.F. party in the neighboring

---

15 Campbell, *et al., The American Voter*, p. 436; see also Chap. 10. This is an issue that still leaves social scientists deeply divided. For a more elaborate discussion of this position, see Converse's excellent essay, "The Nature of Belief Systems in Mass Publics."

16 Lipset, *Agrarian Socialism*, pp. 151–152.

17 See Smelser, *Theory of Collective Behavior*, Chap. 5, and pp. 292ff.

18 Rudolf Heberle, *From Democracy to Nazism* (Baton Rouge: Louisiana State University Press, 1945).

19 Henry W. Ehrmann, "The French Peasant and Communism," *American Political Science Review*, 46 (1952), pp. 19–43.

20 Lipset, *Agrarian Socialism*, pp. 121–124.

21 See Claude Leleu, "La géographie des partis dans l'Isère," in Duverger *et al.*, eds., *Les élections du 2 janvier 1956*, p. 381, pp. 390–393. But if this was not an exception, it was not a general pattern either. (See François Goguel, "Note complémentaire," in *ibid.*, pp. 420–421.) Indeed, it is interesting to note that another pattern was for mass parties to resist more to the Poujadist upsurge than cadre parties. (See François Goguel, "Géographie des élections du 2 janvier," in *ibid.* p. 481.)

22 See Irving, *The Social Credit Movement in Alberta, passim*, esp. Chaps. 8 and 9.

province of Saskatchewan.[23] Within Saskatchewan, in small urban areas, when-ever there was both a Social Credit candidate and a C.C.F. one, they split the protest vote about equally, but when there was only a C.C.F. candidate, almost all the potential Social Credit vote went to the C.C.F. party, not to the Lib-erals.[24]

On the contrary, the conscious and totally organized working class of Ger-many was the only class which in the early thirties successfully resisted the appeals of rising Nazism and remained faithful to its class parties, the Socialist and Communist parties.[25]

In short then, it seems that in the absence of strong organizations based on a well-developed class consciousness, the lower classes when faced with an acute crisis, are likely to follow the first available political movement.[26] In the words of Bendix, such structural conditions lead to "the indetermi-nacy of the relationship between class situation and class action."[27] It should be pointed out that Marx, though believing that in the end the revolution of the proletariat would be "properly" oriented, admitted the possibility of misdirected revolts, which he saw as necessary stages and a manifestation of false consciousness.[28]

23 See Lipset, *Agrarian Socialism*, esp. pp. 121ff. "Many of the farmers . . . did not see vital differen-ces in the program and tactics of these movements (Social Credit, C.C.F., Non-Partison League of North Dakota). . . . Each movement . . . provided a functional definition of the situation within the cultural framework of the wheat belt. Each interpreted the depression as being caused by eastern 'capitalism,' 'vested interests,' or 'financiers.' Within that framework, however, one could apparently build either a leftist or a rightist ideology." (p. 123.)

24 Lipset, *Agrarian Socialism*, p. 161, Table 14. With four parties running, the C.C.F. had 18 percent of the votes, Social Credit, 22 percent, Liberal, 46 percent, and Conservative, 15 percent; with 3 parties, C.C.F. had 23 percent, Social Credit, 25 percent, and Liberals, 52 percent; with two parties only, the C.C.F. got 43 percent and the Liberal, 57 percent (1938 election). See also p. 108, p. 114.

25 Samuel A. Pratt, *The Social Basis of Nazism and Communism in Urban Germany*, (Master's Thesis, Michigan State College, 1948). Note that the "Social Democratic Party in pre-Hitler Germany was said to comprise the workers' entire life, from the cradle (organization for the care of mothers and children) to the grave (proletarian associations for cremation)." Rudolf Heberle, *Social Movements: An Introduction to Political Sociology* (New York: Appleton-Century-Crofts, 1951), p. 291.

26 There may be, however, marginal ideological groups for which this proposition does not hold. The small businessmen may be one of them; their case will be discussed below. The lack of effect of ideology or various attitude configurations in the population at large is discussed at length in Chap. 12. The secondary leaders of the movement (for instance, its candidates) are often also an exception; see Chap. 7.

27 Reinhard Bendix, "Social Stratification and Political Power," in R. Bendix and S.M. Lipset, *Class, Status and Power* (New York: The Free Press of Glencoe, Inc., 1953), p. 600. Bendix, however, failed to limit his proposition to such conditions, as well as to properly evaluate the resistance of the working class to Nazism in Germany.

28 See Karl Marx and Friedrich Engels, *The Manifesto of the Communist Party* in Lewis S. Feuer, ed., *Marx and Engels, Basic Writings on Politics and Philosophy* (Doubleday Anchor, 1959), esp. pp. 15ff. and Karl Marx, *The Class Struggles in France, 1848 to 1850*, in *ibid.*, pp. 281ff. Marx of course stated that class organizations and class consciousness were essential elements to prevent such misdirected revolts; see R. Bendix and S.M. Lipset, "Karl Marx' Theory of Social Classes," in Bendix and Lipset, *Class, Status and Power*, pp. 26–35.

Until 1961, labor unions in Quebec had always limited themselves to the economic sphere; they had never engaged in political action and refused to officially back a party.[29] Furthermore, our data indicate that they have a long way to go before gaining working-class support for such action. When asked, "If the labor unions in the province should recommend to vote for a given party in an election, would this influence you up to a point to vote for that party?" only 5 percent of the respondents answered positively; but what is striking is that this percentage rose to only 6 percent when the workers alone were considered.[30] Moreover, we find that only 53 percent of the workers disagreed with the statement that "labor unions are much more harmful than useful," while 26 percent of them agreed with it.[31]

Given such a weak degree of class consciousness and such a weak identification with their organizations, and considering the record of the latter with regard to political action,[32] we do not find it surprising that the workers should have turned to the first movement available when faced with a crisis. The Social Credit party's concrete appeals may have at times been articulated in terms of its more salient right-wing tendencies, but its central message remained nevertheless a simple claim that it could rapidly better the conditions of all those who were economically dissatisfied.[33] To properly evaluate the party's orientations would have required on the part of the working class a degree of sophistication which, we repeat, studies have shown to be present in very few citizens, let alone the lower classes.[34]

[29] In 1961, one labor organization, the *Fédération des Travailleurs du Québec* (F.T.Q.) joined with the Canadian Labour Congress in the formation of the New Democratic Party (former C.C.F. party).

[30] Workers: yes: 6 percent; no: 79 percent; don't know: 14 percent (N equal to 535); white collars: 4 percent, 82 percent, and 14 percent, respectively (N equal to 316); farmers: 5 percent, 81 percent, and 15 percent, respectively (N equal to 88). (Incidentally, these are indications of the very great cultural homogeneity which exists on class lines, as well as on many other background variables, among French Canadians.)

[31] With 21 percent don't know's or qualified answers (N equal to 533). For the white collars, the figures are: disagree, 49 percent; agree, 30 percent; don't know or qualified answer, 22 percent (N equal to 315); for the farmers: 42 percent, 28 percent, and 30 percent, respectively (N equal to 88).

[32] Only toward the end of the 1962 campaign did the central leaders of the main French-Canadian labor union, the *Confédération des Syndicats Nationaux* (C.S.N.), become worried by the Social Credit's growing popularity among workers; its president publicly warned the workers of the contradictions between the Social Credit's and labor union's philosophies. But it was too late by that time: many local leaders of the union had already passed over to the Social Credit party and had even become its enthusiastic organizers in some districts. (It is interesting to compare this situation with that of Saskatchewan in the thirties: after the defeat of the C.C.F. in 1934, and the victory of Social Credit in Alberta in 1935, many local C.C.F. organizations in Saskatchewan joined the Social Credit movement which started to develop; Lipset, *Agrarian Socialism*, p. 108; see also p. 123.)

[33] A protest movement like Social Credit, which offers immediate and simple cures to economic or other problems, also has an advantage over a movement which, like the N.D.P., proposes more comprehensive, but long-range solutions. On this, see Irving, *The Social Credit Movement in Alberta*, pp. 344–345; Lipset, *Agrarian Socialism*, p. 129, p. 151.

[34] We have no data on deferential attitudes on the part of the working class; but given the type of leadership offered by Social Credit in Quebec, as well as status sentiments on the part of the workers, we doubt very much that deferential attitudes could explain the workers' support of Social Credit. On this, see also Robin, "The Social Basis of Party Politics in British Columbia," p. 206.

WHY WAS THE AVAILABLE PARTY
FROM THE RIGHT?

But to say that the lower classes under the conditions just stated will support the party which is most available tells us nothing about which party will turn out to be the available one. Why was Social Credit, and not the N.D.P., the strongest alternative?

First, it should be mentioned that in fact, on the eve of the 1962 election, these two new parties did not present equally strong alternatives to the electorate. On one side, Social Credit had its leadership deeply rooted in rural districts, precisely where the unrest was brewing. Moreover, since 1958, the party had been reorganized and had been making intense efforts to mobilize the discontented in rural Quebec. In these efforts, the party was reaping the fruits of more than twenty years of intense proselytism by its predecessor, the Union of Electors. The rural electorate was convincingly presented with the image of a new movement, strongly organized and clearly determined to spare no effort in dislodging the old parties.

On the other side, the New Democratic Party, though it had also been revamped at the national level in 1961, had not been making any particularly striking organizational drive in Quebec, let along in rural Quebec. As in the past, it remained highly centralized in Montreal and its leadership was still a faithful representation of the English-speaking tradition of the party in Quebec. And while Social Credit finally succeeded in nominating a candidate in every electoral district of the province, the N.D.P. could not do better than present a slate of 40 candidates, one, to be sure, for every district in Montreal (21), but only 19 for the 54 other districts of the province.

The important point is that this distribution of forces on the part of these two parties was in no way an historical accident. At this level, we think it is correct to resort to ideology as an interpretation. Ultimately, the failure of leftist forces to get organized in Quebec rests with the monolithic conservative ideology of the French-Canadian *elites*, which is strongly rooted in religious and educational institutions and closely tied with their constant preoccupation with nationalist concerns. It is this lack of ideological pluralism which, until very recently, prevented the emergence of a leftist leadership that could constitute more than a marginal and sporadic force in Quebec politics. Insofar as the working man was concerned, class consciousness may not have been very developed, but it was no less developed than in other places on this continent where the workers had not yet been mobilized in class parties through class organizations. There are in fact indications that, had it been presented with leftist alternatives of some strength, the French-Canadian working class could have responded favorably to them.[35]

---

[35] As when a few decades ago their enthusiastic responses to the international unions led the elites, particularly in the Catholic Church, to back the creation of denominational and ethnic unions with a more moderate stance.

In short, it is our contention that the emergence of a rightist, rather than a leftist, alternative can be accounted for mainly by the strong conservative and nationalist values of Quebec's elites and by the ensuing lack of leftist political cadres of any real significance.[36]

THE ROLE OF STRAINS

With these clarifications in mind, we can now turn to the crisis situation which led classes with different and even opposite interests to rally behind the Social Credit party.

We feel that a crucial factor for this sudden and meteoric rise of the Social Credit party in Quebec lies in the worsened economic conditions of large segments of the population. It is our contention that the most general factor of large-scale political movements is to be found in the *changes, and particularly reversals*, occurring in the economic conditions of social groups. We do not claim that poverty *per se* is a source of radicalization; on the contrary, it has often been observed to be a condition of stability.[37] But when the economic conditions of large groups in the population worsen, the likelihood and chances of a political movement are at their best.

There is nothing particularly new in such a thesis. Marx, for instance, stated that the fundamental source of the workers' revolution lies in the constantly worsening conditions of the proletariat under the development of a capitalist economy. According to him, the revolution would be linked to phenomena like "commercial crises (making) the wages of the workers ever more fluctuating," "the modern laborer . . . (sinking) deeper and deeper below the conditions of existence of his own class," "the lower strata of the middle class . . . (sinking) gradually into the proletariat," in short "pauperism (developing) more rapidly than population and wealth."[38] That is, Marx stressed *changes for the worse* in people's economic conditions.

The number of instances in which such factors have led to political revolts could indeed form a very long list. It seems however that the types of economic events which worsen the lot of entire social groups could be classified under a few headings.

[36] This hypothesis has been discussed at greater length in relation to our interpretation of the working class support for the conservative Union Nationale in Quebec provincial politics; see Pinard, "Working-Class Politics: An Interpretation of the Quebec case." The lack of a "working class party tradition" also accounted for the success of Peronism in Argentina, and in turn explains the difference between Italian Fascism and Peronism; see Gino Germani, "Mass Society, Social Class, and the Emergence of Fascism," *Studies in Comparative International Development*, 3 (1967–68), No. 10, pp. 194ff.

[37] Notice in this regard (Table 6.1) that the lower segments of the working class—the unskilled and service laborers—have not been the strongest supporters of Social Credit. We shall examine this point extensively in Chap. 8.

[38] See Marx and Engels, *The Manifesto of the Communist Party*, in *Marx and Engels, Basic Writings*, pp. 15ff. The point is not to see whether these predictions were correct or not, but to indicate what were, according to Marx, the conditions for the revolution of the proletariat.

There are first and above all the economic depressions and recessions, which oppress mainly the lower segments of the industrial sector of the economy, but also the small-holding farmers who are dependent on credit and markets.[39] Marx himself saw the source of revolts that occurred in many countries in Europe in the mid-eighties—France, Germany, Poland, Austria, Hungary, Italy,— in "two economic world events," the potato blight and the crop failures of 1845 and 1846, and the general commercial and industrial crisis of 1847 in England.[40] Similarly, for instance, the postwar depression of the early twenties gave rise, among others, to the Fascist movement in Italy and the Progressive party in Western Canada.[41] The Great Depression of the thirties made the success of the previously stagnant Nazi Party in Germany, assured the rapid rise of the Social Credit Party to power in Alberta, and saw the creation of the C.C.F. movement in Saskatchewan, to mention a few successful instances. Kornhauser's finding in this regard is interesting: considering nine European countries, he found a correlation coefficient of $+.85$ between "the percent of the labor force unemployed at the time of the first election following the onslaught of the depression . . . and the percent change in the Communist vote over the last pre-depression election as an indicator of the extreme response to the crisis."[42]

A second type of economic event which creates economic distress in large social groups is brought about by the processes of rapid industrialization and urbanization. These processes tend to create large pockets in the economy that cannot keep pace with the developments. Small businessmen, small farmers, and generally the remaining population of areas which lag behind are then negatively affected by the differences between their income—either squeezed or maintained—and the rising cost of living. The best documented instance of this we know of is the Poujadist movement in France in the mid-fifties.[43] The support for McCarthyism in the United States is a close analogy to that case.[44] Similarly, in Italy, the Communists have enrolled a larger proportion of party members in less modernized plants.[45] In general, it would seem that even a mild recession could easily be the ultimate push to revolt among such groups.

There are probably other types of economic changes which could trigger political movements if other conditions, like conduciveness, were present.

[39] See V. O. Key, Jr., *Politics, Parties, and Pressure Groups* (New York: Thomas Y. Crowell Company, 1958), pp. 24ff.

[40] Marx, *The Class Struggles in France*, in *Marx and Engels, Basic Writings*, pp. 286ff., p. 293.

[41] Morton, *The Progressive Party in Canada*, passim.

[42] William Kornhauser, *The Politics of Mass Society* (New York: The Free Press of Glencoe, Inc., 1959), pp. 160–61. The correlation increased to $+.93$ when the fascist vote was included.

[43] Stanley Hoffmann, *Le Mouvement Poujade* (Paris: Librairie A. Colin, 1956), esp. Chap. 7. A good illustration of the effects of rapid urbanization upon the rise of millennial movements in the Middle Ages appears in Norman Cohn, *The Pursuit of the Millennium* (New York: Harper Torchbooks, 1961). Notice, however, that in this last case, the affected groups were the peasants moving to the cities and failing to find employment.

[44] See Trow, "Small Businessmen, Political Tolerance and Support for McCarthy."

[45] Mario Einaudi, J. Domenach, and A. Garoschi, *Communism in Western Europe* (Ithaca N.Y.: Cornell University Press, 1951), quoted in Kornhauser, *The Politics of Mass Society*, p. 151.

We will try to mention a few in conclusion. But for the moment, we hypothesize that the two types already mentioned were largely responsible for the
Social Credit upsurge in Quebec.

QUEBEC'S ECONOMIC CONDITIONS
IN THE EARLY SIXTIES

A look at the economic conditions which prevailed among the lower segments of the rural population in Quebec during the four years preceding the
1962 election shows that these conditions had indeed been worsening. In fact,
the economic situation had been deteriorating since 1958 all over Canada. But
the data on monthly unadjusted unemployment rates for Quebec, Ontario,
and Canada, plotted in Figure 6.1, show in detail how particularly bad the
situation was in Quebec from 1958 to 1962. The peaks of the unemployment
rates for Quebec during the winters of these years hovered between 11.3 percent and 15.0 percent, as compared to 9.1 percent and 11.1 percent for Canada
as a whole, and 6.5 percent and 8.6 percent for Ontario. The graph also illus-
trates the very high degree of seasonal variations, particularly strong in Quebec.
These fluctuations, in conjunction with a generally deteriorated situation, were
probably apt to multiply the exasperations of the working class.[46]

Moreover, unemployment in Quebec was highly concentrated in the rural
areas. In a study done in Quebec in 1959 among French-Canadian families of
wage earners,[47] it was found that from 30 to 50 percent of the family heads in
rural areas had been unemployed during the previous twelve months, compared to only 18 percent in the metropolitan areas.[48]

Though the situation had somewhat improved by 1962 (see Figure 6.1),
according to our data, 23 percent of the respondents said that someone in
their family had been unemployed at some time during the preceding twelve
months, and another 5 percent said that someone had been working shorter
hours than usual.[49]

[46] One could wonder why the Maritime Provinces, which had the highest unemployment rates
in Canada during that period, had no protest movements as in Quebec. Recall, however, what we
have said in Chap. 3 about the well-balanced party system in the three old provinces of that region.
And indeed, in two of them, at the provincial level, the traditional opposition parties came to power
during that period: the Conservatives in Prince Edward Island in 1959, for the first time since 1935,
and the Liberals in New Brunswick in 1960. (The Conservatives had come to power in Nova Scotia
in 1956, and at the federal level, all three provinces had turned Liberal pluralities into Conservative
ones in 1957.) (Quebec, of course, had brought the Liberals into power at the provincial level in
1960.)

[47] Farmers were not included in the study.

[48] Specifically, the proportions of families in which the family head had been unemployed are,
by community size, as follows: metropolitan areas, 18 percent; communities of 5,000 or more, 24
percent; prosperous villages, 30 percent; intermediate villages, 46 percent; poor villages, 51 percent
(N = 494, 388, 179, 191, and 208). Adapted from Marc-Adélard Tremblay et Gérald Fortin, *Les
comportements de la famille salariée du Québec* (Québec: Les Presses de l'Université Laval, 1964), Tables
XII-1 and III-6.

[49] N equal to 986.

Figure 6.1

Unemployment rates—Canada, Quebec, and Ontario—1956–1963*

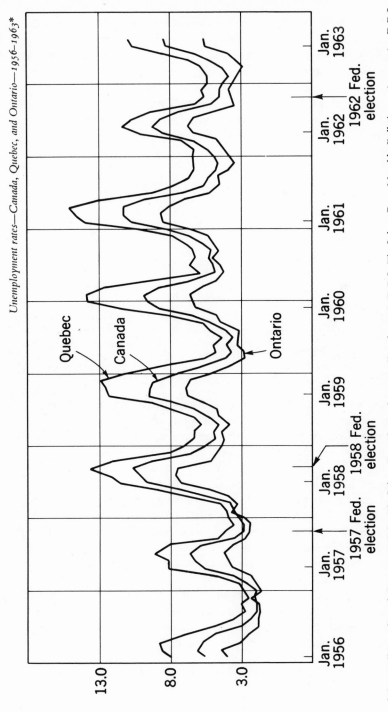

* Seasonally unadjusted. Sources: D.B.S., *The Labour Force,* Monthly Bulletins, 1960 to 1962; D.B.S., *The Labour Force,* September 1960 (Supplement); D.B.S., *The Labour Force,* Monthly Bulletins, 1960 to 1962; D.B.S., *Canadian Statistical Review,* Vol. 36–38.

The detailed data from our sample are presented in Table 6.2 by occupations and regions.[50] It can be seen that 36 percent of the working-class families in the high Social Credit sample districts had had one or more of their members unemployed for some time in the previous twelve months, as compared to 31 percent in other rural districts and 24 percent in Montreal districts. A similar pattern also prevailed among white-collar families, though the overall level is lower. The pattern emerging from these figures thus corresponds to the rural, working-class basis of the Social Credit support.

Table 6.2

Employment Situation of Our Sample By Regions and Occupations

OCCUPATIONAL GROUPS: DISTRICTS:*	WHITE COLLARS			WORKERS		
	I %	II %	III %	I %	II %	III %
*Family Employment Situation:***						
Full Employment	78	82	84	59	60	71
Shorter Hours	2	3	8	5	10	5
One Person Unemployed	14	14	8	20	21	19
Two or More Persons Unemployed	6	1	0	16	10	5
N =	(88)	(96)	(128)	(187)	(131)	(211)

*Districts Groups: I: Rural sample districts with a Social Credit vote of 30 percent or more; II: Rural sample districts with a lower Social Credit vote; III: Montreal sample districts (also with a lower Social Credit vote).
**For index, see Appendix C.

Another good indication of the worsening situation in practically all non-metropolitan areas of the province is afforded by net migration figures for 1951–1956 and 1956–1961; these constitute an excellent measure of the job opportunities in a region. The data (Table 6.3) indicate that except for the new developments of the North Shore-New Quebec region, the Quebec and Montreal Metropolitan areas, and the two Montreal regions, nearly all of the remaining areas in the province had net out-migration rates between 1956 and 1961. Moreover, though the pattern was not new at that time, the gap had been increasing between these two groups of regions: the region which had been decreasing between 1951–1956 went on decreasing, *but all at an increased rate.* Conversely, those which had been increasing (with one exception) went on increasing, but also at an increased rate.

Finally, within rural Quebec, the plight of the farmers was probably the worst of all. Though the farmers themselves may not have been victims of unemployment, they were subjected to serious losses in their income. Indeed, in Eastern Canada,[51] while the per capita disposable income (in 1949 dollars)

[50] The farmers are excluded from this Table. The corresponding data for this group are presented on p. 106, fn. 56.
[51] Quebec and Maritime Provinces.

Table 6.3.

Net Migration by Regions for 1951–1956 and 1956–1961*
(percentages of 1951 and 1956 population)

REGIONS	1951–1956	1956–1961
Gaspe-South Shore	− 5.5	−10.3
Abitibi-Temiscamingue	− 6.2	− 8.5
Quebec	− 5.0	− 7.2
Saguenay-Lake St. John	+ 0.6	− 4.4
Eastern Townships	− 3.7	− 4.2
Three Rivers	− 0.4	− 4.2
Ottawa River	0.0	+ 0.3
Montreal:South	+ 1.0	+ 3.6
Quebec Metropolitan Area	+ 3.4	+ 4.0
Montreal:North	+ 4.2	+ 7.0
Montreal Metropolitan Area	+ 8.3	+ 9.7
North Shore-New Quebec	+15.3	+20.7
Province of Quebec	+ 2.3	+ 2.4

*These percentages were computed from absolute net migration figures in Jacques Henripin et Yves Martin, *La population de Québec et de ses régions, 1961–1981* (Québec: Les Presses de l'Université Laval, 1964), Table VIII, p. 36. I am grateful to Professor Henripin, who made these data available to me in advance of publication.

of all citizens (including farmers) *increased* at an average annual rate of 3.3 percent between 1951 and 1961, the average net income per farm (in 1949 dollars) *decreased* at an average annual rate of 4.5 percent.[52] In Quebec alone, the situation of the farmers was slightly better, but it was certainly far worse than that of other groups; from 1951 to 1961, the average net income per farm (in 1949 dollars) decreased at an average annual rate of 2.6 percent.[53] As should be expected, this was accompanied by large-scale farm desertion. The proportion of the labor force engaged in agriculture decreased by 39.7 percent during that ten-year period.[54]

This implies that for many of the farmers remaining on the farm, the threat of being forced to give up agriculture for some other form of employment was permanent. Since giving up agriculture in turn implies the loss of a trade and of skills which cannot be transferred to other jobs, the likely loss of self-employment and social status, and the loss of a way of life in general, this threat constituted an important additional source of grievances among farmers.[55] If we

52 The average net income per farm, in constant dollars, was slightly above $1,800 in 1951; after a continuous decline over ten years, it was slightly over $1,000 in 1961; see Albert Breton, Claude Bruneau, Yvon Gauthier, Marc Lalonde, Maurice Pinard et Pierre E. Trudeau, "L'agriculture au Québec," *Cité Libre*, XV (July 1965), p. 10.

53 The situation had been improving slightly, however, between 1956 and 1961, since the corresponding decrease was of 1.0 percent only during that period. The Quebec figures were computed by Albert Breton and Georges Dahmen, to whom I am indebted.

54 Computed from Dominion Bureau of Statistics, *The Labour Force*, Cat. No. 71-001, Supplement to March 1965 Report, p. 23.

55 See Breton *et al.*, "L'Agriculture au Québec," pp. 12–13.

also consider that many of the farmers' children and other farm residents were members in the nonagricultural labor force, either full-time or part-time, and that many of them were hit by unemployment,[56] we can easily evaluate the very deep frustrations of that group.

THE EFFECTS
OF THE ECONOMIC CONDITIONS

If our thesis is correct, the worsening economic situation should have had a strong effect on voters' preferences in the 1962 federal election in Quebec. This is indeed the case, as the following data will indicate. We shall consider the effects of economic grievances in the sample as a whole first, and later consider these effects separately for two subgroups of the sample, the small businessmen and the farmers.

Let us turn first to the occurrence of unemployment and part-time work in the respondents' families (Table 6.4). It is clear from these data that unemploy-

Table 6.4

Unemployment Had a Very Strong Effect among Both
*White Collars and Blue Collars**

	FAMILY EMPLOYMENT SITUATION			
VOTE INTENTION	FULL EMPLOY- MENT %	SOME WORKED FOR SHORTER HOURS %	ONE MEMBER UNEM- PLOYED %	TWO OR MORE MEMBERS UNEMPLOYED %
	White Collars			
Social Credit	6	10	27	40
Conservative	20	0	36	40
Liberal	70	80	32	0
N.D.P.	3	10	5	20
N =	(144)	(10)	(22)	(5)
	Blue Collars			
Social Credit	24	29	32	51
Conservative	26	25	18	15
Liberal	47	42	42	28
N.D.P.	2	4	7	5
N =	(253)	(24)	(71)	(39)

*Blue Collars refer to both workers and farmers; for a complete definition of these occupational groups, see Appendix C.

[56] In our sample, 15 percent of the farmers' families had had at least one of their members unemployed for some time in the last twelve months, and 4 percent had had members working only part-time (N = 86).

ment had a very strong effect on whether a Social Credit vote intention[57] was declared or not: it explains about 25 percent of the variation[58] among workers and farmers. This is a much stronger effect than that usually observed in voting studies, apparently reflecting the difference between support of a new political movement in a period of crisis and support of traditional parties during more prosperous times.

Note how the differences between white collars and blue collars tend to disappear when there was unemployment in the family. Differential economic conditions seem therefore to explain in part the difference in voting behavior of these social classes. But when full employment characterized the family, many more workers and farmers than white collars intended to vote Social Credit. This seems to be due above all to a bandwagon effect in the first two groups; notice that the explained variation is greater among the white collars than among the blue collars. Among the latter, as the movement grew stronger, those who turned to it were more undifferentiated.

That such a bandwagon effect took place is revealed by the data, when the time at which the supporters of Social Credit made their decision is considered (Table 6.5). It can be seen that among blue collars, the unemployed turned toward Social Credit disproportionately early during the campaign (first row of the Table), after which the rate of flow seems to have been the same for all

Table 6.5

The Effect of Unemployment Occurred Early among Blue Collars,
Late among White Collars

	WHITE COLLARS		BLUE COLLARS	
	NO UNEM-PLOYMENT*	SOME UNEM-PLOYMENT	NO UNEM-PLOYMENT	SOME UNEM-PLOYMENT
TIME OF DECISION (1962)**	%	%	%	%
Early Social Credit***	4	3	14	24
Late Social Credit	4	23	9	7
Not Social Credit	92	73	76	68
N =	(164)	(30)	(289)	(108)

*No Unemployment: includes full employment and shorter hours.
**Early: a few months before the election; late: a month before or later (see Appendix B, Question 1–51).
***a_1 (effect of unemployment among blue collars in early stages) = .10; $p(a_1^* \le 0) = .02$; a_2 (effect of unemployment among white collars in late stages) = .19; $p(a_2^* \le 0) = .01$.

57 When the index of unemployment is considered, in this and a few subsequent tables, we use the respondents' vote intention rather than their 1962 reported vote since unemployment could have occurred after that election. However, when the 1962 reported vote is used as previously, the same pattern of results obtains, except that the proportion Social Credit among unemployed is slightly lower.

58 The explained variation referred to is simply the difference in Social Credit support between extreme groups, that is the a's presented with most Tables; here: .51 − .24 = .27.

blue collars (second row). Conversely, the effect of unemployment seems to have started later for white collars (compare the first two rows).[59] It seems therefore that, at the beginning, the party got the support of blue collar families *with unemployment*; then, as the bandwagon started rolling in certain districts, it also obtained the support of *all other* blue collars, as well as that of *unemployed* white collars. In short, higher rates of unemployment together with a bandwagon effect would explain why blue collars were more likely to support Social Credit than white collars.

But if unemployment was probably the main source of discontent, it was not the only factor leading to the deterioration of a family's financial condition. A more general picture can be obtained on the basis of two questions from which an index of economic grievances was constructed.[60]

Table 6.6 shows that this factor—which is of course highly related to the employment situation in the family, as the marginal N's indicate—is independently related to a Social Credit vote intention. Note, however, that economic grievances had a much stronger effect among the respondents whose families had an employment problem than among the others. When unemployment was coupled with strong feelings of discontent, the probability that one would cast one's support for Social Credit was highly intensified.

Table 6.6

Other Economic Grievances Also Led to Vote Social Credit
(% Social Credit Vote Intention)

EMPLOYMENT SITUATION	INDEX OF ECONOMIC GRIEVANCES*			
	VERY LOW	LOW	HIGH	VERY HIGH
No Unemployment	13	17	21	23
	(107)	(128)	(177)	(31)
Some Unemployment	17	34	37	52
	(12)	(41)	(65)	(25)

*See Appendix C; very low: index score 0; low: score 1; high: scores 2 and 3; very high: score 4.

Finally, in a situation of crisis, one need not be affected personally or in one's family to feel dissatisfied. The threat that what you see around you might soon

[59] Another finding also supports the interpretation of a bandwagon effect among blue collars: we find that the unemployed blue collars were more likely than the employed ones to have a Social Credit vote intention in the districts where the Social Credit party was the weakest in the 1962 election, that is, in those districts in which the bandwagon effect, if any, must have been small. Conversely, the difference in Social Credit support, between employed and unemployed, appears particularly strong among white collars in the strong Social Credit districts (data not presented).

[60] The two questions were: "So far as your present financial situation and that of your family are concerned, would you say that you are fairly satisfied with them, more or less satisfied, or not satisfied?" and: "Would you say that the financial situation in which you and your family are is better or worse than that in which you were 2 or 3 years ago?" See Appendix C.

affect you may be sufficient to spur you to protest. Moreover, even if you are not afraid that the same thing might happen to you, you may wish to protest against a system that produces such a situation. That these types of protest occurred is clear from the data presented in Table 6.7. We asked our respondents: "Now thinking of the people living in this region of the province, is their financial situation, in your opinion, generally better or worse than that in which they were two or three years ago?"[61] The strong effect the perception of a worsening situation had among those under relatively good economic conditions points again to the process through which such a political movement can reach both the oppressed and the nonoppressed. It is worth noting in this regard that one of the main techniques of propaganda used by Social Credit leaders was to call attention to the deteriorated situation which affected so many people. The appeal was obviously well directed.

Table 6.7

The Perception of a Worsening Situation in the Region Had an Independent Effect
(% Social Credit)

	SITUATION IN THE REGION		
INDEX OF ECONOMIC CONDITIONS*	BETTER	SAME	WORSE
Good Conditions	8	17	31
	(65)	(119)	(26)
Bad Conditions	21	22	36
	(38)	(195)	(110)

*The index of economic conditions combines the index of economic grievances with the employment situation (see Appendix C); good conditions: scores 0 or 1; bad conditions: scores 2, 3, and 4.

CONDUCIVENESS AND STRAINS

In order to view these results from a different angle, but above all to document the independent effects of conduciveness and strains, let us turn once more to aggregate election results.

Census data on net migration constitute a good indicator of the changing economic conditions in a district; the presence of out-migration is a rather clear indication of an oversupply of labor. In France, that seemed to have been one of the factors most clearly associated with the rise of Poujadism.[62] In the case of Social Credit, the relevant data are presented in the first panel of Table 6.8. Since the strength of the Conservative party was shown to be an important

61 This question, as well as those used in the index of economic grievances and some other questions to be presented on economic worry, are inspired from a battery of questions devised at Michigan. See Campbell *et al.*, *The American Voter*, Chap. 14.

62 Hoffmann, *Le Mouvement Poujade*, pp. 197ff.

factor, it is now held constant. The data indicate that both factors were strongly related to the success of Social Credit.

Notice however that in the districts where the Conservative party was strong, out-migration did not trigger a much higher degree of support for Social Credit than in-migration. Actually, the highest vote percentage obtained by a Social Credit candidate in the six strongest Progressive Conservative districts with out-migration was only 27 percent, though these districts had relatively high rates of out-migration (five of them had rates of out-migration of about 10 percent.)[63] Conversely, when out-migration combined with a weak Conservative party, the success of the new movement increased substan-

Table 6.8

Both Political Conduciveness and Economic Strains Are Related to the Rise of Social Credit
(% Districts with Social Credit Victory)*

	NET MIGRATION**	
	IN-MIGRATION	OUT-MIGRATION
1. Strength of Progressive Conservative Party:***		
Strong	20	27
	(5)	(15)
Weak	44	78
	(16)	(18)
2. Political Change at the Provincial Level:****		
Low	11	32
	(9)	(28)
High	36	74
	(14)	(23)

*a_1 (average effect of net-migration in panel 1) = .205; $p(a_1^* \leq 0)$ = .06;
a_2 (average effect of P.C. strength) = .375; $p(a_2^* \leq 0)$ = .002;
a_3 (average effect of net-migration in panel 2) = .295; $p(a_3^* \leq 0)$ = .002;
a_4 (average effect of political change) = .335; $p(a_4^* \leq 0)$ < .001.
Note, however, that Goodman's tests to determine whether the "differences of differences" were significant (that is, to determine, for instance, whether the effect of out-migration was significantly greater with a weak than with a strong P.C. party) all yielded non-significant results at standard levels: p's were equal to .16 in panel 1, and to .21 in panel 2. (For this test, see Leo A. Goodman, "Modifications of the Dorn-Stouffer-Tibbitts Method for 'Testing the Significance of Comparisons in Sociological Data'," *The American Journal of Sociology*, LXVI (1961), pp. 355–363.)
**Net migration from 1956 to 1961. Data from the Dominion Bureau of Statistics, *1961 Census of Canda*, General Review, Bulletin 7.1–1, Table 2. Again, rough adjustments had to be made between census counties and federal electoral districts.
***Strength of P.C. party: strong: P.C. in both 1957 and 1958, or Liberal in 1957 and P.C. in 1958 with more than 54 percent of the votes; weak: Liberal in 1957 and P.C. in 1958 with less than 54 percent of the votes, or Liberal in both 1957 and 1958.
****Political change at the provincial level: low: districts classified in the first, second, and fifth columns of Table 5.1; high: other districts. (The total N is greater in panel 2 than in panel 1, because there are more provincial districts; see notes to Table 5.1).

[63] Results similar in all respects to these are obtained when the factor of economic conditions is added to the survey data presented in Table 2.3 above (see footnote 28, p. 30 above).

tially. This finding reinforces our claim that had the Conservative party been a serious challenger to the Liberals, the electoral success of Social Credit would have been small indeed. In other words, it is the presence of both sets of factors—political and economic—which allowed Social Credit to get a third of the Quebec seats. This supports Smelser's contention that both structural conduciveness and structural strain are necessary conditions for the appearance of a new movement.

Moreover, if we control by the other factor of conduciveness discussed in the previous chapter, that is, political change at the provincial level, we get similar results (second panel of Table 6.8). Both out-migration and political change were favorable conditions for the success of Social Credit,[64] though their joint presence was more particularly effective.

The data presented in the last two sections confirm the hypothesis that the deteriorated economic conditions in Quebec were highly related to the sudden turn of a large number of people toward the Social Credit party. Indeed, about a third of the variation in the support for that party is explained by this factor alone (see, for instance, Table 6.6).

FAMILY SIZE

There were undoubtedly, however, many other grievances which found expression in the support of Social Credit. As an indication of these let us briefly mention two examples.

The first such grievance is family size. One would expect that the number of children—particularly when there are many, as is often the case in rural Que-

Table 6.9

A Large Family Is Always a Strain; A Not So Large Family Can Be a
Strain under Trying Circumstances *
(% Social Credit)

NUMBER OF CHILDREN:	INDEX OF ECONOMIC CONDITIONS**		
	GOOD	SLIGHTLY BAD	VERY BAD
Less than 3	15	13	17
	(123)	(52)	(65)
3 or 4	12	24	32
	(67)	(45)	(50)
5 or more	28	27	34
	(36)	(41)	(77)

*Married respondents only.
**Good: index scores of 0 and 1; slightly bad: score 2; very bad: scores 3 and 4.

64 Introducing the index of economic conditions with the data presented earlier in Table 5.3, we also find both factors to be independently related (though it was impossible to examine all the detailed relationships observed previously with the latter factor, due to sample size).

bec[65]—can constitute a real economic burden for a family, especially if the family is facing a trying period. Table 6.9 presents the relevant data.

These data suggest that a large family (five children or more) is always a strain. Whether the economic conditions of such a family were good or bad, the support for Social Credit tended to be high without much variation. On the other hand, with a medium-sized family (three or four children), the support varied very much with the economic conditions of the family; only bad conditions led to protest. Finally, when the family was small (less than three children), the support for Social Credit tended to be low independently of the economic conditions.[66]

INCREASING TAXES

Other types of grievances were also beneficial to Social Credit. One of these, a political type of grievance, was the increasing burden of taxes,[67] a theme which was constantly stressed by the new party's propaganda.[68] Respondents were asked: "In the last few years, among all the taxes you pay, are there any that have increased?" and, if yes, "Do you feel that your taxes have increased much too much, a little bit too much, or normally?" As many as 85 percent of the respondents said that their taxes had increased in the last few years,[69] and among these, no fewer than 39 percent said they had increased much too much, while another 35 percent said they had increased a little bit too much; only 25 percent said they had increased normally.[70] It seems therefore that the grievances against increased taxation were intense in the population. And not surprisingly, these feelings distinctly manifested themselves in the polling booth (Table 6.10). Indeed, tax grievances were, if anything, even more strongly related to Social Credit support than economic conditions, though both these factors are inter-related (see marginal N's). The appeals of Social Credit were obviously well attuned to people's discontents!

65 While in Montreal and Quebec City, only 14 percent of the married respondents had five children or more, in the rest of Quebec, 35 percent had as many children. (N's equal to 373 and 499 respectively.)

66 This pattern of relationships is not altered when one controls for the urban-rural dimension or for age.

67 Complaints about taxation have always been important in revolutions; see Crane Brinton, *The Anatomy of Revolution* (New York: Vintage Books, 1960), pp. 30, 37.

68 Here is a typical example of Caouette's low-key oratory: ". . . More and more, the people are taxed, the person is taxed, the family is taxed. . . . There are tax increases at all levels of government. Be it in the School Commission, at the municipal, provincial or federal levels: there are tax increases everywhere. . . . Taxes are increased continually, real estate taxes, school taxes, tax on water, tax on electricity, sales taxes, tax on the left, tax on the right, and of all things taxes themselves are taxed." *Réal Caouette vous parle*, p. 51. (Our translation.) Caouette also declared that "income taxes are a confiscation of private property" and that taxation is a "communist principle"; *ibid.*, p. 23, 52.

69 While 9 percent said they had not increased, and 5 percent said they did not know (N equal to 995).

70 The others (2 percent) declared that they did not know (N equal to 850).

Table 6.10

*Tax Grievances Played as Important a Role
as Economic Conditions
(% Social Credit)*

TAX INCREASES	INDEX OF ECONOMIC CONDITIONS*		
	GOOD	SLIGHTLY BAD	VERY BAD
No Tax Increase or Normal Increase	8	15	19
	(99)	(40)	(52)
Taxes Increased a Little Too Much	19	20	29
	(68)	(61)	(69)
Taxes Increased Much Too Much	23	29	35
	(61)	(45)	(95)

*Same categories as in Table 6.9.

SMALL BUSINESSMEN

In previous sections of this chapter, a large part of the difference in white and blue collars' support for Social Credit was explained on the basis of economic dissatisfation. Let us now examine in more detail the support of two special groups, the small businessmen and farmers,[71] to see whether economic factors also account for their strong vote for Social Credit. As previously mentioned, it could be claimed that the support of these two groups—or at least, of the small businessmen—was as much the result of congruence between their ideology and that of the party as the effect of deteriorating economic conditions.

In this regard, it is most interesting to note, however, that while small businessmen were more likely to vote Social Credit than other white collars, *self-employed* blue collars (artisans, etc.) were less attracted to the party than *salaried* blue collars. Only 16 percent of the self-employed workers voted Social Credit, as compared to 27 percent of the latter.[72] It would seem therefore that the ideology of the small entrepreneurs does not necessarily lead to right-wing protest; it may be that it does only when they feel squeezed economically; this may distinguish, for instance, the small grocer from the plumber. And, incidentally, this would lead one to question the suggestion that workers were supporting Social Credit because of their orientation to the small businessmen's class.

71 The proneness of these two groups to social movements is discussed in Kornhauser, *The Politics of Mass Society*, pp. 201–11.
72 N's equal to 32 and 299 respectively; the difference between these two groups (a = .11) is significant at p = .06. (It should be remembered that the self-employed workers are not included in the small businessmen group presently discussed, precisely because of this difference in their political behavior.)

In line with this, our data indicate that the economic grievances of the rural[73] small businessmen were much greater than those of all other rural white collars and that those of farmers were also greater than those of rural workers.[74] Indeed, these two groups, the small businessmen and farmers, were the most dissatisfied of all.

When the small businessmen, however, are compared to the other white collars, their economic grievances do not seem to interpret the difference between the two groups in their support of Social Credit. Though the relationship is not significant, the analysis suggests that with economic grievances constant, small businessmen were still slightly more likely to have voted Social Credit than other white collars while, of course, economic grievances were also related to this support.[75]

One might therefore hypothesize that the typical ideology of small businessmen in America—"nineteenth-century liberalism," as Trow labeled it,[76] and which is characterized by opposition to both big business and labor unions— might interpret their support of Social Credit. This makes sense if one recalls that the leader of the party is himself a rural small businessman—a car dealer— and that the party's ideology stresses a nineteenth-century type of liberalism.[77]

Though we cannot make a rigorous test of this hypothesis,[78] our data suggest that the rural small businessmen are slightly more against social security measures,[79] against labor unions,[80] against nationalization of industries,[81] and

[73] Interestingly enough, almost all the small businessmen in our sample were from rural Quebec: 78 percent of the small businessmen were rural residents as compared to 56 percent of all other white collars (N's equal to 37 and 279 respectively). In the following discussion on small businessmen and farmers, we therefore exclude Montreal interviews to assure a control.

[74] While 76 percent of those in the professional and managerial groups, and 56 percent of those in the clerical and sales groups were low on the index of economic grievances, only 31 percent of the small businessmen were in the same position; and while the corresponding figure is 44 percent among workers, it is only 28 percent among farmers (N = 90, 61, 29, 316, and 85; rural respondents only).

[75] Among those with low economic grievances, 20 percent of the small businessmen, as compared to 9 percent of the other white collars, supported the party (N's equal to 5 and 64); among those with medium or high economic grievances, the proportions are, respectively, 31 and 21 percent (N's equal to 16 and 33). (The average difference between the two groups (.10) is not significant at standard levels; $p = .18$.)

[76] Trow, "Small Businessmen, Political Tolerance and Support for McCarthy."

[77] As we have seen, the party is against big government, against economic concentration and against labor unions, though this last point is not stressed too much, given the party's support! See Chap. 1, and Gérard Pelletier, "Profil d'un démagogue: M. Réal Caouette," *Cité Libre*, 14 (1963), No. 53, pp. 1–9, esp. pp. 6–7.

[78] We have no measure of attitudes towards big business.

[79] Among small businessmen, 17 percent agreed that "there exist too many social security measures," as compared to 14 percent among other white collars, 10 percent among workers, and 14 percent among farmers. (N's equal to 29, 156, 321, and 86, respectively. These and the following data are for rural Quebec only.)

[80] 34 percent of the small businessmen agreed that "labor unions are much more harmful than useful," as compared to 25 percent among the other white collars, 24 percent among the workers and 29 percent among the farmers (N's equal to 29, 157, 320 and 86, respectively).

[81] Among small businessmen, 52 percent disagreed that "the state should nationalize big private companies," as compared to 47 percent among other white collars, 44 percent among workers and 45 percent among farmers (N's equal to 29, 157, 321 and 86, respectively).

against social change in general[82] than all other rural occupational groups. In short, they would be more strongly opposed than others to the major characteristics of a modern industrial society.[83]

And when this tendency is related to Social Credit support, the results are suggestive. While in the population at large, these attitudes made no difference in one's support of the new party,[84] there are indications that opposition to social change among small businessmen tended to push them towards that party.[85] For instance, 50 percent of the small businessmen who were opposed to nationalization voted Social Credit, as opposed to 14 percent among those who favored nationalization.[86]

FARMERS

Insofar as the farmers are concerned, it should be noted that their political behavior in the United States has time and again been shown to be the most unpredictable and variable; it was suggested that this is partly related to the economic vulnerability of the farmers' income.[87]

Recall however, that in our data, the vote of rural workers for Social Credit was stronger than, or equal to, that of farmers (see Table 6.1). Thus in this election, variability—change of party—was not stronger among the latter than among the former.[88]

Furthermore, our data do not indicate that economic grievances—as measured by our index—explain a greater part of the variation among farmers than among workers. However, another indicator of economic hardships, the absence of full employment in the family, bears a very strong relationship to the farmers' vote. It seems to explain more variation in this occupational group than in any other one in rural districts, with the possible exception of the small businessmen. While 25 percent of the farmers with full employment in the family intended to vote Social Credit in the next election, as many as 69 percent of those with some employment problem had this intention.[89]

---

[82] 79 percent of the small businessmen agreed that "it is never wise to want to change rapidly many things," as compared to 65 percent of the other white collars, 57 percent among the workers, and 57 percent among the farmers (N's equal to 29, 157, 318 and 86, respectively).

[83] It is only on the last item mentioned, however, that the difference between small businessmen and other white collars (.14) has some degree of significance ($p = .07$).

[84] See Chap. 12.

[85] Due to sample size, however, we cannot test whether this effect is independent of strains, or whether it is simply an intervening factor which has no effect of its own.

[86] N's equal to 10 and 7 respectively. The difference between the two groups (.36) is significant at .04.

[87] Campbell *et al.*, *The American Voter*, Chap. 15, esp. pp. 416ff.

[88] What seems to have characterized farmers in Quebec provincial politics is their greater tendency to shift their support systematically to the opposition party; on this, see Maurice Pinard, "Classes sociales et comportement électoral," in Lemieux, ed., *Quatre élections provinciales au Québec, 1956–1966*, p. 174: see also Vincent Lemieux, "Quatre décisions collectives," in *ibid.*, p. 210.

[89] N's equal to 55 and 13 respectively. The difference between the two groups (.44) is significant at .001.

The first finding indicates that whenever workers are as affected economically as farmers, they tend to show the same disposition to political change as the latter; this suggests that the source of the farmer's variability has to be attributed primarily to economic, rather than to social factors, contrary to the views of the authors of *The American Voter*.[90]

On the other hand, the presence of a more permanent pattern of variability among farmers indicates that contrary to other occupational groups, the farmers, together with small businessmen, probably entertain long-range grievances against the political system. As shown above, farmers' real income, as well as their share of the labor force, are gradually shrinking. The last finding suggests that when such permanent grievances combine with short-term ones, as, for instance, the presence of some unemployment among their children, their exasperation is likely to become extreme and lead to a very high degree of political ptotest.[91]

Finally, other parts of our data appear to indicate that economic changes among farmers have a peculiar effect. In our sample, both the farmers who said that the profits from their farm products had *increased* in the last four or five years and those who said they had *decreased* were more likely to have voted Social Credit than those who said they had remained about the same.[92] One possible interpretation of this finding is that both those who reported increases in their profits and those who reported decreases were particularly subject to *fluctuations* in their income, and therefore to insecurity and uncertainty about their future income.[93] A slightly different interpretation might be that when one has long-term grievances, a short-term improvement only makes more salient long-term unfulfilled expectations. Whether this effect is due to worry that the improvement will not be maintained or to dissatisfaction with the improvement, or both, cannot be ascertained fully from our small number of cases.[94]

In order to corroborate this surprising finding, we turned again to aggregate data. When the degree of change in the proportion of commercial farms[95] between the 1951 and 1961 census is used as an indicator of the plight of agriculture in a district, we obtain the relationship shown in Table 6.11.

As expected, the data illustrate that deteriorating economic conditions in

[90] They attributed part of the farmers' response to their lack of social integration; see pp. 424ff. On this, see also Kornhauser, *The Politics of Mass Society*, p. 208.

[91] There are no indications that the farmers' attitude toward change would have affected their support of Social Credit in the way this attitude affected the support of small businessmen.

[92] The figures are 36 percent and 36 percent, as compared to 26 percent, respectively (N's equal to 11, 25, and 27). With such small numbers, the finding is not, of course, statistically significant, but a similar kind of relationship is obtained when one takes as the independent variable whether the financial situation of their family is better or worse than it was previously; a similar result, this one statistically significant, is also obtained with aggregate data, as will be shown presently.

[93] See Lipset, *Agrarian Socialism*, p. 29.

[94] To the degree that we can test it, the first of these interpretations is supported by our data.

[95] A commercial farm is defined by the Census as a farm reporting $1,200 or more for its sales of agricultural products for a 12-month period.

Table 6.11

*Both a Decrease and a Large Increase in the Proportion of Commercial Farms
Between 1951 and 1961 Led to a High Social Credit Vote*

SOCIAL CREDIT VOTE	CHANGES IN THE PROPORTION OF COMMERCIAL FARMS		
	DECREASE %	SMALL INCREASE* %	LARGE INCREASE %
50% or more	46	10	19
30% to 49%	27	30	50
Less than 30%**	27	60	31
N (districts) = ***	(11)	(20)	(16)

*Small increase: less than 5%; large increase: 5% or more.
**Considering the districts with a Social Credit vote of less than 30% against all others, the curvilinearity of the relationship is statistically significant: the departure from linearity has a χ^2 of 4.348 with 1 d.f., and $p < .05$. (This follows A.E. Maxwell, *Analysing Qualitative Data* (London: Methuen, & Co. Ltd. 1961), Chap. 4, esp. pp. 63–69).
***Six districts were combined two by two since the Census data on commercial farms was not detailed enough to make adjustments between electoral districts and census counties. The urban districts (Longueuil, and those of Montreal and Quebec cities) are excluded. The data on the proportion of commercial farms was computed from Dominion Bureau of Statistics, *1961 Census of Canada, Agriculture: Number and area of farms*, Bulletin SA-1. Due to a change in the definition of a farm in 1961, the figures in this Bulletin were supplemented by figures comparable to 1951 made available to this author by the D.B.S.

agriculture strongly influenced a turn towards Social Credit.[96] But again notice that, as with the individual data, the relationship is not linear: a relatively large increase in the proportion of commercial farms also exerted a push, though weaker, towards that party.[97] Therefore, though in general we find that an improvement in one's economic conditions pushes one away from political protest—that is, the relationship is linear[98]—the situation is apparently different among farmers. At both the individual and aggregate levels, the same curvilinear relationship appears. This suggests, as mentioned before, that fluctuations in one's profits or the combination of long-term grievances with short-term improvements increase the tendency to protest.[99]

[96] Since he found no strong linear relationship between Social Credit support and level of income, Lemieux has suggested that while the farmers may have supported Social Credit because of their economic conditions—"un crèditisme piutôt économique"—workers would have done it because of status grievances—"un crèditisme plutôt social"; see "Les dimensions sociologiques du vote créditiste au Québec," pp. 183–85. The data presented so far suggest on the contrary that economic grievances were important for both groups, as indeed Lemieux also suggested elsewhere; see his "The Election in the Constituency of Lévis," p. 51. As for the relationship with income, it is in fact curvilinear, and this also for both groups, as will be discussed in Chap. 8.

[97] The curvilinearity of this relationship was maintained when subjected to a series of controls, such as the change in the proportion of total farms, net-migration, and strength of the Progressive Conservative party.

[98] See Table 6.6 for instance.

[99] This would imply a qualification of Durkheim's classic proposition "that even fortunate crises, the effect of which is abruptly to enhance a country's prosperity, affect suicide like economic disasters": short-term improvements alone, at least in the area of collective behavior, would not be sufficient to lead to deviance; they would need to follow a long-term period of deterioration to have this effect; see Émile Durkheim, *Suicide* (New York: The Free Press of Glencoe, Inc., 1951), p. 243.

CONCLUSIONS

The results presented above reveal the existence of strong relationships between changes in economic conditions and the support of a new political movement. Whether we looked at the effects of economic adversities as such or considered other grievances, such as a large family or the burden of taxes,[100] the relationships observed are strong enough to indicate that we uncovered a major factor of support for new movements.

In general, the types of economic changes which lead people to turn to new political paths can apparently be summarized in a few categories. The most important seems to be short-term deteriorating conditions after relatively long-term periods of prosperity. An example of this situation is the recession of the early sixties after the relative prosperity prevailing, by and large, since the end of World War II. How strong the people's responses will be depends on, among other things, how deep and how long the deterioration goes on, that is, how complete the despair of the people becomes. This first type of change and its effects are best exemplified in our data by the case of the blue collars in general (mostly workers).[101]

A second type of change is the long-term regular lowering of one's financial position. This is usually exemplified by groups whose economic pursuits run contrary to the main streams of economic development; the cases of the small businessmen and the small farmer fit this pattern perfectly. If they are relatively few—the former group does usually meet this condition—or if the decline is relatively slow, however, the discontent may not crystallize easily into organized protest. But the conditions of these groups becomes really exasperating when long- and short-term deterioration are combined; the potential for revolt then reaches its highest point. Unemployment in farmers' families exemplifies this situation.

It even seems that within this second type of change—long-term deteriorating conditions—fluctuations of any kind are worse than steady decline. A sudden steep decline, but also short-term improvements, produce uncertainty; or, if these improvements are not trusted to last, they just make more salient the gap between where one comes from and where one is going. Contrary to Durkheim's generalization with regard to suicide, it would seem that only in such cases—long-term deterioration—would short-term improvements lead to the search for new means of political action. Our data, on the other hand, clearly show that for those in already satisfactory financial conditions, short-term improvements detract one from any kind of political protest.[102]

---

[100] Growing families, as well as increasing taxes, are not stable conditions, but imply changes for the worse in one's financial position.

[101] These are exactly the conditions which, according to Davies, lead to revolutions; see James C. Davies, "Towards a Theory of Revolution," *American Sociological Review*, 27 (1962), pp. 5–18.

[102] It may be, however, that under certain situations, short-term as well as long-term improve-

A third type of situation might also lead to protest movements. This occurs when the gradual improvement of a group's lot, though expected to continue, finally levels off. In their paper on separatist movements in Quebec, the Bretons suggest that some of these movements appear in periods of prosperity as well as during depressions, when at the end of their course they engender "rigidities and institutional plateaux," characterized by the strangulation of channels of occupational mobility, the stabilization and even diminution of profit rates, and the stabilization and reduction of remuneration rates at the top of the occupational structure.[103]

More generally, if there is one general proposition that can be suggested by the above considerations, it is that political movements are *a response to gaps created between a group's expectations and its actual conditions*.[104] Whether this gap results from the types of changes just described, or from other sources, does not matter too much.

What matters, however, is that a large number of people be similarly affected and that effective means be used for the *mobilization* of the people. The thesis here developed also implies that long-endured *poverty*, to the extent that it does not involve changes in one's economic conditions, is not a factor of political movements. The problems centering around these last two themes will be our concerns in the next two chapters.

---

ments lead one to develop even greater expectations, thus creating an unfulfilled gap conducive to grievances and revolt. See Brinton, *The Anatomy of Revolution*, Chap. 2; Arthur L. Stinchcombe, "Social Structure and Organizations," in James G. March, ed., *Handbook of Organizations* (Chicago: Rand McNally & Co. 1965), p. 174.

103 Raymond Breton and Albert Breton, "Le séparatisme ou le respect du statu quo," pp. 17–28; see also Crane Brinton, *The Anatomy of Revolution*, p. 68.

104 See Daniel Bell, *The End of Ideology*, rev. ed. (New York: Collier Books, 1962), p. 31.

The
Mobilization
of
the
Discontented

CHAPTER SEVEN

If strains can engender much discontent and stimulate strong outcries against parties and governments, and eventually lead to an overthrow of the incumbents in a healthy two-party system, they cannot alone, or even coupled with conducive conditions, produce a new political force. For this, leaders must emerge, a new movement must be created, and the discontented must be led to believe in it and be mobilized into it.[1]

The emergence of leaders and the creation of the new Social Credit movement in the 1957–1958 period have already been briefly described in Chapter 1. For a more detailed account of these aspects of the movement, the interested reader is referred to Stein's study.[2] Here we would like to concentrate our attention on the mobilization of a following to the movement.

A HISTORICAL DIMENSION

The first aspect to be dealt with brings us back to the long history of intense proselytism by Social Credit groups in Quebec, which Lemieux has referred to as the "partisan dimension" of the new movement.[3] One would expect that the efforts of the old Union of Electors had not been completely vain, and that despite its electoral failure, the seeds of the movement had not been completely

---

1 N.J. Smelser, *Theory of Collective Behavior*, esp. pp. 296ff.
2 M. B. Stein, *The Dynamics of Political Protest.*
3 Vincent Lemieux, "Les dimensions sociologiques du vote créditiste au Québec," p. 181.

blown away by other political winds. Was the new movement after all an actual outgrowth of these previous efforts?

Actually, the mobilization efforts of the previous decades did finally bear fruits. In his analysis, Lemieux found that there was a strong relationship between the results which Social Credit obtained in Quebec during the forties and its success in 1962. For instance, the votes (4.5%) which the party obtained with 43 candidates in the 1945 federal election were concentrated in the districts which turned out to give Social Credit a strong support in 1962: sixteen of the seventeen districts with a vote of more than 6 percent in 1945 gave the party more than 30 percent of their votes in 1962. Similarly, the relative success of the Union of Electors in the 1948 provincial election (it obtained 9.3 percent of the votes) was also concentrated in districts which gave a strong vote to Social Credit in 1962. Finally, there is a close coincidence between the areas with the largest number of subscriptions to the movement's newspaper (*Vers Demain*) in 1946, and the party's strongholds in 1962. Put differently, only a few of the strongest Social Credit districts of 1962 had not already been areas of strength before.[4]

There is therefore a historical dimension to the new party's success, which should not be overlooked. Its recent victories in Quebec were apparently related to its relatively unsuccessful efforts of the forties.[5]

CAOUETTE'S TELEVISION APPEALS

The immediate mobilization drive which, however, multiplied many times the number of old supporters was in a very large measure due to Réal Caouette, the leader of the new movement, and, to a lesser extent, also to his party's secondary leaders and candidates.[6]

Let us first consider the very effective recruiting drive of the movement's leader. Réal Caouette possessed many qualities which are typical of a charismatic leader. He was a brilliant demagogue[7] and a talented populist speaker; his speeches transpired a sense of righteous anger for people's conditions, of utter sincerity to the cause, and of deep conviction that very easy solutions were at hand, if only politicians wanted to implement them.

His appeals reached the people primarily at home through one media, television, in quarter-hour broadcasts, which started in some rural areas on a bi-

---

4 *Ibid.*, pp. 181–83.

5 It should be ascertained, however, whether the 1940's successes had an effect independent of other factors, in particular one-party dominance and strains.

6 We shall be considering here only the formal aspects of mobilization by the party's organization. More will be said about informal mobilization through social participation in Chaps. 10 and 11.

7 See Gérard Pelletier, "Profil d'un démagogue." Demagogic appeals seem to go hand in hand with leadership of political movements, if not of modern political parties; on this see Max Weber, "Politics as a Vocation," in H. H. Gerth and C. Wright Mills, ed. and trans., *From Max Weber: Essays in Sociology* (New York: Oxford University Press, 1958), pp. 77–128.

monthly basis soon after the formation of the party in 1958, and were gradually extended to cover many regions of the province.[8] The program rapidly became very popular and gradually changed the early skepticism of many viewers into attraction and even enthusiasm.[9] Actually, it is this enthusiasm which made so extensive a TV coverage possible, since the very high costs of extended coverage were paid with the money collected from membership fees and newspaper subscriptions. It has been reported that by the winter of 1961–62, the movement had recruited 12,000 members and was using nine TV stations.[10]

The remarkable effectiveness of these television programs can be easily demonstrated with our data. Respondents were asked for how long and how regularly they had watched these programs. From Table 7.1, it can be seen that the difference in Social Credit support between those who reported a very high degree of exposure to the party's TV propaganda and those who reported only a very low degree of such exposure is nothing less than 36 percent.[11] Even if in all likelihood this represents a two-way relationship—those who already favored Social Credit were selectively exposing themselves to its propaganda as well

Table 7.1

The Social Credit TV Propaganda Was Most Effective

	INDEX OF EXPOSURE TO S.C. PROPAGANDA*				
VOTE IN 1962	VERY LOW %	LOW %	MOD- ERATE %	HIGH %	VERY HIGH %
Social Credit	7	19	28	30	43
Conservative	31	35	29	34	22
Liberal	59	44	40	36	33
N.D.P.	3	1	2	1	2
N =	(212)	(77)	(163)	(104)	(60)

*For the index, see Appendix C. Very low: index scores 0 and 1: low: score 2; moderate: score 3; high: score 4; very high: score 5.

[8] The broadcasts were started in the Rouyn-Noranda and Saguenay-Lac Saint-Jean regions (with Grégoire rather than Caouette appearing regularly in the latter region), then extended to the Sherbrooke and Quebec City areas, and finally to the Bas-du-Fleuve region. (Plans to extend the coverage to the Gaspé region and to Montreal and Three Rivers were finally abandoned due to a shortage of funds); see Stein, *The Dynamics of Political Protest*, and "The Structure and Function of the Finances of the Ralliement des Créditistes," pp. 426–32.

[9] See Regenstreif, *The Diefenbaker Interlude*, p. 115; Lemieux, "The Election in the Constituency of Lévis," p. 37; Stein, *The Dynamics of Political Protest*.

[10] J. Murray Beck, *Pendulum of Power: Canada's Federal Elections* (Scarborough, Ont.: Prentice-Hall of Canada, Ltd., 1968), p. 342.

[11] Other leaders of modern political movements had also been most successful in their use of modern means of communication. We have already mentioned the effective use of radio by Aberhart in Alberta; Key mentions the case of Long in Louisiana. See Irving, *The Social Credit Movement in Alberta;* Key, *Southern Politics*, p. 162.

as the other way around[12]—there can be no denying that the broadcasts were very successful.[13]

Moreover, this factor tends to explain part of the difference in Social Credit support between Montreal and the rest of the province. Another tabulation (not presented here) revealed that among those with a very low degree of exposure—which was characteristic of Montreal respondents—4 percent supported Social Credit in Montreal as compared to 11 percent in rural districts.[14]

STRAINS AND MOBILIZATION

Finally, as one would expect, the television programs were particularly effective among the discontented groups (Table 7.2). Among those who had no unemployment problems, *exposure* increased the support for the new party by only 20 percent while among those whose families had suffered from unemployment, it increased support by no less than 41 percent. Conversely, *unemployment*, under conditions of low exposure, increased Social Credit support by

Table 7.2

Both Strains and TV Propaganda Were Effective, with Each Factor Intensifying the Other's Effect
(% Social Credit Vote Intention)

	EMPLOYMENT SITUATION	
EXPOSURE TO SOCIAL CREDIT PROPAGANDA*	NO UNEMPLOYMENT	SOME UNEMPLOYMENT
Low**	10 (216)	19 (53)
Moderate	21 (115)	32 (40)
High	30 (109)	60 (48)

*Low: scores of 0, 1, and 2; moderate: score of 3; high: scores of 4 and 5.

**a_1 (difference of differences, i.e., effect of unemployment in the high exposure group minus same effect in the low exposure group) $= .30 - .09 = .21$; $p(a_1^* \leq 0) = .02$;

a_2 (difference of differences, i.e., effect of exposure in the unemployed group minus same effect in the employed group) $= .41 - .20 = .21$; $p(a_2^* \leq 0) = .02$. (This test follows Leo A. Goodman; see footnote to Table 6.8.)

12 It has been shown that in routine politics people tend to expose themselves to their own partisan side, and that the greater the amount of exposure, the higher the proportion of exposure to one's own partisan side. Bernard R. Berelson, Paul F. Lazarsfeld, and William N. McPhee, *Voting* (Chicago: University of Chicago Press, 1954), p. 339.

13 The strength of this relationship is not at all reduced when rural districts alone are considered.

14 N's equal to 124 and 88 respectively; when the degree of exposure was more intensive than that, however, the difference remains large: only 8 percent voted Social Credit in Montreal as compared to 33 percent in rural districts (N's equal to 67 and 337 respectively).

only 9 percent, while under conditions of high exposure, it increased support by as much as 30 percent. In short, although both factors acted independently, they mutually intensified their effect. This suggests that Smelser's model is correct again in its assertion that both strains and mobilization are necessary factors for the success of a new movement. Finally, notice how these two factors together explain a very high proportion of the variation in Social Credit support (50 percent, i.e., 60 minus 10 percent).[15]

Blumer has severely criticized writings which tended to generalize the findings of studies reporting little effect of the mass media in general, and especially in electoral campaigns. Our own findings support his position, particularly when he asserts that researchers should pay attention to variations which exist "in the sensitivity or responsiveness of the people touched by mass media," which may differ between people and "more importantly in given people through time." We certainly concur with him when he insists that "account must be taken of a collective process of definition which . . . may settle into a stable set of views, images, and positions, (but) is always subject to movements in new directions as people, collectively, face new situations, meet new problems and crises. . . ."[16]

THE SOCIAL CREDIT CANDIDATES

Turning to the organization of the movement and its other recruiting activities during the 1962 campaign itself, again we have little to add to Stein's descriptions and our own brief account in Chapter 1. In many ways, the 1962 Social Credit campaign followed the patterns of electioneering of traditional parties, with conventions, public meetings, publicity, and so on. But, as could be expected in such a new movement, it aimed at the development of a "mass," rather than a "cadre" party; thus the organizers spent a lot of energy in recruiting a membership and gathering subscriptions to *Regards*, in order to educate the followers into the movement's doctrine, and above all, to build the financial resources necessary to prepare for an election. To do this, however, the movement could soon feed on the enthusiasm it was itself generating. Following the old Union of Electors' pattern, it had voluntary activists engaged in door-to-door canvassing to recruit members and sell subscriptions to the movement's newspaper. The enthusiastic efforts of these activists certainly played a large role in the diffusion of the movement; thanks in large part to their zeal, the

---

15 This proportion is reduced to only 41 percent when Montreal interviews are excluded. It should be repeated, however, that exposure to the party's propaganda is not a purely independent factor. Notice moreover that exposure is itself dependent on strains (see the marginal N's in Table 7.2).

16 Herbert Blumer, "Suggestions for the Study of Mass-Media Effects," in Eugene Burdick and Arthur J. Brodbeck, *American Voting Behavior* (New York: The Free Press of Glencoe, Inc., 1959), pp. 197–208; (citations at p. 199 and 202).

movement could reap a large measure of success with a budget averaging less than $1000 per constituency.[17]

Although these activities will not be given further attention, we would like to analyze more systematically two aspects of the role of the leaders at the constituency level. These two aspects concern a description and an interpretation of the social background of the new party's candidates, and the effect this background exerted on the mobilization of supporters.

First, given that the party was so strongly based on the working and farming classes, one would expect the party's leadership structure to mirror this support. The Social Credit candidates should have been more closely linked to these two classes than the candidates of the old parties.[18]

This is in fact what the data reveal.[19] If the occupations of the candidates in Quebec in the 1962 federal election are classified according to the Socioeconomic Index worked out by Duncan,[20] we find that the average social status of the Social Credit candidates was much lower than that of the old parties' candidates. The average Social Credit candidate had a score of 53.7, while the average Conservative and Liberal candidates had scores of 72.1 and 73.0 respectively. Their New Democratic Party counterpart, on the other hand, had a score of 55.6, which is close to that of the average Social Credit candidate.[21]

These figures can be given more substantive meaning when the distribution of each party's candidates on the Edwards occupational scale[22] is considered (Table 7.3). Although the distributions for the two old parties are quite similar, with typically more than half of their candidates in the occupational group with the highest status—professionals and kindred workers[23]—they differ sub-

17 See Stein, "The Structure and Function of the Finances," pp. 430–32; Lemieux, "The Election in the Constituency of Lévis," pp. 36–39.

18 This is indeed what Lipset found in the case of the C.C.F. movement in Saskatchewan; *Agrarian Socialism*, Chap. 9.

19 The data on the occupations of the candidates are from the *Report of the Chief Electoral Officer, 1962 Election* (Ottawa, The Queen's Printer). Though certainly far from precise and accurate, we do not think that they invalidate the propositions to be made.

20 Otis Dudley Duncan, "A Socioeconomic Index for All Occupations," in Albert J. Reiss, Jr., *Occupations and Social Status* (New York: The Free Press of Glencoe, Inc., 1961), Chap. 6 and Appendix B. (This is an extension of the classic North and Hatt prestige scale, which has been found to be highly correlated with similar scales in other countries.)

21 N's equal to 75, 73, 73, and 40, respectively. The mean scores we obtained for the 1962 election compare well with those obtained by Kornberg from a sample of candidates for the period 1945–1962: see Allan Kornberg, *Canadian Legislative Behaviour: A Study of the 25th Parliament* (New York: Holt, Rinehart & Winston, Inc., 1967). Table 3-2.

22 Which is the American Census occupational scale, also used to classify our respondents (see Appendix C).

23 "The professional occupations have played a crucial role in political life since the beginning of modern politics. . . . (They) have increasingly formed the political elite. . . ." S. M. Lipset and Mildred A. Schwartz, "The Politics of Professionals," in Howard M. Vollmer and Donald L. Mills, ed., *Professionalization* (Englewood Cliffs, N.J.: Prentice-Hall, Inc., 1966), p. 299, and bibliographical sources cited therein.

Table 7.3

Social Credit Candidates Were Unrepresentative of Both Their Supporters
and Traditional Parties' Candidates

	CANDIDATES*				ELECTORATE**	
	CONSERVA-TIVE %	LIBERAL %	N.D.P. %	SOCIAL CREDIT %	SOCIAL CREDIT %	TOTAL SAMPLE %
Professionals and Technicians (S.E.I. = 75)***	56	56	38	25	3	6
Managerials, Officials, and Proprietors (S.E.I. = 57)	19	27	15	27	6	13
Sales Workers (S.E.I. = 49)	15	8	2	17	5	6
Clerical workers (S.E.I. = 45)	1	4	2	3	3	8
Craftsmen and Foremen (S.E.I. = 31)	3	3	32	21	24	23
Operatives and Service (S.E.I. = 18 and 17)	1	0	10	4	31	25
Laborers (S.E.I. = 7)	0	0	0	0	9	8
Farmers (S.E.I. = 14)	4	1	0	3	18	9
N (Candidates) =	(73)	(73)	(40)	(75)	(131)	(939)

*Data not available for 2 Conservative and 2 Liberal candidates; the N.D.P. had only 40 candidates. (Source: see footnote 19, p. 125.)
**Data from the present study sample.
***For the occupational groups, see Appendix C. The S.E.I. figures under each group represent the Socioeconomic Index of the major occupational groups computed from aggregate data for males in the United States; they indicate the relative status of these groups (Duncan, "A Socioeconomic Index for All Occupations," p. 155).

stantially from the candidates of the Social Credit party and the N.D.P.[24] The
latter two parties have many fewer professionals and many more workers.[25]

Moreover, from Table 7.4, it can be seen that even the middle class candidates the of two new parties quite different from those of the old parties. For
one thing, they occupy the lower echelons within the occupational groups of
that class, which indicates a lower degree of social status or prestige. Other interesting observations also emerge from this tabulation.[26] The legal profession,

Table 7.4

The New Parties' White Collar Candidates Have a Lower Social Status
Within Each White-Collar Occupational Group

	SOCIAL CREDIT %	CONSER-VATIVE %	LIBERAL %	N.D.P. %
Professionals and Technicians*				
1. Lawyers and Notaries	5	54	54	13
2. Other traditional and presti-gious professions	26	24	12	0
3. Nontraditional or less prestigious professions, and technicians	68	22	34	87
N (candidates) =	(19)	(41)	(41)	(15)
Managers, Officials and Proprietors				
1. Managers, Officials and Manu-facturers	25	50	40	33
2. Proprietors	70	50	60	0
3. Union Officials	5	0	0	67
N (candidates) =	(20)	(14)	(20)	(6)
Sales Workers				
1. Brokers and Kindred	15	64	50	—
2. Salesmen and Agents	85	36	50	—
N (candidates) =	(13)	(11)	(6)	(1)

*Other traditional and prestigious professions include physicians and dentists (9), engineers (7), architects (2) and pharmacists (2); nontraditional or less prestigious professions, and technicians include professors and teachers (13), accountants (7), journalists (6), social scientists (6), draftsmen (3), and others (14); managers, officials, and manufacturers include managers and executives (9), manu-facturers (9), public officials (2), and others (2); proprietors include merchants and businessmen (28), and contractors (5); brokers and kindred include insurance brokers (8), other brokers (3), and others (2); salesmen and agents include various salesmen (traveling salesmen, sales clerks, etc.) (12) and insurance agents (6).

24 The range is however slightly larger for the N.D.P.: they have more professionals and more workers as candidates than Social Credit.

25 Relatively similar findings had been reported for Canada as a whole with regard to the candi-dates in the 1957 federal election; see Meisel, *The Canadian General Election of 1957*, Chaps. 6 and 10. The similarity between the Canadian MP's of the two old parties has also been documented for the past; see Norman Ward, *The Canadian House of Commons: Representation* (Toronto: University of Toronto Press, 1950), pp. 135–36.

26 The order in which the subgroups are presented in Table 7.4 represents quite clearly a decreas-ing degree of social status or prestige (except for the first two subgroups among professionals and technicians).

which characteristically occupies a predominant position in the two old parties[27]—in each case, 30 percent of all their candidates are lawyers or notaries—
is practically unrepresented in the two new parties.[28] The latters' candidates in
the professional group tend to be engaged in new[29] or less prestigious, rather
than in traditional and prestigious, professions, or in technical occupations.
Moreover, among the Social Credit candidates, there is a relatively smaller
proportion of managers, officials, and manufacturers, and a slightly larger proportion of less important proprietors or businessmen.[30] Finally, among the sales
workers, the Social Credit candidates tend to be simple salesmen and agents,
rather than brokers.[31]

In short, the old parties' candidates are recruited in the very top echelons of
the middle class, if not the upper class, with the legal profession dominating in
its traditionally unparalleled fashion. More generally, no fewer than 96 percent
of the Liberal candidates and 92 percent of the Conservative ones were members
of the middle class or above,[32] (while only a third of the electorate belong to
that class). The new parties, on the other hand, found their candidates in the
new professions and, in general, in lower echelons of the middle class, but also
in the top layers of the working class.[33] That is not to say, however, that the

[27] As in most other democratic countries; see Weber, "Politics as a Vocation"; see also, for instance, Mattei Dogan, "Political Ascent in a Class Society" in Dwaine Marvick, *Political Decision-
makers* (New York: The Free Press of Glencoe, Inc., 1961), pp. 69–70. In the Canadian House of
Commons, law has usually accounted for approximately one-third of the total membership, from
1867 to 1945, though Quebec used to rely more heavily on lawyers than the rest of Canada; see Ward,
The Canadian House of Commons, pp. 131–136. The situation has not changed much lately, as far as
the old parties are concerned; for Canada as a whole, the two old parties had 27 percent of their
candidates as lawyers in the 1957 election, while Quebec had 33 percent; see Meisel, *The Canadian
General Election of 1957*, pp. 126ff. Lawyers are even more overrepresented among the federal Cabinet ministers and provincial premiers; see Porter, *The Vertical Mosaic*, pp. 391–393. Finally, lawyers
are more likely to win than many others; see Kornberg, *Canadian Legislative Behavior*, p. 44.

[28] Again, this represented a Canadian pattern among the candidates elected in the 1949 election;
neither minor party elected lawyers as MP's; see John R. Williams, "Representation in the House
of Commons of the Twenty-First Parliament: Party and Province," *The Canadian Journal of Economics and Political Science*, XVIII (1952), p. 82.

[29] The group of teachers and professors (13) occupies an important position here: there were four
in each of the two new parties, and the Liberals and Conservatives had three and two respectively.
(In Quebec, to engage in teaching as a profession is a relatively new field for lay people: the profession had long been monopolized by the religious orders.)

[30] Though we have no data on the size of these businesses, it would not be surprising to find that
the Social Credit businessmen are small compared to those of the two old parties. Notice that the
N.D.P. has no representative here.

[31] It is interesting to note here that no fewer than fourteen candidates were insurance brokers or
agents, which makes this profession the most represented one after law and business. Notice that
generally the members of these professions are highly "economically dispensable," an important
condition to engage in politics; on this, see Weber, "Politics as a Vocation," p. 85.

[32] The candidates of the two old parties in Quebec, as well as these of the N.D.P.—but not those
of Social Credit—have tended to have a higher social status then their respective counterparts in the
rest of Canada; see Kornberg's data, *Canadian Legislative Behavior*, Table 3.2, p. 46.

[33] Notice that no party has a strong representation of farmers. This is characteristic of Quebec;
see Meisel, *The Canadian General Election of 1957*, pp. 127ff. Except for the absence of farmers among
Social Credit candidates in Quebec, their occupational distribution bears a striking resemblance to

Social Credit candidates even approximated a fair image of that party's electoral support (as indeed no party has ever done); although three out of four Social Credit candidates (72 percent) are members of the middle class, with the typical Social Credit candidate best described as a lower-middle class person, only 17 percent of their supporters belong to the middle class (see Table 7.3). Nevertheless, these candidates represented a fairer image of the discontented than those of the old parties.

One could ask: What are the processes through which the party differences we have observed have emerged? It seems to us that at least three kinds of explanation could be suggested to account for the lower status of the new parties' candidates.

The first one is obvious and is implicit in what precedes. It is natural, one could argue, that those who were more closely linked to the disgruntled segments of the population should have been more aware of[34] and responsive to their grievances (if not affected themselves), and that they should have chosen to represent them out of some sense of solidarity. This is after all one of the basic processes through which each social group gives rise to its natural leaders. But I am not sure that a sense of solidarity was the most important factor here, though no data are available to support this claim.

A shared ideology with a given party could be a second factor explaining the class position of those recruited to be its representatives. As suggested in the previous chapter, and as will be discussed in Chapter 12, ideology may not play an important role among the masses, but it nevertheless often guides the political options of large segments of the elites. A shared ideology is certainly determinant in the case of strongly ideological parties, and was no doubt very important in the case of a large majority of N.D.P. candidates.[35] It was also important in the case of many Social Credit leaders, particularly among the old *Créditistes*, as documented by Stein.[36] The large number of lower-middle class persons,

---

that of Social Credit MLA's in British Columbia; see Robin, "The Social Basis of Party Politics in British Columbia," pp. 206–207. See also Irving, *The Social Credit Movement in Alberta*, pp. 196ff.

[34] It is interesting to note that when the members of our sample were asked if the financial situation of the people living in their region was better or worse than it had been a few years before, among professionals—that is, the main pool of candidates for the old parties, and for these alone—a smaller proportion answered that it was worse (10 percent) than in the other occupational groups; in these other groups, the proportions were around 20 percent, with the exception of the small businessmen and farmers, among whom the proportions were 30 percent. Similarly, the professionals were much less likely to have been aware of a serious unemployment problem in their community than all other groups, which were quite similar.

[35] The number of workers (17), union officials (4), professors (4), and social scientists (2) (altogether 68 percent) among the N.D.P. candidates is highly suggestive here. Meisel reports that in 1957 at least 40 percent of the C.C.F. candidates in Canada belonged to a labor organization; see *The Canadian General Election of 1957*, p. 219. Similarly, this accounts, for instance, for the high proportion of workers and teachers in the Communist party in France; see Dogan "Political Ascent in a Class Society," pp. 66ff.

[36] Michael B. Stein, *The Dynamics of Political Protest*, Part 3 and 4, *passim;* see also Kornberg, *Canadian Legislative Behavior*, pp. 74ff.

and in particular the number of businessmen and salesmen among Social Credit candidates[37] may also be significant in this regard, given our findings about small businessmen in the previous chapter. But our impression is that for a great many Social Credit candidates—particularly among the newcomers to the movement—ideology was not the prime source of their attraction to Social Credit, and their class background cannot be accounted for primarily in terms of the philosophy of the party.[38]

The process which we think was more important for a large number of them —as well, incidentally, as for most candidates of the old parties—follows from the assumption that for many,[39] the decision to run or not to run as a candidate for a party is largely determined by the rational calculation of their own political self-interest. Let us assume there existed in the Quebec population a pool of people who were eager to become Members of Parliament. Let us further assume that parties (except perhaps strongly ideological ones) are always looking for the candidates who are the most prestigious in all regards, including social status.[40] This means that those in the pool who had a relatively high social status had better chances than the others to be nominated as candidates of these parties. Add to this that the high-status aspirants were more likely to perceive their chances of being elected to be better as candidates of the old parties than as Social Credit candidates, because they were more socially separated from the discontented, and therefore less aware of the forthcoming Social Credit surge. Given their imperfect knowledge, their self-interest therefore prescribed them to remain faithful supporters of the old parties and to try to be nominated as their candidates. On the other hand, those in our pool who had a lower social

---

[37] They represented 34 percent of all candidates. The Social Credit had slightly more candidates in the business category (43 percent) than the Conservatives (39 percent) or the Liberals (35 percent) in the 1957 election. (The C.C.F., with 16 percent only, was quite different from all other parties); Meisel, *The Canadian General Election of 1957*, p. 230.

[38] When a group of Social Credit leaders were asked in an open-ended question what their reasons were for joining the movement, only about three out of ten answered first in clearly ideological terms (in terms of congruence between the doctrine of the movement and their individual beliefs). To a structured question asking them if the most important reason was the doctrine, the shortcomings of the two old parties, or the members of the movement, only about half gave only the doctrine as their reason; see Stein, *The Dynamics of Political Protest*, Chap. 4. Kornberg, however, finds ideology to have been a more frequent motive for becoming a Social Credit candidate—ideology was in fact more often stated by the latter than by those of all other parties, including the N.D.P. (*Canadian Legislative Behavior*, pp. 74ff). It should be stressed, however, that in both studies, ideological motivations are determined on the basis of the respondents' own self-assessment; given the strong normative context of what is a proper motivation, particularly in a new movement, we suggest that the role of ideology may have been overestimated, especially among Kornberg's Social Credit MP's.

[39] A third of the MP's Kornberg interviewed were motivated to become a candidate "by an apparent simple and powerful desire to become MP's"; since this is based on the respondents' own admissions, we suspect the real figure to be much higher: at least, this desire may have been a part of the motives of others; see *Canadian Legislative Behavior*, p. 67.

[40] See Mattei Dogan, "Political Ascent in a Class Society," p. 68. The efforts of Social Credit leaders to recruit prestigious candidates are described in Stein, *The Dynamics of Political Protest*, Chap. 7. The old Union of Electors was an exception, as they were looking for authentic *Créditistes* rather than prestigious ones; see Stein, "The Structure and Functions of the Finances," pp. 422ff.

status tended to perceive their chances of being nominated by the old parties as relatively slim, while at the same time they were more likely to be aware of the potential Social Credit tide. They were thus more likely to be eager to become candidates of that party.[41]

From this model, the following proposition can be derived: the weaker the chances of a party appear to be (particularly if it is not strongly ideological), the lower in the social structure that party will have to descend to recruit its candidates. This simple proposition can be tested in various ways. First, the findings just presented support it. We did find that the Social Credit candidates were of a lower status than those of the old parties,[42] and furthermore that the N.D.P. candidates were more likely to be from the working class than the Social Credit ones.[43] These findings probably correspond to the order in which the chances of the parties were estimated by our pool members prior to the 1962 election.

Secondly, we find that the Social Credit candidates in Montreal had on the average a lower score on the socioeconomic index (50.1) than those in rural Quebec (55.1),[44] which again undoubtedly corresponds to the potential candidates' expectations regarding that party's chances in these respective areas.

Third, these expectations must have increased after the 1962 success. We should therefore expect that whenever Social Credit came out with *new* candidates in the following federal election (1963), it must have been able to recruit people with higher social status than those they were replacing. We do find that the candidates who did not reappear in 1963 had an average socioeconomic score of 52.9 in 1962, while the new ones had a corresponding score of 61.9.[45] Indeed, the new candidates had a higher social status than the former ones in twenty-seven out of thirty-seven cases.[46] It is interesting to note that with these new candidates, Social Credit was closing by about one-half the gap of 1962

41 It is interesting to note in this regard that many of Stein's respondents had considered other parties or movements before joining Social Credit, and that the most often named alternative was the C.C.F./N.D.P.; Stein, *The Dynamics of Political Protest*, Chap. 4.

42 The Conservative and Liberal parties were quite identical in this regard; though we have described the Conservative party as much weaker before, it must be remembered that in the short run this party must have been appealing to potential candidates, given its 1958 successes (it had obtained 50 deputies as compared to 25 for the Liberals). On the other hand, it is interesting to note that in the 1957 election, when the Conservative party was much weaker in Quebec, its candidates in that province were less likely to be professionals than the Liberal ones; and Meisel commented that "Quebec Conservatives were probably able to attract fewer professional people than the Liberals because of the seemingly hopeless position of their party in French Canada"; see *The Canadian General Election of 1957*, p. 133.

43 Although the N.D.P. candidates' average S.E.S. score was slightly higher than the Social Credit candidates' score. We have noted that the variance is greater for the former and that this may be linked to ideological factors. But even in an ideological party, a number of candidates are moved by opportunism, rather than ideology.

44 N's equal to 21 and 54 respectively.

45 N's equal to 37 in each case. The candidates who remained the same in 1962 and 1963 had an average score of 54.5 (N equal to 37).

46 The party lost seats in 1963 (from 26 to 20) and in the 1965 election, its new candidates had an average score of 52.2, while those they replaced had a corresponding score of 60.5 (N's equal to 46 in each case). Thus the drop in social status probably reflected lower expectations.

between its candidates' and the old parties candidates' average scores. This is not surprising when you remember that even in the socialist Labor party of England the *embourgeoisement* of the leadership was directly related to its successes.[47]

Finally, we find that the weaker the Conservatives had been in rural districts —and therefore the better the chances of Social Credit—the higher the Social Credit candidates' socioeconomic status tended to be. In the weak Conservative districts, 69 percent of the candidates had a high status score (56 or more), while in the intermediate and the strong Conservative districts, the corresponding percentages are 56 and 14 percent respectively.[48] Thus, where Social Credit was the only real alternative to the Liberals, it could recruit much more prestigious candidates than where the Conservatives were also an alternative.

These data, therefore, strongly suggest that the relatively lower status of the Social Credit candidates can probably in large part be explained by the inherent weakness of the new party in the eyes of prospective candidates. Their political interest prescribed to aspirant MP.'s of high status that they remain faithful to the old parties, and the Social Credit party was left with a less prestigious pool of candidates to choose from.

Instead of asking why the two new parties had lower status candidates, one could have asked: Why were there so few workers and farmers among these candidates? The answer is in part found in what precedes. Parties are always trying to recruit the most prestigious candidates from the available pool, and a lower-middle class candidate is better in this regard than a worker or a farmer. In fact, the latter are conscious of the handicap their low status would entail if they were to become candidates. To this we may add that workers and farmers are far less economically dispensable to live "for" politics than some of the other groups. But another factor also seems important.

Just as the poor do not possess the ability to be the early joiners of a new movement, even in as simple a mode of participation as voting,[49] so the working class in general (including most small farmers) do not have the ability to engage in the more elaborate forms of participation implied by becoming the candidate of a party. Despite their grievances, they lack, together with the financial resources, the educational, oratorical, and organizational skills required for such roles. Thus, in the same way we found that active participation in direct forms of action in the civil rights movement in the United States was almost totally restricted to middle-class people, to the relative exclusion of upper-class and the almost complete absence of working-class people,[50] similarly the secondary leaders of the new party tended to be from the lower-middle class, rather than from the working class or from a higher class.

47 See W. L. Guttsman, "Changes in British Labour Leadership," in Dwaine Marvick, *Political Decision-makers*, pp. 99ff.

48 For the definition of the Conservative strength in rural districts, see Chap. 2, pp. 23ff. N's equal to 13, 34, and 7, respectively.

49 This will be substantiated in the next chapter.

50 Maurice Pinard, Jerome Kirk and Donald Von Eschen, "Processes of Recruitment in the Sit-In Movement," *The Public Opinion Quarterly*, 33 (Fall 1969), pp. 355–369.

THE CANDIDATES' SOCIAL STATUS
AND MOBILIZATION

w gave less
ing figure is
igh.[54]

irection of   ;ocial Credit affected the type of people who were
e potential   :s, one could also expect that the status of the can-
permitted   an effect on the actual mobilization of supporters.
e affecting   this is presumably one reason why the parties strive
ay causal   ;ious candidates.
aintained   fact more successful in the rural districts in which it
h of the   ous candidates?[51] The data indicate that, for all rural
ant, the   ar positive relationship between the social status of the
here is a   iportion of supporters recruited by Social Credit (panel
didates,   ever, when not only the Montreal districts, but also nine
one for   real region are excluded (panel 2), there appears to be a
of the   ionship between these two variables.[52]
7.6.   intreal and Montreal region districts are concerned, we find
                     nship,[53] though it is not statistically significant: 41 percent of

ble 7.6

nt, the   Table 7.5
ined*

There Is a Positive Relationship between the Candidates' Social Status
and the Social Credit Vote in the More Rural Areas

	CANDIDATES' S.E.S.		
DIT VOTE IN 1962	LESS THAN 50 %	50–69 %	70 OR MORE %
	Rural Quebec*		
20%	35	18	29
%	35	24	29
hore	30	59	43
cts) =	(23)	(17)	(14)
	Rural Quebec, Excluding Montreal Region**		
ian 20%	33	7	0
to 39%	33	27	33
40% or more***	33	67	67
N (districts) =	(21)	(15)	(9)

*The Montreal districts excluded.
**The Montreal districts and 9 Montreal region districts, which are mainly the suburbs of Mon-
treal, are excluded; see footnote 11, p. 24.
***a_1 (effect of candidates' S.E.S. on Social Credit vote, comparing extremes) = .34; $p(a_1^* \leq 0) = .04$.

51 Meisel did find that in the 1957 election the candidates of higher occupational prestige or more
education were more successful than their respective counterparts; see *The Canadian General Election
of 1957*, p. 127, p. 135.
52 The absence of a clear relationship before the exclusion of the Montreal region districts is due to
the fact that in the latter, the candidates had relatively high S.E.S. scores and low support. When these
districts are pooled with those of Montreal, however, the situation is different, as presently discussed.
53 Identical relationships were also obtained for both the Liberals and the Conservatives, in
Montreal as well as in rural Quebec.

the districts in which the candidates' socioeconomic scores `were l
than 5 percent of their votes to Social Credit, while the correspond
only 23 percent for the districts in which the candidates' score was l

To ·be sure, on the basis of the model presented above, the d
causality in these relationships is not obvious; it could have been th
strength (as indicated by the actual strength) of the new party which
the recruitment of more prestigious candidates, rather than the prestig
the actual strength of the party. To assess whether these were two-w
relationships, the potential Social Credit success can be indirectly m
constant by controlling for strains (net-migration) or for the streng
Conservative party; we can assume that when these factors are cons
potential support of the new party also tends to be constant, and if t
variation in actual support with a variation in the social status of the car
the latter factor, being antecedent, becomes the causal factor. This was d
the most rural districts (those of the second panel of Table 7.5), and one
relationships (that in which strains are controlled) is presented in Table

Ta

With the Potential Success of Social Credit Consta
Original Relationship Is Maint

NET-MIGRATION	IN-MIGRATION		OUT-MIGRATION	
CANDIDATES' S.E.S.	LESS THAN 56 %	56 OR MORE %	LESS THAN 56 %	56 OR MORE %
Social Credit Vote in 1962:				
Less than 20%	25	17	33	0
20% to 39%	25	17	33	38
40% or more**	50	67	33	62
N (districts) =	(8)	(6)	(15)	(16)

*The Montreal districts and 9 Montreal region districts are excluded.
**a_1 (average effect of candidates' S.E.S.) = .23; $p(a_1^* \leq 0)$ = .07.

With the potential success of Social Credit maintained constant (by controlling for net-migration), we still find that the candidates' status is positively
related to the actual vote for Social Credit.[55] (However, when the strength of
the Conservatives is used as an indicator of the potential success of Social Credit,
the original relationship disappears among the weak[56] Conservative districts,
though not among the others.)

[54] A low score is a score of fifty-five or less. N's equal to 17 and 13 respectively. The difference
(a_1 = .18) as not significant at standard levels (p = .14).

[55] Notice that in Table 7.6, the original relationship between net-migration and the Social Credit
vote (see Table 6.8) disappears. It seems that this is due to the fact that the poor districts, which had
large out-migration rates, resisted the new movement, as will be discussed in the next chapter.

[56] As defined in Table 6.8.

In short, a large part of the data suggests that the more prestigious candidates of Social Credit were more successful in mobilizing a mass support than the less prestigious ones.[57] It has been argued that the masses in Quebec had become alienated against *all* traditional elites, and that the Social Credit upsurge was a manifestation of that disaffection. The results we have just presented cast serious doubts on this interpretation. That alienation against political leaders and, to a lesser extent, against intellectuals had an effect on the Social Credit vote is supported by our data.[58] But, on the other hand, we find that the voters were more attracted by candidates of the elites than by candidates of lower status. Indeed, the data lead us to suggest that if Social Credit had been able to recruit a slate of candidates as elitist as that of the old parties, it would have been even more sussessful. But since the elites were not very likely to risk their political fortunes for a party which they considered too unpromising, it is unlikely that it could have recruited such a slate.

To summarize this chapter briefly, let us simply mention that on the one hand, the Social Credit leader's appeals on television were a most effective factor of mobilization, while on the other hand the relatively low social status of the party's candidates was prejudicial to its success. In the next chapter, we shall turn our attention to the effects of another factor which, surprisingly, was also prejudicial to the party—that is, the effects of poverty.

[57] Our single indicator of the prestige of the candidates was their occupational status. It can be assumed that if we could have secured a more global measure of their prestige—based, for instance, on their prior political activities and formal social participation, on their age, on their wealth, on their education—we would have observed even stronger relationships. It is interesting to note in this regard that many of the Social Credit candidates were quite active in various political, professional, and other voluntary organizations: in a mimeographed pamphlet of the party, which presented the biographical sketches of its candidatates, 49 of the 75 candidates reported a total of 54 memberships and 47 positions in various organizations. (Those who did not report any were not necessarily non-participants.)

[58] See Chap. 12.

The
Response
of
the
Poor*

CHAPTER EIGHT

Thus far, in considering the impact of economic strains, we have seen that changes in people's economic conditions—and, above all, deteriorating conditions—had a strong effect on Social Credit support. But what about poverty *per se*? Does relatively extreme destitution produce the same effect? More generally, do the poor form the basis on which protest movements are built?

It is the hypothesis of this chapter that the poor, though they may come to form an important element in political movements and even to be disproportionately represented in them, are not their first recruits. If political movements are understandably often not successful among the rich because they are economically satisfied, it seems that at first such movements are not successful among the poor because, paradoxically, they are too dissatisfied. This dissatisfaction prevents them from developing the ability to translate their grievances politically, or, in Smelser's terms, the ability to develop a gereralized belief and to mobilize others or be mobilized for action. In short, we suggest that the poorer segments of the population are not the first joiners, but late joiners of mass movements.[1] We are not of course the first to suggest this, though there is little sound empirical evidence on the question and a great deal of confusion surrounding it. Analysts usually fail to distinguish permanent strains—steady

---

*A shorter version of this chapter appeared in *Social Problems*, 15 (Fall 1967), pp. 250–263.

[1] If this is correct, it challenges the mass theory of politics, since the poor are likely to be the most atomized and alienated segments of the population. The theory will be criticized more fully in Chaps. 10 and 11.

poverty being a good example—and reversals in people's conditions. The purpose of this chapter is to present some evidence concerning this problem and to try to interpret it.

That misery is not a sufficient condition for protest action has been suggested by many. Trotsky for instance wrote: "In reality, the mere existence of privations is not enough to cause an insurrection; if it were, the masses would always be in revolt."[2] Closer to us in time, Key anticipated the themes of Chapter 6 and this chapter when he wrote: "A factor of great significance in the setting off of political movements is an abrupt change for the worse in the status of one group relative to that of other groups in society. The economics of politics is by no means solely a matter of the poor against the rich; the rich and the poor may live together peaceably for decades, each accepting its status quietly."[3] Similarly, Bell, discounting the importance of mass society in the rise of extremist movements, wrote: "It is not poverty *per se* that leads people to revolt; poverty most often induces fatalism and despair, and a reliance, embodied in ritual and superstitious practices, on supernatural help. *Social tensions are an expression of unfulfilled expectations.*"[4] And Turner and Killian argued that "frustration by itself is never a guarantee of receptivity to movements. Long-continued frustration characteristically leads to hopelessness which mitigates against participation in the promotion of any reform. Frustration from *recent* losses or the experience of *improving* conditions is more likely to make receptive individuals than long-continued frustration".[5] Lipset commented in *Agrarian Socialism:* "It is possible to adjust to a continuously low income and standard of living, as do many farmers in the Maritime Provinces. . . . But it is the 'boom and bust' character of wheat production that unhinges life's plans."[6] Finally, the proposition we have hypothesized seems to hold true in all forms of non-routine politics, including revolutions, as already implied in Trotsky's statement. Davies claimed that "revolutions ordinarily do not occur when a society is generally impoverished—when, as de Tocqueville put it, evils that seem inevitable are patiently endured . . . because the physical and mental energies of people are totally employed in the process of merely staying alive. . . . Enduring poverty makes for concern with one's solitary self or solitary family at best and resignation or mute despair at worst."[7]

---

[2] Quoted by Brinton, *The Anatomy of Revolution*, p. 34.

[3] *Politics, Parties, and Pressure Groups*, p. 28.

[4] *The End of Ideology*, p. 31; italics in original.

[5] Ralph H. Turner and Lewis M. Killian, *Collective Behavior* (Englewood Cliffs, N.J.: Prentice-Hall, Inc., 1957), p. 432; italics in original.

[6] *Agrarian Socialism*, p. 29; see also his *Political Man*, p. 63, pp. 258ff.

[7] James C. Davies, "Toward a Theory of Revolution," p. 7. See also Wm. Bruce Cameron, *Modern Social Movements* (New York: Random House, Inc., 1966), pp. 39–40; W. G. Runciman, *Relative Deprivation and Social Justice* (Berkeley and Los Angeles: University of California Press, 1966), esp. pp. 25–26; Eric Hoffer, *The True Believer: Thoughts on the Nature of Mass Movements* (New York: Mentor Books, 1951), Chap. 5.

Let us try to document this general proposition by showing that the poor were relatively weak supporters of Social Credit in Quebec, and more generally that the poor have not usually been the early joiners of other political movements *whether they were rightist or leftist movements.*

THE POOR AND SOCIAL CREDIT

Recall first that we found in Chapter 6 that the poorer segments of the working class (unskilled and service workers) had been less inclined to vote Social Credit than the middle segments of that class (semiskilled workers) (see Table 6.1). If now poverty is defined as a net income of less than $3,500 a year,[8] the survey data clearly indicate that the poor were not the strongest supporters of the new movement (Table 8.1). The relationship is clearly curvilinear in the group of those whose family was not hit by unemployment. Those above the poverty level, not those who live in poverty, were the first joiners in the Social Credit upsurge in Quebec. Notice, however, that this does not hold among those whose family had at least one person unemployed; this is very interesting and we shall return to it shortly.[9]

The hypothesis can also be documented in a different way for a subgroup in the population. Among farmers, if we consider farm size as an indicator of wealth, we find that those with medium-size farms were the most likely to have voted Social Credit: 50 percent of those with farms ranging from 70 to 180 acres supported the new movement ($N = 22$). Among those who possessed larger farms (180 to 400 acres, and 400 acres or more), the support was relatively smaller: 26 and 18 percent of these, respectively, voted Social Credit ($N = 19$ and 17 respectively). But those with very small farms (less than 70 acres) were barely more favorable than the latter: only 25 percent of them voted Social Credit ($N = 20$).[10]

---

[8] In 1962, the Conference of Economic Progress stated, on the basis of studies by the U.S. Department of Labor, that families in the U.S.A. with an income below $4,000 "live in poverty," while those with an income between $4,000 and $5,999 "live in deprivation." See Conference on Economic Progress, *Poverty and Deprivation in the United States: The Plight of Two-Fifths of A Nation* (Washington, 1962), esp. Chap. 3. It is interesting to note that the main break in the data is at a net income of $3,500, which is close to the above definition for the poverty level.

[9] In his analysis of Gallop poll data, Alford reports that "the emerging Social Credit party took over the votes of the poorer Quebeckers." This divergent finding may be due to a loose definition of socioeconomic status (interviewers' ratings from A to D) and/or to the fact that he does not control for immediate strains in the respondents' families as we do. (Our relationship remains curvilinear, however, even without this control.) Robert R. Alford, "The Social Basis of Political Cleavage in 1962," in John Meisel, ed., *Papers on the 1962 Election*, pp. 219–220. However, using aggregate data, Irvine reports a finding similar to ours (see below, Table 8.2); W. P. Irvine, "An Analysis of Voting Shifts in Quebec," in *ibid.*, pp. 131–132.

[10] It is interesting in this regard to note that rural sociologists have repeatedly found size of farm (or other measures of status) to be positively related to the adoption of new farm practices. Though this could be attributed to the fact that poor farmers cannot afford to secure new practices, Lionberger notes that "the fact that low-income farmers are slow to adopt practices that they could well afford suggests that factors other than income are operative"; H. F. Lionberger, *Adoption of New Ideas and Practices* (Ames: The Iowa State University Press, 1960), pp. 100ff. This generalization of the relation-

Table 8.1

The Relationship Between Social Credit Support and Income Levels Is Curvilinear

VOTE IN 1962	INCOME GROUPS*		
	LOW %	MIDDLE %	HIGH %
	No Unemployment in the Family		
Social Credit**	16	27	11
Conservative	40	29	25
Liberal	44	42	61
N.D.P.	1	2	3
N =	(140)	(176)	(150)
	Some Unemployment in the Family		
Social Credit***	36	32	21
Conservative	27	28	45
Liberal	32	38	34
N.D.P.	4	2	0
N =	(69)	(50)	(29)

*Low Income: a yearly net income of less than $3,500; middle income: between $3,500 and $5,000; high income: $5,000 or more. Actually in the above as in other tables to be presented, in order to increase the case base and to make income comparable, those who refused to give their income are classified according to the rent or property value of their home and farmers are always classified according to the size of their farms; for details, see Appendix C. The relationship presented in the above Table holds of course without these modifications; among those with no unemployment, the proportion Social Credit by income groups are: less than $3,000: 18%; $3,000 to $3,499: 16%; $3,500 to $3,999: 28%; $4,000 to $4,999: 24%; $5,000 or more: 7% (N's equal to 84, 64, 79, 76, and 81, respectively).

**Comparing those who voted Social Credit against all others, the probability that this curvilinear relationship could have resulted from chance is smaller than .001. This test follows Maxwell, *Analysing Qualitative Data*, Chap. 4, pp. 63–69.

***The variation due to linear regression gives a χ^2 of 2.099 with 1 d.f. and $p = .15$. The probability that this relationship is curvilinear is very far from being significant (departure from regression line has a χ^2 of 0.129 with 1 d.f., and $p = .72$); that is, if the probability of a linear relationship is not too strong, that of a curvilinear one must be rejected. Note that Coleman's test, comparing extremes on income, gives an effect parameter of .15, with $p = .05$.

The relationships observed at the individual level also obtain with aggregate data, which provide independent tests of the hypothesis. Remember that in Chapter 6 we found that economic *reverses* in a district—as indicated by net out-migration rates—were a factor leading to the success of the new party. If now we consider the economic *level* of the same districts, we find the same curvilinear relationships as for the survey data.

When the rural districts of the province are classified according to their average levels of income (Table 8.2), it can be seen that the support for the new movement came disproportionately from the districts of middle income, while the poorer districts gave much weaker support.[11]

ship between status and adoption is extended by Rogers to non-farmers as well on the basis of his review of the literature; Everett M. Rogers, *Diffusion of Innovations* (New York: The Free Press of Glencoe, Inc., 1962), pp. 174ff.

11 This finding holds when we control for one-party dominance as well as for strains.

Table 8.2

Social Credit Obtained Only Weak Support in the Poorer Rural Districts

% SOCIAL CREDIT VOTE	AVERAGE TOTAL FAMILY INCOME (MALE HEADS) IN DISTRICT*		
	LOW %	MIDDLE %	HIGH %
40% or more**	18	59	36
20% to 40%	46	29	27
less than 20%	36	12	36
N (districts) =	(11)	(17)	(22)

*Low: less than $4,000; middle: $4,000 to $4,750; high: more than $4,750. Calculated from D.B.S., *1961 Census of Canada*, Vol. IV, Bulletin 4.1-6, Table F.6. As previously, rough adjustments had to be made between Census counties and electoral districts. The districts from Montreal (21) and Quebec (4) cities are excluded, since adjustments cannot be made. The data are not available for smaller units.

**Considering the districts with a Social Credit vote of 40 percent or more against all others, the relationship is curvilinear with $p < .05$. (The departure from linearity has a χ^2 of 4.464, with 1 d.f.)

If the proportion of commercial farms, rather than the average family income is taken as an indicator of the wealth of a district, similar results are obtained. Though in Chapter 6, we found that a *reduction* in the proportion of commercial farms was positively related to Social Credit support, we now discover a curvilinear relationship. While we find that 81 percent of the rural districts with a moderate proportion of commercial farms gave a vote of 30 percent or more to Social Credit, the corresponding figures for the districts with a small and a large proportion of commercial farms are only 58 and 68 percent respectively.[12] In short, as seen in Chapter 6, the districts where the conditions on the farm were worsening turned to Social Credit; on the other hand, we find now that the districts in which agriculature was in a state of poverty did not.[13]

In short, while curvilinear relationships are found in this chapter when indices of *steady poverty* are used, the data of Chapter 6 revealed monotonic positive relationships between *economic reversals* and the proportion favoring Social Credit. If poverty prevents one from joining a new movement, changes for the worse in one's economic conditions do not.

An obvious objection could be raised against our interpretation of these

[12] N = 16, 12, and 21 respectively. Proportion of commercial farms: small: less than 55 percent; moderate: 55 percent to 69 percent; large: 70 percent or more. Calculated from D.B.S., 1961 *Census of Canada, Agriculture: Number and Areas of Farms*, Bulletin SA-1. As previously, rough adjustments had to be made between the census counties and the electoral districts. The district from Montreal (21) and Quebec (4) cities and the district of Longueuil are all excluded since they are completely urban. If we break the dependent variable as in Table 8.2, we get similar results, though the relationship is weaker.

[13] It has been argued that the Gaspésie and Bas-du-Fleuve regions resisted the Social Credit tide because they had been less exposed to the Social Credit TV propaganda. Since this is one of the poorest regions, part of the explanation seems to be their income level.

data. One could say that Social Credit is a conservative party, or more properly a party with populist appeals based on an ideology of the right, very much like Father Coughlin's movement in the United States during the thirties. It therefore failed to recruit the most disinherited strata of the population and instead attracted the support of the middle class. In other words, the party's support would reflect the party's ideology.

We do not think that this objection is correct. First, middle-class observers tend to overestimate the role of ideology among the masses, as discussed above; this is even more so among the poor. Secondly, the category of "middle-class support" would have to be substantially extended to cover the present instance. In occupational terms, the party got the bulk of its support from the working class and farmers, not from the middle class. Our use of the term middle-income group (or category) should not be taken to refer to the middle class, as the empirical cutting points on our income scale clearly indicate (see note to Table 8.1).

Moreover, the data demonstrate that the party was particularly successful among workers who identify with the working class and not among those who identify with the middle class (Table 8.3). Indeed, in all three occupational groups—non-manual, worker, and farmer—the party got disproportionate support from those who identified with the working class.[14] We also found that it got disproportionate support among the unionized segments of the working class (see Chapter 11). One cannot, therefore, interpret the greater support of the middle-income group as resulting from a middle-class ideology.[15]

Another set of facts also stands contrary to the objection. The phenomenon

Table 8.3

Working-Class Identifiers Were More Likely to Vote Social Credit than Middle-Class Identifiers
(% Social Credit)

CLASS POSITION	CLASS IDENTIFICATION	
	MIDDLE-CLASS*	WORKING CLASS
Non-manuals	7 (124)	20 (70)
Workers	19 (100)	28 (227)
Farmers	20 (25)	39 (46)

*a_1 (effect of class identification) = .137; $p(a_1^* \leq 0) < .001$.
a_2 (effect of class identification for workers) = .09; $p(a_2^* \leq 0) = .03$.

14 The relationship is maintained if only those without unemployment in the family are concerned.
15 Actually, the data support the hypothesis of a relationship between identification with a group and behaviors distinguishing members of this group from non-members; Campbell *et al.*, *The American Voter*, p. 307.

we observed in the case of Social Credit in Quebec can also be shown in the case of other political movements, whether they have a leftist, a center, or a rightist ideology.

THE POOR IN OTHER MOVEMENTS

THE C.C.F. MOVEMENT

In his study of the socialist C.C.F. party in Saskatchewan, Lipset observed that the doubling of rural backing for the party between 1934 and 1944 did not reflect an extension of support from "extremely poor farmers" to more conservative "middle-class agrarians," but "the exact opposite": "C.C.F. supporters in 1934 came from the groups in the rural population which had the highest social and economic status. The party's vote was highest in prosperous farm areas where land-tax assessment was high and tenancy was low," while "in the election of 1944 the party made most of its electoral gains from the low-status groups, the poorer and non-Anglo-Saxon farmers."[16]

Lipset also presents some data showing that in the 1934 election, the C.C.F. vote in Regina was lower in areas populated predominantly with unskilled workers (20 percent) than in those populated predominantly with skilled workers (33 percent), while middle-class areas were also low (19 percent).[17] Notice that in 1944, the relationship became linear, the corresponding figures being 62, 61, and 32 percent, respectively.[18] This last relationship will be discussed below.

THE POUJADIST MOVEMENT

If we consider the Poujadist movement in France during the fifties—a movement, as mentioned before, which has many similarities with Social Credit—the same type of curvilinear relationship obtains. Though some have reported the movement's strength to lie in the poorer and economically stagnant *Départements*,[19] many have also mentioned that it's main support comes from small merchants, artisans, and peasants.[20] In his study of the movement, Hoffman

[16] *Agrarian Socialism*, pp. 163–165. This would seem to indicate that the relationship between wealth and C.C.F. support was first positive, then negative, but not curvilinear. However, some of the empirical data presented show clearly a curvilinear relationship in the first period, as will be presently indicated.

[17] Basically similar results regarding the class basis of the N.D.P. were more recently found in one Ontario constituency; see John Wilson, "Politics and Social Class in Canada: The Case of Waterloo South," *Canadian Journal of Political Science*, 1 (1968), pp. 299–300.

[18] See *ibid.*, p. 168, Table 18. These findings are all the more interesting if we consider that at the time the movement was reaching the most dispossessed, it was becoming less radical.

[19] See for instance Lipset, *Political Man*, p. 159.

[20] See, for instance, François Goguel, "Géographie des élections du 2 janvier," pp. 467–505, esp. pp. 477–482; Jean Stoetzel et Pierre Hassner, "Résultats d'un sondage dans le premier secteur de la Seine," in Duverger *et. al.*, eds., *Les élections du 2 janvier 1956*, pp. 199–248, esp. pp. 224–225; Lipset, *Political Man*, p. 160.

observed that richer *départements* of France—as measured by per capita production and per capita income—did not offer strong support to Poujadist candidates. But he was puzzled by the fact that the relationship was weaker at the other end of the continuum, and concluded: "If it is certain that Poujadism has but little succeeded in penetrating *départements* with a high per capita production or income, it cannot on the contrary be said that it has particularly well succeeded in the least productive and poorer *départements*."[21]

A reanalysis of Hoffman's data for the 1956 French election yielded the results presented in Table 8.4. A curvilinear relationship similar to that observed in the Quebec data is apparent. The relatively poorer *départements* were more resistant to Poujade's movement than those of moderate wealth.

Table 8.4

The Same Curvilinear Relationship Appears with Regard to the Poujadist Success in the 1956 French Election

| | INDEX OF PER CAPITA INCOME** | | |
| | LOW | MIDDLE | HIGH |
POUJADIST VOTE	%	%	%
13% or more***	29	41	4
10% — 12 %	24	30	21
Less than 10%	48	30	75
N (*départements*) =	(21)	(37)	(24)

*Recalculated from S. Hoffman, *Le mouvement Poujade*, Annex X, pp. 205–208.
**Index of per capita income: low: less than 75; middle: 75 to 94; high: 95 or more (France = 100); eight *départements* without Poujadist lists are excluded.
***Considering the *départements* with a Poujadist vote of 13 percent or more against others, the relationship is curvilinear with $p < .02$. (The departure from linearity had a χ^2 of 5.980, with 1 d.f.)

It is interesting to note that in his analysis of one *département*, Leleu commented that "it is peculiar to observe that the poorest regions are not those which brought more votes to the U.F.F. (Poujade). The extreme poverty of the South-East region of the *département* made it the least permeable to Poujadism. And it is precisely in the most disinherited canton of the *département* that the U.F.F. obtained its weakest rural percentage of the votes."[22] Then the author went on to show that in that *département* as a whole—as in Quebec—the Poujadist success was attributable to an economic crisis (here in the textile industry and in agriculture).[23] Finally, in Paris, a survey done in part of the city found

21 Hoffman, *Le mouvement Poujade*, pp. 194ff., p. 196 (my translation). The author having assumed a linear relationship then went on to show that when one considers migration figures, the relationship was indeed more clearly linear, as we also found in Chap. 6, since this is a measure of changes in the economic conditions. *Ibid.*, p. 197.
22 Claude Leleu, "La géographie des partis dans l'Isère," in Duverger *et al.*, (*Les élections du 2 janvier 1956*, pp. 393ff. (my translation).
23 *Ibid.*, p. 394.

that the Poujadist movement had the smallest proportion of rich people of all parties except the Communists, and the smallest proportion of poor people of all parties.[24]

MCCARTHYISM

The analysis of the support for McCarthyism in the United States yields a similar curvilinear relationship. On the basis of data collected in a nationwide Gallup survey in 1954, there are indications that the people most likely to have a favorable opinion of Senator Joseph McCarthy occupied some intermediate position in the class structure. According to the first panel of Table 8.5, they were underrepresented in the *lower social-economic rating* subgroup, and while they seemed to come in relatively equal proportions from the other subgroups of that scale,[25] the second panel clearly indicates that they were also underrepresented in the *highest educational* subgroup. Both those low and those high in class position seem to have resisted McCarthyism.[26] This, incidentally, is at

Table 8.5

The Support for McCarthy Tended to Decrease at the Extremes of the Social-Economic Rating or Educational Scales*

OPINION OF McCARTHY	SOCIAL-ECONOMIC RATING				
	UPPER %	ABOVE AVERAGE %	AVERAGE %	BELOW AVERAGE %	LOWER %
Favorable**	39	38	56	40	34
Unfavorable	61	62	44	60	66
N =	(33)	(368)	(16)	(507)	(142)

	EDUCATIONAL LEVELS			
	OVER 12 YRS. %	9—12 YRS. %	UP TO 8 YRS. %	NO SCHOOL %
Favorable***	31	40	45	36
Unfavorable	69	60	55	64
N =	(239)	(582)	(258)	(11)

*Recomputed from Nelson W. Polsby, "Toward an Explanation of McCarthyism," in Nelson W. Polsby, Robert A. Dentler, and Paul A. Smith, *Politics and Social Life* (Boston: Houghton Mifflin Company, 1963), Tables VIII and IX, pp. 818–819.
**a_1 (difference between "below average" and "lower" subgroups) = .06; $p(a_1^* \leq 0)$ = .09.
***a_2 (difference between "over 12 years" and "9—12 years" subgroups) = .09; $p(a_2^* \leq 0)$ = .01.

[24] Stoetzel et Hassner, "Résultats d'un sondage dans le premier secteur de la Seine," p. 225.
[25] If we disregard the "average" subgroup, which has only 16 cases.
[26] Since in these data Republicans were more likely to be favorable to McCarthy and since they tended to be of a higher social status, this would have to be controlled to ascertain more fully these relationships.

odds with Polsby's own analysis.[27] Lipset, on the other hand, obtained results
similar to ours, even though the interpretation he gave differs from ours.[28]

THE GOLDWATER MOVEMENT

If we consider Goldwater as the representative of a right-wing conservative
movement, it is also noteworthy that Goldwater adherents (those who, regard-
less of party preference, selected Goldwater, from many Republicans, as the
Republican nominee) were not predominantly white-collar workers, but
farmers. Further, "there appears to be a tendency for Goldwater support to peak
at the $3,000 to $4,999 income bracket" among both white-collar and blue-
collar people in all regions.[29] Both poorer and richer people were less likely to
support him.

FRANCE'S EIGHTEENTH CENTURY REBELLIONS

With regard to revolutionary activity, recent historical research in France
indicates that the privileged classes as well as the more destitute classes of
unskilled workers and proletarians were substantially under-represented in the
popular rebellions of 18th century France.[30] "The findings imply very little
participation in either ordinary political activity or revolutionary outbursts
by misfits, outcasts, nomads, the truly marginal, the desperately poor."[31] The
activists were a "working-class elite" of tradesmen and craftsmen, who were in
turn, however, strongly stimulated by the misery of the poor and other inactive

27 Polsby percentaged these data in the direction of the dependent variable and concluded that
there were tendencies for the support of McCarthy to come from the lower class and the less educated
parts of the population. ("Toward an Explanation of McCarthyism," p. 186). Sokol also found the
support of McCarthyism to be inversely related to education and occupation; however, his sample
came from "a generally upper-middle-class suburb," so that in his analysis he presents no subgroup of
poor people; Robert Sokol, "Power Orientation and McCarthyism," *The American Journal of Sociology*, 73 (1968), pp. 443-452.
28 Lipset reported that the least educated and the lower occupational groups were *more* likely to
support McCarthy, but that, when socioeconomic status was taken as an indicator of class, the lower-
status persons were *less* likely to support him; and he added that with occupation or education constant, "*the higher the socioeconomic-status level, the greater the proportion of McCarthy supporters*" (author's
italics). He concluded that "perhaps the *higher-income people within lower occupational or educational
strata* were precisely those who were most drawn to an ideology that attacked as pro-Communist
both liberal lower-class-based politics and moderate, conservative old upper-class-elitist groups"
(italics supplied); S. M. Lipset, "Three Decades of the Radical Right: Coughlinites, McCarthyites,
and Birchers (1962)" in Daniel Bell, ed., *The Radical Right* (Garden City, New York: Doubleday
Anchor, 1964), pp. 398ff., pp. 401-402. As argued in this chapter, we suggest that the ideology of this
movement is not the important intervening variable. Moreover, Lipset's comments suggest that income is probably the most discriminating variable (as it is in our own data).
29 Irving Crespi, "The Structural Basis for Right-Wing Conservatism: The Goldwater Case,"
The Public Opinion Quarterly, XXIX (Winter 1965-1966), pp. 523-543, esp. pp. 529, 533.
30 Charles Tilly, "Reflections on the Revolutions of Paris: An Essay on Recent Historical
Writing," *Social Problems*, 12 (1964), pp. 111ff., p. 113; for other revolutions, see also Brinton, *The
Anatomy of Revolution*, pp. 102-105.
31 Tilly, "Reflections on the Revolutions of Paris," p. 114.

groups, as well as by their own personal privations.[32] The indications are that modern revolutionary movements today in underdeveloped areas are more likely to find their early base in even higher strata of the population.[33]

THE AMERICAN CIVIL RIGHTS MOVEMENT

The same curvilinear relationship was observed in a study of the Negro sit-in movement in Baltimore. Though the participants were almost all middle-class (96 percent), when they were classified by an extended North-Hatt prestige scale the data showed that those of middle status were more likely to have joined the movement a year or more ago (36 percent) than those of lower status (27 percent) or of higher status (27 percent).[34] It is well-known that the support of lower-class Negroes for desegregation movements has been conspicuously low. The processes to be discussed here can certainly account for much of this phenomenon.[35]

This varied array of data, to which more could easily be added,[36] strongly document the proposition that the poorer segments of the population are not the supporters of new movements. The generality of this finding is all the more impressive when one considers that it was found in quite different contexts.

But if it is interesting to show that the poor are not the initiators of political movements, it is also important to determine the causes of such a phenomenon. The set of findings presented go a long way in answering the question: Why are there so few revolutions in developing countries? We still have to answer, however, another question: Why do the poor fail to revolt?

WHY NOT THE POOR?

Let us first give a negative answer. The lower support of the poor is certainly not due to lower degrees of deprivations. Objectively they are the most deprived; but they are also the most deprived in subjective terms. Studies have

32 Tilly, "Reflections on the Revolutions of Paris," p. 116. Compare with our analysis, pp. 108ff. This historical research confirms the importance of economic adversities, as opposed to long-endured misery, in triggering these rebellions. See *ibid., passim*.

33 Watnick has argued that both Communist and non-Communist movements in underdeveloped areas appeal first and foremost to the rootless intelligentsia and professional groups; Morris Watnick, "The Appeal of Communism to the Peoples of Underdeveloped Areas," in R. Bendix and S. M. Lipset, *Class, Status, and Power*, 2nd ed. (New York: The Free Press of Glencoe, Inc., 1966), pp. 428–436.

34 N's equal to 161, 45, and 97 respectively; see Maurice Pinard, Jerome Kirk, and Donald Von Eschen, "Processes of Recruitment in the Sit-In Movement." The form of participation in this movement (sit-in, picketing, etc.) being more elaborate than in others so far mentioned, the peak of the curvilinear relationship appears accordingly at a higher status level.

35 See also the interpretations and data presented in *ibid.*

36 For instance, Morrison and Steeves reported, on the basis of a review of 13 studies, that the members of a farmers' movement, the National Farmers' Organization, were not, "on the average, among the most economically deprived farmers"; Denton E. Morrison and Allen D. Steeves, "Deprivation, Discontent, and Social Movement Participation: Evidence on a Contemporary Farmers' Movement, the NFO," *Rural Sociology*, 32 (1967), p. 422.

shown that the poor are not only more likely to be hit by adverse economic conditions, but also more likely to have complaints about their life than others.[37] This is also supported by the present data: respondents in the lower-income group were hit by unemployment in their family much more often than others, and independently of this, had more grievances than others. Unemployment during the preceding twelve months had hit 31 percent of the families in the low-income group, as compared to 22 and 16 percent in the middle and high-income groups respectively.[38] And if we consider only the respondents not subjected to unemployment, we find that the poor were, subjectively, more dissatisfied: in our three income groups, starting with the latter, 24, 18, and 12 percent, respectively, scored high on the index of economic grievances.[39] Thus the relationship between wealth and grievances is linear and negative. One must therefore look elsewhere to find the reasons for their low degree of protest.

Moreover, the fact that the poor feel more dissatisfied economically goes against the theory that their weak response stems from a lower degree of relative deprivation.[40] Actually, in our survey, the respondents were asked: "Comparing yourself with people living around here, would you say that your economic situation is better or worse than theirs?" Though most answered "the same" (74 percent) and few said "worse" (only about 8 percent), this proportion was higher in the low-income group than in the middle one (11 percent vs. 4 percent). When this factor was controlled, we found that the curvilinear relationship of Table 8.1 among the employed respondents was maintained (though the number of cases are at times small), except, surprisingly enough, among the relatively *satisfied*—those who answered "better." Under that condition, the poor were as likely supporters of Social Credit as the middle-income respondents. Seen differently, among the poor, the relatively *satisfied* were the most likely Social Credit supporters, while in the middle-income category the relationship ran in the other direction, with the relatively deprived being the most likely supporters of the new movement. Relative deprivation stimulated the latter, while it *restrained* the poor, in a pattern to be repeated in many other data to be presented below.[41]

37 See for instance Genevieve Knupfer, "Portrait of the Underdog" in Bendix and Lipset, *Class, Status and Power*, pp. 255–263, esp. p. 262; Alex Inkeles, "Industrial Man: The Relation of Status to Experience, Perception and Value," *The American Journal of Sociology*, LXVI (1960), pp. 1–31. Even if he found that the poor were not necessarily the most relatively deprived in certain respects, Runciman nevertheless found them to be the most economically dissatisfied; see Runciman, *Relative Deprivation and Social Justice*, Chap. 10, esp. pp. 205–207.

38 N's equal to 340, 344, and 269 respectively.

39 N's equal to 228, 263, and 225 respectively.

40 See Morrison and Steeves, "Deprivation, Discontent, and Social Movement Participation," pp. 422–427; Runciman, *Relative Deprivation and Social Justice*.

41 The proportions supporting Social Credit among the poor, the middle-income and the high-income categories, respectively, are as follows: 26, 24, and 6 percent, among those who answered "better" (N's equal to 19, 25, and 34); 14, 28, and 11 percent, among those who answered "the same" (N's equal to 105, 146, and 103); 18, 33, and 37 percent, among those who said "worse" (N's equal to 11, 3, and 8).

Finally, *severe and sudden deprivations of the kind implied by unemployment seem actually to be a sufficient condition to lead the poor to protest to an even higher degree than those of middle income.* The reader is referred back to the second panel of Table 8.1. While we found in Chapter 6 that sudden changes in one's economic conditions were a strong element in the Social Credit success, these data now show this relationship to be all the more true, the lower one's income; for those whose family was hit by unemployment, the relationship between wealth and vote for a new political movement seems no longer curvilinear.[42] It may be that any sudden economic reversal is a sufficient condition to make the poor one of the group—if not the group—most likely to support a new movement. This finding throws an interesting light on the ease with which movements of protest arise during periods of acute depression. Such a situation means that both the poor *and* those immediately above them find themselves in intolerable conditions which make a very large mass of people easily attracted to new movements. This, incidentally, may account for the linear negative relationship between socioeconomic status and the presence of favorable attitudes toward Coughlin[43] and Townsend[44] during the thirties in the United States. This also partly accounts, we suggest, for the failure of millennial movements in the Middle Ages among poor peasants—presumably living in steady poverty—and their success among poor rural and urban *migrants*, whose fate was also poverty, but whose migration often produced unemployment or worsening conditions.[45]

Short of a very severe crisis, however, the poor seem to lack the ability which facilitates the growth of a strong movement, and, relatively, too few above them have sufficient grievances to be attracted. With these qualifications in mind, let us now turn to a consideration of the elements leading generally to a low degree of protest among the very poor.

Formally, the curvilinear relationship observed suggests a multiplicative model;[46] the curvilinearity would result from two linear relationships, but with

---

[42] However, when using "vote intention" instead of "past vote," in order to respect the time order of the variables when considering unemployment (see fn. 57, p. 107), the relationship is no longer linear even among the unemployed group: the proportions with a Social Credit vote intention in the low, middle, and high income groups are 34, 44, and 29 percent respectively. On the other hand, there is now a strong tendency to support the N.D.P. in the low income group (the proportions N.D.P. in the three groups are 11, 4, and 0 percent respectively), and if the votes for the two third parties are added together, there is practically no difference between the low and the middle income groups among the unemployed (N's equal to 64, 52, and 28 respectively). (Incidentally, we have a suspicion that some respondents—and interviewers, despite clear warnings—confused the "new" party, Social Credit, with the New Democratic Party!)

[43] See Lipset, "Three Decades of the Radical Right: Coughlinites, McCarthyites and Birchers," pp. 382–384. (Notice however that the relationship is not clearly linear among Catholics.)

[44] See Hadley Cantril, *The Psychology of Social Movements* (New York: John Wiley & Sons, Inc., Science Editions, 1963), pp. 192–193. The more active participants, however, were not poor; see *ibid.*, p. 190.

[45] Or at least, an increasing gap between their expectations in migrating and their actual conditions (see p. 119 above). For these data on millennial movements, see Norman Cohn, *The Pursuit of the Millennium*, pp. 21ff.

[46] I am indebted to Arthur Stinchcombe for this suggestion.

one positive and one negative. That is, the relationship between wealth and grievances, as was just seen, in linear and negative, while the relationship between wealth and ability to translate one's grievances politically would be linear and positive, and the multiplicative result could therefore yield a curvilinear relationship.[47] This is shown with hypothetical data in Table 8.6. The low degree of protest among the poorer people would result from their low ability to translate their grievances politically, while the low degree of protest among the richer people would result from their low number of grievances.

Table 8.6

The Curvilinearity Observed Suggests a Multiplicative Model

	INCOME GROUPS		
	LOW	MIDDLE	HIGH
$P_g^* =$	.8	.5	.2
$P_t =$	.2	.5	.8
$P_p = P_g \cdot P_t =$	.16	.25	.16

*P_g: probability of having grievances; P_t: probability of being able to translate them politically; P_p: probability of taking some political action.

THE PSYCHOLOGICAL AND SOCIAL WORLD OF THE POOR

Substantively, what are the more concrete elements in the poor's life which explain their inability to translate their grievances in political terms? The literature suggests four clusters of factors which might account for the weak response of the poor. We shall discuss each of them and try to determine whether they explain our findings.

WORRY AND HOPELESSNESS

It has been suggested that poverty generates a high degree of worry which detracts from any consideration of long-term solutions to problems. A worried person becomes a self-centered individual, and everything outside his immediate and urgent needs is of little relevance.[48]

47 Though not necessarily of course; for instance, if one of the relationships is strong and the other is weak, the result could still be a linear relationship.

48 See the quotation from Davies' paper above. In trying to explain why some workers in France and Italy are not Communist voters, Cantril wrote that many are too much concerned with their own daily personal problems and "just don't see any point in worrying about the political scene because their own private worries are so pressing"; H. Cantril, *The Politics of Despair* (New York: Basic Books, 1958), pp. 119–120. Lipset also suggests that the insecurity of the lower classes prevents them from taking a long-term view of the political process and thus prevents them from being early joiners of political movements; *Political Man*, p. 150ff.; also p. 113ff. On the "narrowed outlook" and the "lack of effort to control the environment" of the low-status groups, see Genevieve Knupfer,

Closely related to the worry is the hopelessness, fatalism, and despair of the very poor that they will ever escape their miserable conditions. They have usually experienced these conditions for so long that they have lost faith in overcoming them, either by individual or by collective action. Unless something happens that can reactivate their hope, they are not likely to turn to political action. They abstain from politics altogether and become chronically apathetic.[49] In short, the poor are unable to develop the generalized belief necessary for the appearance of a social movement.[50] Are these actually some of the processes accounting for the low support of Social Credit among the poor in Quebec?

Surprisingly, no difference is found in the degree of worry of the low- and middle-income groups: 27 percent of the first group as compared to 28 percent of the second group[51] said they were much worried "about how [they] would get along financially in the next year."[52] Nevertheless, the consideration of worry as an additional variable is interesting, in that it specifies the curvilinear relationship in a suggestive way. As shown in the first panel of Table 8.7, the lower one's income, the less likely one is to be led to protest as a consequence of worry. Though "much" worry has some depressing effect in the middle-income group as well, the level of protest in that group is still higher in such a case than when there is no worry. On the contrary, much worry seems to lead to the lowest level of protest within the low-income group. In short, worry enhances one's tendency to protest in higher-income groups, while it hampers it in the

---

"Portrait of the Underdog," in Bendix and Lipset, *Class, Status and Power*, pp. 255–263; see also Donald R. Whyte, "Sociological Aspects of Poverty: A Conceptual Analysis," *The Canadian Review of Sociology and Anthropology*, 2 (1965), pp. 175–189. Lane also attributes to "financial worry" the low political participation of low-status people; R. E. Lane, *Political Life* (New York: Free Press, 1959), pp. 224–225.

[49] These themes are developed by Turner and Killian, Bell, and Davies in the quotations above. "Hopes" and "faith" are also crucial factors in Cantril's explanation of workers' adherence to the Communist Party. Cantril, *The Politics of Despair*, esp. Chap. 4. And Kahl, in his analysis of the values of the various classes writes that "the lower-class persons . . . react to their (conditions) by becoming fatalistic, they feel that they are down and out, and that there is no point in trying to improve, for the odds are all against them. They may have some desires to better their position, but cannot see how it can be done." Joseph A. Kahl, *The American Class Structure* (New York: Rinehart and Co., 1957), p. 211. See also Oscar Lewis, "The Culture of Poverty," *Scientific American*, Oct. 1966, pp. 19–25, esp. p. 23.

[50] Strictly speaking, they are unable to reach the positive stages of envisioning alternatives. They go through the negative steps of losing faith in a given normative set-up, but fail to develop the vision of a movement as an omnipotent cure. See Smelser, *Theory of Collective Behavior*, esp. Chap. 5. Blumer also wrote that social movements "derive their motive power on one hand from dissatisfaction with the current form of life, and on the other hand, from wishes and hopes for a new scheme or system of living." H. Blumer, "Collective Behavior," in A. McClung Lee, ed., *Principles of Sociology* (New York: Barnes & Noble, 1951), p. 199.

[51] N's equal to 232 and 261 respectively; for the high-income group, the figure is 21 percent (N equal to 223). (Unemployed excluded.)

[52] In these data, as in all data presented in the rest of this chapter, the "unemployed" group of Table 8.1 is excluded in order to provide a control; as we have seen, among the unemployed the curvilinear relationship does not hold.

Table 8.7

*The Effects of Income on Social Credit Support under Various Conditions (I)
(% Social Credit)**

| | | INCOME GROUPS** | | |
		LOW	MIDDLE	HIGH
1.	Worry: Much***	9	27	23
		(34)	(45)	(30)
	A little	20	35	12
		(70)	(81)	(51)
	Almost none	16	16	4
		(32)	(45)	(69)
2.	Party has chances	50	56	31
		(28)	(43)	(29)
	Don't know	13	28	4
		(38)	(40)	(23)
	Party has no chances	4	9	5
		(81)	(70)	(84)
3.	Index of Political Information:† Low††	10	26	9
		(68)	(76)	(43)
	High	21	28	11
		(72)	(100)	(107)
4.	Index of Primary Group Participation:††† Low††††	12	24	13
		(34)	(33)	(23)
	High	18	27	10
		(103)	(139)	(125)

*All percents in this Table are percents voting Social Credit in 1962, except in the second panel of the Table, where they are percents with a Social Credit vote intention (see text).

**Unemployed excluded; see fn. 52 p. 150 above.

***a_1 (effect of worry on low-income respondents, comparing extremes, and testing whether the proportion Social Credit is significantly lower among those who worry) $= -.07$; $p(a_1^* \geq 0) = .19$; a_2 (effect of worry on medium and high-income respondents, comparing extremes and testing the opposite relationship) $= \frac{1}{2}(.11 + .19) = .15$; $p(a_2^* \leq 0) = .006$.

†For index, see Appendix C; low: scores 0 and 1; high: scores 2, 3, 4.

††a_3 (effect of information on low-income respondents) $= .11$; $p(a_3^* \leq 0) = .03$.

†††For index, see Appendix C; low: score 0; high: scores 1 and over.

††††a_4 (effect of primary groups participation in the low-income group) $= .06$; $p(a_4^* \leq 0) = .29$.

low-income group. This suggests that worry means something different among the poor than among the other groups: for the poor, a state of worry seems to be a permanent psychological state which paralyzes them, while for people of the middle and high-income groups, worry apparently stimulates them to protest, rather than restrains them. Worry—and presumably worry of a permanent type—seems to be at least one of the reasons for the poor's low ability to protest.

This relationship seems to account for an otherwise surprising finding. Consider Table 8.8 (first panel): according to these data, economic grievances

Table 8.8

The Effect of Worriness: A Case of Specification
(% Social Credit)

	INCOME GROUPS		
	LOW	MIDDLE	HIGH
Low Economic Grievances*	16	24	8
	(58)	(82)	(107)
Moderate or High Grievances	15	30	16
	(78)	(91)	(43)
Not much worry:			
Low Grievances	16	22	9
	(51)	(68)	(93)
Moderate or High Grievances	20	35	4
	(49)	(57)	(27)
Much worry:			
Low Grievances	20	36	7
	(5)	(11)	(14)
Moderate or High Grievances	7	21	38
	(28)	(33)	(16)

*Index scores 0 — 1. Unemployed excluded.

(other than severe ones, like unemployment) would have no effect among the poor, while as should be expected, they are positively related to protest in the two other groups. But when the degree of worry is introduced as a control factor, this result does not hold any longer (second panel). Instead, the pattern appears the same among both the poor and the middle-income group, though possibly with stronger effects among the former. In the absence of worry, both groups are likely to respond to economic grievances by a higher degree of protest; but when much worried about the future, both groups do just the contrary: the more grievances they have, the less they tend to protest.[53]

This suggests that economic grievances would tend to lead to worry, which in turn would engender a state of hopelessness and resignation, and hence a low degree of political protest. These ideas are supported indirectly by findings in *Agrarian Socialism*. As reported earlier, when the C.C.F. party became successful in Saskatchewan, the poorer farmers and workers rushed to it, though they had failed to do so previously. We suggest that their hopes were reawakened by the growing success of the movement.[54]

More convincingly yet, Lipset shows that the weaker the Communist parties

53 The latter generalization is based on few cases in some cells, since grievances and worries are so closely related. But a more equal break on grievances in that last case yields the same results.
54 Lipset suggests that they were brought out by the upswing in the business cycle (*Agrarian Socialism*, p. 167). But the cases of the Nazi party and the Communist parties to be discussed below cannot be interpreted this way. It may be, however, that an economic upswing is *one* of the ways which lead to a reawakening of hopes and a desire for change.

are in various countries, the less surely can they win the support of the poorer workers:

> The available evidence from Denmark, Norway, Sweden, Canada, Brazil, and Great Britain supports this point. In these countries where the Communist party is small and a Labor or Socialist party is much larger, Communist support is stronger among the better paid and more skilled workers than it is among the less skilled and poorer strata. In Italy, France, and Finland, where the Communists are the largest party on the left, the lower the income level of workers, the higher their Communist vote.[55]

Lipset's explanation is that the lower strata tend to "choose the least complex alternative." But he also writes that "where the party is small and weak, it cannot hold out the promise of immediate changes in the situation of the most deprived."[56]

Let us document the effects of hopelessness more directly from our survey data. The respondents were asked if they thought the Social Credit party would have some chances of winning the next *provincial* election, were they to present candidates at that level too. If someone answers negatively, he can be considered as hopeless: for him the party cannot secure power and change things. Interestingly enough, the data indicate that the poor respondents were more likely to be hopeless than the middle-income ones (see the marginal N's of the second panel in Table 8.7).

This may, of course, reflect the lower Social Credit vote in 1962 in the former group. But it is interesting to note the effect of this factor on the respondents' vote intention (Table 8.7, second panel). Among both those who are hopeful and those who are hopeless, the curvilinearity tends to disappear. If we add that the curvilinear relationship remained among the hopeful when the respondents' *past vote* was considered, the present results with vote intention indicate some effect of the Social Credit success in the low-income group.[57] So far, therefore, the data support the hypothesis that worry and hopelessness are among the factors which reduced the support for the new party among the poor people.

POLITICAL INFORMATION

It has also been suggested that the lack of sophistication is one of the factors accounting for the inability of the poor to translate their grievances into politi-

---

[55] Lipset, *Political Man*, p. 123.

[56] Lipset, *Political Man*, p. 122–123. Notice that these data fail to support Blumer's view that reform movements tend to enlist the allegiance of the middle class (by awakening their vicarious sympathy for the oppressed), while revolutionary movements would be movements of the lower class (enlisting the latter by agitation). Blumer, "Collective Behavior," p. 213.

[57] The curvilinearity remains strong among the "don't knows," but we suspect this might be due to two different possible meanings of a don't know answer: I have never thought about it; or, I am not sure if they have a chance or not. It may be that more of the latter type are found in the middle-income group.

cal terms.[58] With low sophistication, a voter is more likely to abstain[59] or follow a traditional path of protest.[60] That sophistication could indeed be a spur to engage in new movements among the less privileged is suggested by findings of the Freedom Rides study. Respondents of the lowest status group were more likely than others to be the early joiners only when they were ideologues; ideology—an extreme form of sophistication—can therefore be seen as a sufficient condition to lead the most deprived to protest.[61]

But such a high degree of sophistication is rather rare in the population.[62] Does, however, the lack of a certain degree of political information account for the low-income group's inability to protest? First, as one would expect, the data do indicate that political information is positively related to income level. For instance, when asked for the names of those occupying four Cabinet posts, 39 percent of the respondents in the low-income group could not report any name correctly, as compared to 28 and 18 percent in the middle- and high-income groups respectively.[63]

When the degree of the respondents' information is introduced to interpret the poor's low degree of protest, it can be seen that this factor again does not, strictly speaking, interpret the relationship (Table 8.7, panel 3). At equal degrees of information, the poor remain less likely to support the new movement than the middle-income group, though this is particularly true when the degree of information is low. However, the lack of information does reduce the ability to protest among the poor, while it does not among the other income groups. In other words, only the poor people are hampered by the lack of information, in somewhat the same way that they are the only ones seriously restrained by worry. This is again an interesting specification of the original relationship.

SOCIAL PARTICIPATION

A third cluster of factors which has been suggested as reducing the poor's ability to protest covers various aspects of social participation. Formal social participation, which permits the development of skills and means which are crucial to building a new political organization, is characteristically lower in the lower classes. And Lipset attributed in part the early C.C.F. support of the

[58] Students of diffusion have found "mental ability," "ability to deal with abstractions," and information to be positively related to innovativeness; Rogers, *Diffusion of Innovations*, pp. 177ff.

[59] The lack of some of the "skills required for participation" is "largely concentrated in the lower ranges of the working class"; Lane, *Political Life*, p. 232. Also Lipset, *Political Man*, pp. 190ff. Ideological sensitivity was also found to be an important factor of political participation in the I.T.U.; see Lipset, Trow, and Coleman, *Union Democracy*, pp. 92–102, 333–335.

[60] Lipset, *Political Man*, pp. 150–151; see also pp. 122ff.

[61] Maurice Pinard, Jerome Kirk, and Donald Von Eschen, "Processes of Recruitment in the Sit-In Movement." pp. 363–365.

[62] It was found that only 2.5 percent of a national sample could be characterized as "ideologues" and only an additional 9 percent as "near ideologues." Campbell *et al.*, *The American Voter*, pp. 216ff., p. 249.

[63] N's equal to 235, 267, and 227 respectively. (Unemployed excluded.)

well-to-do farmers to their high degree of participation in various farmers' organizations.[64] The degree of informal social participation is also more restricted in the lower classes. This may possibly contribute to the poor's inability to protest by making the world outside their immediate concern less meaningful. Furthermore, a social movement, like any other idea, must be diffused and in all likelihood through some of the same processes as other items of diffusion. And diffusion studies have shown the crucial importance of a rich social life for early adoption.[65] In short, the interpretation here is that the poor lack the degree of social participation required for their mobilization into a movement.

To test these ideas, let us consider first the effect of different degrees of informal social participation (primary groups contacts). Notice first that in the present data, there is no difference in the amount of primary contacts of the two lowest income groups. From the low- to high-income groups, we find that 20 percent, 19 percent, and 16 percent, respectively, had a low degree of informal social contacts.[66] And when this variable was introduced to interpret the low degree of Social Credit support among the poor, a relationship of the same type as many of the previous ones obtained (Table 8.7, last panel). Primary group participation, while it fails to interpret the relationship, that is, to remove the curvilinear relationship, would seem to specify the result once more, though the relationship is not significant. The lack of social contacts would reduce the support of Social Credit among the poor, but not among those who are better off.

The same pattern of results is obtained when participation in voluntary associations of various sorts[67] is considered. However, a more specific type of participation, that is, participation in labor and trade associations, seems to have different effects. First, the data indicate that the middle-income group is much more likely to participate in such organizations than the other two groups: 43 percent in the former group are union or trade association members, while only 24 percent and 17 percent are members of such associations in the low- and high-income groups respectively.[68] But when this factor is controlled, the curvilinear relationship with income does not disappear (Table 8.9, first panel). Notice, however, how participation in labor and trade organizations fails to produce a higher degree of support in the low-income group, while it stimulates the middle- and high-income groups, which exhibit then a higher degree of support for Social Credit. Here, the low-income group fails to respond to a

---

64 Lipset, *Agrarian Socialism*, pp. 166–167.

65 For a summary of such findings, see Lionberger, *Adoption of New Ideas and Practices*, esp. Chap. 6; Rogers, *Diffusion of Innovations*, esp. Chaps. 6 and 8. The mass theory of politics, on the other hand, stresses the restraining effects of social participation. This will be discussed in Chaps. 10 and 11.

66 N's equal to 233, 261, and 223 respectively. (Unemployed excluded.) Notice some differences, however, among those who revealed the party they voted for (see marginal N's of Table 8.7, last panel).

67 This factor is discussed in more detail in Chap. 10.

68 N's equal to 259, 234, and 223 respectively. (Unemployed excluded.)

stimulating factor, and this accounts in part for their overall lower support for the new movement.

Finally, the mobilization of the poor may be affected by the structural context of their social participation. In small communities, the poor tend to be more or less integrated with the other social classes and, in particular, with members of our middle-income category. In larger communities, they tend to form sub-communities of their own—social ghettoes—which are literally separated from all other social classes. We should expect in the latter situation that it would have been particularly difficult to mobilize the poor into a movement developing in a social world with which they maintain little contact.[69]

The data presented in the second panel of Table 8.9 support this expectation. If we do not consider Montreal, where the Social Credit support was minimal, the data indicate that the smaller the community the smaller the differences in Social Credit support between the middle-income group and the other two groups. Indeed, while Social Credit support increases with size of community in the middle-income group (except for Montreal), it decreases in the other groups. Thus the more integrated a community, the more widespread was the new party's support; and the less integrated, the more it was concentrated in the middle-income group. This indicates that the social structure of a community may be important for the development of a new movement. We will examine this problem in more detail in Chapter 11.

EXPOSURE TO SOCIAL CREDIT

Finally, on the basis of our previous findings as well as of diffusion studies, one might suggest that the low degree of Social Credit support among the poor might be related to their low degree of exposure to the new party's propaganda, either directly, in the mass media, or indirectly, by participating in different social milieux.

With regard to direct exposure to the Social Credit propaganda on television, the data however do not reveal that the poor were less exposed than the middle-income group; if anything, it was the other way around. While only 52 percent in the low-income group had only a low degree of exposure, 57 percent and 56 percent in the middle and high-income groups were as little exposed.[70]

But when this variable is introduced as a test factor (Table 8.9, third panel), a relationship quite similar to a previous one emerges: while all those not exposed to the propaganda were low in their Social Credit support, whatever their income level, we find that when people had been exposed to it, the middle-income group was much more responsive to it than others. Thus the poor, while not less exposed to the party's propaganda, failed to be as much stimulated

---

[69] For a related hypothesis based on a similar social mechanism, see MacRae, "Occupations and the Congressional Vote, 1940–1950," pp. 333–334; Lipset, *Political Man*, pp. 248–252.

[70] N's equal to 229, 259, and 220 respectively. (Unemployed excluded.)

Table 8.9

The Effects of Income on Social Credit Support Under Various Conditions (II)
(% Social Credit)

		LOW		MIDDLE		HIGH	
		INCOME GROUPS*					
1.	Membership in Labor and Trade Associations:	No**	16		22		8
				(112)		(92)		(106)
		Yes	15		33		31
				(26)		(78)		(26)
2.	Size of Locality:						
	Less than 1000 Electors†	24		34		19	
				(25)		(29)		(31)
	1000–5000	21		39		16	
				(24)		(31)		(19)
	5000 or more	19		41		7	
				(47)		(61)		(44)
	Montreal	4		2		7	
				(44)		(56)		(56)
3.	Index of Exposure to Social Credit Propaganda:***	Low††	10		10		9
				(58)		(87)		(75)
		Moderate	14		45		3
				(42)		(47)		(31)
		High	20		46		20
				(35)		(39)		(40)

*Unemployed excluded; members of professional associations also excluded in the first panel (too few cases).

**a_1 (effect of membership in the middle-income group) $= .11$; $p(a_1^* \leq 0) = .05$.

a_2 (effect of membership in the high-income group) $= .23$; $p(a_2^* \leq 0) = .01$.

***For index, see Appendix C; low: scores $0 - 2$; moderate: score 3; high: scores $4 - 5$.

†a_1 (effect of size of locality, comparing those with less than 1000 electors with those of 5000 or more, among middle-income respondents) $= .07$; $p(a_1^* \leq 0) = .26$.

a_2 (same effect, among both low and high-income respondents) $= -.085$; $p(a_2^* \leq 0) = .10$.

††a_1 (difference of differences, i.e., effect of exposure of middle-income respondents (.36) minus effect of exposure of low-income respondents (.10) $= .26$; $p(a_1^* \leq 0) = .01$. The test applied here to see if the difference is significantly greater among middle-income respondents than among low-income ones follows Leo A. Goodman, "Modifications of the Dorn-Stouffer-Tibbitts Method for 'Testing the Significance of Comparisons in Sociological Data'," *American Journal of Sociology*, LXVI (1961), pp. 355–363. (We compare only extremes on exposure, considering this variable as a dichotomy).

by it. We suspect that the other factors considered above might account for this, in particular, worry and hopelessness.

Exactly the same type of relationship results when we look at the effect of having social contacts within the groups most partisan to the new party. When the respondents' friends were from occupational groups[71] which were low in

---

71 Based on data on the occupations of the respondents' three best friends. This factor is discussed in more detail in Chap. 11.

their support of the new movement, the respondents from all income groups were themselves low in that support too. But when the poor's friends were from occupational groups which were high in their support for Social Credit,[72] the poor themselves were less responsive to this influence than the middle-income group.[73]

CONCLUSION

The data presented support the hypothesis that the Social Credit party in Quebec failed to enlist the support of the poor, as did other political movements of both the left and the right, at least as long as these movements remained relatively weak. These findings suggest that the masses are not easily won to non-routine politics. Indeed, successful political movements with mass support are a relatively rare phenomenon if we consider the extent of deprivations of large segments of the population in the world. An exception to this generalization is when the poor themselves are adversely affected by changes in their economic conditions. The data indicate that in that situation—and in that situation only—the poor are among the earliest recruits of a new movement. This is obviously a most important qualification, since it means that in periods of very acute economic crisis, the poor might be early to flock to political movements in disproportionately large numbers. In other situations, the poor tend to be later recruits.

In trying to account for this generalization, many other factors have been considered. In only one instance has the factor introduced tended to wash out the curvilinear relationship; this is when the condition of hopelessness of the poor was considered. The lack of hopefulness seemed to account for the lower degree of support for the new party among the poor. In all other cases, the introduction of control factors led to the emergence of new relationships.

First we found that worry, while reducing the support of the poor, tended to increase that of the other income groups, suggesting that worry is of a different type among the poor than among the others. The other control factors generally produced two different kinds of relationships. On the one hand, in the

[72] Though in general, as in the present data, social participation tends to take place within or close to one's socioeconomic group. It has also been found that personal influence is largely confined within status levels; E. Katz and P.F. Lazarsfeld, *Personal Influence* (New York: The Free Press of Glencoe, Inc., 1955). As suggested below, this is probably the more so the larger or the more stratified the social system; and studies of rural diffusion do seem to indicate a larger social distance between influencer and influencee than the above quoted study; see Lionberger, *Adoption of New Ideas and Practices*, pp. 84ff.

[73] The same type of relationship also emerges with political alienation: the middle-income person is more likely to respond to alienation by voting Social Credit than the poor. Alienation therefore seems to take a retreatist form among the poor, a rebellious one among others. (The role of alienation will be discussed at length in Chap. 12.) Finally, let us mention that age did not affect the original relationship: the poor, whether young, middle-aged or old, were always less likely supporters of Social Credit than members of the middle-income category of the same age group.

presence of some elements, the middle-income group's support for the new movement was greatly intensified, while those factors failed to produce such a strong
effect among the poor. This is what tended to happen in the presence of participation in labor and trade organizations, of exposure to the new party's propaganda, of contacts with occupational groups manifesting a strong sympathy for
the movement, and of political alienation.[74]

On the other hand, in the *absence* of other elements, while the support of the
poor was reduced, that of the other income groups was not affected: the lack of
political information and of social participation exemplified this type of relationship. *In short, the poor negatively react to intensifying conditions and positively
react to restraining conditions*, with the end result in both cases that their support is
lower than what might be expected on the basis of their grievances alone.

Finally, our findings raise interesting sociological problems. For instance, it
would be instructive to examine more attentively than has usually been done the
response of the poor to social movements other than political. Are the poor, for
instance, more prone than others to join religious movements, as has often been
suggested?[75] Or do they show the same resistance to such movements as to others
as some findings indicate?[76]

Indeed could it be claimed that the poor, in order to alleviate their deprivations, would turn to religion rather than to political protest?[77] Our data do not
support this last view, in that the poor were not more religiously inclined than
members of the middle-income group (though those of the high-income group
were slightly more so); in addition, among the poor, the more, not the less,
religiously inclined were more likely to be Social Credit supporters.[78]

[74] These elements may not all have independent effects, but it is impossible to test for that here.

[75] See, for instance, Elmer T. Clark, *The Small Sects in America*, rev. ed., (New York: Abingdon
Press, 1949), pp. 16ff., pp. 218ff.; H. Richard Niebuhr, *The Social Sources of Denominationalism*
(Cleveland and New York: The World Publishing Co., 1957), Chaps. 2 and 3; Norman Cohn, *The
Pursuit of the Millennium*, pp. 26ff., pp. 89ff.; J. Milton Yinger, *Religion in the Struggle for Power* (New
York: Russell and Russell, 1961); S.D. Clark, "The Religious Sect in Canadian Politics," in Bernard
R. Blishen *et al.*, *Canadian Society*, rev. ed., (Toronto: Macmillan Co. of Canada, Ltd., 1964), p. 290.
These authors, however, do not seem to differentiate between poverty *per se* and economic adver-
sities. (On Cohn's data, see page 148 above.)

[76] S.D. Clark has mentioned elsewhere that "it is not the slum population which affords support
to new sectarian movements"; "The Religious Sect in Canadian Economic Development," in Bernard
R. Blishen *et al.*, *Canadian Society* (New York: The Free Press of Glencoe, Inc., 1961), p. 384. Similarly
Mann has observed about Alberta's sects that "in neither city nor country were (the sectarians)
generally found among the extremely poor, although a few small congregations, and certain members
of other congregations, were probably very underprivileged economically. The movement seems to
have found support among people of average working-class income in the cities, and slightly less than
average farm income in the rural areas"; W.E. Mann, *Sect, Cult, and Church in Alberta* (Toronto:
University of Toronto Press, 1955), p. 36. (Cults, on the other hand, recruited people of a middle-
class economic level; *ibid.*, p. 41).

[77] Notice that here we are asking whether religion and political protest are functional alternatives,
not whether religion, once adopted, acts to inhibit or stimulate political protest; on the latter point,
see below, Chap. 11, where it will be shown that among the poor, at least, religiosity was positively
related to Social Credit support.

[78] See fn. 77.

More generally, is the curvilinear relationship we have observed here also found in other forms of collective behavior, such as, for instance, hostile outbursts? Couch has presented as a stereotype the idea "that crowds tend to be composed of the lower echelons of society"; "those protesting are seldom if ever representatives of social categories with the lowest prestige and fewest rights."[79]

But what about crazes?[80] Is the relationship observed also to be found in other forms of deviance? Durkheim's proposition that poverty is a protection against suicide[81] and Merton's hypothesis that the lower-lower class is subject to retreatism rather than to other forms of deviance[82] come readily to mind in this context.

Finally, does this pattern also occur in routine politics, when under conditions of unrest, the population turns against the party in power to elect the traditional opposition party? It might very well be that the poor are again not the initial

[79] Carl J. Couch, "Collective Behaviour: An Examination of Some Stereotypes," *Social Problems*, 15 (1968), pp. 317–19. The data we have examined does not certainly support unambiguously the view that the poorest ghetto residents are the more prone to engage in riots. According to the Kerner report, for instance, rioters, though as poor as non-rioters, were more educated than the latter. Lieberson and Silverman found no relationship with Negro income in their study of U.S. riots between 1913 and 1963, but found that the proportion of Negroes in traditional occupations (unskilled and service.) was lower in riot cities. In their studies, Brink and Harris, and Feagin reported that the poor were less riot prone or violence oriented than those immediately above the poverty level. (Of course, rigorous tests should control for the stages of a riot (early vs. late involvement) as well as for age and the presence of predisposing strains (e.g., worsening conditions). See *Report of the National Advisory Commission on Civil Disorders* (Bantam Book Edition, 1968), pp. 128ff.; Stanley Lieberson and Arnold R. Silverman, "The Precipitants and Underlying Conditions of Race Riots"; *American Sociological Review*, 30 (1965), pp. 894ff.; William Brink and Louis Harris, *Black and White: A Study of U.S. Racial Attitudes Today* (New York: Simon and Schuster, Inc., 1967), Table 18 (i), p. 266; J.R. Feagin, "Some Sources of Support for Violence and Nonviolence in a Negro Ghetto," *Social Problems*, 15 (Spring 1968), Table 2 and pp. 437–438. (It may be, however, that for the more elementary forms of collective behavior, the peak of participation in the income distribution is at a lower level (though not the lowest) than in social movements.)

[80] We would not expect the panic to manifest such a relationship, since it is such a "passive" response to threats; and indeed it was found that the lower the income, the greater the vulnerability to panic; see H. Cantril, *The Invasion from Mars* (Princeton: Princeton University Press, 1940), p. 157. In fact, some of the elements found in that study to be conducive to panic—worry, lack of critical ability—were shown here to be inhibitive factors. *Ibid.*, Chaps 5 and 6.

[81] Durkheim wrote: "What proves still more conclusively that economic distress does not have the aggravating influence often attributed to it, is that it tends rather to produce the opposite effect. (. . .) *Poverty may even be considered a protection* (. . .) Poverty protects against suicide because it is a restraint in itself. No matter how one acts, desires have to depend upon resources to some extent; actual possessions are partly the criterion of those aspired to. So the less one has, the less he is tempted to extend the range of his needs infinitely." Durkheim here seems to imply, however, that the poor are less dissatisfied, which is not generally the case, as we have seen. E. Durkheim, *Suicide* (New York: The Free Press of Glencoe, Inc., 1951), p. 245 and 254. (Italics are ours.)

[82] Merton wrote that "one should not . . . expect a linear correlation between crime and poverty"; Robert K. Merton, *Social Theory and Social Structure* (New York: The Free Press of Glencoe, Inc., 1957, new ed.), p. 147n; see also pp. 153ff.

source of such institutionalized political change, when they fail to perceive the opposition as a likely winner.[83] At any rate, these are important problems which deserve much more careful attention than they have so far received.

[83] There are indications that the middle class was the first to turn Conservative in Canada in the 1957 federal election, after some twenty years of Liberal administration (see, for instance, Robert R. Alford, *Party and Society: The Anglo-American Democracies* (Chicago: Rand McNally & Co., 1963), Table 9.1, pp. 264–265). The middle class was also apparently the first to become Liberal in the 1960 Quebec provincial election, which came after sixteen years of Union Nationale administration (see Maurice Pinard, "Classes sociales et comportement électoral," in Vincent Lemieux, ed., *Quatre élections provinciales au Québec*, p. 151). In each case, it seems that the working class followed only in the subsequent election, 1958 at the federal level, and 1962 at the provincial level.

An
Upsurge
of
the
Young

CHAPTER NINE

Studies of political socialization have stressed the very high degree of continuity in party identification which exists between generations,[1] and the crucial role of the family in creating political attachments.[2] In the United States, it was found that people voting for the first time are very likely to follow their parents' political affiliation; in general, it seems that at least three out of every four first voters support the party of their parents,[3] and the number of those switching to one of the main parties is probably close to the number of those switching to the other party. On that basis, one should not expect the party distribution of each generation to vary much. Indeed the political continuity between generations should be very great.

Yet these observations have generally been made during periods of high political stability, characterized by routine contests between traditional parties. There are, however, times when elections produce major political realignments or at least important shifts from one traditional party to another or from traditional parties to new political movements. Are these periods characterized by the same degree of political continuity between generations?

Students more concerned with the dynamics of political life have tended to give a negative answer to that question, and for that purpose, have developed

---

[1] See for instance Herbert H. Hyman, *Political Socialization* (New York: The Free Press of Glencoe, Inc., 1959), Chap. 4; Robert E. Lane and David O. Sears, *Public Opinion* (Englewood Cliffs, Prentice-Hall, Inc., 1964), Chap. 3.

[2] So that families tend to vote as units; see Berelson *et al.*, *Voting*, pp. 92–93.

[3] Estimated on the basis of data presented in *ibid.*, p. 89, and data reported in Hyman, *Political Socialization*, pp. 74ff.

the theory of "political generations." According to this, each generation enters the political arena under the influence of common social experiences which mark their political outlook in specific ways.[4] In general, the hypothesis seems to be supported by the observation that important shifts between traditional parties appear to be the result of disproportionate change among the younger generations. It has been shown, for instance, that the general shift to the Democratic party during the Great Depression of the 1930s involved a greater proportion of the young voters than of the old ones.[5]

The process by which, under the impact of serious alterations in social conditions, new generations become prime artisans of political realignments would appear at least as relevant to the study of new political movements as to the study of traditional politics. Yet this problem has received little empirical attention. The purpose of this chapter is to try to fill at least part of this gap in our knowledge.

We would like to try to answer the following set of questions. Which generations were more likely to support Social Credit? Is the pattern observed in this movement a pattern common to all social movements? To this descriptive account, can we add an interpretation of the disproportionate support of some age groups for Social Credit? Does such an analysis throw some light on the observations concerning other movements and does it provide some elements toward the elaboration of a theory linking generations to social movements?

To begin let us immediately mention that on the basis of the available evidence, no overall generalization seems possible. If many movements have been predominantly based on the younger generations, some, on the contrary, have found greater support among the older generations. Let us consider the evidence.

MOVEMENTS OF THE YOUNG

Social Credit, for one, exhibited the former pattern. As can be seen in Table 9.1, there is a strong negative relationship between age and support for that political movement: Social Credit obtained 24 percent more votes among the youngest age group (voting for the first time in a federal election) than it did among the oldest age group. Indeed, this is one of the strong relationships observed in the present study.[6] Without the young people's strong support, the movement's success would have been much more limited. And if we assume that the parents of the youngest age group were in their forties or above, the

[4] See Karl Mannheim, "The Problem of Generations," in his *Essays on the Sociology of Knowledge* (London: Routledge and Kegan Paul Ltd., 1952), pp. 276–322; Heberle, *Social Movements*, Chap. 6, pp. 118–127; Lipset, *Political Man*, pp. 264–270; Hyman, *Political Socialization,* Chap. 6.

[5] See Campbell *et al.*, *The American Voter*, pp. 150ff.

[6] A similar relationship in that election has been independently reported, on the basis of Canadian Institute of Public Opinion data, by Robert Alford; see his "The Social Bases of Political Cleavage in 1962," pp. 223–224; see also Lemieux, "The Election in the Constituency of Lévis," p. 38.

Table 9.1

Social Credit Drew a Disproportionate Support from the Younger Age Groups

	AGE GROUPS				
VOTE IN 1962	24 OR YOUNGER %	25–34 %	35–44 %	45–59 %	60 OR OLDER %
Social Credit	38	26	21	19	14
Conservative	22	28	34	32	30
Liberal	35	44	43	48	54
N.D.P.	5	2	2	1	2
N =	(40)	(145)	(178)	(161)	(101)

data suggest that the high continuity in party choices between parents and first voters so often observed in normal periods did not prevail in this election.[7] Whether this break from parents' affiliations will represent a permanent departure in party alignments remains a moot question; it is clear, however, that people's reactions to the conditions of the time were significantly related to their age.

Moreover, the disproportionate support of the young for Social Credit is but one of the manifestations of the youth's unrest in Quebec today. Available data indicate that the separatist movement in Quebec is also more likely to recruit young people. In a survey taken in 1963, it was found that among those aware of the movement, 22 percent of the youngest age group (eighteen to twenty-four years old) favored the separation of Quebec from the rest of Canada, while only 10 percent of those sixty and over had the same attitude.[8] The violent wings of the separatist movement—the F.L.Q. in particular—have depended almost entirely on young people. Similarly, the young people in Quebec are more likely to favor the establishment of a neutral (nonreligious) school system than older people.[9] They have been quite involved in various leftist political groups, and they have struggled to renew the literary and artistic life of French Canada. More recently, Quebec's youth has shown no less enthusiasm for the goals and means of the student movement than the youth of other countries.

The support of the young generation for all these social movements is of course not peculiar to Quebec. In a recent national sample of the Canadian urban public, there were some signs[10] that the young people were more likely to be

---

7 This is particularly true if one considers that our observation is one of net change between these age groups. We have no data to compute the exact proportion of the first voters' choices which were at odds with those of their parents.

8 From data gathered by the Social Research Group in August 1963 (N's = 137 and 113 respectively). For a brief report of the survey, see *Maclean's Magazine*, Nov. 1963.

9 Among those eighteen to thirty years old, 21 percent favored such a school system, while only 11 percent of those sixty and over did the same. (N = 195 and 120 respectively.) From data gathered by the Social Research Group in May-June 1964 from the non-farm Quebec population.

10 Young Canadians favored placing restrictions on American investments in Canadian companies

nationalist and exhibit anti-American attitudes than the older generations.[11]
Similarly, other political movements in other countries have been particularly successful among the young generations. Again the student movement is but the last in a long series. The Communist party, for instance, seems to be successful in recruiting its members, as well as its voters, among the youth in many countries,[12] if not everywhere. The Nazi party in Germany appealed to the young; its members have been shown to be younger than the population in general.[13] The neo-Fascist movement in Italy has the same appeal to youth.[14] A similar characteristic existed among the supporters of the Poujadist movement in France.[15] In a study of a group of about 150 Russian Communist party members, it was found that the peak age of first revolutionary activity was between sixteen and eighteen and that the peak age of joining the revolutionary party was at twenty.[16]

In the United States, the younger generation clearly dominates in the activi-

---

and thought the Canadian government should pass laws encouraging Canadians to purchase American-owned or controlled companies in Canada. For instance, 79 percent of those eighteen to thirty years of age favored placing restrictions on American investments, as compared to 69 percent of those sixty and over. (On the other hand, young Canadians were not more opposed to political or to economic union with the United States.) From data gathered by the Social Research Group in March 1964. For a brief report of that survey, see *Maclean's, Magazine*, June 1964.

11 There does not seem to exist any data on the age composition of earlier political and social movements in Canada. But there are indications that the New Democratic Party (former C.C.F.) at least now does not draw a disproportionate support from the young people in Saskatchewan, the land of its first success. Indeed, it is apparently now disproportionately supported by the older generations. The party also seems to draw its largest support from the middle-age group in Ontario, Manitoba and British Columbia, three provinces where it has been relatively successful for some time. But in the Maritime provinces where it is still weak, it is more successful among the young voters than among others. Similarly, Social Credit draws equally from all age groups in Alberta and British Columbia, two provinces where it has been in power for some time (1935 and 1952 respectively); but again the age composition of its early support is not known (See Alford, "The Social Basis of Political Cleavage in 1962," p. 224).

12 See Gabriel A. Almond, *The Appeals of Communism* (Princeton: Princeton University Press, 1954), pp. 217ff. See also Stoetzel and Hassner, "Résultats d'un sondage dans le premier secteur de la Seine," p. 205; Pratt, *The Social Basis of Nazism and Communism in Urban Germany*, Chap. 10.

13 See Hans H. Gerth, "The Nazi Party: Its Leadership and Composition," in Robert K. Merton, *et al.*, *Reader in Bureaucracy* (New York: The Free Press of Glencoe, Inc., 1952), pp. 107ff.; Abel, *The Nazi Movement*, pp. 63, 81.

14 See Lipset, *Political Man*, p. 165.

15 See Stoetzel and Hassner, "Résultats d'un sondage dans le premier secteur de la Seine," p. 224. But see also: "Les résultats du scrutin dans l'Aisne," (author not indicated) in Duverger *et al.*, *Les élections du 2 janvier 1956*, pp. 405ff., where it is reported that in Soissons, the newly registered voters, predominantly young, supported the leftist parties rather than the rightist ones, including the Poujadists.

16 Jerome Davis, "A Study of One Hundred and Sixty-Three Outstanding Communist Leaders," *American Sociological Society Publications*, 24 (1929), pp. 42–55, quoted in Raymond G. Kuhlen, *The Psychology of Adolescent Development* (New York: Harper & Row, Publishers, 1952)), pp. 449–450. It is interesting to note that the age at political conversion largely corresponds to the age at religious conversion, though the latter probably tends to occur earlier: in studies done around 1900, the peak was found to be between fifteen and twenty, and in 1928, it was found by Clark to be at approximately twelve; E. T. Clark, *The Psychology of Religious Awakening* (The Macmillian Company, 1929), quoted in Kuhlen, *ibid.*, pp. 446–447. (The same data are also briefly presented in Leonard Broom and Philip Selznick, *Sociology* 3rd ed., (New York: Harper & Row, Publishers, 1963)), pp. 412–413).

ties of the student movement, the peace movement, and the more dynamic organizations fighting for racial integration (e.g., the Student Non-Violent Coordinating Committee, the Congress of Racial Equality). If the older movements (the National Association for the Advancement of Colored People, the National Urban League) have many older members, students and young people in general predominate in the new movements. In the study of a Freedom Ride in Baltimore mentioned earlier, it was found that only 23 percent of the participants were twenty-six years of age or older, and only 11 percent were thirty-three years of age or older.

MOVEMENTS OF THE OLD

On the other hand, there are pieces of evidence indicating that certain political and social movements were or are particularly successful among the older generations. In some cases, this is easily understandable. No one is surprised to find that older people were more favorable to the Townsend Movement,[17] since it aimed at relieving old peoples' distressing conditions by the development of a pension plan. But this movement is not an exception. The Gaullist *Rassemblement du Peuple Français* (R.P.F.) in France was also backed by the older people.[18]

In Germany, the Nazi movement, whose *members*, as we have seen, were predominantly young, apparently got disproportionate support from older *voters*.[19]

In the United States, movements of the radical right have also been generally successful among older citizens. An analysis presented by Lipset shows that Father Coughlin's supporters, as well as supporters of the John Birch Society— though in this last case the relationship is less clear—were older citizens.[20] Both Polsby and Lipset have reported that elderly people were more likely to be supporters of McCarthy.[21] On the other hand, at the national level, the support for Goldwater as a Republican presidential candidate (over other Republican contenders) was practically unrelated to age; however, in the South, the region where his support was the greatest, the *young* were slightly more favorable to

---

[17] See Hadley Cantril, *The Psychology of Social Movements*, pp. 192–193.

[18] See Lipset, *Political Man*, p. 156. But MacRae reports no association between age and R.P.F. support; actually, he finds that in general shifts in political preferences are not related to age in France; see Duncan MacRae, Jr., *Parliament, Parties, and Society in France*, pp. 276–278.

[19] See Pratt, *The Social Basis of Nazism and Communism*, Chap. 10. There is a possibility, however, that Pratt's finding with ecological data might be spurious, since he found that members of the lower classes were younger and anti-Nazis. See also Lipset, *Political Man*, pp. 149–152.

[20] See Lipset, "Three Decades of Radical Right: Coughlinites, McCarthyites and Birchers," pp. 384, 425 (Table 21) and p. 429 (Table 24).

[21] See Nelson W. Polsby, "Toward an Explanation of McCarthyism," p. 814; Lipset, *ibid.*, p. 395, pp. 400–401. See also Raymond E. Wolfinger *et al.*, "America's Radical Right: Politics and Ideology," in David E. Apter, *Ideology and Discontent* (New York: The Free Press of Glencoe, Inc., 1964), pp. 267–268.

him than the other age groups.[22] The strong organizational support Goldwater received from young supporters, and in general the revival of right-wing movements among the young has too often been noted to allow us to make too easily the assumption that the ideology of a movement determines its age composition. Indeed some of the movements of the young mentioned in the previous section were not leftist movements—Social Credit being only one of those instances.

In short, it is not easy to detect age patterns in the support of social and political movements.[23] Moreover, the patterns are not more consistent in routine politics.[24] In this regard, it is noteworthy that, though diffusion studies have generally found younger people to be more open to new ideas and practices, there are exceptions.[25]

If no overall generalization can easily be arrived at, is it possible at least to explain the disproportionate support of the young for Social Credit? Some partial explanations can be derived from our data, and as will be seen, they will allow us to gain insights into the instances which deviate from this pattern.

FORMER POLITICAL COMMITMENTS

A first line of explanation possibly lies in the differential degree of commitment to, and identification with, the old parties among the various age groups. Older people should have developed a greater degree of partisanship for the old parties and, moreover, a partisanship which should have grown more intense with age. As the authors of *The American Voter* wrote:

> Individuals become increasingly identified with their political party the longer they have remained committed to it psychologically . . . (young people) are less likely to evaluate political objects in party terms and show less affective involvement in the fortunes of any particular party *qua* party. . . . Like farm people, they are rather free psychologically to shift their vote from party to party. . . . In time of crisis, they may suddenly flock to the polls in proportions that create great surges in the electoral support of a party promising salvation. And they may in crisis depart from the traditional party structure entirely.[26]

22 See Irving Crespi, "The Structural Basis for Right-Wing Conservatism," pp. 528–529.

23 It would be very useful to have data on a larger number of social, political and even religious movements. But many studies of such movements fail to report their age composition.

24 See, for instance, Lipset, *Political Man*, pp. 221–222. Lipset wrote: "In some countries and historical periods, the young voters (or the aged) are likely to be found on the left, in others they are more conservative. Different age groups react to their political environment according to the significant experiences of their generation." *Ibid.*

25 Lionberger, *Adoption of New Ideas and Practices*, pp. 96–97; Rogers, *Diffusion of Innovations*, pp. 172–174.

26 Campbell, *et al.*, *The American Voter*, p. 497. See also *ibid.*, p. 156, pp. 161–165. Interestingly enough, it is the length of party identification, rather than age proper, that accounts for the greater strength of party identification. Indeed, at equal length of party identification, the latter is stronger among the young than among the old. *Ibid.*

The present data do indicate that young voters were less partisan of the old parties than their elders.[27] Does this explain the disproportionate shift of the young to Social Credit? It does in part, as can be seen in the first panel of Table 9.2. Actually the results are quite interesting.

Among nonpartisans, the various age groups differ little in their support of the new party and all were about equally strong supporters. But on the other hand, among partisans, the young were much more likely to have supported

Table 9.2

The Relationships between Age and Social Credit Support Under Various Conditions (I)
(% Social Credit)

	AGE GROUPS		
	34 OR YOUNGER	35–49	50 OR OLDER
Partisans*	29	13	6
	(73)	(103)	(113)
Nonpartisans	29	29	24
	(106)	(136)	(80)
Partisans:			
Opinion Leaders**	42	10	5
	(26)	(41)	(44)
Non-Leaders	22	15	7
	(46)	(62)	(69)
Nonpartisans:			
Opinion Leaders	38	40	40
	(16)	(10)	(5)
Non-Leaders	27	29	23
	(88)	(126)	(74)
Index of S.C. Enthusiasm:			
Low***	9	8	5
	(86)	(118)	(105)
Moderate	26	32	12
	(31)	(41)	(32)
High	65	45	41
	(54)	(67)	(39)

*In answer to question: "What about yourself: would you say you are a convinced partisan of a provincial political party?"

**In answer to question: "Do you happen to try to convince others of your own political beliefs?"

a_1 (average effect of opinion leadership among nonpartisans) = .13; $p(a_1^* \leq 0)$ = .10.

a_2 (effect of opinion leadership among young partisans) = .20; $p(a_2^* \leq 0)$ = .04.

a_3 (average effect of non-leadership among the two older groups of partisans) = .035; $p(a_3^* \leq 0)$ = .19.

***For index of Social Credit enthusiasm, see Appendix C; low: scores 0 and 1; moderate: score 2; high: scores 3 and 4.

[27] There were 17 percent more partisans among the old voters (fifty years of age or older) than among the young (thirty-five or younger); see marginal N's of the first panel of Table 9.2. A similar finding is also reported by Lane, *Political Life*, pp. 300, 341.

Social Credit than the old; to put it differently, we find that partisanship did not entail any restraining effect among the young, but that it did among the old. In part, this probably reflects, among the partisans, the increasingly intense party identification which develops with age, as just suggested. Unfortunately this is difficult to test since our data do not provide any direct measure of intensity of partisanship. However, it is not certain that the sheer lack of intense identification is the only factor which prodded the support of the young even when they were partisans. Consider, for instance, the effects of opinion leadership (Table 9.2, second panel) where both partisanship and opinion leadership are controlled.

Among nonpartisans, again age has no effect; but we find that within each age group, opinion leaders were more likely to have voted Social Credit than followers. That opinion leaders should have preceded the latter in the absence of commitment to older parties, is indeed what you would expect on the basis of the two-step flow of communication hypothesis,[28] since political opinion leaders tend to be more exposed to mass media and more cosmopolitan in this exposure,[29] they should be earlier adopters than those who take their cues from them.[30]

On the other hand, among partisans, while age still maintains its effect, we expected opinion leaders to resist Social Credit more firmly since partisans who are also opinion leaders must be quite intense in their identificaion to the old parties. This expectation is borne out among the two older groups,[31] *but not among the young*. What we find among the latter—and among them only—is that opinion leaders were, despite their partisanship, *more* likely to have voted Social Credit than non-leaders. The behavior of the young, therefore, appears intriguing and suggests that some other processes were at work to stimulate the young in favor of the new party. So far, we find that partisanship did not affect them and that, when coupled with opinion leadership, it did in fact intensify their support of Social Credit.

THE ROLE OF ENTHUSIASM

A second mechanism which could have affected the behavior of the different age groups consists of a complex of related attitudes. Young people are presumably more likely than their elders to develop enthusiasm for, and emotional attraction towards, a new movement and its leader.[32] They are more likely to

28 See Elihu Katz and Paul F. Lazarsfeld, *Personal Influence* (New York: The Free Press of Glencoe, Inc., 1955), esp. Chap. 2 and Chap. 14.

29 *Ibid.*, pp. 310ff.

30 This is what has generally been found in studies of diffusion; see, for instance, Rogers, *Diffusion of Innovations*, pp. 242ff.

31 Though the relationship is weak and not statistically significant; but it is worth noting that the relationship is not positive among them.

32 Heberle, *Social Movements*, pp. 96–97.

adopt a utopian vision of the world,[33] and to join in the defense of a "cause." Older people, on the contrary, are presumed to be more "rational" and more realistic; they tend to be more suspicious of new political ventures.[34] Closely related to that is the idea that the young are capable of stronger rebellious feelings, or, to put it differently, of a greater degree of rebellious alienation.

Concerning the role of enthusiasm, the data show that the young who voted for the new party were somewhat more enthusiastic about Social Credit than the old supporters of the party. But what is more interesting is the effect of enthusiasm for the party (Table 9.2, third panel). Among the relatively non-enthusiastic voters, age does not make much of a difference (4 percent only). But as enthusiasm increases, so does the effect of age. Among the very enthusiastic, the young were more likely to have supported the new party by a proportion of 24 percent. Put differently, the young when enthusiastic, were 56 percent more likely to have voted Social Credit, while among the middle-aged and the old, enthusiasm increased the support of the new movement by 37 percent and 36 percent only. In short, enthusiasm was more frequent among the young voters, and when present, was a more effective spur to action than among the old voters. This is another interesting specification of the relationship.

REBELLIOUS ALIENATION

A similar situation appears when one considers political alienation. First, as found elsewhere,[35] the data indicate that older voters were more politically alienated than younger ones.[36] But the revealing finding, as can be seen from the first panel of Table 9.3, is that alienation seemed to produce no effect among the old, while it clearly incited the young voters to join the new political venture. Seen otherwise, the relationships which now result are no less surprising. In the absence of alienation, the young voters, contrary to the overall pattern of Table 9.1, are no longer the strongest Social Credit supporters—indeed the data indicate that the relationship is now, if anything, reversed. It is only when they are characterized by a high degree of political alienation that the young become very much more likely to be Social Credit supporters. The original (zero-order) difference of 15 percent between the three age groups becomes nothing less than a 35 percent difference when considering only the very alienated.

The interpretation we are inclined to make of this last set of relationships is that, as suggested before, among the young, alienation tends to generate rebellious tendencies, while among the old, it leads them to give up, to withdraw.

---

[33] Lane, *Political Life*, p. 217; see also S.M. Lipset, "University Student Politics," in S.M. Lipset and S.S. Wolin, *The Berkeley Student Revolt: Facts and Interpretations* (Garden City, New York: Doubleday, Anchor Books, 1965), p. 3.

[34] Campbell *et al.*, *The American Voter*, p. 497.

[35] See Lane, *Political Life*, p. 151, 168.

[36] The difference is about 10 percent; see marginal N's of the first panel of Table 9.3.

Table 9.3

*The Relationships between Age and Social Credit Support
under Various Conditions (II)
(% Social Credit)*

	AGE GROUPS				
	34 OR YOUNGER		35–49		50 OR OLDER
Index of Alienation:*					
Low	6		12		13
		(48)		(57)	(39)
Moderate	25		20		14
		(72)		(88)	(71)
High	49		30		14
		(65)		(97)	(85)
Index of Economic Conditions**
and Employment Situation					
Good	20		14		9
		(84)		(78)	(76)
Bad, but without Unemployment	37		21		12
		(43)		(96)	(60)
Bad, with Unemployment	33		34		22
		(54)		(64)	(58)
Worry:
Much***	40		23		12
		(45)		(79)	(57)
A little	31		26		19
		(87)		(97)	(73)
Almost none	16		17		8
		(51)		(63)	(62)

*For index of political alienation, see Appendix C; low: scores 0 to 2; moderate: scores 3 and 4; high: scores 5 and 6.

**Index of Economic Conditions: good: scores 0 and 1; bad: scores 2, 3, and 4.

a_1 (difference of differences, i.e. difference between first two lines among the young (.17), minus same difference among the old (.03)) = .14; $p(a_1^* \leq 0) = .08$.

***a_2 (stimulating effect of much worry, comparing first two lines among the young) = .09; $p(a_2^* \leq 0) = .15$;

a_3 (average restraining effect of much worry, comparing first two lines among the middle-aged and the old) = .05; $p(a_3^* \leq 0) = .13$.

Presumably, there are two types of alienation which, following Erbe, can be labelled rebellious and retreatist alienation;[37] the young would more likely exhibit the former, while the old would more likely be affected by the latter.

37 See William Erbe, "Social Involvement and Political Activity: A Replication and Elaboration," *American Sociological Review*, 29 (1964), pp. 198–215, esp. p. 206; see also below, Chap. 12, where the effects of alienation are examined in greater detail. Our questions on alienation, however, do not allow us to distinguish between the two types of alienation (see the questions in Appendix B). In order to measure rebellious alienation, one would need items like the following: "If the people join together in protest, they can induce the politicians to consider their problems," or: "Nothing can be changed by voting for new parties."

ECONOMIC CONDITIONS AND WORRY

Differences in economic situations or, at least, differences in reactions to similar economic conditions, could be another source of the unequal support of the various age groups for the new party. However, according to our data, the economic recession of the early sixties—an important factor of Social Credit support, as we have seen—did not disproportionately affect the young people. We find, for instance, that they had not been subjected to unemployment to any greater extent than the other age groups. Moreover, the young were as likely to declare that they were satisfied with their financial situation and that of their family as the old—the middle-aged group being the group less likely to do so. Actually, the young were much more likely than the other two groups to say that their financial situation had improved in the previous two or three years.

There is, however, another side to this picture. At the early stages of their life cycle, people are generally placed under heavier financial burdens than at later stages. In particular, the young tend to have more debts, or at least a larger ratio of debts to assets than older people. This has been considered as one of the factors accounting for the predominance of the young in the Quebec separatist movement.[38] Unfortunately, we have no data which would permit us to test this idea.[39]

Is it not possible, on the other hand, that the young, though in many respects objectively better off than the old, might *react more easily ˉand/or sooner* to a worsening plight? Actually the data of Table 9.3 (second panel) indicate that generally bad economic conditions were influencing each age group to a somewhat similar extent, which at first sight suggests that the greater support of the young is not due to greater reactions to similar conditions. But the data suggest an important qualification to this generalization. The indications are that the younger you were, the less severe the strains needed to be to incite you to support the new party: in comparing the first and second rows in the second panel of Table 9.3, it can be seen that the effect of moderately bad conditions (bad, but without unemployment) was greater among the young than among the others. Therefore the data suggest, not a stronger, but an easier or earlier reaction to strains among the young; their threshold seems to be lower.

But why were the older respondents not reacting as readily to bad conditions? It may be that among the old such conditions lead to a state of worry that

[38] Albert Breton made this point in a seminar presented in the Department of Sociology and Anthropology at McGill University in 1963.

[39] If we assume that homeownership could constitute a particularly heavy financial burden among younger people, we should find a particularly strong age difference in support of the new party among homeowners. Actually, the data indicated a slightly larger difference among nonowners; the reason is that, among the old, if anything, the homeowners tended to be more responsive to Social Credit than non-owners. (The urban-rural dimension was simultaneously controlled here, given previous findings; see p. 91 fn. 1.)

is paralyzing, somewhat as it was found to be among the poor. And in fact, in Table 9.3 (third panel), it can be observed (though the relationships are not significant) that much worry tends to have a depressing effect among the middle-aged and the old, but not among the young.[40] The more worried the young voters were, the more likely they were to support Social Credit; conversely, among the middle-aged and the old voters, those who were very worried were slightly less likely to vote Social Credit than those who were only moderately worried. The latter were the most likely supporters in these two age groups. So that among those who were very worried, the young were 28 percent more likely to have voted Social Credit than the old, while the differences decrease to only 12 percent among those who worried only a little, and to 8 percent among those who had almost no worry.[41] In short, worry does not produce the same effect among the young as among the others: it is an incitation to protest among the former, but it restrains the latter.[42]

SOCIAL CREDIT AND OTHER MOVEMENTS

So far, we have specified some of the conditions which permitted Social Credit to have a particularly strong appeal among young voters. Presumably these conditions should also account, at least in part, for a similar pattern of support in many other movements. However, as we have seen, in some movements, the support seemed to increase, rather than decrease, with age. Does our analysis throw some light on these latter instances? Before we answer this question let us first summarize our results.

Under certain conditions, the support for Social Credit tended to be about *equally high* among *all* age groups. This was particularly the case when voters were not partisans of the old traditional parties, and more particularly so when,

[40] Though these relationships are not statistically significant, the depressing effect of worry among the old and its stimulating effect among the young are strikingly analogous to its effects among the poor and the rich respectively (except that the latter relationships were stronger); see pp. 150ff.

[41] However, when worry was introduced as an additional control variable in the data of the second panel of Table 9.3, it failed to interpret that relationship.

[42] A few other possible interpretations deserve at least a brief mention. For instance, one might argue that the weaker support of the older age group for Social Credit reflects their conservatism. Our data do reveal the older to be somewhat more resistant to change. But in the same way this attitude did not affect the vote (see Chap. 12), it did not interpret the initial age relationship either. One could also argue that the older citizens tend to have greater responsibilities and are therefore more likely to be prudent in their decisions, to be "responsible"; this should be manifest, among other things, in their more negative attitudes toward new political ventures. Actually, considering the number of children in a family as an indicator of its degree of responsibilities, we find that it does not explain the original age relationship; indeed, as the number of children increases, the age differences in support of the new party increase, the young respondents with a large family having been particularly prone to support Social Credit. Finally, one could suggest that the young, and particularly the students, are disproportionately attracted to social movements because they are less subjected to social constraints. We have no data to test this here, though it is very plausible; see Donald Von Eschen, Jerome Kirk, and Maurice Pinard, "The Conditions of Direct Action in a Democratic Society," *The Western Political Quarterly*, 22 (1969), p. 315.

while nonpartisans, they were also opinion leaders in political matters. Under other conditions, *all* age groups tended to be *equally low* in their support of Social Credit. This happened if people were not very enthusiastic about the new party, or else, if they were not politically alienated; (if anything, under this condition, the original relationship with age was even reversed).

Finally, in the remaining cases, we *specified* the circumstances under which the young voters were more likely—indeed, much more likely since the initial relationship was then usually strengthened—to give their support to the new movement. It was thus specified that when they were partisans, voters were much more likely to favor Social Credit if they were young than if they were old—and this was particularly the case again if they also happened to be opinion leaders. The same thing happened if voters were enthusiastic about the new movement, or more particularly, if they were politically alienated. Finally, this same pattern was observed if the voters were not too severely dissatisfied economically, or if they were much worried about their future financial situation. In short, partisanship and worry tended to *produce restraint only among the old respondents*, while enthusiasm, alienation and, in some way, economic dissatisfaction tended to *stimulate only the young*.

If we compare these conclusions with those concerning the response of the poor, formulated in the previous chapter, it becomes apparent that the poor's reactions to political movements present many similarities to those of the old. Both groups tend to be immune to intensifying conditions and sensitive to restraining ones.

To be sure, on the basis of these results alone, very little can be said about movements which found a greater support among older citizens. The most we can suggest is that if the conditions under which all age groups tended to give an equally low or an equally high support should prevail, you should not find much of a difference in each generation's support of a movement.

But when pushed one step further, the analysis provides some additional clues. Remember that we found some indications of a possible reversal in our initial relationship, under conditions of low political alienation (see Table 9.3, first panel). Now when more than one of our control factors (partisanship, alienation, etc.) are considered simultaneously, we find that these reversals are maintained and even reinforced. Consider for instance the following data where the effects of two of the control factors—alienation and economic conditions—are analysed simultaneously (Table 9.4). It can be seen that there is apparently a reversal in the initial relationship under certain conditions. The older voters appear to have been *slightly more likely* to support Social Credit when they were under conditions of both *severe* strain and *low* alienation. Seen otherwise, the data of Table 9.4 indicate that among the young, political alienation and strains are both independently and positively related to the support of Social Credit. But this is not the case among the old; under bad economic conditions, alienation becomes *negatively* related to such support in that age group.

Table 9.4

Older Participants, When under Strain, but Not Alienated,
Were Stronger Supporters of Social Credit
(% Social Credit)

	AGE GROUPS		
	34 OR YOUNGER	35-49	50 OR OLDER
Low Alienation*:			
Economic Conditions:			
Good**	5	12	0
	(41)	(32)	(29)
Bad***	14	25	26
	(22)	(44)	(27)
High Alienation:			
Economic Conditions:			
Good	35	17	15
	(43)	(47)	(46)
Bad	41	26	14
	(76)	(117)	(91)

*Alienation: low: scores 0 to 3; high: scores 4 to 6.
**Economic Conditions: good: scores 0 and 1; bad: 2 to 4.
***a_1 (effect of old age under low alienation and bad conditions, comparing extremes) = .12; $p(a_1^* \leq 0) = .14$.

In addition, when three of the control factors were introduced (adding partisanship), the results confirmed the above generalizations, while adding some new specifications. (Data not presented.) We found that the important reversal of the previous table was maintained, whether voters were partisans or not. Among the low alienated, severely deprived voters, the old were more likely to have been supporters of Social Credit than the young, even when they were partisans of the old parties. On the other hand, and in line with our previous findings, the data indicated that the support of the old—and of the old only— was particularly low when partisanship and political alienation combined together.

To be sure, these reversals are not self-explanatory and one may now wonder why under conditions of low alienation and high deprivations the aged become the most likely Social Credit supporters. Our own interpretation is that the old, when under strain, while not too alienated, may be more intolerant than the young about conditions they may have experienced more often than the young. Under such conditions, their threshold may in fact be lower than that of the young. When alienated, on the other hand, the old people would be paralysed by resignation or even fatalism.

If we now return to our inquiry concerning the movements of the aged, we realize that in the present population strains tended to be associated with high political alienation, so that there were few people presenting the combination of high strains and low alienation (see the marginal N's of Table 9.4); it is not surprising therefore that we found the zero-order relationship between age and support of the new movement to be negative. But it is not inconceivable that at other times one might find large pockets of people characterized precisely by that combination of severe deprivations and low alienation (or at least, alienation recently developed). This may have been the case, for instance, during the depression of the thirties, when so many people were suddenly severely strained; hence the disproportionate support of the aged observed during that period in the Nazi party and the Coughlin movement.[43]

If moreover we add that in Germany the Nazi party recruited its supporters mainly from the center parties,[44] and that the number of parties was so large[45] that the degree of partisanship must have been weak—and thus not too disproportionately restraining among the old—these findings may be less perplexing. In general, therefore, we suggest that the chances that a new political movement will obtain greater support among the old are good if it appears in a period of very widespread (and perhaps sudden) deprivations, when the population is not too alienated (or only recently alienated), and when the alienated are not too strongly attached to traditional parties.[46]

On the other hand, if the new movement is not a political party and therefore does not meet the restraints of prior partisan attachments, the young people should not be disproportionately represented in it. In this regard, recall the relatively weaker relationships with age found in the other recent social movements in Canada, as reported earlier.

To be sure, our findings do not account for all deviant cases, and particularly for the McCarthy and John Birch movements. But again notice that these movements were not new parties. Moreover, both movements were particularly successful among Republican voters,[47] and these tend to be older.[48] Therefore, the reported disproportionate support of the aged for these movements may represent a spurious finding.

In conclusion, it can be tentatively hypothesized that when appealing to groups in which nonalienated but severely deprived people clearly dominate, a movement is likely to be particularly successful among the older generations.

[43] On the other hand, the strains were certainly less widespread at the time of many of the other movements which fit the Social Credit pattern, as for instance the other movements in Canada today, or the present or recent communist, neo-fascist and poujadist movements, or even the membership— as opposed to the voters—of the German Nazi movement (since many of these members were probably recruited before the Great Depression).

[44] See Lipset, *Political Man*, pp. 140ff.

[45] Recall that there were thirty-eight parties in Germany at the time.

[46] Another factor may be involved in the case of the Nazi party (which is also relevant in the case of de Gaulle's party). The disproportionate support of the aged may reflect the young's prior recruitment in, and attachment to, the mass parties of their respective countries—the Communist and the Socialist parties.

[47] See Polsby, "Toward an Explanation of McCarthyism," pp. 815ff. and Lipset, "Three Decades of Radical Right," pp. 395ff., pp. 422ff.

[48] See Campbell *et al.*, *The American Voter*, pp. 153ff.

This will be all the more true if the movement does not have to fight against strongly entrenched partisan attachments. But if the population is alienated—and more particularly, if it has also created partisan attachments to traditional parties—the success of a new party will be relatively more limited among the old; it will characteristically be a movement of the young. Since, moreover, as we have seen, the young people are more likely to be stimulated by their enthusiasm, by deprivations, and by conditions which worry them, the youth's support for the new movement in that case will tend to be particularly strong. These are some of the reasons, we propose, for the success of Social Credit among the younger generations in Quebec.

In the last four chapters, we have considered many social and economic factors which proved crucial for the rise of the new party. We have disregarded, however, what many consider to be the crucial social factor in the rise of political movements, that is the "mass" characteristics of modern democratic societies. The lack of attachments between the individual and his society, the rootlessness of modern man, become in the mass theory of politics the prime source of political movements. Certain of the findings presented so far would already lead us to suspect that this theory is in need of qualification: it can certainly not explain, for instance, the slow response of the poor, one of the most detached groups in modern society. It cannot explain either our finding of this chapter that opinion leaders, who are obviously more integrated in the polity than their followers, were generally more attracted to Social Credit than the latter. In the next section, the theory will be theoretically examined and its many shortcomings will lead us to a reformulation. The new model will then be subjected to an empirical test, a task which mass theorists have rarely attempted.

IV

MASS

SOCIETY

AND

POLITICAL

MOVEMENTS

A
Reformulation
of the
Mass Society
Model[*]

CHAPTER TEN

In the contemporary social sciences, the theory of mass society has become a very popular theoretical perspective for the analysis of modern society and in particular, of modern political movements. For many, this theory is held to be the most pertinent statement of the genesis of mass movements. It has been argued that class analysis is not appropriate to understand crisis politics and should be reserved for the analysis of routine politics; mass analysis is presented as the most useful tool to explain crisis politics.[1] The overall perspective and the findings of the previous section—in particular, in Chapters 6 and 8—are a challenge to that thesis: class analysis did prove very useful in understanding the rise of Social Credit. Should this lead us, however, to reject mass analysis as failing to contribute to our understanding of crisis politics? The answer to this question will gradually unfold in this and the following chapter, as we proceed with a theoretical and empirical examination of the political effects of mass society.

The purpose of the present chapter, therefore, is to summarize some of the claims of that theory and to present a critique of these views.[2] This will lay the

---

[*]This chapter previously appeared in a slightly different form in *The American Journal of Sociology*, 73 (1968), pp. 682–90.

[1] Kornhauser, *The Politics of Mass Society*, pp. 14–16.

[2] It is not our purpose, however, to assess the accuracy of the *description* of modern societies as dominated by the masses and mass behavior, nor to examine the contention that modern trends toward bureaucratization and concentration of power undermine the presumed strength of a pluralist system. On these questions, see E.V. Walter, "'Mass Society': The Late Stages of an Idea," *Social Problems*, 31 (1964), pp. 391–410. (This paper also presents an interesting analysis of the roots and history of the theory.)

ground for a reformulation of the model, which will take into account a wider range of theoretical as well as of empirical concerns.

THE CLAIMS OF MASS THEORY

According to mass theory,[3] the source of the proliferation of mass behavior and mass movements[4] in modern society must be sought in the characteristics of its social structure, more specifically, in the weakness of modern societies' integrative functions. Very large segments of the population—the masses—are highly vulnerable to political movements, it is claimed, because of the weakness of the set of intermediate structures between the individual (or the primary group) on the one hand, and large scale national organizations on the other hand. The local community, a primary source of integration in feudal or communal society, has lost its function; the occupational community is weak, when not altogether absent; religious, political, and other voluntary associations play an integrative role—and a weak one, at that—for relatively few people. For some, even primary attachments are weaker in mass society, and atomization of the individual prevails.[5]

RESTRAINING EFFECTS

But what are the mechanisms through which strong intermediate structures are assumed to prevent the growth of political movements? Many can be suggested, but let me summarize them immediately under a single heading: strong attachments and identification to social groupings produce *restraining effects* on people. The mechanisms through which this is achieved can be enumerated briefly.[6] First, if there is a strong network of secondary groups, these groups will tend to check one another, and their members will be more selective in their political participation; without these groups, the non-elites feel less restrained in

---

[3] We are relying mainly on Kornhauser, *The Politics of Mass Society*. But see also Philip Selznick, *The Organizational Weapon* (New York: The Free Press of Glencoe, Inc., 1960).

[4] We shall make no distinction here between reform, mass, totalitarian, or other forms of political or social movements. (For such distinctions, see Kornhauser, *The Politics of Mass Society*, p. 50.) The reason for our decision is presented later, pp. 191–192.

[5] Though Kornhauser does not see personal isolation as conducive to mass movements (see *The Politics of Mass Society*, pp. 90–93, pp. 217–218), he differs on this with others; see, for instance, Hannah Arendt, *The Origins of Totalitarianism* (Cleveland and New York: World Publishing Company, Meridian Books, 1958), Chap. 10. esp. pp. 318, 323–324.

[6] For a summary of many of these mechanisms, see Donald Von Eschen, Jerome Kirk and Maurice Pinard, "The Organizational Substructure of Disorderly Politics," *Social Forces*, forthcoming. This chapter complements that paper in two main respects: while the paper examined the relevance of mass theory for an incipient movement with strong cadres but a weak following, the present chapter is concerned with social movements having a mass support; moreover, the paper was primarily concerned with the role of alienated organizations, while here we are considering as problematic the role of the entire intermediate structure.

their appeals to the elites.[7] Second, intermediate organizations are likely to create a structure of social attachments and loyalties between the elites and the non-elites and thus lead to social restraints in the latter's demands from the elites and in their evaluation of the elites' decisions.[8] Third, secondary groups are likely to socialize their members to accept the rules of the game and to struggle for their goals through discussions, negotiations, and compromises, rather than through the use of radical means. Participation into organizations is also apt to transmit knowledge and understanding about the nature and complexity of distant issues and to render people "reasonable" in their expectations from the elites. Forth, organizations enlarge the range of proximate concerns of their members and are the source of various cross-pressures with regard to the latter's objectives; they thus prevent the development of a single overriding goal and ideology so characteristic of a social movement.[9] Fifth, organizations can be a source of sanctions for members who might be tempted to engage in a social movement to secure their goals outside the routine channels approved by the organization. Sixth, participation in an elaborate set of intermediate groups is likely to foster the development of a sense of political efficacy, while the opposite engenders alienation and anxiety and the search for political ventures.[10] Finally, secondary groups can be the source of rewarding primary attachments and thus procure a more satisfactory life and a greater readiness to accommodation with the *status quo*.[11]

In short, the main proposition of mass theory states that a society with mass tendencies, because it lacks restraining mechanisms,[12] cannot prevent its members from turning to mass behavior and to mass movements.

A CRITIQUE OF MASS THEORY

Some of the findings reported in the foregoing chapters fail to support a mass analysis of Social Credit. In particular, the party's success in rural areas, where community attachments are stronger, raises questions about the presum-

---

7 Kornhauser, *The Politics of Mass Society*, p. 82.

8 *Ibid.*, p. 67; see also Coleman, *Community Conflict.*

9 Kornhauser, *The Politics of Mass Society*, p. 64.

10 *Ibid.*, p. 32. See also Arthur G. Neal and Melvin Seeman, "Organizations and Powerlessness: A Test of the Mediation Hypothesis," *American Sociological Review*, 29 (1964), pp. 216–222. The mediation hypothesis is empirically examined in Chap. 12.

11 Another important effect of organizational integration must be mentioned: Organizations can act as channels for the redress of their members' grievances and thus prevent the recourse to non-routine means of solving their problems. But this is a different function of secondary groups and will be dealt with later.

12 One of the criticisms made by Gusfield is that mass societies also have restraining mechanisms, albeit of a different sort (see Joseph R. Gusfield, "Mass Society and Extremist Politics," *American Sociological Review*, 27 (1962), pp. 19–30). This may be in part valid, but as pointed out by Perrow, this brings us back to the mass society perspective (see Charles Perrow, "The Sociological Perspective and Political Pluralism," *Social Research*, 31 (1964), pp. 411–422.)

ed restraining effects of these attachments. Similarly, the generalization that the poor are not easily recruited to new movements, even though they constitute one of the most atomized segments of the population, suggest that mass theory is in need of reconsideration.

In fact, this theory has already been subjected to severe criticisms. We would like to recast some of these criticisms and present additional ones, but in a way which will permit a reformulation of the theory, something that has rarely been done before.[13] As it now stands, the theory suffers from observational and theoretical biases.

To start with, a specification must be entered. Mass theory seems to be assuming that all the groupings of a strong intermediate structure would always and in all areas of their members' lives, act as important *reference groups*. Research indicates, however, that a large number of organizations do not actually represent reference points for their members, even in small rural communities.[14] In this regard, a pluralist society with a proliferation[15] of autonomous intermediate groups could be relatively little more restraining than a mass society. It would seem, in fact, that if restraining effects are to be ascribed to the intermediate structure, primary groups and the social networks of small communities, rather than most associations and organizations, are the groupings to be considered, since they are more likely to act as reference points.

MOBILIZING EFFECTS

But even if we assume that the various components of the intermediate structure are taken as reference points, we must still raise a major criticism: It seems to us that the claim that primary and secondary groups exert restraining effects on their members implies a one-sided view of the role of intermediate groupings. To be sure, no sociologist would question the fact that these groups may

13 Criticisms of the theory can be found, in particular, in Gusfield, "Mass Society and Extremist Politics,"; Bell, "America as a Mass Society: A Critique," in his *The End of Ideology*, Chap. 1; Perrow, "The Sociological Perspective and Political Pluralism." A reformulation concerning the role of an alienated organizational substructure can be found in Von Eschen *et al.*, "The Organizational Substructure of Disorderly Politics." We know of only one other attempt at an overall reformulation, that of Gino Germani; see his "Mass Society, Social Class, and the Emergence of Fascism," *Studies in Comparative International Development*, 3 (1967–68), no. 10. Germani has in particular noted the neglect of class in mass theory and has presented an alternative theory which departs drastically from the latter; although it is developed along different lines than ours, we think the two reformulations do not contradict one another. Germani places a strong emphasis on the role of strains, in particular on the lack of incorporation of newly mobilized strata, but on the other hand he pays little attention to the central concern of modern mass theorists, that is, the role of the intermediate structure as such; this will be our prime concern in this chapter.

14 See David E.W. Holden, "Associations as Reference Groups: An Approach to the Problem," *Rural Sociology*, 30 (1965), pp. 63–74.

15 Though mass theorists tend to have an idealized view of pluralist societies in this regard; actually, social participation tends to be quite limited; on this, see Perrow, "The Sociological Perspective and Political Pluralism," pp. 415–416.

exert such effects. But with regard to new political ventures, they may also exert just the opposite type of effects: the intermediate structure may actually, under circumstances discussed below, exert *mobilizing*, rather than restraining, *effects*. By this, we mean that certain intermediate groups, because of their positive orientations to the means and goals of a social movement, can be a strong force acting to *motivate* and *legitimate* individual as well as group participation in a movement. Between these two extremes, certain groupings may maintain neither a positive nor a negative stand, but simply a neutral, indifferent stand toward a new movement. In short, the effects of primary and secondary groups can empirically be located at any point on a continuum, ranging from strong restraining to strong mobilizing effects, with an intermediate neutral point.

Mass theorists do not always deny the possibility that primary attachments in fact can play a mobilizing role. Actually, this is the main effect some assign to primary groups.[16] However, this is a bias in the opposite direction; it neglects the potential restraining effects of primary groups, which must also be considered.[17]

But what constitutes a major shortcoming of mass theory is its failure to recognize that secondary groupings can also exert neutral or mobilizing functions. It may be empirically true that a very large number of organizations in affluent societies will usually exert restraining effects, but not all organizations under any circumstances will do so. Mass theory fails here because it makes the unwarranted assumption that the various components of the intermediate structure are always and in all spheres of activity characterized by conformist or constraining orientations and therefore opposed to non-institutionalized means of action. In this regard, it is as if mass theorists were equating pluralist to communal or feudal societies, with their strongly hierarchical and integrated social structure. In fact, in pluralist societies at least, there are always institutionalized components of the intermediate structure which exhibit a diffuse orientation of alienation vis-à-vis most or all features of the larger society, and there are certain other components which are alienated against specific aspects of the society, that is, which perceive their subjective interests as well as their norms and goals in harmony with those of a social movement. Obviously, such groups will stimulate rather than restrain participation in social movements.

That this should have been overlooked is in fact surprising, given the often made observation that social movements and revolutions are built upon the foundations of elites and organizations displaying some form of alienation against

16 Kornhauser, *The Politics of Mass Society*, pp. 90ff. Kornhauser writes: ". . . the individual is more likely to engage in new ventures when he receives support from his close associates. . . ."; *ibid.*, p. 93. See also Walter, "'Mass Society': The Late Stages of an Idea," pp. 403ff.

17 In an excellent case study of an hysterical contagion, the authors also distinguished the two opposite types of effects; the primary groups were seen as both "resistors" and "conductors"; see Alan C. Kerckhoff, Kurt W. Back, and Norman Miller, "Sociometric Patterns in Hysterical Contagion," *Sociometry*, 28 (1965), pp. 2-15.

the larger society. This was as true in the great revolutions of the nineteenth century as it was in the emergence of socialism in Western Canada or in the civil rights movement in the United States, to mention but a few examples.[18]

Still this only implies a static view of organizational life. All organizations are not necessarily *always*, and to the same degree, conformist *or* alienated. Organizational analysis often stresses the tendency for organizations to move from alienation to conformity. Little attention, however, is usually paid to the opposite process, a change from conformity to alienation, whether diffuse or specific. Under certain conditions, some organizations, or sections of them, may *become* alienated, at least with regard to specific social arrangements, and they will then positively sanction non-routinized ways of behavior. In the United States, for instance, one has witnessed the participation in sit-ins and other civil rights demonstrations of many organizations which had previously been rather conformist in their approach to this problem; the role of certain segments of the organized churches is an excellent example. In French Canada, the process of redefinition of one's orientation with regard to separatism is currently the major concern of almost all organizational elites. Many other examples could easily be mentioned. Let me only recall the revolt of the French settlers in Algeria against the metropolitan French government, backed as it was by the organizational network of the French colons and the French army, formerly the most conformist strongholds against change.

In short, whenever pre-existing primary and secondary groupings *possess* or *develop* an ideology or simply subjective interests congruent with that of a new movement, they will act as mobilizing rather than restraining agents toward that movement. And their members will be, not late joiners, but the early joiners of the movement, much earlier than the atomized masses.[19]

DIFFUSION THEORY

These are not the only functions of the intermediate structure which have to be taken into consideration in a reformulated model. The theory of mass society also disregards the accumulated propositions of diffusion studies[20] as well as

18 See Brinton, *The Anatomy of Revolution*, esp. pp. 41ff., pp. 106ff.; Tilly, "Reflections on the Revolution of Paris," pp. 113ff; Lipset, *Agrarian Socialism*, Chap. 10; Lipset wrote that "the rapid acceptance of new ideas and movements in Saskatchewan can be attributed mainly to the high degree of organization" (p. 206). See also Smelser, *Theory of Collective Behavior*, pp. 274ff., pp. 282ff. The impetus given to the civil rights movement by the preexistence of a substructure of alienated organizations (pacifist, socialist, liberal organizations) has been specifically documented in Von Eschen *et al.*, "The Organizational Substructure of Disorderly Politics".

19 See Von Eschen *et al.*, "The Organizational Substructure of Disorderly Politics," for data supporting this.

20 Surprisingly, the sociology of diffusion and that of collective behavior, though both are concerned with the appearance of new items in a culture, tend to develop independently of one another. For a notable exception, however, see Alan C. Kerckhoff, Kurt W. Back, and Norma Miller, "Sociometric Patterns in Hysterical Contagion." Their conclusions are not very different from ours.

some propositions of the theory of conflict; both sets of propositions, however, would lead one to make predictions which in important respects are opposite to those of the former theory.[21]

With regard to diffusion theory, mass society theorists overlook the fact that a social movement is basically a new item in a culture and that as such its adoption implies the processes of diffusion. But as the studies of diffusion have shown, the adoption of new ideas and practices, and therefore of new social movements does not take place in a social vacuum.[22] If there is in that field one firm empirical generalization which can be made, it is that the higher the degree of social integration of potential adopters, the more likely and the sooner they will become actual adopters, and that, on the other hand, near-isolates tend to be the last to adopt an innovation.

Thus diffusion studies have shown that there are "positive correlations between participation in formal social groups and the adoption of new farm practices";[23] that "farm practice adoption rates were higher in communities that had community clubs than in those that did not"; and that "farmers and wives who participated in community clubs adopted more improved farm and home practices than those who did not";[24] that opinion leaders, who characteristically have "a greater degree of both formal and informal social participation,"[25] "are generally more innovative than their followers";[26] that in general informal participation was highly conducive to diffusion;[27] and that "the degree of a doctor's integration among his local colleagues was strongly and positively related to the date of his first use of a new drug."[28]

Two important mechanisms of the intermediate structure overlooked by mass theory would seem to account for the proposition that social integration is conducive to diffusion. First, of course, are what we have called the mobilizing effects of social groupings, that is, their motivation and legitimation effects. In modern societies experiencing a high rate of social change, a great many items of diffusion are likely to induce mobilizing rather than restraining effects on the part of the intermediate structure. Hence the finding of a positive relationship between integration and adoption in American studies of diffusion. The possibility of resistance to innovation in certain other cultures should not, however, be overlooked.

21 For two syntheses of the empirical generalizations in the field of diffusion, see Lionberger, *Adoption of New Ideas and Practices,* and Rogers, *Diffusion of Innovations.* With regard to conflicts, we have in mind some of the propositions in Coleman, *Community Conflict.*

22 A similar idea, from a different point of view, is also expressed by Lewis M. Killian; see his "Social Movements," in Robert E. L. Faris, *Handbook of Modern Sociology* (Chicago: Rand McNally & Co., 1964), p. 431.

23 Lionberger, *Adoption of New Ideas and Practices,* p. 84.

24 Lionberger, *Adoption of New Ideas and Practices,* p. 73.

25 Rogers, *Diffusion of Innovations,* pp. 240–241.

26 Rogers, *Diffusion of Innovations,* p. 243; also pp. 184ff.

27 Rogers, *Diffusion of Innovations,* pp. 217ff.

28 James S. Coleman, Elihu Katz, and Herbert Menzel, "The Diffusion of an Innovation among Physicians," *Sociometry,* 20 (1957), p. 257.

COMMUNICATING EFFECTS

But a second mechanism can be fruitfully distinguished from the former one at the analytical level. I suggest that one important mechanism which produces the positive association between integration and adoption is what I shall call the *communicating effects* of the intermediate groupings. Organizations and social networks are excellent channels of communication, transmitting information about new ideas and practices. More generally, they contribute in developing among their members a certain degree of sophistication: they enlarge their members' field of attention and perception, as well as contribute to the development of leadership and other organizational skills. Thus, participants in various social groupings, particularly in primary groups, should be more likely to learn about a new social movement—its leadership, its goals, its successes in recruiting members—than atomized people.[29] It is important to note that here we do not distinguish whether the intermediate groupings have a positive or a negative orientation toward the new movement; all groupings, whether characterized by a restraining, mobilizing, or neutral potential, can exert communicating effects and as such can be conducive to the rise of new movements.[30]

Similarly, certain aspects of the theory of community conflict are at odds with mass theory.[31] Notice first that community conflicts are typically uninstitutionalized ways of coping with a given problem, as are social and political movements. But Coleman describes a community conflict as something that usually originates between the administration of a community and some center of active opposition while the majority of the people remain passive. It is only after the administration has committed some blunders or after the climate of opinion has deteriorated that the masses become available for recruitment.[32] Moreover, Coleman states that the *more* integrated among these people will be the *first* to join into the controversy; lower-status people, for instance, lacking identification with and attachment to the community and its leaders, will less often and less easily be drawn into a conflict.[33] This is in direct contradiction with what mass theory would predict.

[29] In at least one case study, the failure of a new movement was actually attributed in part to communication failure, due to the lack of pre-existing organizational networks complementing the primary groups and the mass media; see Maurice Jackson, Eleanora Peterson, James Bull, Sverre Monsen, and Patricia Richmond, "The Failure of an Incipient Social Movement," *The Pacific Sociological Review*, 3 (1960), pp. 35–40.

[30] Indeed, among collective behavior theorists, mass theorists are an exception in their oversight of the importance of communication for the development of collective behavior. Consider, for instance, Blumer's stress on circular reaction, milling, collective excitement, and social contagion, or Smelser's stress on the necessity of communication channels for the development of collective behavior. Blumer, "Collective Behavior," esp. pp. 170–177; Smelser, *Theory of Collective Behavior*, passim. See also Ralph H. Turner's review of the field, "Collective Behavior," in Faris, *Handbook of Modern Sociology*, pp. 382–425, esp. pp. 397–409.

[31] See Coleman, *Community Conflict*.

[32] Coleman, *Community Conflict*, pp. 8–9.

[33] Coleman, *Community Conflict*, pp. 21–22. This model was substantiated in routine politics: it was found that more integrated communities were more likely to back a fluoridation referendum

Notice, however, that Coleman also states that "when and if" the least integrated are drawn into a controversy, they are likely to make it degenerate into a "fight to the finish," while the more integrated citizens, though more easily recruited, are more likely to be restrained because of various cross-pressures.[34] This is apparently more in agreement with mass theory; the reason is that, while conflict theory distinguishes between *attraction* to a conflict and *intensity of participation* into it, mass theory fails to make such a distinction. Basically we think the propositions of mass theory are sound to account for what happens after—but only after—the least attached are drawn into a conflict or a social movement:[35] communicating and mobilizing effects are no longer effective, but the restraining effects of other groups could still affect their modes of participation. What primarily concerns us here, however, is attraction to a new movement, not the modes of participation in it.[36]

In short, the theory of community conflict contradicts mass theory insofar as the processes of emergence of a conflict—or of a social movement—are concerned. This, we suggest, is because conflict theory considers as crucial what we have called the communication and mobilizing effects of the intermediate structure.[37] Since community conflicts are likely to arise during situations of crisis, when important areas of people's lives are threatened,[38] that is, under conditions of strain, the predictions of conflict theory are more sound than those of mass theory, as shall presently be discussed.

THE ROLE OF STRAINS

So far, it has been argued that under certain circumstances, components of the intermediate structure can exert mobilizing effects rather than restraining effects. The specification of one major set of such circumstances leads us to another important criticism of mass theory. Basically, mass theory, even with the quali-

---

than less integrated ones, presumably because of the greater restraining effects in the former; but when communities of the first type defeated the proposition, they were more likely to do so with greater unanimity than those of the second type, presumably because of greater mobilizing and communicating effects; see Maurice Pinard, "Structural Attachments and Political Support in Urban Politics: The Case of Fluoridation Referendums."

34 Coleman, *Community Conflict*, pp. 21ff.

35 Indeed, Kornhauser quotes Coleman, stressing his proposition on the modes of participation, which he implicity applies to the attraction to the movement, though not making any distinction between the two; see *The Politics of Mass Society*, pp. 66–67.

36 This is indirectly supported by findings of our study of the sit-in movement. It was found that the least integrated participants, as revealed by their lower social status, were late joiners of the movement, but once they had joined they were the most active participants; see Pinard, Kirk, and Von Eschen, "Processes of Recruitment in the Sit-in Movement"; see also Lipset, *Agrarian Socialism*, p. 167.

37 Coleman, *Community Conflict*, pp. 18ff. "Formal and informal associations in the community also make their influence felt through the very fact of association. Word-of-mouth discussions within organizations do more than communicate information; they influence and persuade, often far more effectively than more formal channels. . . ." *Ibid.*, p. 18.

38 Coleman, *Community Conflict*, pp. 4–6.

fications made above, deals at most with *some* of the conditions for the rise of social movements. In terms of Smelser's model, it deals mainly with three determinants, or rather some aspects of them—conduciveness, mobilization for action, and social control,[39] or, more concretely, communicating, mobilizing, and restraining effects. As such, mass theory is a more limited model than it pretends to be: the intermediate structure can limit or foster the rise of political movements, but it is not, in itself, a sufficient condition for their appearance. In particular, the presence of strain is a crucial condition. To be sure, the lack of social participation and in particular, the lack of primary group ties, can itself be a source of strain; but this is at times overemphasized.[40]

Once these distinctions are made, one soon realizes that the crucial and necessary element of strain, as distinct from other determinants, tends to be seriously underestimated in mass theory.[41] To be sure, some sources of strain are considered—economic crises, for instance—but they are only part of a large set of forces, such as the processes of democratization, industrialization, and urbanization, and these forces all lead to mass movements, not primarily because they produce deprivations of various sorts but above all because they weaken the system of attachments of the non-elites to the elites. In other words, conditions of strain are only one type of factor, among many others, which can bring about a mass society, and it is *because* all these factors bring about such a society that they lead to mass movements.[42]

Contrary to this, we subscribe to the idea that strains are *per se* a necessary independent factor and a more important one than the restraining effects mass theory deals with.[43] Moreover, and this is theoretically important, we claim that strains will affect the various functions of the intermediate structure which have been discussed so far, or, to put it differently, that *strain will affect the conduciveness, mobilization, and social control potential of the intermediate structure.* Under severe strains, and given that no other institutionalized channels for the redress of grievances are available (another condition of conduciveness to be discussed), conformist components of the intermediate structure can become elements which encourage, rather than limit, the growth of a new movement.

[39] See Smelser, *Theory of Collective Behavior*, pp. 274ff, pp. 282ff., p. 298.

[40] Relatively few people, after all, are isolated to the point of serious discomfort, and we doubt that severe strains frequently develop from the lack of participation in secondary groupings. As Germani puts it, "mass theory has exaggerated the 'loss of community' effect"; see "Mass Society, Social Class and the Emergence of Fascism," p. 193.

[41] Students of diffusion also tend to overlook the role of strains or, at least, to assume their existence, though Lionberger explicitly states that dissatisfaction with conditions as they exist is necessary for adoption. *Adoption of New Ideas and Practices*, p. 14.

[42] See Kornhauser, *The Politics of Mass Society*, pp. 119–174, esp. pp. 162–167. From this stems much of the confusion about mass theory; on this particular point, see Perrow, "The Sociological Perspective and Political Pluralism," pp. 419–420.

[43] Germani's reformulation makes, in this regard, an important contribution (see "Mass Society, Social Class and the Emergence of Fascism," esp. pp. 193–194). We would not, however, go as far as Daniel Bell who seems to discount completely the role of the intermediate structure: ". . . It is not the mass society, but the inability, pure and simple, of any society to meet impatient popular expectations that makes for a strong response to radical appeals." *The End of Ideology*, p. 32.

On the one hand, under severe strains, individuals may withdraw psychologically and/or physically from the intermediate groups likely to exert restraining effects on them[44] and turn toward more neutral or mobilizing agents as reference groups, while at the same time becoming very susceptible to the communicating effects of all the groups they participate in.[45]

On the other hand, and of greater consequence, conformist secondary groups, under severe strains, can develop some degree of alienation, oppose certain aspects of the *status quo* and, if no other alternatives are opened, adopt a neutral or even a positive orientation to a new movement.[46] This brings us back to an earlier point. We have seen that intermediate groupings can become a source of positive, rather than negative, sanctions regarding non-routine politics. We now add that the appearance of strains is a major determinant of such changes, whether these strains are economic strains affecting the membership of the organization, or a feeling on the part of the organization that it is powerless in meeting its goals, or any other form of strains.[47] The important thing is that organizations which were permanently and diffusely alienated are now joined by newly and specifically alienated groups in exerting mobilizing effects. If we add to this that, given the social unrest engendred by these strains, the communicating effects of these groups will be particularly strong, one can see that, under these conditions, the growth potential of a new movement will be substantially improved.

STRAINS AND TYPES OF MOVEMENTS

Before we conclude, two additional points must be clarified. It should be emphasized that the severity or mildness of the strains should be considered relative to the strength of the restraining effects of conformist organizations. Obviously, strains will need to be more severe to break strong restraining effects than weak ones. Conversely, the strength of the restraining effects will in large measure depend on the evaluation which is made of the new movement: the more negative the evaluation of its ideology, of its means and goals, the stronger

44 Turner mentions the possibility of "neutralization or inapplicability of existing norms"; Turner, "Collective Behavior", p. 390.

45 For a study which exemplifies these processes, see Jeffrey K. Hadden and Raymond C. Rymph, "The Marching Ministers," *Trans-action*, Sept. Oct., 1966, pp. 38–41.

46 An excellent case study of such a process, which was instrumental in our rethinking of this problem, is Alvin W. Gouldner's *Wildcat Strike* (Yellow Springs, Ohio: The Antioch Press, 1954). Notice that the wildcat strike was started not by atomized workers, but by a disenchanted clique of the workers' union.

47 Gusfield enumerates four situations in which pluralism invites non-routine behavior: situations of "disenfranchised classes," of "doomed and defeated classes," of hostility of public opinion to a group's interests, of inability of political elites to deal with crises. He concludes that in each, "extremist politics is developed and conducted by well-structured groups, representing discrete and organized parts of the social structure, acting to secure goals related to group needs." Joseph Gusfield, "Mass Society and Extremist Politics," pp. 24–26. In a similar vein, Perrow states that mass theory "minimizes the role of power in society, and overlooks the role of economic interest." Charles Perrow, "The Sociological Perspective and Political Pluralism," pp. 416–417.

will be the restraining effects. Hence, an extremist or a "mass" movement may require more severe strains to attract the integrated segments of the population than a mildly reformist movement. But this does not mean that one must have different models to deal with these different types of movements. Moreover, since the leaders of new movements usually tend to hide the latter's unfavorable charactieristics[48] and since, historically, the average citizen, not to mention those above him, has not been particularly keen in foreseeing the negative aspects of certain movements, the qualification we have made should not be overemphasized. One tends to forget that despairing people frantically looking for solutions to their problems will usually lack the sophistication necessary to pass a sound judgment, an ability which often is available to few but the historians of tomorrow.

ORGANIZATIONS AS CHANNELS
FOR THE REDRESS OF GRIEVANCES

Finally, when the mechanisms which, according to mass theory, lead to restraining effects were enumerated, an important one was temporarily put aside. Let us return to it. It can be argued that an elaborate intermediate structure constitutes a barrier against social movements for the simple reason that it provides channels for the redress of grievances. For instance, associations and organizations can act as pressure groups or otherwise help people work routinely toward the solution of their problems.[49]

From what precedes, it should already be clear that we do not mean to disregard this function of the intermediate structure. If mass theory simply stated that in a mass society movements arise because of the lack of channels for the redress of grievances, then the theory, though incomplete, would be sound in that respect.[50] But mass theory states much more than that, and this is where it fails, as we have tried to show. The pressure-group function of the intermediate structure is of a different type than the restraining functions discussed above: the restraining functions deal with the socializing role of intermediate groupings, while the pressure-group function deals with their instrumental role. Not all components of the intermediate structure are fit to work toward the redress of a given set of grievances (think of the primary groups, the community social networks, leisure and religious associations in a modern society facing an economic depression), while potentially all can act as communication and mobilization centers for a new movement. More importantly, even those groupings

---

[48] On this, see Killian, "Social Movements," pp. 434–436.

[49] Kornhauser, *The Politics of Mass Society*, p. 82.

[50] According to Smelser, the lack of routine channels for the redress of grievanes is an important condition of conduciveness for collective behavior; see *Theory of Collective Behavior, passim.* The reader will recall that this proposition was substantiated in Chaps. 2 and 3 above, where it was shown that the lack of alternatives in systems of one-party dominance had been important in the rise of third parties in Canada. See also Germani, "Mass Society, Social Class and the Emergence of Fascism," pp. 193–194.

which might act as channels of redress will not necessarily be effective in that role: they may fail in their efforts and turn with their members to non-routine means. It is our claim that a society which has a highly pluralist structure, but no channel, or no effective channel, for the redress of a given set of grievances will turn faster and more easily to social movements than a society with a mass structure.[51] A mass society may be more likely to lack effective channels for the redress of grievances, but it will also lack the extensive networks of attachments and organizations on which new movements arise.

A REFORMULATED MODEL

To conclude, let me summarize the factors and processes which a reformulated theory of mass politics must take into account; some general new propositions will then be stated.

First, the various elements of the intermediate structure (primary groups, communal ties, occupational groups, associations, and organizations of all sorts), must be taken as reference groups by their members, in order to exert any kind of normative effects, either positive or negative. Their mere existence is no assurance that they act as such. Moreover, under certain circumstances, some groups may cease to be regarded as legitimate reference points.

Second, the components of the intermediate structure which are taken as reference groups may be found at any point of the alienation–conformity continuum and their position may change over time. Their ideology as well as their short-term interests may lead them to be conformist, neutral, or alienated, in diffuse or specific ways: accordingly, they can exert on their membership restraining, neutral, or mobilizing effects toward a new movement.

Third, all components of the intermediate structure, whatever their normative orientation, are likely to exert communicating effects on their members. In this regard, a pluralistic society is always more conducive to social movements than a mass society, and well-integrated individuals are easier targets than atomized ones.

Fourth, strains must be considered as an important independent factor; they can also affect the conditions of the intermediate structure. Under severe strains, integrated individuals can elude the restraining effects of intermediate groupings, while becoming particularly susceptible to their communicating effects, and intermediate groupings can themselves move toward an alienated position, exerting both communicating and mobilizing influences.

On the basis of these ideas, it is now possible to make some general propositions regarding the fate of social movements in societies or among individuals varying according to their degree of social integration. This new theory, however, cannot be as simple as the previous one.

51 This is directly related to some of the points made by Gusfield and Perrow; see footnote 47, p. 191.

The outcome, obviously, depends on the relative strength of the various, and opposite, types of effects discussed above. And it seems that one of the crucial variables here will be the severity and the generality of the existing strains.

If the strains are severe and widespread, alienated groups will tend to be particularly active; moreover, either conformist groups will tend to move from a restraining position to a more neutral or even to a mobilizing position, or their members will tend to elude their restraining effects. Their communicating role, on the other hand, will be working fully. To the extent that this prevails, I would predict that integrated individuals and pluralist societies will be more prone to social and political movements than atomized people and mass societies. This prediction, of course, is just the opposite of that made by mass theorists.

If, on the other hand, strains are not severe or widespread, then restraining effects will tend to predominate over mobilizing effects, and communicating effects will be weak since there is no need for a new movement. Under such circumstances, any new movement, if it should appear, will of course be weak; but to the extent that it succeeds in recruiting some people, the basic proposition of mass theory should hold: the lower the degree of integration, the greater the proneness to social movements. So far, therefore, mass theory appears to be sound, paradoxically, only when strains are limited, that is, when the success of a movement is highly problematic to start with.

At this point, however, a final qualification must be entered. In their study of the diffusion of a new drug, Coleman, Katz, and Menzel identified an interesting process of diffusion: they found that the social networks in which doctors were integrated contributed to the adoption process only in the early stages of the diffusion of the new drug; later on, they seemed "completely *inoperative* as chains of influence. The social structure seemed to have exhausted its effect."[52] This would suggest that the communicating and mobilizing effects which we have postulated should be particularly effective during the early stages of a new movement, but should become inoperative during later stages when the movement has become well-known and has gained a large degree of legitimacy in the population. To the extent, and only to the extent, that the permanent restraining effects of some intermediate groupings might still prevail at these later stages, one would then predict, with mass theorists, a negative relationship between social integration and the success of social movements at that stage.

Finally, let us repeat that this model is primarily concerned with the processes of recruitment to new movements. It is consistent, however, with the idea that the least integrated, once members of a movement, may be more extremist in their behavior than more integrated people.

---

[52] Coleman, Katz, and Menzel, "The Diffusion of an Innovation among Physicians," p. 266. Italics in original. The authors found that the social networks seemed inoperative when no distinctions between stages were made.

Mass Society and Social Credit

CHAPTER ELEVEN

The propositions of mass theory, in its traditional form, have rarely been subjected to severe empirical verification. In the present chapter, we intend to test some of the new propositions suggested in the previous chapter with both survey and aggregate data. In so doing, two purposes will be fulfilled. At a more explanatory level, the data to be presented will try to assess the role of the intermediate structure—primary groups, community structures, organizations and associations in the rise of new political movements. At the same time, at a more descriptive level, the data will throw some light on many empirical questions which may be considered as directly relevant to this particular movement: Given the conservative philosophy of Social Credit, was it weakly backed by members of labor unions? Given the religious character of the Social Credit movement in Alberta and in its early phases in Quebec, was the movement particularly strong among the devout Catholics? Though a predominantly rural movement, was it more successful in very small villages or in the relatively large towns and cities of Quebec? Such questions are of primary interest; the answers provided may be helpful in considering, for instance, the relationship between the ideology of a movement and its mass following.

INFORMAL GROUPINGS

The best way to start is to consider the effects of different degrees of primary group participation, that is, social interaction with relatives and friends, since these are the components of the social structure which should have exerted the stronger effects. Indeed, primary groups should more likely constitute reference groups than formal associations and organizations, since in the latter participation has a much more remote character. Primary groups should be the milieu where social integration exerts its clearer and stronger effects.

As brought out in the previous chapter, there is no agreement among mass theorists as to what the effects of informal networks should be. Some of them claim that the lack of primary attachments has the same effects as the lack of secondary attachments, both being likely to lead to political extremism;[1] others disagree with that position. On the one hand, Arendt writes, for instance, that "totalitarian movements depended less on the structurelessness of a mass society than on the specific conditions of an atomized and individualized mass . . .";[2] and that the total loyalty that such movements demand "can be expected only from the completely isolated human being who, without any other social ties to family, friends, comrades, or even mere acquaintances, derives his sense of having a place in the world only from his belonging to a movement, his membership in the party."[3] Kornhauser, on the other hand, states that "the individual who is *totally* isolated . . . for long periods is not likely to possess that minimum of personal organization required by collective activity," and therefore should be led to personal deviance rather than mass behavior.[4] Indeed, according to Kornhauser, "participation in small but isolated groups (i.e., isolated from the common life of the larger society) . . . may even be favorable to participation in mass movements, since the individual is more likely to engage in new ventures when he receives support from his close associates, and because the member of even a small group is a more accessible target for mass agitation than is a completely unattached person."[5]

This last view is, of course, one of the basic premises adopted in the reformulation of the mass society model. With respect to primary attachments, Kornhauser recognizes now the possibility of mobilizing and communicating effects which he does not consider in the case of secondary affiliations; on the other hand, he now disregards the possibility of restraining effects. As suggested above, the hypotheses we advanced are the same in the case of primary contacts as in the case of secondary groupings. Both types of social integration can exert restraining as well as mobilizing and communicating effects; we simply add that these effects may be more intense when primary contacts rather than secondary affiliations are concerned.

In his study of Social Credit support in one electoral district, Lemieux implicitly identified the communicating, mobilizing, and restraining effects of primary contacts which we postulated. He wrote: ". . . the propagation of Social

[1] So that Gusfield presents this position as that of mass theory; see, "Mass Society and Extremist Politics," pp. 20–21. See for instance Hannah Arendt, *The Origins of Totalitarianism*, enl. ed. (Cleveland New York: The World Publishing Co., Meridian Books, 1958).

[2] Arendt, *The Origins of Totalitarianism*, p. 318.

[3] *Ibid.*, pp. 323–24.

[4] Kornhauser, *The Politics of Mass Society*, pp. 90–91. Italics in the original.

[5] *Ibid.*, p. 93. See also Walter, "'Mass Society': The Late Stages of an Idea," pp. 401–404.

Credit seemed to have occurred in places where men meet and are united by social ties. . . . Our interviews suggest that this diffusion through primary groups met with astounding success among workers at (certain plants). . . ." But he also reported: "In certain places, several voters who favored Social Credit did not dare to declare their support openly. This accounted for some Social Credit organizers being among the most surprised at the success of their party. . . . On this point, (the winning Social Credit candidate) told us of having received numerous telephone calls from unknowns, pledging him their vote and apologizing for not being able to say it in public because of pressures on them from the 'old-line' parties . . . . This 'hidden créditisme' confirms our hypothesis that Social Credit doctrines were disseminated mainly by primary groups. . . ."[6]

In our survey each respondent was asked how many times, during the seven days preceding the interview, he had "visited other people at their homes," how many times "people visited (him) at (his) home," and how many times he had been "out with other people to go somewhere else than at relatives' or friends' homes." From these data, an index of primary group participation was constructed. When related to the respondents' vote in 1962, the results of Table 11.1 were obtained. They reveal the presence of a curvilinear relationship between the degree of primary group participation and Social Credit support.

Table 11.1

A Moderate Degree of Primary Group Participation Seemed Most Conducive to Social Credit Support

VOTE IN 1962	INDEX OF PRIMARY GROUP PARTICIPATION*		
	LOW %	MODERATE %	HIGH %
Social Credit	19	27	19
Conservative	42	28	27
Liberal	39	42	52
N.D.P.	0	3	3
N =	(134)	(174)	(309)

*For index, see Appendix C. Low: score 0; moderate: score 1; high: scores 2 and 3.

Both those who had been socially isolated in the week preceding the interview (i.e., those low on the index) and those who had been most socially active were less likely to have voted Social Credit than those who had been moderately active.[7] These results indicate that overall, the diffusion of the new movement

6 Vincent Lemieux, "The Election in the Constituency of Lévis," pp. 37–38; see also Irving, *The Social Credit Movement in Alberta*, p. 249.

7 Since the amount of informal social participation is related to occupational status and to age, both factors were controlled, but it did not affect this basic relationship. When the *number of times* one visited others or was visited by others or went out is used as an indicator (rather than whether or not he did any of these things), the same relationship is obtained.

was hampered among isolates,[8] as diffusion studies would have led us to expect, but contrary to the predictions of many mass theorists.

It is interesting to compare this finding with one reported by Couch. In a study of Michigan county farmers, among whom "there was rather widespread discontent" and, presumably, a high degree of alienation, a positive association was discovered, at the zero-order level, between interaction with peers and participation in an agrarian protest movement, the National Farmers Organization. Among those who received no sociometric choices from their peers, only 18 percent were members of N.F.O., while among those who received one choice, or received more than one choice, the proportions were 24 and 29 percent respectively.[9] Again the isolates were lagging behind others; but while we find that the most socially active were not the strongest supporters of Social Credit, Couch reports that these were the most likely members of N.F.O. We suggest that the positive association found by the latter probably reflects the climate of widespread alienation prevailing among the farmers studied, as in fact the author himself reports.[10]

Indeed, we have suggested that the alienated or conformist position of intermediate groupings should determine the kind of effects they will exert. In our sample, which is a cross section of the entire population, and not only of a segment of discontented people, it is not as easy to evaluate whether an informal grouping is conformist or alienated as it is for a given subgroup or for a secondary association, and we have no direct measure of the climate of the primary groups in which our respondents were participating. Nevertheless we have an indirect measure and it permits us to differentiate conformist from alienated social networks. It is based on the respondents' reports of the occupations of their three best friends. If a respondent's best friends were from an occupational group which offered strong support to Social Credit, we may assume that this respondent's social network was relatively alienated and favorable to Social Credit. Conversely, if his friends were from an occupational group which was weak in its support of the new party, he can be assumed to have been a member of a social network which was relatively conformist and unfavorable to that party.

First, it is clear from Table 11.2 that the climate of one's primary group played an important role in the mobilization of support for the new movement. Since one's occupational level is strongly related to that of one's friends, the former is held constant in that tabulation.

[8] Note how the isolates disproportionately favored the Conservatives, the traditional opposition party, and were the least likely to vote Liberal.
[9] Recomputed from Carl J. Couch, "Interaction and Protest," a paper read at the 62th Annual Meeting of the American Sociological Association, San Francisco, 1967, Table 2 (N's equal to 158, 100, and 75 respectively). Quoted with Professor Couch's permission.
[10] Findings similar to those of Couch, and presumably due to the same reasons, are reported by Marx regarding Negro militancy; see Gary T. Marx, *Protest and Prejudice: A Study of Belief in The Black Community* (New York: Harper Torchbook, 1969), p. 71.

Table 11.2

The Primary Group Climate Had a Strong Effect on Social Credit Support
(% Social Credit)

RESPONDENTS' OCCUPATIONAL GROUP	INDEX OF PRIMARY GROUP CLIMATE*		
	FAVORABLE	INTERMEDIATE	UNFAVORABLE
White Collars	24	15	9
	(17)	(46)	(121)
Skilled Workers and Farmers	33	27	13
	(70)	(97)	(47)
Semi-skilled Workers	38	29	16
	(45)	(31)	(19)
Unskilled and Service Workers	36	26	17
	(14)	(31)	(18)

*For index, see Appendix C.; favorable: scores 6 to 9; intermediate: scores 3 to 5; unfavorable: scores 0 to 2.

It can be seen that independently of the effect of the respondents' own occupational status, which are only slightly reduced, the primary group climate exerted a relatively strong influence, accounting for an average difference in support of 19 percent (compare first to third column in Table 11.2). Notice, incidentally, how the climate effect was stronger among workers and farmers, and conversely, how the occupational status effect was stronger under a favorable climate; put differently, the two factors were reinforcing each other.

But, as expected, the primary group climate had another more important effect as far as our model is concerned. This can be seen in Table 11.3. If understandably a strong climate effect can again be observed (compare rows in the Table), the relationships between primary group participation and Social Credit

Table 11.3

The Degree of Primary Group Participation Has Opposite Effects,
Depending on the Primary Group Climate
(% Social Credit)

PRIMARY GROUP CLIMATE:	INDEX OF PRIMARY GROUP PARTICIPATION		
	LOW	MODERATE	HIGH
Favorable*	29	32	36
	(35)	(47)	(63)
Intermediate	20	33	22
	(49)	(66)	(92)
Unfavorable	15	14	8
	(41)	(49)	(123)

*a_1 (Effect of favorable networks, comparing extremes) $= .36 - 29 = .07$; $p(a_1^* \leq 0) = .24$;
a_2 (Effect of unfavorable networks, comparing extremes) $= .15 - .08 = .07$; $p(a_2^* \leq 0) = .13$.

support are of greater interest now (compare columns). Though not statistically significant, these relationships are clearly running in opposite directions: *when the primary group climate was relatively favorable, the more socially active the respondents had been, the more likely they were to have voted Social Credit:*[11] The initial curvilinear relationship becomes *monotonic* and *positive.* On the other hand, *when the social climate was relatively unfavorable, the relationship becomes monotonic* and *negative: the more active the respondents had been, the weaker the support for the new movement.* Clearly, it does not seem sound therefore to make any overall prediction with regard to the role of primary groups; as contended in the previous chapter, it must first be determined whether these groups are alienated or conformist (favorable or unfavorable) in order to determine whether they will exert mobilizing or restraining effects.[12] As can be seen from these data, both types of effects are possible, and both took place in Quebec in 1962. The blanket assertion that social isolation is at the roots of mass movements is therefore clearly misleading. But so is the assertion that primary groups will exert only mobilizing effects.[13]

COMMUNITY STRUCTURE

Local communities constitute another important component of the intermediate structure. The way they affected the outcome of the election in 1962 has already been briefly considered. Recall that we found that in small—and presumably more integrated—communities, the support for Social Credit was more uniformly distributed in all income groups, while in larger rural communities, it was concentrated in the middle-income group.[14] This suggests that the diffusion processes vary according to the degree of integration of a community.

Turning now to the new model, the impact of community structure will be tested more thoroughly with aggregate data.   While in general primary groups are likely to be the most important reference groups for most people, the closely-knit social structure of rural communities may also provide a set of important

---

[11] This is the same type of relationship as that observed in Couch's data (p. 198).

[12] And, it might be added, whether the restraining effect of conformist groups will be strong enough to paralyze the communicating effects of these groups, as they presumably do in the unfavorable subgroup of Table 11.3. Notice, however, that the relationship remains curvilinear in the intermediate subgroup. This may be the result of some multiplicative model between the restraining and communicating effects: the probability of voting Social Credit would be the result of the product of the probability of being free from restraining effects, which would decrease with conformist interaction, and the probability of being influenced by communicating effects, which would increase with interaction. (Compare to the model presented in Chap. 8, Table 8.6.)

[13] The two opposite types of effects observed would challenge the view that primary groups have lost their autonomy under the forces of mass society; on this, see Walter, "'Mass Society': The Late Stages of an Idea," pp. 404–405.

[14] See Table 8.9 and comments.

reference points. At the extreme, small communities of a few hundred people constitute large sociometric networks of closely-bound individuals, where everyone is at least an acquaintance of everyone else and where social control is particularly strong. If mass theory were correct, these communities should be much more difficult to win to a new movement than large, loosely-knit communities where there is a much greater degree of social atomization and of freedom from community norms.

To test the reformulated model, we computed the proportions of the votes obtained for each party in each community of the province in the 1962 federal election. Moreover, indicators of social integration and of economic strains were obtained. With regard to the former, the size of the communities[15] was used; it can readily be assumed that overall and despite variations in class structures, small communities are more integrated than large ones,[16] because in the former the interactions are more frequent and the contacts are closer in the pursuit of people's daily activities.[17] As an indicator of economic strains, the net migration between 1956 and 1961 for each federal district was obtained from the 1961 Census[18] and assigned to every community in a district.[19] As suggested before, a high degree of out-migration in a district is a good indicator of a labor force surplus and of lagging economic conditions. Finally, as an indicator of the stage of growth of the new movement in each district, we used the actual proportion of votes the new party obtained in 1962 in that district.

The theory of mass politics would lead one to predict a positive relationship

15 As indicated by the number of electors in 1962 in each community (all Canadians 21 years of age and older are registered in a door-to-door canvass prior to each election). Since the size of communities was taken as an indicator of social integration, "sociological" communities rather than "legal" ones had to be considered. Adjacent legal communities (e.g., separated by a street) in a larger community had therefore to be grouped together. This was done on the basis of personal knowledge and with the aid of detailed maps. In some cases, however, it was difficult to reach a judgment, and therefore some errors were certainly introduced in the process. Further, some communities belonged in part to two or more districts, the Montreal Metropolitan area being an outstanding example: these were left out of the analysis (which meant that all the legal communities of the Montreal and Quebec Metropolitan areas were excluded, with a few others). This was done since it would have been questionable to add the votes of a given party cast for different candidates in different districts. With these excluded, the coding process of communities yielded a N of 1609 communities, which is used in the foregoing analysis.

16 In the case of communities, however, one could distinguish between two types of social integration: the within-community integration, which is here considered, but also the between-communities integration, that is, the extent to which a community is integrated with the larger social system. We are implicitly assuming the same degree of the latter type of integration for all communities; for instance, we assume that the new movement diffused to all communities at the same time, and we look at what happened then within each community. But it is not unlikely that some small remote communities were reached later by the new movement.

17 The size of the communities as an indicator of social attachments, though a remote one, was used in Pinard, "Social Attachments and Political Support in Urban Politics."

18 Recomputed from data given by counties. Dominion Bureau of Statistics, *1961 Census of Canada*, Bulletin 7.1-1, Table 2.

19 Obviously, this is only a very rough indicator; it would have been much better to get the net migration for each community, since large communities tend to be more prosperous (see Lemieux, "The Election in the Constituency of Lévis," p. 50). But the data are not available.

between community size and support of a new movement: the larger the community, the more atomized its population is; hence the greater the chances of a new movement.[20] When community size in rural Quebec was related to the percentage who voted Social Credit, however, no relationship emerged at that crude level.[21]

To test our own model, on the other hand, we would need to differentiate communities in terms of their social climate; but no such data are available. It was suggested, however, that under severe strains, the community climate should become alienated. Under such circumstances, the more integrated communities—the small communities—should become stronger supporters of the new movement during its early stages of growth, due to greater mobilizing and communicating effects. Only under mild strains, during the early stages, would we expect integrated communities to better resist a new movement, because of stronger restraining effects.

To test this, each of the fifty electoral districts retained for this analysis was classified according to the existing degree of strains and to the stage of growth of the movement (Table 11.4). Then correlation coefficients between the percent Social Credit in the communities and their size were computed *for each district*. It can be seen from that table that in the early stages of growth of the new movement, when strains were mild, it tended to be more successful in *large* communities than in small ones, as indicated by the preponderance of positive

Table 11.4

*During the Early Stages, When under Strains, Small Communities Were
Stronger Supporters of Social Credit than Large Ones*

STAGES OF GROWTH IN DISTRICT*	STRAINS IN DISTRICTS**	% DISTRICTS WITH A POSITIVE CORRELATION COEFFICIENT BETWEEN COMMUNITY SIZE AND PROPORTION SOCIAL CREDIT	
Early	Low	64	(11)
"	Medium	56	(9)
"	High	17	(6)
Late	Low	100	(6)
"	Medium	67	(9)
"	High	67	(9)

*Stages of growth: early: Social Credit obtained less than 35 percent of the votes in the district; late stages: it obtained more than 35 percent.

**Strains: low: net in-migration between 1956 and 1961 in the district; medium: net out-migration smaller than 8 percent; high: net out-migration of 8 percent or more.

[20] For some qualifications regarding urbanization, however, see Kornhauser, *The Politics of Mass Society*, pp. 143–50.

[21] The correlation coefficient between the size of each community and its percent Social Credit was +.01.

correlation coefficients. But with the presence of strains, the proportion of posi-tive correlation coefficients declines sharply, indicating that *small* communities were relatively stronger supporters of the new movement than large ones. Finally, as stated in the previous chapter, at later stages, correlation coefficients tended to be generally positive: large communities again became stronger sup-porters of the new movement, suggesting that integration was no longer neces-sary for diffusion.[22] These findings clearly support the new model. At the beginning, when there are no strains, the movement is more successful among less integrated communities, as predicted by mass theorists; but it remains weak. On the other hand, if the strains are severe, at that stage, integrated communities appear as more conducive grounds for the diffusion of the movement, contrary to the claims of mass theorists. Only later do large communities regain their greater conduciveness.

There is another way of looking at these data. We should expect that wher-ever the new party remained very weak, the restraining effects must have been strong, and particularly so the smaller the community. Under such circum-stances, the new party, though weak, should have been slightly more successful in large communities and operationally our correlation coefficients should be more clearly positive. However, where the diffusion of the new party started gaining momentum, our correlation coefficients should tend to become negative, due to stronger mobilizing and communicating effects in small communities. Finally, wherever the party became very strong, the diffusion through social networks must have come to an end and the remaining restraining effects should render small communities again less responsive to the new movement; that is, the coefficients should tend to become positive again. This is what Table 11.5 establishes. The mean correlation coefficients go from positive in the early stages to negative in the intermediate stages to positive again in later stages.[23]

In short, it is *only when a new movement is weak* or *when the social diffusion is more or less completed* that well-integrated communities are more resistant to it than less-integrated ones. *When a movement is in its period of intense growth, well-integrated communities become in fact easier targets than others.*[24]

---

22 The details of these computations can be found in the author's doctoral dissertation, *The Rise of a Third Party*, The John Hopkins University, 1967, Table 11.13. Instead of computing correlation coefficients, one can cross-tabulate the outcome in each community (the party obtaining the plurality) by the size of the community, holding constant both stages of growth and strains, as in Table 11.4. This procedure yielded the same relationship (see *ibid.*, Table 11.14).

23 The drop in the mean correlation coefficient in the "very late" stage may indicate that beyond a certain point, the community structure should cease having any effect whatsoever.

24 It is not correct, therefore, to conclude that in general "the city (was) needed as the hub for the communication of Social Credit propaganda"; see Irvine, "An Analysis of Voting Shifts in Quebec," p. 133. Nor can Lemieux' opposite finding of a negative relationship between size and percent Social Credit in one district be generalized; see Lemieux, "The Election in the Constituency of Lévis," pp. 42ff., p. 50. Notice that Lemieux relates his finding to both greater strains and easier diffusion due to stronger attachments in small communities. *Ibid.*, p. 50.

Table 11.5

*Small Communities Were More Conducive to Social Credit during the
Stages of Intense Growth*

STAGES OF GROWTH*	MEAN CORRELATION COEFFICIENT BETWEEN COMMUNITY SIZE AND PERCENT SOCIAL CREDIT	N (districts)
Very Early	+.09	(6)
Moderately Early	+.05	(7)
Early	−.13	(8)
Late	+.10	(5)
Moderately Late	+.17	(12)
Very Late	+.07	(7)

*Stages of growth: very early: actual Social Credit vote in district smaller than 15 percent; moderately early: between 15 and 24 percent; early: between 25 and 34 percent; late: between 35 and 44 percent; moderately late: between 45 and 54 percent; very late: 55 percent or larger.

This, as already mentioned, is in agreement with Irving's account of the upsurge of Social Credit in Alberta during the thirties. Given the depression, the new movement, he reports, spread in rural areas "like a prairie fire",[25] with Social Credit "groups (springing) up like mushrooms."[26] This is also in agreement with Pratt's finding that the Nazi party in Germany was more successful in 1932 (again during the Great Depression) in rural than in urban areas and in smaller than in larger cities.[27] As Lipset put it, these findings "sharply challenge the various interpretations of Nazism as the product of the growth of *anomie* and the general rootlessness of modern urban industrial society."[28]

These data, furthermore, shed some additional light on the relative weakness of Social Credit in the Montreal metropolitan area. Recall for instance that the highest percentage the new movement obtained in the twenty-one districts of the Island of Montreal was 17 percent in Montreal-Mercier.[29] The huge size of this community[30] and its more highly atomized social structure certainly

[25] Irving, *The Social Credit Movement in Alberta*, p. 109.

[26] Irving, *The Social Credit Movement in Alberta*, p. 105. Notice that the core of the movement originated in a large community, Calgary, but the problem considered here is that of the early success in mass recruitment.

[27] Pratt, *The Social Basis of Nazism*. Similar findings are reported in Heberle, *Social Movements*, p. 232.

[28] Lipset, *Political Man*, p. 146. Lipset also reports that the supporters of Father Coughlin's movement during the thirties came disproportionately from rural areas and small towns. See his "Three Decades of the Radical Right: Coughlinites, McCarthyites and Birchers," p. 384.

[29] While the party's vote ranged between 6 and 11 percent in ten other districts, and was 5 percent or less in the remaining ten districts.

[30] According to the 1961 census, the Montreal metropolitan area had a population of 2,109,509, that is 40 percent of the population of the province of Quebec (5,259,211).

makes for a very low degree of social restraints; but at the same time the diffusion of a new movement could not but be extremely slow in such a loosely-knit structure.[31]

HIGH CONSENSUS IN SMALL COMMUNITIES

In addition to the analysis just presented, the community data allow us to test an inference from the revised model. If it is true that a more integrated social system can be both a source of greater constraints against a new social movement and a more appropriate milieu for mobilization and communication, that is, that integrated communities can develop both stronger negative and positive norms, and if it is also true that depending on the amount of grievances, one of the two opposite sets of effects will dominate, one should expect smaller communities to exhibit a higher degree of consensus or unanimity for or against a new movement than larger communities. In other words, due to these two strong sets of effects, one would expect a negative relationship between the size of the communities and the degree of voting consensus.[32] These ideas have been substantiated in routine politics. Lipset, Trow, and Coleman found a greater degree of voting consensus in small union shops than in large ones.[33] Similarly, in a study of fluoridation referendums, we found that small communities were more likely to be strongly for or strongly against fluoridation than large ones.[34]

Furthermore, since conversion to a new movement under conditions of strains is more likely to produce intense sentiments[35] and passionate debates than the choice between old parties—and the more so, the smaller the community—

[31] To be sure, many movements have generally been more successful in urban than in rural areas, as, for instance, socialist and communist movements. This, we suggest, is due to many other factors which counteract the conduciveness of rural social structures under strains. Examples of such factors are the emergence of leadership for these movements in urban areas, their organizational strength, and their mobilization drive in such areas, as well as differences in ideology (affecting mainly the elites). Our point, however, is that, with everything else constant, under conditions of strains, a movement will grow bigger and faster in rural than in urban areas. Compare with Lipset, *Political Man.* pp. 145-146, 249-252 and with Kornhauser, *The Politics of Mass Society*, pp. 143-150.

[32] As mentioned before, an interesting aspect of this greater consensus in small communities was revealed by the finding that in these communities the movement was less likely than in large communities to be confined to the middle-income group (Table 8.9).

[33] Lipset, Trow, and Coleman, *Union Democracy*, pp. 166ff.

[34] Pinard, "Social Attachments and Political Support." In that paper, however, we failed to specify the conditions under which smaller communities would be strongly for *or* strongly against the proposal; see also Heberle, *Social Movements*, p. 228.

[35] On this, see Jean Burnet, *Next-Year Country* (Toronto: University of Toronto Press, 1951), pp. 147-148; Irving, *The Social Credit Movement in Alberta*, pp. 283-288. Part of these intense sentiments may be due to the ambiguity or uncertainty accompanying the adoption of a new party, and Coleman and his colleagues reported that under conditions of greater ambiguity, group solidarity in the decision tended to be stronger; see James S. Coleman, Elihu Katz, and Herbert Menzel, *Medical Innovation: A Diffusion Study* (The Bobbs-Merrill Company, Inc., 1966), Chap. 8, esp. pp. 120ff.

we should expect the negative relationship to be stronger when the communities turned Social Credit (for instance, gave a majority to that party) than when they favored one of the old parties.

These ideas can be tested with the aggregate data. To measure the degree of voting consensus, an index of voting unanimity in the 1962 federal election was computed for each community of the province of Quebec.[36] The higher the value of this index, the greater is the degree of unanimity. The data presented in Table 11.6 substantiate the first inference. Though the index is subject to greater variations in small communities, it is clear that unanimity was greater in small than in large communities.[37]

Moreover, when the communities were divided into three groups, according to which party obtained the plurality in a community, the same relationship

Table 11.6

The Degree of Unanimity Was Greater in Smaller Communities

INDEX OF VOTING UNANIMITY*	NUMBER OF ELECTORS					
	LESS THAN 100 %	100– 249 %	250– 499 %	500– 999 %	1000– 2499 %	2500 OR MORE %
Very Low	27	17	16	18	14	19
Low	19	31	37	38	43	43
Medium	24	34	32	35	36	34
High	30	18	14	9	8	3
N (communities) =	(111)	(369)	(472)	(430)	(169)	(58)

*See footnote 36, below; very low: less than .34; low: .34 to .39; medium: .40 to .49; high: .50 or more.

[36] The index of voting unanimity, the values of which range between o and 1, is as follows:

Let a community divide its votes between i candidates, each one receiving $n_1, n_2, \ldots, n_i$ votes.

Each member of any n_i group of voters acted in a way consistent with all other members of that group, so that the number of consistent vote relationships for any i candiate is:

$$n_i(n_i - 1);$$

and the total number of consistent vote relationships for all candidates of a community is:

$$R_c = \sum_1^i n_i(n_i - 1).$$

But the total number of vote relationships in a community is simply the total number of potential relationships in a community, that is:

$$R_t = n(n - 1),$$

(while the number of inconsistent vote relationships is $R_t - R_c$).

The index of voting unanimity is the number of consistent vote relationships divided by the total number of vote relationships, that is:

$$I = R_c/R_t.$$

I am indebted to James S. Coleman who suggested this index.

[37] For the data presented in that Table, we obtained a correlation coefficient of $-.07$ (N = 1609). Since large values of our independent variable have strong effects on r, all communities with 2,500 electors or more were then excluded and a correlation coefficient of $-.12$ was obtained (N = 1550).

was clearly maintained (Table 11.7). But the main interest of this last Table lies elsewhere: it indicates, as predicted, that when Social Credit obtained the plurality in a community, this community was more likely to approach unanimity than when one of the two old parties did. For every community size, a larger proportion of communities reached a high degree of consensus when Social Credit obtained the plurality than when one of the two old parties did; and the smaller the communities, the greater the differences.[38] The community norms were more effective and the consensus reached was greater when a community was under the spell of the new movement than when it was dominated by traditional parties. The inferences drawn from the reformulated model are therefore strongly supported by community data.

Table 11.7

The Degree of Unanimity Was Greater When the Community
Gave a Plurality ot Social Credit

INDEX OF VOTING UNANIMITY*	NUMBER OF ELECTORS				
	LESS THAN 100	100– 249	250– 499	500– 999	1000+
	Social Credit Plurality in Community				
Low	38	44	48	52	49
Medium	19	29	27	34	40
High	43	27	25	14	12
N (communities) =	(53)	(168)	(218)	(168)	(111)
	Conservative Plurality in Community				
Low	54	50	56	53	64
Medium	31	42	39	40	33
High	15	8	5	7	4
N (communities) =	(26)	(105)	(131)	(137)	(52)
	Liberal Plurality in Community				
Low	53	54	60	65	70
Medium	28	32	34	31	30
High	19	14	6	4	0
N (communities) =	(32)	(96)	(123)	(125)	(64)

*Low: less than .40; medium: .40 to .49; high: .50 or more.

OCCUPATIONAL ORGANIZATIONS

As mentioned earlier, for some proponents of mass society theory, what characterizes a mass society is the weakness of the intermediate relations, "no-

[38] These relationships were maintained when the degree of strains (net-migration in the districts) was introduced as an additional control, though the relationships were much stronger under severe strains.

tably the local community, voluntary association, and occupational group."[39] Some aspects of the impact of the local community have just been considered. Let us now turn first to the influence of occupational organizations and then to that of other associations and organizations.

With regard to occupational organizations, consider first the data of Table 11.8. They strongly challenge the idea that all occupational groups act as a rampart against a new movement. If non-manuals were more likely to resist Social Credit when members of professional associations,[40] the relationship runs significantly in the opposite direction among farmers and workers. Participants in farmers' associations and labor unions were *more* likely to have voted Social Credit than nonparticipants, contrary to the prediction of mass theory.[41] Notice, furthermore, that in the working-class groups, the lower the status, the greater the differences between members and nonmembers.[42] In addition, other parts of our data indicate that in these two groups, *active* members of occupational organizations were more likely to have voted Social Credit than *nonactive* members.[43]

With regard to farmers and working-class groups, our findings support, we suggest, the proposition that members of *alienated* organizations are more likely to support a social movement than nonmembers, and that the greater the integration into an alienated organization, the greater the likelihood that they will do so. Given the severe strains prevailing in these two groups, labor unions and farmers' organizations, already not too conformist, became seriously alienated, according to the process described above. During the election campaign, many of their secondary leaders, at the local level, became strong supporters and even

39 Kornhauser, *The Politics of Mass Society*, p. 74; see also pp. 177ff., pp. 207ff.

40 Comparing white-collars who were nonmembers with white-collars in professional associations only (see note of Table 11.8), the difference (.13) is highly significant ($p < .0001$).

41 Alford also reports that Quebec respondents who had a trade union member in the family were more likely to intend to vote Social Credit (41 percent) than others (24 percent) (N's equal to 138 and 412 respectively); see Alford, "The Social Bases of Political Cleavage in 1962," pp. 222–223. The paradox of the success of this anti-union party among union workers had also been noted at an earlier period; see Pierre E. Trudeau, "La Province de Québec au moment de la grève," in Pierre E. Trudeau, ed., *La grève de l'amiante*, p. 71.

42 Since union workers are in many respects different from non-union workers, many test factors were introduced in the relationship of Table 11.8. For instance, union workers are more likely to be in the middle-income group (while non-members are more concentrated in the lower and higher-income groups); they are more likely to identify themselves as working-class, have a higher degree of political information, and are more politically involved than non-union workers. However, none of these factors changed the initial relationship. (We have seen however in Table 8.9 that membership in labor and trade associations did not increase the Social Credit support of low-income respondents who were not affected by unemployment).

43 Considering farmers and workers as one group, the proportions who voted Social Credit are 37 percent (N = 68) among the active members and 31 percent (N = 93) among the nonactive members (22 percent (N = 238) of the nonmembers voted Social Credit). Activity is defined in terms of attendance at the meetings of the organization and of interest in the latter. Notice that in the Freedom Rides study, we also found that members of more than one alienated organization were more active and earlier joiners than members of only one such organization. Von Eschen *et al.*, "The Organizational Substructure of Disorderly Politics."

Table 11.8

Participation in Occupational Organizations Did Not
Necessarily Prevent Voting Social Credit

OCCUPATIONAL GROUPS:	NON-MANUALS		FARMERS		SKILLED WORKERS		SEMI-SKILLED WORKERS		UNSKILLED & SERVICE WORKERS	
MEMBERSHIP IN OCCUPATIONAL ORGANIZATIONS:*	NO %	YES %	NO %	YES %	NO %	YES %	NO %	YES %	NO %	YES %
Social Credit**	13	9	30	42	21	24	24	39	12	44
Conservative	34	20	37	8	29	32	35	30	40	12
Liberal	51	68	33	50	47	42	37	32	42	44
N.D.P.	2	2	0	0	3	2	4	0	5	0
N =	(147)	(44)	(60)	(12)	(92)	(66)	(46)	(57)	(40)	(25)

*Membership in a professional association, a trade association, or a labor union. In the case of the non-manuals 13 are in professional associations (none of whom voted Social Credit), and 31 are in trade associations or labor unions (13% of whom voted Social Credit).

**a_1 (negative effect of occupational groups among non-manuals) = .04; $p(a_1^* \leq 0)$ = .22 (see also footnote 40, p. 208);

a_2 (average positive effect of occupational groups among workers and farmers) = $\frac{1}{4}(.12 + .03 + .15 + .32)$ = .155; $p(a_2^* \leq 0)$ = .003.

organizers of the new party.[44] The economic situation previously described was considered so bad that it pushed the organizations themselves into alienation; hence the positive effect on Social Credit support, as predicted. To be sure, the central leadership of labor unions in Quebec came to realize, though relatively late in the campaign, what was going on in their locals and started their own campaign against Social Credit. They emphasized that the new movement was a right-wing party opposed to almost everything unions stood for and that their members should oppose it.[45] But presumably it was already too late; with the low ideological sophistication of their members, a split had divided the unions between central leadership on one side and local leadership and following on the other side.[46]

It is interesting to note that existing organizations played a similar role in the rise of the C.C.F. in Saskatchewan, though it is a party which stands at the opposite end of the traditional political spectrum. Lipset convincingly argues that the high degree of participation in various community organizations was an important condition for the rise of the C.C.F. party, and he found that "the members of class organizations were the leaders and first supporters of the C.C.-F."[47] And he added that "when the attitudes of a class are in flux, because of changing social and economic pressures, those who are most thoroughly integrated in the class through formal organizations are the first to change. In Saskatchewan it was the *local* leaders of the Wheat Pool, of the trade-unions, who were the first to join the C.C.F. . . . The unorganized mass became C.C.F. supporters only gradually, following the organizationally active members of their class. . . . When a large social class or group is changing its attitudes, the normal integrated leaders of the class are the first to change. They are more exposed to the social pressures on the class than are marginal, deviant, or apathetic members."[48]

It is of interest, moreover, to note that participation in alienated organizations seems to be a sufficient condition to join a movement. As can be seen in

[44] This assessment is based on newspaper reports. At least four of the Social Credit candidates (out of 75) were union members or union organizers, according to biographical sketches of the candidates published by the Social Credit Montreal organization (mimeo, no date).

[45] A last-minute denunciation of Social Credit was made by Mr. Jean Marchand, then Chairman of the C.S.N. (*Confédération des Syndicats Nationaux*) on June 11, only one week before the polling of June 18. He was followed by some other union leaders on the last days of the campaign (as well as by some other civic leaders). (See Léon Dion, "The Election in the Province of Quebec," p. 120). One may wonder, however, if these last-minute appeals did not reveal a state of panic on the part of the elites and thus strengthened the belief, among followers and waverers, that the movement was a strong potential alternative to the old parties.

[46] Following the election, a public discussion took place between the central leaders and the local leaders who had supported Social Credit. While some of the latter revised their position, many stood by it.

[47] Lipset, *Agrarian Socialism*, Chap. 10. Quotation from p. 197.

[48] Lipset, *Agrarian Socialism*, pp. 197-198 (italics provided). The same thing holds in the case of the farmers' parties; and again it seems that the local leadership was the first to veer away from routine politics. This is at least what happened during the rise of the United Farmers of Alberta; see Macpherson, *Democracy in Alberta*, esp. pp. 38ff.

Table 11.9, all members of trade associations or labor unions tended to be strong supporters of Social Credit, whether under strains or not. On the contrary, nonmembers had to be under strains to become strong supporters. Therefore a pluralist society with an elaborate intermediate structure, but where there are serious grievances, can see many of its organizations become alienated. To the extent that their membership is large and given that relatively large proportions of this membership, whether deprived or not, tend to be strongly attracted to a new movement, a pluralist society is highly susceptible to such a movement.[49]

Table 11.9

Strains Are Not Necessary among Members of Alienated Organizations
(% Social Credit)

WORKERS' AND FARMERS' PARTICIPATION IN OCCUPATIONAL ORGANIZATIONS:	STRAINS*		
	LOW	MOD-ERATE	HIGH
Yes	40 (50)	33 (46)	30 (63)
No	12 (77)	22 (58)	30 (99)

*Index of economic conditions: low: scores 0 and 1; moderate: score 2; high: scores 3 and 4.

VOLUNTARY ASSOCIATIONS AND OTHER ORGANIZATIONS

If workers' unions and farmers' associations became alienated and served as bases on which the new movement rose, what about the voluntary associations and other organizations which are said to be so crucial in preventing the rise of political movements?

In this study, respondents were asked if apart from occupational organizations, they "belong to other associations, clubs or various movements, such as social, religious, cultural, civic, or political associations" and if there were "other groups which (they) meet quite regularly, such as card clubs, golf clubs, recreation centers, or similar groups." These two questions provide us with a measure of voluntary association participation. Moreover, our data allow us to consider two other specific forms of organizational participation. On the one hand, since practically all our respondents, as expected, mentioned some religious affiliation, we also measured their degree of religious involvement with the following two questions: "In general, people are not all religiously inclined

[49] It is also noteworthy that the positive relationship between membership and Social Credit support among workers and farmers stands independently of whether these people were in a favorable or unfavorable primary group climate. Also see Von Eschen et al., Proposition 3 and Table 3.

to the same degree: as for yourself, do you go to church more than once a week, once a week, not every week, rarely, or never?" and "Apart from going to church, do you happen to pray God practically every day, a few times a week only, a few times a month only, less often, or practically never"?[50] On the other hand, we have measures of the degree of involvement in the polity and in particular, measures of political opinion leadership and of political information.[51] The latter data, in particular, should constitute a hard test for the theory of mass politics: indeed, involvement in the polity itself should be one of the strongest sources of restraints against political movements. However, if even those who are politically active citizens can at times be early recruits of a new political movement, then some other variables than organizational restraint must be taken into account by the theory.

As mentioned before, Lipset's analysis of the rise of the C.C.F. in Saskatchewan strongly suggests that this is necessary. He attributed much of the success of the new movement to an especially high degree of grass-roots participation in community organizations, which "provides direct channels of communications between the mass of farmers and their leaders." But this structure of organizations "in turn provided a structural basis for immediate action *in critical situations.*"[52] Moreover, there are suggestions that even membership in an incumbent political party does not render one immune to a new political movement. In his analysis of the rise of Social Credit in Alberta, Irving reports that in some locals of the incumbent party, the United Farmers of Alberta, "the entire membership, apart from the officials (went) over en masse to the Social Credit movement." But even the officials were not completely immune: ". . . In a number of instances most or even all of the officials of U.F.A. locals rejoined their followers by rushing into the Social Credit movement with them, thus leaving the U.F.A. without even a skeleton organization in their communities."[53] Similarly, in his study of one electoral district in Quebec, Lemieux found that "several organizers had left the Conservative for the Social Credit party before the campaign began."[54]

[50] Since 93 percent of the respondents are Catholics (the Quebec population, according to the 1961 census, was 88 percent Catholics), and since none of the non-Catholics in the sample (most of them are Montreal Protestants) voted Social Credit, only Catholics will be considered when analyzing these data.

[51] As a direct measure of political involvement, one would wish to consider membership in any of the two old political parties. But since Canadian political parties are cadre parties and membership is restricted to very few, this is not possible. (A recent study indicates that only 4.3 percent of all Canadians belong to a political organization; see John Meisel and Richard Van Loon, "Canadian Attitudes to Election Expenses 1965–1966," in Committee on Election Expenses, *Studies in Canadian Party Finance* (Ottawa: Queen's Printer, 1966), p. 46).

[52] Lipset, *Agrarian Socialism*, p. 203, p. 206. (Italics provided.)

[53] Irving, *The Social Credit Movement in Alberta*, p. 273. We have mentioned earlier the very high degree of formal social participation reported by Social Credit candidates (see Chap. 7, p. 135, footnote 57). See also Stein, *The Dynamics of Political Protest*.

[54] Lemieux, "The Election in the Constituency of Lévis," p. 39. Lemieux adds: "One of them . . . told us how, when people saw him coming into a house, they would say, believing that he was still a Conservative: 'This year, we are not voting for you, we are voting for Social Credit.' He would reply that he, too, was voting Social Credit!" *Ibid.*

More generally, it was found that radical right crusaders were more likely to be members (and to have a somewhat higher level of membership) in all kinds of organizations than other people.[55] Similarly, militancy in the Black community was found to be positively related to social participation and, in particular, to organizational membership.[56] Moreover, given the widespread view that American ghetto riots reflected the lack of *social* integration of the Negro lower-class, it is interesting to report that in one study, it was found that isolated ghetto dwellers were not necessarily more likely to think that violent means would be necessary to enable Negroes to attain equal rights. If active church members were less violence-oriented than others, active participants in other types of associations were *more* violence-oriented than nonparticipants, and so were regular newspaper readers.[57] The type of effects observed, therefore, varied with the presumed orientation to violence of these components of the intermediate structure.

Turning to our data, the results are presented in Table 11.10. In two instances —membership in voluntary associations and opinion leadership—there appears to be no relationship between integration into the intermediate structure and support for the new movement. In a third instance—religious involvement— the relationship is partly positive:[58] both the ritualists and the devouts were more likely to have voted Social Credit than the lukewarms[59] (who are incidentally in a small minority and were probably considered as deviants, at least in rural areas).[60] With the last measure—political information—the relationship appears to be curvilinear.[61] How can we interpret this set of apparently inconsistent zero-order relationships?

55 In fact, they were more active than usually active people, that is, business, professional, and white-collar respondents; see Raymond E. Wolfinger, Barbara Kaye Wolfinger, Kenneth Prewitt, and Sheila Rosenback, "America's Radical Right: Politics and Ideology," in David E. Apter, ed., *Ideology and Discontent*, p. 276.

56 Gary T. Marx, *Protest and Prejudice*, pp. 70ff. Similarly, Black nationalist sympathizers, though an infinitesimal minority, were more active participants than conservative Negroes; *ibid.*, Table 74, p. 121.

57 J. R. Feagin, "Social Sources of Support for Violence and Nonviolence in a Negro Ghetto," *Social Problems*, 15 (Spring 1968), pp. 432–41, esp. pp. 438–39. These results, moreover, do not seem to be an artifact of differential educational achievement since the less educated were more violence-oriented than the more educated (except possibly for the very small college group in that sample); *ibid.*, p. 430.

58 This finding seems to be different from that reported in other instances. For example, the Catholic Church was one of the strongest restraining factors in the rise of Hitlerism. See Samuel A. Pratt, *The Social Basis of Nazism and Communism*. But it must be added that the Catholic Church in Germany was complemented by a Catholic party, as well as by its own trade-unions, peasants' associations, and people's unions in the cities; see *ibid.* In Quebec, of course, all parties are *de facto* Catholic.

59 The ritualists are those who adhere to the formal norms of the Catholic Church, which prescribes that members go to church once a week and pray God daily; the lukewarms do less than that and the devouts go to church more often; for details, see Appendix C.

60 That religiosity can act to inhibit as well as to inspire protest has often been noted; for a recent statement, see Gary T. Marx, "Religion: Opiate or Inspiration of Civil Rights Militancy among Negroes?," *American Sociological Review*, 32 (1967), pp. 64–72.

61 When income is introduced as a test factor, this curvilinear relationship is not affected at all; it does not seem therefore to be simply an alternative demonstration of the curvilinear income relationship.

Table 11.10

The Impact of Various Forms of Organizational
Participation on Social Credit

	INDEX OF MEMBERSHIP IN VOLUNTARY ASSOCIATIONS*		
	NONE	YES-ONCE	YES-TWICE
% Social Credit	22 (392)	22 (166)	19 (64)

	INDEX OF RELIGIOUS INVOLVEMENT (Catholics only)**		
	LUKEWARMS	RITUALISTS	DEVOUTS
% Social Credit	16 (111)	26 (311)	23 (154)

	POLITICAL OPINION LEADERSHIP***	
	FOLLOWERS	OPINION LEADERS
% Social Credit	22 (479)	20 (146)

	INDEX OF POLITICAL INFORMATION****				
	VERY LOW	LOW	MODERATE	HIGH	VERY HIGH
% Social Credit	21 (153)	22 (101)	28 (195)	15 (88)	16 (92)

*The indices are described in Appendix C. Index of membership in voluntary associations: none: score 0; yes, once: score 1; yes, twice: score 2.
**Index of Religious Involvement: lukewarms: scores 4 to 7; ritualists: score 3; devouts: scores 1 and 2.
***In answer to Q. 1-75, in Appendix B; those who answered "no" are classified as followers; those who answered "yes," as opinion leaders.
****Index of Political Information: very low: score 0; low: score 1; moderate: score 2; high: score 3; very high: score 4.

First, these results are far from giving unambiguous support to the mass society theory. There is no consistent pattern of negative relationships between involvement in the organizations and Social Credit support.

But the reader will remember that according to the new model the effect expected depends first on the climate of the organization or institution considered, but also, if the organization is conformist, on the amount of strains and on the stage of growth or diffusion of the new movement. In the present instance, we do not possess any direct measure of these organizations' climate in the respondents' immediate environment, even though it is common knowledge that the traditional religious, civic and political elites were not, at the higher levels at least, favorable to the new movement; in fact they often remained neutral. Short of such a measure, we shall shortly consider the effects of these organizations in conjunction with the climate of the respondents' primary group, a factor which was shown earlier to be very important. We do possess, however, a measure of strains endured by our respondents and a measure of the stage of growth of the movement in each respondent's community.

Recall that when aggregate measures of these last two factors at the district level were introduced in the analysis of the effects of community structures, the lack of relationship at the zero-order level gave way to a set of relationships predicted by the new model: in the early stages, under strains, integration was found to be positively related to Social Credit support; it was negatively related under other conditions (see Table 11.4). When these two factors are now considered simultaneously with the data of Table 11.10, the results which emerge, however, do not allow any firm conclusion.

With regard to voluntary association participation, these additional variables barely affect the zero-order relationship (see Table 11.11, first panel) and though the data tend to replicate the predicted set of relationships observed in Table 11.4,[62] the relationships are very weak and generally not statistically significant. Insofar as religious involvement is concerned, the additional variables also do not generally affect the positive association observed at the zero-order level (Table 11.11, second panel). To be sure, there is, as expected, a reversal to a negative relationship in the absence of strains during the early stages, but it is not statis-

Table 11.11

The Effects of Voluntary Associations and Religious Involvement
with Strains and Stages of Growth Constant
(% Social Credit)

STRAINS:*	LOW		HIGH	
STAGES OF GROWTH:**	EARLY	LATE	EARLY	LATE
Membership in Voluntary Associations:***				
No	10	32	11	48
	(105)	(37)	(151)	(94)
Yes	2	30	14	39
	(54)	(43)	(66)	(64)
Religious Involvement:****				
Lukewarms	13	25	10	32
	(32)	(12)	(48)	(19)
Others	8	33	13	47
	(102)	(69)	(152)	(136)

*Index of economic conditions: low: scores 0 and 1; high: scores 2 to 4.
**Stages of growth: early: actual Social Credit vote in the respondents' *community* smaller than 30 percent: late: larger than 30 percent.
***a_1 (effect of voluntary associations in early stages, under low strains) = .08; $p(a_1^* \leq 0)$ = .01. (This is the only effect of voluntary associations which is significant at the .05 level.)
****None of the effects of religious involvement is significant at the .05 level.

62 In particular, the slightly positive relationship between involvement in voluntary associations and Social Credit support during the early stages of growth and under strains. For a related finding of the same nature, see pp. 240–241 and Table 12.9.

tically significant and there are no reversals at later stages. Finally, with regard to opinion leadership and political information, the relationships of Table 11.10 were not clearly altered by the introduction of these two additional variables.[63]

Table 11.12

Specification of the Effects of Organizational Participation According to Primary Group Climates
(% Social Credit)

	INDEX OF PRIMARY GROUP CLIMATE		
	UNFAVORABLE*	INTERMEDIATE	FAVORABLE**
Membership in Voluntary Associations:			
None	10	26	30
	(125)	(136)	(97)
Yes—Once	11	25	38
	(53)	(59)	(39)
Yes—Twice	11	21	45
	(36)	(14)	(11)
Religious Involvement (Catholics Only):			
Lukewarms	12	19	17
	(41)	(32)	(29)
Ritualists	12	26	41
	(92)	(120)	(82)
Devouts	10	36	35
	(58)	(45)	(31)
Opinion Leadership:			
Followers	12	26	31
	(154)	(168)	(108)
Opinion Leaders	8	24	38
	(61)	(41)	(40)
Political Information:*			
Low	14	24	28
	(72)	(83)	(75)
Moderate	10	31	48
	(62)	(78)	(44)
High	9	18	26
	(82)	(50)	(31)

*a_1 (negative effect of opinion leadership, under unfavorable climate) = .04; $p(a_1^* \leq 0)$ = .21; a_2 (negative effect of political information, under unfavorable climate, comparing extremes) = .05; $p(a_2^* \leq 0)$ = .15.

**a_3 (positive effect of voluntary associations, under favorable climate, comparing "none" to all "yes") = .40 − .30 = .10; $p(a_3^* \leq 0)$ = .11.

a_4 (positive effect of religious involvement, under favorable climate, comparing extremes) = .18; $p(a_4^* \leq 0)$ = .05.

a_5 (positive effect of opinion leadership, under favorable climate) = .07; $p(a_5^* \leq 0)$ = .21.

***Index of Political Information: low: scores 0 and 1; moderate: score 2; high: scores 3 and 4.

[63] With regard to opinion leadership, the results were like those obtained with voluntary association participation, and with regard to political information, the relationships remained curvilinear.

However, if instead of strains and stages of growth, the climate of each respondent's primary group is introduced as an additional variable, some quite interesting and consistent relationships emerge (Table 11.12). What were the inconsistent relationships of Table 11.10 give way to two striking patterns. On the one hand, when the primary group climate was presumably unfavorable to Social Credit, organizational involvement seems to have had either no effect at all or a slight negative effect (though the negative effects are not significant at standard levels). On the other hand, when the climate among the respondents' best friends was favorable to the new movement, positive relationships tend to emerge between organizational involvement and Social Credit support.[64] In particular and although the relationships fall short of standard significance levels, it is interesting to notice the effects of primary group climate on political opinion leaders. Clearly these opinion leaders are more strongly integrated in the polity, in mass theory terms, than their followers. We find that while under an unfavorable climate, opinion leaders were weaker supporters of Social Credit than followers, the contrary holds when they were under a favorable climate. Recall that we also found previously that among the young, opinion leaders were stronger supporters of the new movement than followers, and that this was also true under certain circumstances among older voters (Table 9.2). In other words, opinion leaders always conform more closely to the primary group's climate than followers, but in so doing and despite their greater degree of social integration, they are at times resistors, and at other times initiators, of change. This incidentally throws light on what might be called the leaders' paradox, that is, their ability to be both greater conformist to group norms and greater deviant than followers. The primary group's climate seems to be a key to this paradox.

In general, these findings suggest that whatever effect organizations exerted was via the channels of the respondents' primary groups and varied according to the climate of these groups. They further suggest that contrary to such intermediate groupings as primary groups, community structure and the polity, voluntary associations and the Church, in this specific instance, may have exerted little restraining pressure or else were avoided as reference groups,[65]

---

[64] Notice that these patterns are very similar to those of Table 11.3. In this regard, it is noteworthy that in Couch's study, there was a very strong positive association between interaction with peers and N.F.O. membership, when farmers had no or few contacts with extension agents (the latter were strongly committed to the status quo); but the association disappeared completely when the amount of contacts with agents was moderate or high. Thus, in the first case, among those who received no peer choices, one choice, or two or more choices, the proportions who were N.F.O. members were 20, 33, and 67 percent respectively (N's equal to 100, 49, and 21); in the second instance, these proportions were 15, 15, and 14 percent respectively (N's equal to 61, 52, and 55). Recomputed from C. J. Couch, "Interaction and Protest," Table 4. Quoted with Professor Couch's Permission.

[65] Mass theorists, to be sure, could argue that this makes one of their points: in modern mass societies, they would claim, these voluntary associations are too weak to refrain people from nonroutine politics. But our contention is either that they are too weak to exert *any* effect at all or, if they are strong enough, that they can, like primary groups, exert positive as well as negative effects; moreover, the effects they could exert in truly pluralist societies seem exaggerated. On this, consider again the negative findings of Holden in small rural communities; David E. W. Holden, "Associations as Reference Groups."

as often such associations seem to be.[66] They all could, however, under a favorable climate, exert mobilizing and/or communicating effects, which at times proved quite strong. All of this is highly consistent with the new model developed.

Before we conclude, a last comment on the effect of religious involvement must be entered. One could suggest that the success of Social Credit among the more religiously inclined Catholics is as should have been expected.[67] The movement was first introduced in Canada by a lay preacher and school teacher, William ("Bible Bill") Aberhart through the religious activities of his Bible Institute in Alberta, and up to this day the Alberta branch of the party has always kept some of its religious flavor.[68] Similarly, in the province of Quebec the early branch of the party, the *Union des Electeurs*, also developed the character of a religious-political movement. Though decreasingly political and increasingly religious, this movement still exists; as we have seen, it publishes a newspaper and it holds meetings throughout the province which are some form of Catholic religious revivals.

It must be stressed, however, that the movement, although supported by members of the clergy at the beginning, had its conflicts with the Catholic Church later on.[69] Moreover, since Réal Caouette and a few followers broke from that group to form the *Ralliement des Créditistes* in 1958, they abandoned completely the religious character of the former movement;[70] they definitely secularized it. Nevertheless, one could claim that the positive association between religious involvement and Social Credit simply reflects these religious aspects of the movement.

There may be some truth in this argument. It should not however be overemphasized, because of the Church's cool attitude toward the religious stances of the movement and because Caouette's appeals were totally secular. Moreover, the effects of religious involvement observed in the last tabulation are not different from the effects of other forms of organizational participation; in particular, religious involvement was ineffective under an unfavorable primary

---

[66] See *ibid.*

[67] Irvine commented that "there may even have been a religious aspect to this movement of the right. Many of the areas showing greatest Social Credit strength are places where the Roman Catholic clergy and hierarchy have kept to their traditional ideas with growing uneasiness caused by the attitudes of Cardinal Léger and Pope John XXIII"; W. P. Irvine, "The Analysis of Voting Shifts in Quebec," p. 130.

[68] Premier Aberhart and his present successor, Premier E. C. Manning, an early disciple, never gave up their weekly Sunday Bible lectures on radio; see also Meisel, *The Canadian General Election of 1957*, pp. 229–230.

[69] See Stein, *The Dynamics of Political Protest*.

[70] One of Caouette's prime reasons for breaking from the Union was its tendency to mix religion with politics; see Stein, *The Dynamics of Political Protest*. Caouette insisted in his public speeches that the two movements should be clearly distinguished, describing his ex-colleagues as "lunatics." ("Don't get fooled," he said in one of his speeches, "by people who believe in reaching Social Credit in the moon. Let us leave the lunatics to the moon, and let us be practical. . . .") See *Réal Caouette Vous Parle*, pp. 55–56.

group climate. All this leads us to believe that religious involvement acted at least in part like other forms of social participation and that the relationship between the former and Social Credit support probably did not result exclusively as a consequence of the religious orientations of the early branches of the movement.

CONCLUSIONS

Various views regarding the effects of mass conditions on political movements have been empirically tested with our data on Social Credit. It is clear, on the one hand, that the results do not support the unqualified propositions of the theory of mass society. From our evidence, it appears unwarranted, both theoretically and empirically, to hypothesize that social atomization is at the source of modern political movements.

We have, on the other hand, presented a set of data which go a long way in establishing the soundness of the reformulated model. In particular, all the propositions of our model have been supported when tested with aggregate data on community structures: thus we have verified the hypothesis that when strains are severe and widespread, a new movement is more likely to meet its early success among the more strongly integrated citizens. Similarly, the effects of primary groups and occupational organizations were in conformity with the new model. However, when employing data on participation in other organizations, the relationships we expected did not always result or, when they did result, were not statistically significant. Some would argue that that part of the new model is unsound. Our own sentiment, given the results just mentioned, is that the effects of these organizations were relatively weak, although they did not follow the predictions of mass theory. Further investigations are certainly needed on this point.

It must be stressed, however, that we have consistently shown the importance of the social climate prevailing in primary as well as secondary groupings. We have repeatedly demonstrated that under a favorable climate, the most integrated were the strongest supporters of Social Credit, while the contrary tended to be true under an unfavorable climate. This is an aspect of the new model which can certainly no longer be overlooked.

All in all, it seems that the prime role attributed to mass conditions in the genesis of mass movements represents a distortion. Many other factors discussed in previous chapters and in particular, class factors, were more important. To the extent that social integration played an important role, this role was not in keeping with the claims of mass theory. We are led to conclude that the image of modern society mass theorists have developed is seriously biased by ideological preconceptions, and that these preconceptions, whether conservative or radical, are largely responsible for the favor the theory continues to obtain.

V

SOME

PSYCHOLOGICAL

FORCES

Authoritarianism,

Conservatism,

and

Alienation

CHAPTER TWELVE

It is often assumed that the followers of new political movements are characterized by a particular psychological complexion, if not by some psychopathological traits, and this would be particularly true, presumably, in the case of extremist movements which reject the democratic process.[1] This view is held not only by psychologically- and psychoanalytically-oriented analysts, but also by most mass theorists, for whom the personal disorganization of the individual is the psychological consequence of structural disintegration, and at least an intervening variable in the process of recruitment to mass movements.[2]

[1] An early proponent of these ideas is Gustave Le Bon; see his *The Crowd: A Study of the Popular Mind* (New York: Compass Books, The Viking Press, 1960), originally published in France in 1895 under the indicative title of *La Psychologie des Foules*. A good example of such an orientation is Eric Hoffer's *The True Believer: Thoughts on the Nature of Mass Movements* (New York: Mentor Books, The New American Library, 1951). The idea that authoritarians were potential recruits of fascist movements was a basic assumption of Adorno and his colleagues: see T.W. Adorno *et al.*, *The Authoritarian Personality* (New York: Harper and Brothers, 1950), p.i. See also S.M. Lipset, *Political Man*, Chap. 4. For an extensive review of studies along these lines, see Thelma H. McCormack, "The Motivation of Radicals," in R.H. Turner and L.M. Killian, *Collective Behaviour*, pp. 433–440; Roger Brown, *Social Psychology* (New York: The Free Press, 1965), Chap. 10, esp. pp. 527ff. See also K. Lang and G.E. Lang, *Collective Dynamics* (New York: Thomas Y. Crowell Company, 1961), pp. 275–289. Among those who criticize the psychological view, see Theodore Abel, *The Nazi Movement*. Introduction and pp. 186ff.; R. Heberle, *Social Movements: An Introduction to Political Sociology*, pp. 104–117; Crane Brinton, *The Anatomy of Revolution*, pp. 111ff., esp. p. 127; Nelson W. Polsby, Robert A. Dentler, and Paul A. Smith, *Politics and Social Life*, pp. 164–172; Maurice Zeitlin, "Revolutionary Workers and Individual Liberties," *American Journal of Sociology*, 72 (1967), pp. 619–632.

[2] The position of mass theorists is summarized by J.R. Gusfield, "Mass Society and Extremist Politics," p. 21–22. We shall distinguish below, however, political alienation from other clusters of

In this chapter, we turn our attention to the effects, or lack of effects, of such psychological forces. First, we will consider some personality factors and examine their impact on the recruitment of Social Credit supporters, even though this movement is not an extremist movement. The two related personality factors to be considered here are authoritarianism and ethnocentrism; both are factors which have received wide attention in the literature. Following this, we will examine the effects of two sets of political attitudes, conservatism and political alienation. Though these attitudes are not conceived of as dimensions of the personality proper, they constitute socio-psychological forces which are often assumed to be relevant to the study of social movements.

PERSONALITY FACTORS

With regard to personality factors, the general hypothesis we are working with is that the psychological complexion of the followers of a movement is less important in accounting for their recruitment than is often believed. For one thing, the studies presenting the psychological thesis have clearly eschewed a sociological context, as noted by Thelma McCormack:

> With few exceptions (these studies) are not related to an actual social movement. And in no case are they related to the type of historical situation which generates a radical movement. . . . American investigators have not had the opportunity to study radicalism except *in vacuo* . . . they may have unwittingly studied a selected group of radicals: those whose radicalism stems primarily from inner personal needs rather than from environmental pressure. . . . Whether or not it is true of the mass in a social movement . . . is still to be determined.[3]

In particular, we believe that the psychological complexion of the followers has very little, if any, significance in explaining the success of political movements arising as a response to economic crises and whose main overt goals are the redress of economic grievances. As Turner and Killian wrote:

> Frequently, elaborate pathological explanations are offered to account for susceptibility to . . . control movements. However, in the face of a widespread feeling that (a) conditions could not be much worse than they are, and that (b) there are no real alternatives, nothing is more normal than to cast one's lot with a movement that appears at least capable of drastic action.[4]

---

attitudes, which is not done by mass theorists. Kornhauser indeed tries to substantitate his thesis by showing that the more detached people are usually more authoritarian and less likely to support a multi-party system; see *The Politics of Mass Society*, pp. 68–72. The inference, following the "fallacy of retrospective determinism," is that they are more likely joiners of mass movements. (Notice, however, that this author also develops the idea that personal disorganization leads to personal deviance rather than to mass movements; see *ibid.*, pp. 90ff.)

[3] "The Motivation of Radicals," pp. 439–440. For the scanty evidence available, see Brown, *Social Psychology*, pp. 529ff.

[4] *Collective Behavior*, p. 363. A control movement is one devoted to dominating society, while

Such protest movements are the only ones we have in mind in the following pages. They include class movements and mainly, but not exclusively, those of the reform type (as opposed to the extremist type); socialist movements in general, but also conservative ones, such as Social Credit and the Poujadists, would also fall in this group; even fascist movements arising in periods of·economic crises would fall in this category.[5]

We do not see how such political movements could recruit a disproportionately large number of people characterized by pathological personality traits. For one thing, deep psychological traits are not necessarily translated into political beliefs, and the connections of these two with political action is not as simple as is often implied.[6] Moreover, people afflicted by these traits are relatively few in the general population and, above all, the strains that these traits produce in the personality are too constant to account for the sudden emergence of large-scale movements. If such a movement were to draw only on such people, it would be small indeed and very marginal.[7] It is possible that such people may flock to a larger movement emerging on the basis of more widespread economic strains, but their small number will not strongly affect the general configuration of its mass support.[8]

More specifically, we do not think that such movements particularly attract people who are characterized by attitude configurations such as authoritari-

---

leaving its value objectives flexible and undefined. But the authors seem to hold a different view with regard to participation-oriented movement, that is movements in which participation is for the sheer satisfaction so derived; see *ibid.*, pp. 440–441.

5 At the other extreme, if one considers "status" movements whose overt goals are to maintain or promote some form of racial or ethnic bigotry, or the like, the situation might very well be different. We think here of movements like the Ku Klux Klan, the John Birch Society, or McCarthyism. Indeed, it was actually found that the support for McCarthy was partly dependent on authoritarianism, but mainly among the better educated, and that John Birch supporters were more likely to be prejudiced toward ethnic and religious minorities and intolerant with regard to civil liberties. On the distinction between class and status politics, see S.M. Lipset, "The Sources of the 'Radical Right' (1955)," in D. Bell, ed., *The Radical Right*, pp. 308ff. For the findings just reported, see S.M. Lipset, "Three Decades of the Radical Right: Coughlinites, McCarthyites, and Birchers (1962)," in *ibid.*, pp. 411ff., pp. 434ff. Notice however that the relationship between support for McCarthy and anti-Semitism is not clear (see Lipset, *ibid.*) and that the relationship of the former with political tolerance "almost or wholly disappears" holding formal education constant (see M.A. Trow, "Small Businessmen, Political Tolerance and Support for McCarthy," p. 272). Sokol has also reported a relationship between intolerance of ambiguity, as a measure of authoritarianism, and support for McCarthy in an upper-middle-class suburb; R. Sokol, "Power Orientation and McCarthyism," *American Journal of Sociology*, 73 (1968), pp. 443–452. See also R. E. Wolfinger *et al.*, "America's Radical Right," p. 285.

6 Fred I. Greenstein, "Personality and Political Socialization: The Theories of Authoritarian and and Democratic Character," in Calvin J. Larson and Philo C. Wasburn, eds., *Power, Participation and Ideology* (New York: David McKay Co., Inc., 1969), pp. 372–388, esp. pp. 380–382.

7 We do not say that such movements do not exist; some marginal movements do give the impression of having such a basis. But they seem to remain marginal, and if social conditions become such as to make the movement grow beyond their first marginal core, then the peculiar psychological complexion which formed the very early basis of support will gradually vanish. On this, see Heberle, *Social Movements*, p. 110.

8 To say that criminals are attracted by large cities is not to say that urbanization is the product of a high incidence of criminality.

anism or ethnocentrism. Such value configurations may fit perfectly with the organizational character of a movement (as, for instance, a fascist or any extremist movement), and/or they may be more or less important parts of its ideology, but we do not think this is sufficient to give rise to a congruent mass following. When such values fit with the organizational character of the movement, we would have to assume that the mass of the population is attentive enough to that character to perceive, even more or less consciously, the congruence it has with their attitudes. The very great majority of the population lack the degree of intellectual sophistication and of ability to perceive accurately which this would require.[9] When these values are but marginal parts of a more or less coherent ideology, they will often be formulated by very small groups and will be held almost exclusively by the more ideological members of its leadership. Such leaders may try to diffuse their values, but more often, in such movements, the appeals will be in "bread and butter" terms. Even if they make serious efforts to diffuse them, they face among their followers the lack of sophistication and the lack of attention we have just mentioned.[10]

In short, we would agree with Bendix when he writes:

> I question . . . whether much light is shed on the conquest of power by a totalitarian movement when a study of its social composition is combined with a psychological analysis. . . . The fallacy of retrospective determinism applies here also: we study a group whose support swept a totalitarian movement into power, we find that it is authoritarian, and we infer that the second fact caused the first (among many other factors, to be sure). But ethnocentric people were always authoritarian, long before they became supporters of a movement. . . . The issue is not whether people of an authoritarian bent will support a totalitarian regime more wholeheartedly than others, once it is in power. The question is rather whether, under trying circumstances, people of such character will jump on the band wagon, as well as despair, earlier than people of a more permissive disposition. I believe that we lack the necessary comparative evidence to answer this question properly.[11]

In the pages which follow, we shall limit this inquiry to the effects of authoritarianism and intolerance.

---

[9] See Campbell *et al.*, *The American Voter*, Chap. 8–10.

[10] We would classify Father Coughlin's movement in the thirties as an example of the type of economic movement we are now considering. And although he was an anti-Semite, it seems, according to Lipset, "that Coughlin was never perceived by the bulk of the American people as a Fascist and anti-Semite, and that much of his support came from people who disapproved of much of what he advocated." His "support was due in large part to economic dissatisfaction." There are some indications, however, though indirect ones, that his "backers were probably more anti-Semite than the population in general." Lipset, "Three Decades of the Radical Right," pp. 381, 386, 389–390.

[11] R. Bendix, "Social Stratification and Political Power," in R. Bendix and S.M. Lipset, *Class, Status and Power*, p. 608. The same points are also made by N. Glazer and S.M. Lipset, "The Polls on Communism and Conformity," in D. Bell, ed., *The New American Right* (New York: Criterion Books 1955), pp. 141–165, esp. pp. 159–162. For some evidence in this regard, see Lipset, *Agrarian Socialism*, pp. 196–198.

AUTHORITARIANISM AND INTOLERANCE
OF MINORITIES

Of all the attitudinal configurations considered in relation to extremist movements, authoritarianism and, to a lesser extent, intolerance toward minorities, are probably the ones which have received the greatest attention.[12] This is not surprising since the organizations of extremist movements usually display some of the characteristics of the authoritarian and the ethnocentric, such as intolerance and affinity to strong leadership.

The Social Credit movement was no exception in this regard. It had a tradition of anti-Semitism,[13] as well as a tradition of strong, autocratic leadership.[14] The Quebec leader, Réal Caouette, was also a charismatic and authoritarian leader; a few months after the election, when asked by a journalist to name his political heroes, he did not hesitate to reply, "Mussolini and Hitler,"[15] an answer which created a national uproar.[16]

However, for the reasons given above, we hypothesized that authoritarianism and tolerance toward racial and religious minorities would not be related to Social Credit support. As we have seen before, Social Credit was an answer to widespread economic deprivations, and the propaganda of the party was directed mainly to that problem and to the presentation of the party's economic solution.[17] The foregoing set of attitudes should not therefore explain the new movement's success.[18]

This hypothesis is supported by the data of Table 12.1. There are no relation-

12 See for instance Lipset, *Political Man*, Chap. 4.; Kornhauser, *The Politics of Mass Society*; Lang and Lang, *Collective Dynamics*; Trow, "Small Businessmen, Political Tolerance and Support for McCarthy".

13 See Macpherson, *Democracy in Alberta*, pp. 210ff.; Irving, *The Social Credit Movement in Alberta*, p. 7. Also see Chap. 1 above.

14 See Irving, *op. cit.*, *passim*; Macpherson, *op. cit.*

15 And though he went on to disavow fascism because it was a dictatorship, he added that he admired the leadership qualities of Mussolini; he also admired the economic reforms of Hitler, though regretting he had employed the ideas he had for war rather than peace. See H. Pilotte. "Réal Caouette, Führer ou Don Quichotte?" *Le Magazine Maclean*, Sept. 1962, p. 38.

16 See, for instance, *The Montreal Star* and *La Presse* (Montreal), August 23, 1962. To the *Montreal Star*, he commented on his *Maclean* interview as follows: "Those who may have been led to believe that my admiration for Hitler and Mussolini gives any measure of my political aspirations are in complete error. What I have said is that I admired greatly both Hitler and Mussolini for their immense quality of leadership, particicularly in the manner in which they could identify themselves with their people and enrapture huge crowds," adding however that no one "in his right mind could believe I would condone their wars, their race laws, their absolute ignorance of human self-respect, their gas chambers, their concentration camps, their sheer vanity." *The Montreal Star*, August 23, 1962, p. 1.

17 Though, as we have seen in Chap. 1, a larger part of that propaganda was also devoted to the spread of the traditional Social Credit philosophy of extreme individualist conservatism. Caouette's astonishing declaration quoted above was made after the 1962 election. To this author's knowledge, no such content could be found in his usual propaganda.

18 Zeitlin found that authoritarianism was not related to support for the Cuban revolution; Maurice Zeitlin, "Revolutionary Workers and Individual Liberties," pp. 629–631.

Table 12.1

*Authoritarianism and Intolerance toward Minorities Bear No
Relationship to Social Credit Support*
(% *Social Credit*)

	AGREE	DISAGREE*
Authoritarianism:		
1. A strong leader is better for a country than all the laws and talk.	21	22
	(345)	(244)
2. The most important thing to teach children is strict obedience to their parents.	22	22
	(481)	(139)
Intolerance toward Minorities		
3. Generally Jews take up too large a position in the Province of Quebec.	23	18
	(325)	(240)
4. Jehovah's Witnesses should not be allowed to hold activities in the Province of Quebec.	22	21
	(452)	(169)

*In this table, as in the following ones, the "disagree" answers include the "qualified" answers.

ships between the responses to items[19] deemed to measure authoritarianism[20] and the support for the new movement[21] and there is only a 5 percent difference in one of the two items used to measure intolerance, which is even reduced when controlling for socioeconomic status.[22]

These findings are important since by choosing only certain pieces of the present data, one could have fallen victim of the "fallacy of retrospective determinism," to use Bendix' term. First the data reveal that the Quebec population rates relatively high on both attitude configurations[23] and this is the province

[19] These statements, as well as others in the present study, are borrowed verbatim from previous American studies when they were thought to fit the present population. A few were slightly adapted and some were written specifically for this study.

[20] When an index of authoritarianism is constructed with the two items of Table 12.1, the results are not altered; with this index broken into four groups (agree, score 2; qualified answer and don't know, score 1; disagree, score 0), we find that the proportions who voted Social Credit, from low to high authoritarians, are 22, 21, 23, and 21 percent, respectively (N = 77, 172, 95, 284).

[21] In Table 12.1, as in the following tables we present only the proportions who voted Social Credit since these attitudes do not bear any relationship either to other parties.

[22] The 5 percent difference is reduced to an average 2 percent difference within the three income groups. None of the differences are statistically significant at the .05 level.

[23] The Quebec population and, specifically, the French Canadians are generally thought of as more authoritarian and more intolerant than other Canadians, though no comparative Canadian data are available (within Quebec, French Canadians actually fit this description, though we do not know to what extent this reflects differential socioeconomic status). Moreover, the Quebec population is probably more authoritarian and intolerant than the United States population. The proportions in the present study who agreed to the four statements of Table 12.1 (as opposed to those who disagreed, gave qualified answers or did not know) are, respectively, 56, 75, 51 and 68 percent (N's = 998). On the cult of the strong man in Quebec, see, for instance, Trudeau, "La Province de Québec au moment de la grève," pp. 24–25.

where Social Credit made its surprising upsurge in 1962.[24] Moreover, as elsewhere,[25] the low-educated in the above data are slighty more authoritarian and are more intolerant than the better-educated,[26] and on the other hand, the former gave a disproportionate support to Social Credit. It is therefore obvious that any direct inference could be quite misleading: the relationship of socioeconomic status to both attitude configurations and to support for the new movement does not mean that the latter two variables are themselves related to each other.

However, a note of caution should be entered at this point. There are serious methodological difficulties with the use of questionnaire items of the agree-disagree type. It might very well be that these simple questionnaire items failed to measure in an heterogeneous population the authoritarian syndrome which was clinically observed in a more homogeneous (well-educated) population. There are some suggestions that this syndrome can more readily be picked up at the college level. Among those who are less educated, these questions are more liable to a "response set," and a positive response does not necessarily imply an authoritarian syndrome.[27]

With regard to the 1952 election, the authors of *The American Voter* generally found no relationship of authoritarianism to shifts of party allegiances to Eisenhower or to attitudes on policy issues, except among the college-educated with regard to the latter attitudes.[28] In the present survey, when education was introduced as a control, the relationships observed in Table 12.1 with items one and three were not altered, and with items two and four, we observed what appears to be inconsistent relationships.[29] Therefore, unless we did not really measure these syndromes, it seems that they did not affect Social Credit support.

It might be mentioned that two alternative and contradictory hypotheses

24 Though the party first gained ground a long time ago in western, English-speaking Canada.

25 See Lipset, *Political Man*, Chap. 4.

26 For those who gave a party preference, i.e., for those considered in Table 12.1, we found that the less educated were 6 and 8 percent more authoritarian than those with a higher level of education, for items 1 and 2 respectively. In the case of items 3 and 4, the differences were 14 and 15 percent respectively (a low education is one of less than 9 years).

27 See Campbell *et al.*, *The American Voter*, pp. 512ff. Campbell and his associates found that with a sub-battery of reversed items, the relationship of authoritarianism and education was reversed and *positive*. Removing the response set by considering only those who were authoritarian (or not) on both subsets of the battery (direct and reversed items), they nevertheless found that the less-educated were more authoritarian. But different aspects of their findings did not convince them that the corrected index of authoritarianism was still meaningful for the 80 percent segment of less educated people; see also Brown, *Social Psychology*, pp. 510ff.

28 *The American Voter*, pp. 508ff., pp. 510ff. Lipset also found the strongest relationship between authoritarianism and support for McCarthy in the college-educated group; see "Three Decades of the Radical Right", p. 413. See also Berelson *et al.*, *Voting*, Chap. 9.

29 Among the less-educated, the non-authoritarian and the tolerant were greater supporters of Social Credit (differences of 9 and 8 percent with each item respectively), while among the more-educated, the relationship was opposite (differences of 7 and 6 percent with each item respectively); (these differences are not statistically significant at the .05 level). These relationships were not consistent either when occupation or income were controlled. But compare with Gabriel A. Almond, *The Appeals of Communism* (Princeton N.J.: Princeton University Press, 1954), pp. 244ff.

were also considered. First, as suggested by both Heberle and the Langs, it is possible that the recruits of a movement in its early stages might more likely be those whose personality characteristics presumably make them more susceptible to a new movement, while in later phases, the movement following would more likely be heterogeneous in this regard.[30] On the contrary, one might suggest that the tendency to be conformist, rigid, and submissive to existing authorities, which are presumably characteristic traits of the authoritarians, would render them less likely to be the early recruits of a new political venture: indeed, when there is near-unanimity around them, authoritarians are more likely than nonauthoritarians to exhibit a high degree of conformity to the prevailing views.[31] As a test of these ideas, the stages of growth of the movement were introduced as a control and the new relationships were again weak and inconsistent from item to item. Neither of the two alternative hypotheses can therefore be accepted, and the null hypothesis must be retained. Notice, however, that when there is no unanimity around them (here, when the movement was in later stages), authoritarians, though more likely to consistently side with the same people[32] (which become their ingroup), are faced like others with the dilemma of choosing one side, that is, of choosing who will be their ingroup. Thus far, the argument of those who claim a positive relationship between authoritarianism and support of new movements is that authoritarians side with new movements on the basis of the latter's authoritarian tendencies. However, on the basis of the last study cited, the authoritarians' choice can also be made and, we suggest, is more likely to be made on the basis of other ingroups and outgroups which are so defined by the authoritarians themselves (for instance, primary contacts), and by which their behavior is more likely to be influenced. But then, if other more significant nonpolitical groups guide the authoritarians, the overall effect of such a process may well be the absence of relationships found in Table 12.1.

Finally, the position that the lack of structural integration is associated with authoritarianism[33] is also supported by the present data, though the relationship is weak.[34] But given the zero-order curvilinear relationship between primary group participation and support for the new movement, it is no longer clear what one should expect by also considering authoritarianism or intolerance towards minorities. At any rate, the three-variable tabulations indicated that the

---

30 See Heberle, *Social Movements*, p. 113; Lang and Lang, *Collective Dynamics*, p. 287.

31 See I.D. Steiner and H.H. Johnson, "Authoritarianism and Conformity," *Sociometry*, 26 (March 1963), pp. 21–34. But notice that again this experiment was conducted with college students.

32 *Ibid.*

33 See p. 223.

34 For instance, on item 2 of Table 12.1, if we compare those with a low, a moderate, and a high degree of primary group participation, we find among those with grade school education or less that 86, 79 and 78 percent agreed respectively (N = 132, 173, 235); among the better-educated, the proportions are 77, 73, 69 percent respectively (N = 60, 109, 237). (The average effect of primary group participation, comparing extremes = .08; p = .02.)

curvilinear relationship was maintained, while the relationships between the attitude items and Social Credit support were basically unchanged (items 3 and 4) or inconsistent from one to the other (items 1 and 2).[35]

In short, therefore, we think we are warranted to accept the proposition that authoritarianism and intolerance did not affect the Social Credit upsurge in Quebec.

POLITICAL ATTITUDES: CONSERVATISM

Although the authoritarian and intolerant traits of the new movement were not stressed in its propaganda, the same cannot be said of the party's conservative social and economic philosophy. Of course, as expediency required, the party did not stress its opposition to labor unions, to the right to strike, to union fees withheld at source, to all social security measures—at least until after the election.[36] But it did express its opposition to all forms of government control, to government planning, to big government, to state hospitalization and health insurance plans, which were all labeled as forms of "communistic socialism," the enemy that was relentlessly attacked. These were all depicted as ways by which the state was crushing the individual. The party also expressed its faith in the free enterprise system, in the freedom of the individual. To be sure, it seems that much more stress was put on the burden of taxes, on the high unemployment rates, on people's economic difficulties, but the conservative themes were often linked to the latter.

Nevertheless, we did not expect to find a relationship between conservatism or traditionalism, and support for Social Credit. In a large-scale movement of economic protest, as argued before,[37] we suggest that such political attitudes should not have much importance among the rank and file citizens.

Previous studies of the impact of these attitudes in routine politics gave ground to this expectation. McClosky, for instance, found that conservatism as a form of resistance to change, though strongly related to other personality and related attributes, was correlated only at a "fairly low" level with party affiliation and the like. He concluded that for the general population, as opposed to some of the more articulate groups, "political divisions . . . appear to be more affected by group membership factors than by personality."[38] The same set of items were also administered by the authors of *The American Voter*, and

---

35 The same results were obtained when political information (as an index of political integration) was used instead of primary group participation.

36 On this, see *Le Devoir*, August 20, 1962, pp. 1–2; *Magazine Maclean*, Vol. 2, No. 9, Sept. 1962, pp. 17ff. *La Presse*, Oct. 5, 1962, p. 12.

37 See Chap. 6.

38 H. McClosky, "Conservatism and Personality," in N.W. Polsby *et al.*, *Politics and Social Life*, p. 231.

they found "no significant correlation between conservatism and party identification" in the total sample.[39]

On the other hand, it has often been found that those who were liberal on economic issues tended to support the parties of the left.[40] But the authors convincingly argued that this pattern of attitudes was more a reflection of self-interest than of liberal ideologies. Moreover, we would suggest that these attitudes become linked to partisan choices only over time, and only if the parties have clearly differentiated images in this regard.[41]

In the present study, we administered to our sample three of McClosky's items (slightly adapted) to measure "resistance to change," together with more general items deemed to measure non-economic as well as economic conservatism.[42] The zero-order relationships are presented in Table 12.2.

The *resistance to change* items bear no definite relationships to support for Social Credit:[43] the conservative respondents (those who agreed with the items) were on the average only one percent more favorable to the new movement than the liberals.[44] This therefore supports our contention. But though a positive answer to the resistance-to-change items is congruent with the Social Credit opposition to changes brought about by industrialization and economic growth, it might be suggested that a negative answer would be more congruent with the support of a new political movement, since this in itself implies a form of change. Thus two opposite set of forces might produce the null relationships observed. This difficulty is less serious, however, when the other items of the conservative attitude configuration are considered. What do the data reveal in that instance?

With regard to the items of *non-economic conservatism*, the data do not indicate any clear positive relationship between the latter and Social Credit support. Although the conservatives were on the average 5 percent more likely to be supporters of the new movement,[45] the effect is a rather weak one,[46] and is statistically significant at standard levels in only one case.

---

[39] Campbell, *et al.*, *The American Voter*, pp. 210ff. However, they did find a relationship in a sub-group of the population, i.e. among those who had shifted their party identification later in life on political grounds (as opposed to social influence); the shifts tended to be made in agreement with traditional party orientations (*Ibid.*, pp. 213–14). But this small subgroup probably constituted a very articulate segment of the electorate.

[40] See for instance, *ibid.*, pp. 101ff.

[41] The relationship of conservatism and traditionalism to partisan choices in Quebec provincial politics is discussed in Pinard, "Working-Class Politics: An Interpretation of the Quebec Case."

[42] On the distinction between these two types of conservatism, see Lipset, *Political Man*, pp. 101ff.

[43] Neither do they bear relationships to support for the other parties.

[44] These data indicate that the well-educated were less conservative than the less-educated, but only on items 2 and 3 (differences of 14 and 13 percent respectively). The well-educated were 9 percent *more* conservative than the others on item 1. A negative relationship between education and conservatism was found by McClosky ("Conservatism and Personality," pp. 223–224) and Campbell and his colleagues (*The American Voter*, p. 210). When an education control was applied to the data of Table 12.2, the relationships were not affected at all.

[45] Notice that items 5 and 6 are reversed items so that a disagree answer is a conservative answer. (The same goes for item 9.)

[46] Various controls (socioeconomic status, region, religion) did not change these relationships.

Table 12.2

Conservatism Bears No Definite Relationship to Social Credit Support
(% *Social Credit*)

	AGREE	DISAGREE*
Resistance to Change:		
1. It is never wise to want to change rapidly many things in a society.	20 (423)	22 (179)
2. The organization of society is so complicated that if one starts changing things, one risks much of upsetting everything.	22 (357)	21 (238)
3. If one starts changing what already exists, one usually makes things worse.	24 (331)	19 (279)
Non-Economic Conservatism:		
4. Newspapers, radio and television enjoy too much freedom in Quebec.	24 (196)	20 (416)
5. Film censorship should be less severe in the Province of Quebec.**	17 (290)	25 (322)
6. Politicians should not introduce religion into politics.	21 (522)	24 (97)
Economic Conservatism:		
7. Labor unions are much more harmful than useful.	19 (175)	23 (412)
8. Nowadays, there exist too many social security measures, such as family allowances, old age pensions, etc.	23 (79)	21 (549)
9. The State should nationalize the big private companies and thus become their owner.	22 (194)	22 (374)

*See note of Table 12.1.
**a_1 (effect on item 5) = .08; $p(a_1 \leq 0)$ = .01.

Finally, with regard to items of *economic liberalism* (whether they are considered as measures of self-interest or not), no clear relationship is apparent either way (with or without controls).[47] In general, therefore, the basic thesis of this chapter is upheld, whatever the type of variables considered thus far. One must look elsewhere to account for the success of Social Credit.[48]

[47] In particular, favorableness or opposition to labor unions (item 7) did not affect the vote strongly. Given the stronger support of union members found previously, this last finding would indicate that the union members' support was not given on grounds of ideological commitment to their organizations, but because, as suggested before, unions were an appropriate milieu for the spread of alienation.

[48] The lack of effects of another set of political attitudes—nationalist feelings—was also documented in Chap. 5.

POLITICAL ALIENATION

But if the attitudinal configurations just considered were not expected to be related to the support of the new movement, the situation is different with regard to political alienation. Indeed, one would expect attitudes of alienation to be strongly related, at least at the zero-order level, with our dependent variable. As was shown earlier, there were serious economic grievances at the source of people's vote; one might therefore expect that the discontented were highly dissatisfied with the existing parties and politicians and that statements devised to tap this dissatisfaction and political alienation in general would be related to Social Credit support.[49]

Table 12.3

Political Alienation Is Positively Related to Social Credit Support
(% Social Credit)

	AGREE	DISAGREE*
1. Generally our elected deputies soon lose touch with the people.	24 (464)	12 (130)
2. Generally governments do not care what most people think.	26 (395)	13 (208)
3. Intellectual take up too large a position in our governments.	25 (244)	19 (334)
4. It is more and more difficult to trust the people with whom we deal.	24 (483)	12 (137)

*See note of Table 12.1.

The data presented in Table 12.3 show that the two are related; observe moreover how both political alienation (or powerlessness) (items 1 to 3) and a more general measure of alienation (or anomie) (item 4) are equally strongly related. Actually the only surprising finding is the weakness of the relationships; the average difference between those who agreed and those who did not is only about 11 percent.

To better assess this effect, a simple index of political alienation was constructed with the first three items of Table 12.3. This permits one to distinguish different degrees of political alienation. Table 12.4 clearly shows that the greater the degree of political alienation, the larger was the Social Credit support, with a difference of about 20 percent between extremes.[50]

[49] This is at least what the literature on alienation and on mass society would suggest. See, for instance, Melvin Seeman and John W. Evans, "Alienation and Learning in a Hospital Setting," *American Sociological Review*, 27 (1962), pp. 772–782, and other papers of Seeman cited below; Kornhauser, *The Politics of Mass Society*.

[50] Notice that the Conservatives also gained from the voters' alienation, while all the loss was suffered by the Liberals (a difference of 35 percent between extremes).

Table 12.4

The Greater the Degree of Alienation, the Larger the Social Credit Support

| | INDEX OF POLITICAL ALIENATION* | | | | | |
| | LOW | | | | | HIGH |
VOTE IN 1962	0–1 %	2 %	3 %	4 %	5 %	6 %
Social Credit	10	11	24	19	31	29
Convervative	20	37	22	29	29	35
Liberal	69	51	54	49	38	34
N.D.P.	2	2	0	3	2	2
N =	(51)	(95)	(54)	(178)	(90)	(179)

*For index, see Appendix C.

POLITICAL ALIENATION, SOCIOECONOMIC STATUS, AND STRAINS

What are the sources of this political alienation? The literature on alienation, and more generally on anomie, has traditionally stressed the social roots of these attitudes. But, as pointed out and demonstrated empirically by McClosky and Schaar, anomie—and presumably alienation—are also highly conditioned by personality factors.[51] They found in particular that the latter factors had an effect on anomie independently of social influences. This suggests that alienation would have an effect on Social Credit support independently of social factors such as socioeconomic status[52] and economic strains.

To be sure, our data indicate that the latter two factors are related to political alienation, the relationship with economic strains being slightly stronger (Table 12.5). Together, socioeconomic status and strains explain more than 25 percent of the variation in political alienation.[53]

When these three factors are simultaneously related to Social Credit support, we find that the effects of political alienation are maintained, but mainly among those not subjected to strains; its effects are substantially reduced among those adversely affected by economic conditions (Table 12.6). (This pattern is true for all categories of income.) Moreover, it is worth noting that strains have no further effect when alienation is high. One can therefore summarize these two

51 Herbert McClosky and John H. Schaar, "Psychological Dimensions of Anomy," *American Sociological Review*, 30 (1965), pp. 14–40.

52 The relationship between socioeconomic status and alienation has been repeatedly found; see, for instance, William Erbe, "Social Involvement and Political Activity: A Replication and Elaboration," *American Sociological Review*, 29 (1964), pp. 198–215, and other citations mentioned there (p. 200).

53 That is, there is a difference of 28 percent in alienation between those of high socioeconomic status and good economic conditions and those of low socioeconomic status and bad economic conditions.

Table 12.5

Political Alienation Is Related to Both Strains and Socioeconomic Status
(% Highly Alienated*)

	INCOME GROUP**		
STRAINS***	LOW	MIDDLE	HIGH
Low	36	34	23
	(94)	(114)	(152)
Medium	47	43	34
	(74)	(99)	(51)
High	51	51	52
	(168)	(127)	(64)

*High alienation: index scores 5 and 6.
**Income Groups: see Appendix C.
***Index of economic conditions: low: index scores 0 and 1; medium: score 2; high: scores 3 and 4.

Table 12.6

Political Alienation Is Independently Related to Social Credit Support, with Income
and Economic Conditions Controlled
(% Social Credit)

		POLITICAL ALIENATION*		
STRAINS**	INCOME	LOW	MODERATE	HIGH
Low	Low	9	19	24
		(21)	(16)	(17)
	Middle	9	32	38
		(32)	(22)	(26)
	High	2	3	23
		(48)	(29)	(26)
High	Low	26	15	31
		(31)	(48)	(72)
	Middle	27	31	32
		(33)	(42)	(69)
	High	16	12	24
		(25)	(17)	(33)

*Political alienation: low: scores 0 to 3; moderate: score 4; high: scores 5 and 6.
**Index of economic conditions: low: scores 0 and 1; high: scores 2 to 4.

findings by saying that alienation is effective only when there are no strains, and strains are effective only when there is no alienation.[54]

[54] Notice how, when alienation is low, the curvilinear relationship between income and Social Credit support disappears; it is only when they are moderately or (in the case of low strains) highly alienated that the poor become less likely to protest than those of middle income; the poor, like the rich, are therefore less responsive than the middle-income people to the incentive effect of alienation; on this see Chap. 8. (Note however that the unemployed respondents are included here.)

POLITICAL ALIENATION AND
SOCIAL INTEGRATION:
THE MEDIATION HYPOTHESIS

Seeman and his associates have repeatedly established that political aliena-tion—powerlessness—encourages poor learning of control-relevant information and they have suggested that it might similarly induce participation in social movements.[55] As was just shown, the present data demonstrate that this is correct: those who were politically alienated were much more likely to have voted Social Credit than the nonalienated.

But these authors have also established that at least one of the sources of alienation can be located in the lack of social integration: participation in occu-pational organizations was found to prevent the development of a sense of powerlessness.[56] Finally, Seeman found that participation in such organizations increased knowledge of relevant information. On the basis of this set of relation-ships—alienation led to poor learning and, presumably to mass behavior, lack of integration led to alienation, and lack of integration led to poor learning and, presumably, to mass behavior—it was suggested[57] that alienation was the inter-vening variable between lack of integration, or mass conditions, and the growth of social movements. This, as they pointed out, is in agreement with mass society theory, in which in fact this is a central theme.[58]

In our data, social integration does not bear any simple relationship to aliena-tion (Table 12.7). If, as in these studies, we find that the greater the integration of non-manual respondents (whether in primary groups, occupational, or voluntary associations), the less alienated they were, the situation is different among workers and farmers. Among these, there is no clear relationship with regard to primary group participation; moreover, contrary to Seeman's findings, the data establish that those workers and farmers who were members of occupational organizations (labor unions, trade or professional associations) were slightly more alienated than nonmembers. Finally, while participation in

---

55 See Melvin Seeman and John W. Evans, "Alienation and Learning in a Hospital Setting"; Melvin Seeman, "Alienation and Social Learning in a Reformatory," *American Journal of Sociology*, 69 (1963), pp. 270–284; Melvin Seeman, "Powerlessness and Knowledge: A Comparative Study of Alienation and Learning," *Sociometry*, 30 (1967), pp. 105–123; see also Kornhauser, *The Politics of Mass Society* esp. pp. 107–113.

56 See Arthur G. Neal and Melvin Seeman, "Organizations and Powerlessness: A Test of the Me-diation Hypothesis," *American Sociological Review*, 29 (1964), pp. 216–226; Melvin Seeman, "Aliena-tion, Membership, and Political Knowledge: A Comparative Study," *Public Opinion Quarterly*, 30 (1966), pp. 353–367.

57 *Ibid.*, in particular in the 1962 and 1966 papers. Notice, however, that these authors have rarely conducted any trivariate analysis, bringing together organization, alienation, and their consequences; they usually correlate them only two at a time, though the first paper (1962) is partly an exception.

58 Kornhauser wrote that according to democratic critics, "mass society is objectively the *ato-mized* society, and subjectively the *alienated* population"; *The Politics of Mass Society*, p. 33 (italics in the original).

Table 12.7

Social Integration Always Reduces Alienation among Non–Manuals,
but Often Increases It among Blue Collars
(% Highly Alienated*)

	INDEX OF PRIMARY GROUP PARTICIPATION		
	LOW	MODERATE	HIGH
Non-Manuals	40 (47)	24 (78)	22 (184)
Workers and Farmers	43 (144)	53 (194)	45 (269)

	MEMBERSHIP IN OCCUPATIONAL ORGANIZATIONS**	
	NO	YES
Non-Manuals	28 (231)	20 (71)
Workers and Farmers	45 (375)	52 (235)

	INDEX OF MEMBERSHIP IN VOLUNTARY ASSOCIATIONS		
	NO	YES ONCE	YES TWICE
Non-Manuals	31 (174)	20 (80)	15 (54)
Workers and Farmers Nonmembers of Occup. Organ.	47 (274)	42 (84)	36 (14)
Members of Occup. Organ.	50 (153)	55 (56)	54 (24)

*As in Table 12.5.
**a_1 (positive effect of membership in occupational organizations on alienation among workers and farmers) = .07; $p(a_1^* \leq 0)$ = .05. (This is the only significant relationship at the .05 level among workers and farmers.)

voluntary associations reduced alienation among blue collars who were not members of occupational organizations, it seemed to increase it among members.[59]

So far, therefore, our data indicate that the generalizations of alienation studies are at least subject to qualifications. As seen in Chapter 11, organizations, and in particular, occupational organizations, can in fact induce mass behavior;

[59] The same is true of the few non-manuals who were members of labor or trade associations (as opposed to members of professional associations and nonmembers): those who were also members of voluntary associations were more likely to be highly alienated than those who were not (32 as compared to 18 percent; N's equal to 19 and 28 respectively).

and now we find that they also can increase political alienation.[60] The findings of Seeman and his associates, in both the United States and Sweden, do not therefore hold unequivocally in Quebec. Since they did not hold unequivocally in the American sit-in movement either, we suggest that this is not due to differences in political culture, but to differences in political and economic conditions. In a situation of crisis, there are social and political processes which are not necessarily those prevailing under routine conditions. While social integration may normally reduce alienation, it may also act to increase it in a situation of severe discontent, where nonroutine politics takes over.

On the other hand, given the reformulated model of mass society and the findings supporting it which were presented in the preceding two chapters, it becomes obvious that the so-called mediation hypothesis is also in need of reconsideration. In order to take into account the effects of alienation, it is not necessary, we suggest, to alter the model presented: it is proposed that political

Table 12.8

Alienation Increases Social Credit Support in All Groups,
Whether Integrated or Not
(% Social Credit)

	POLITICAL ALIENATION		
	LOW	MODERATE	HIGH
Primary Group Participation:			
Low	14 (37)	14 (37)	27 (60)
Moderate	12 (57)	27 (41)	39 (75)
High	14 (104)	17 (98)	26 (106)
Membership in Occupational Organizations:			
White Collars* : No	8 (66)	18 (79)	
: Yes	5 (21)	13 (23)	
Workers and Farmers: No	19 (62)	20 (71)	26 (104)
: Yes	27 (33)	29 (42)	39 (85)

*For the white collars, moderate and high alienation are collapsed due to the small N's among the members of occupational organizations.

60 In the sit-in movement, it was found that alienated organizations increased alienation among ideologues and reduced it only among nonideological participants; but the latter finding was interpreted as a result of the effectiveness of the alienated organizations in setting the routine system in motion. It is interesting in this regard that it was also found in that study that participation in sit-in demonstrations increased optimism about desegregation; see Von Eschen et al., "The Organizational Substructure of Disorderly Politics."

alienation, at the individual level, acts simply as an additional incentive to join political movements (with one important qualification to be made below). This is indeed what the data of Table 12.8 reveal. For instance, whatever the amount of primary group participation, the greater the alienation, the larger was the Social Credit vote; similarly, among both non-manual and manual workers, whether members of an occupational organization or not, alienation is positively related to support for the new movement.

The proposition that alienation is what pushes the atomized people to political movements is certainly not supported by these data. On the one hand, among non-manuals, there is no indication that alienation interprets the slightly greater Social Credit support among the nonorganized.[61] On the other hand, to the extent that there is a correct proposition, it is that alienation is in part what pushed the *organized* workers and farmers to Social Credit.[62]

So far, it was suggested that alienation simply increased the probability one would join a political movement. This proposition, however, requires one important qualification. Recall that it was hypothesized in Chapter 10 that during the early stages of growth of a movement, under conditions of strains, the organized people would be the early joiners. Though this was not always clearly supported in the previous chapter,[63] we find here that under these conditions, the alienated ceased to be more easy recruits (Table 12.9). The basic

Table 12.9

During the Early Stages of Growth, under Strains, the Alienated Are
No Longer Easier Recruits
(% Social Credit)

STAGES OF GROWTH*	STRAINS	POLITICAL ALIENATION		
		LOW	MODERATE	HIGH
Early	Low	1	5	21
		(74)	(43)	(42)
	High	12	14	11
		(52)	(66)	(101)
Late	Low	17	36	43
		(29)	(25)	(28)
	High	37	33	55
		(41)	(43)	(75)

*See notes of Table 11.11.

[61] The non-significant 4 percent difference found between members and nonmembers (see Table 11.8) becomes 3 percent among those with a low degree of alienation, and 5 percent among those with a moderate and high degree of alienation (combined) (Table 12.8).

[62] The proposition is supported to the extent that when under low or moderate alienation, the differences in Social Credit support between the organized and the non-organized were relatively small (8 and 9 percent respectively), while the corresponding difference among the highly alienated increased to 13 percent. (The original difference, without alienation, was 12 percent.)

[63] See pp. 202ff. and pp. 214ff.

idea that under these circumstances, a movement reaches more easily the non-atomized, as well as the nonalienated, masses is thus worth careful consideration.

RETREATIST AND REBELLIOUS ALIENATION

Our findings, as well as the literature, suggest that alienation can have two opposite types of effects. On the one hand, political alienation has repeatedly been found to be negatively associated with political participation.[64] In the present case, we find that alienation led to active support of a new party, except in the interesting situation we have just mentioned. The apparent contradiction stems from the fact that alienation can both refrain someone from acting or incite him to protest, depending in part on whether it occurs in routine or nonroutine politics. It seems, following Erbe, that one can distinguish between what he calls, on the basis of their effects, "retreatist" and "rebellious" alienation,[65] and that each, at least among the nonideological masses, are manifested mainly in these two types of politics respectively.[66] The dissatisfied masses develop an alienation which leads them to give up and withdraw[67] up to the point where the political situation gives new signs of hope, as when a new political movement emerges.[68]

[64] In a recent article, Erbe cited no less than nine studies reporting this relationship, with partial reversals in only two of these; see William Erbe, "Social Involvement and Political Activity: A Replication and Elaboration," p. 200. It is true, however, that alienation has also been found to be related to political opposition; see, for instance, Edward L. McDill, and Jeanne C. Ridley, "Status, Anomie, Political Alienation and Political Participation," *American Journal of Sociology*, 68 (Sept. 1962), pp. 205–13.

[65] *Ibid.*, p. 206, fn. 26. See also Germani, "Mass Society, Social Class and the Emergence of Fascism." He distinguishes two types of responses to disintegration and release: withdrawal or apathy, and psychological availability.

[66] Erbe also reports that socioeconomic status and organizational involvement are positively associated with political participation, but that when one introduces these two variables together with alienation, the latter no longer has any effect on political participation. ("Social Involvement and Political Activity," pp. 203ff.) In the present data, we find, contrary to Erbe, that at least certain forms of organizational involvement (e.g., participation in alienated labor unions) *increased* alienation. And controlling at the same time socioeconomic status (cocupational level), participation in occupational organizations and alienation, we find that the latter has still some effect on the support of Social Credit, although this effect is reduced.

[67] To be sure, sudden adverse conditions may similarly produce rebellious alienation in routine politics; this is at least what the findings of a positive association between alienation and political opposition would suggest.

[68] Retreatist alienation can be transformed into rebellious alienation not only by new hopes born out of the appearance of a strong movement, or adverse economic conditions, but also, among the elites, by ideology. In the sit-in movement (a weak movement compared to Social Credit), it was found that alienated ideologues were earlier joiners and more active participants than nonalienated ideologues, while the effect of alienation was reversed among nonideologues (the latter finding probably suggesting that the movement was still too weak to transform this nonideological alienation into a rebellious one); see Pinard, Kirk, and Von Eschen, "Processes of Recruitment in the Sit-In Movement," pp. 365ff.

SUMMARY AND CONCLUSIONS

Many psychological interpretations of the rise of political movements have been proposed in the literature. In the present chapter, it was suggested that the role of personality variables had been overstated. We hypothesized that in the case of successful political movements appearing as a response to economic crises and proposing the redress of economic grievances as their overt goals, personality factors such as authoritarianism and political intolerance, and attitudes such as conservatism in its many forms were not important. The data presented did support the idea that these factors could not account for the Social Credit upsurge in Quebec. Although personality factors may be helpful to explain why people hold certain sets of beliefs (including political beliefs), or support certain types of social movements not considered here (though this has yet to be fully demonstrated), and although they may help to account for the numerous and varied political behaviors of political leaders—whether in routine or nonroutine politics—they seem to be of little relevance in explaining the political choices of an electorate backing a protest movement such as Social Credit.[69]

On the other hand, as suggested by the literature, it was found that alienation in general (anomie) and political alienation in particular were related to the new party's support, and particularly to the desertion of the Liberals, the traditional party of French Canadians. It was also found that this effect generally remained when other variables were controlled.

Moreover, it was established that social integration did not always prevent political alienation. In particular, the data showed that occupational organizations increased alienation among workers and farmers; this led us to findings suggesting that the mediation role alienation is deemed to play in mass behavior is seriously open to question. We also suggested that in the future, it might be useful to distinguish between retreatist and rebellious alienation.

---

[69] Some of these points are also made by Polsby and his colleagues; see Polsby *et al.*, *Politics and Social Life*, pp. 164–72.

VI

CONCLUSIONS

Social Credit in Quebec: Determinants and Prospects

CHAPTER THIRTEEN

When considered in comparative perspectives, one of the salient characteristics of party politics in advanced democratic nations is their relatively high degree of stability. The number of parties which vie for power and the strength of the contending forces may vary from nation to nation, but the pattern exhibited by any one nation has recently been relatively stable. In fact, the party systems that have developed tend to appear as traditional systems. Moreover, there is a very high degree of stability with regard to the social bases of the existing parties. This has meant that the social sciences have accumulated little hard data on emerging new parties.

Thus it was fortunate that a new movement, which obtained a quarter of the votes almost overnight, could be studied with modern research tools. We have sought to establish the bases of its mass support and the factors behind its surprising success and, more generally, to bring to empirical tests some of the ideas developed in the social sciences about such parties and movements. We will close our inquiry with a brief summary of our findings and some forecasts about Social Credit's future in Quebec politics. But first some theoretical notes are in order.

THE THEORETICAL PERSPECTIVE

As could be seen throughout our analysis, Smelser's *Theory of Collective Behavior*, and more specifically, his so-called value-added scheme, with its unique combination of determinants, proved most adequate to our task. We shall now summarize our results in the light of that scheme, after we have made a few comments.

First, it should be realized that Smelser's value-added scheme is formulated at a rather abstract level. The set of determinants he proposes—conduciveness, strain, generalized belief, precipitating events, mobilization for action, social control—are cast at such a high level of abstraction, even within the study of each type of collective behavior, that they do not easily engender substantive predictions, except of a very general character. Nevertheless, as should prove obvious from what precedes, this does not vitiate the scheme, on the contrary. In fact, it is most helpful in sensitizing the analyst to the various elements he should consider in the search of an explanation to some episode of collective behavior. In the present instance, the scheme gave us a way to bring together findings and theories that at first sight proved disparate.

With regard to the recruitment of a mass following into a movement like Social Credit—a typical protest or "surge" movement—we are not certain, however, that these determinants should all be given equal weight, or even that all of them should be considered as independent determinants.

In our mind, the two crucial independent factors here are strain and conduciveness; and although strain is a basic element because it creates *readiness among participants* for some alternative pattern of action, conduciveness is also of great importance, in that it generally determines which courses of action are *structurally possible*.[1] Once these are given, however, the three other basic determinants (generalized belief, precipitating factor, and mobilization)[2] will in part follow, as far as the recruitment of a mass following in that type of movement is concerned. This is particularly true of the generalized belief: it will largely be produced or at least be activated as a consequence of the presence of strain and conduciveness,[3] so that it can be conceived of as a psychological intervening factor[4] in an episode of collective behavior. To be sure, things might be quite different for ideological cadres or in strongly ideological movements; in these instances, the presence of a strongly articulated ideology—a particularly sophisticated type of generalized belief—could constitute a factor, if not the factor, of paramount importance for recruitment.[5] But we do not think this applies here.

Similarly, once the conditions are ripe with strain and conduciveness, these

---

[1] But even some aspects of conduciveness are themselves dependent on strain; an example of this was discussed in Chaps. 10 and 11, when it was suggested that strains could alter the conduciveness of the intermediate structure.

[2] We could even add social control, though this is a different type of factor, which "arches over all others," and is important in its own right; Smelser, *Theory of Collective Behavior* p. 17.

[3] Smelser does seem to realize this since he writes at times about generalized beliefs in these terms; see *Theory of Collective Behavior*, pp. 80–81, 112, 292.

[4] The argument that Smelser's model is too "sociological" fails to realize this.

[5] See for instance Morris Watnick, "The Appeal of Communism to the Peoples of Underdeveloped Areas."

will be in part responsible for the setting of precipitating events[6] and even, to a certain extent, mobilization for action. Of course, many other factors may also be involved in the activation of the other determinants, but we suggest that strain and conduciveness can be two important causes of these determinants. Moreover, we do not imply that the latter determinants are not necessary factors in protest movements, but simply that they are not wholly independent factors, and therefore, not as fundamental as strain and conduciveness.

The preference for Smelser's scheme and the ensuing neglect of other schemes for the analysis of social movements stems in part from a basic orientation which leads us to concentrate on the factors behind such phenomena. We ask: Why and under what conditions do social movements occur? Why and under what conditions do people join them? As pointed out by Janowitz, a distinguishing characteristic of the value-added approach in collective behavior, as opposed to previous "natural history" approaches, is that it clearly differentiates between dependent and independent variables.[7] The natural history approach is much more concerned with the description of an episode of collective behavior and the study of its transformation through time (for instance, emergence of new institutions, changes in leadership composition, creation of homogeneity and morale, and the like), together with what is happening to people once they have engaged in collective behavior.[8] Too often, these concerns lead to an emphasis on description over explanation and hence, among other things, to a strong interest in the development of typologies,[9] often elaborated for their own sake. In this analysis, we chose to emphasize explanation and generalization, rather than description.

THE FINDINGS

Since our findings have usually been summarized at the end of each chapter, we can now be relatively brief. With regard to the crucial factor of strains, we showed in Chapter 6 the role played by the recession of the early sixties in accounting for the class base of the movement. Economic deprivations were a significant factor behind the support for Social Credit. Unemployment was particularly important, but other grievances were also involved; among them,

6 For instance, to decide to hold an anticipated election. The presence of a precipitating factor appears at any rate less important in social movements than in elementary forms of collective behavior.

7 Morris Janowitz, "Collective Behavior and Conflict: Converging Theoretical Perspectives," *Sociological Quarterly*, 5 (1964), p. 114.

8 Discussing the psychological complexion of the following, Killian writes, for instance, that "what happens to the members as a consequence of their interaction within the movement is vastly more important than the reasons why they first came into the movement," Lewis M. Killian, "Social Movements," in Robert E. L. Faris, *Handbook of Modern Sociology* (Chicago: Rand McNally & Co. 1964), p. 445.

9 An example of this is Killian's essay (*ibid.*); he develops there at least five typologies (typologies of leaders, of followers, of objectives, of strategies, of values).

we must mention the declining incomes and the shrinking economic position of two doomed classes, small businessmen and farmers. A high level of discontent over rapidly increasing taxes also proved an important factor, as well as the grievances of those who had to provide for the wants of large families.[10] All these factors, together with class and community solidarity, and bandwagon effects, accounted for the rural, agricultural and working-class basis of Social Credit in 1962.

The findings of Chapter 6, together with those of Chapter 8, led us to important generalizations which, though suggested before in the literature, had rarely, to the best of our knowledge, been seriously tested. We established that not all kinds of economic strains acted as an incentive to join new political movements. If changes for the worse[11] in one's economic status, in the short run as in the relatively longer run,[12] coupled in particular with fluctuations in income,[13] can exert that effect, steady deprivations such as poverty, on the other hand, seem unable to provide a basis of recruitment, at least during the early stages of growth of a movement. Data on Social Credit in Quebec, as well as a reanalysis of the Poujadists' support in France, of the McCarthyites' and the Birchers' support in the United States, among others, were used to establish this generalization. When the poor are spurred by sudden additional adversities (unemployment, for instance) they may respond as other discontented groups, but short of this, they seem too hopeless to find the energies which could lead them to protest. They remain immune to what intensifies others' reactions (in particular, participation in social networks or organizations favorable to the new movement, exposure to propaganda, and alienation), and are alone to be restrained by conditions which do not affect others (like social isolation and political information). These are important findings, given the image many have that revolutions and political movements are produced by the most destitute elements of society.

Many conducive elements were also involved in the rise of Social Credit, but the most important was certainly the conduciveness of the party system. As established in Chapters 2 to 4, the traditional weakness of the federal Progressive Conservative party in Quebec, which was itself the result of Canada's ethnic cleavages, had a few times before created the structural conditions for the appearance of third parties and again opened the avenues for the rise of Social Credit. Given the strains, the lack of any viable alternative to the Liberals left the electorate of many districts with no other choice but to turn to a new party. Thus one-party dominance proved a most important condition of conduciveness for the appearance of a third party. If we add that this condition

---

[10] Logically, we cannot, of course, claim to have exhausted the list of grievances which led people to embrace the new party; but these at least seemed the most important.

[11] Including stabilization of income after a period of steady rise.

[12] The case of the suddenly unemployed, as opposed to the case of groups whose income is gradually declining.

[13] The case of some farmers.

seems to have prevailed in similar occurrences in the United States and that the data accumulated in Chapter 3 strongly suggest that it was an important factor in the rise of third parties in other provinces or regions of Canada, it seems that we have discovered a very general and important factor in the rise of new political parties. The new political model we have presented in Chapter 4 seems therefore of a more general character than former models.

It was also established in Chapter 5 that political change, once under way, becomes itself a conducive condition for further political change. Those who had previously severed their ties to a traditional party at the provincial level were more ready than stable voters to switch to an altogether new party at the federal level in 1962. Moreover, the general unrest which prevailed at that time on the larger political scene in Quebec was also conducive for the rise of the new movement: this is at least what the positive association between separatist support and Social Credit (as well as N.D.P. support) suggests, even though it involved very few people. But each of these conditions was less important than the system of one-party dominance prevailing in Quebec federal politics. Finally, we have shown, contrary to what has been suggested in some quarters, that the Social Credit upsurge could not be construed as another manifestation of French-Canadian nationalism. The strains involved were basically economic, not ethnic. If Quebec alone witnessed this upsurge in 1962, it is because Quebec alone assembled at that time two important conditions, as we have seen, that is, political conduciveness and strains.

Turning to social as opposed to political conduciveness, the analysis indicates that in one respect—the role of mass society—this type of conduciveness was not as important as often suggested. The belief that the conditions of life in modern mass societies, with their ensuing social atomization, anonymity, and alienation, are the crucial forces accounting for political movements in modern times was certainly not supported by our findings. We proposed instead another model in Chapter 10 and suggested that social integration can be conducive or nonconducive to political movements depending on the orientation of the integrative institutions or groups considered, and on the amount of strains and the stages of growth of a movement. In Chapter 11 we saw that the role of primary groups, community structure, and various other organizations conformed in the main lines to the new model. Conditions of mass society were certainly not the prime determinant of the Social Credit upsurge: they were a positive element of conduciveness only under some specific conditions, and a weak one at that; under other conditions, a weak intermediate structure actually meant immunity against the new movement.

But another social factor—youth—proved very conducive to recruitment. The new movement's greater success among the young, though not a pattern found in all movements, was certainly not an exceptional instance. It was established in Chapter 9 that this pattern is in part the result of weaker or at least less restraining partisan allegiances among young voters. It is also the result of the greater ability of the young to be spurred to action by economic adversities and worry, enthusiasm, and alienation, in somewhat the same way the middle-income groups are.

Concerning what might be called psychological conduciveness, we have shown in Chapter 12 that contrary to some theses, political movements of protest which aim at the redress of economic grievances are not the particular refuges of the authoritarians, the politically intolerant, or even the conservatives; this is so despite the conservative and at times intolerant character of the new movement, and despite its strong charismatic leadership and its bent for easy solutions. Political alienation, on the other hand, turned out to be an important element of the generalized belief, though not in all circumstances. We have shown in turn that this alienation was itself in part the product of strains, low socioeconomic status, and participation in alienated organizations.

Finally, in Chapter 7, we have given some attention to mobilization and the spread of the belief in the new movement,[14] though our data on these counts were rather limited. On the basis of our analysis, it seems that Caouette's long personal campaign on television was most effective in transmitting a conviction that Social Credit was the cure to people's economic problems. With regard to the effects of the recruiting and propagandizing work of his lieutenants, we know little; we presented some data, however, which showed that the relatively low social status of the Social Credit candidates—which was itself largely due to the inherent weaknesses of a new party in the eyes of potential candidates— was prejudicial to its success. If the discontented were alienated against the present political leaders, they were not alienated against all elites. Our findings suggest that a more elitist slate of candidates would have increased the Social Credit proportion of the votes.

All in all, our findings do not support the popular image of the following of political movements as consisting of the dregs of society—the rootless, the poor, the marginal, the psychologically affected. In this instance at least, the typical supporter tended to be the common man: the respectable upper-lower-class worker or farmer, relatively young, generally well-integrated in primary groups and occupational associations, but dissatisfied with his present lot.

THE PROSPECTS
OF SOCIAL CREDIT IN QUEBEC

Since the 1962 election, there have been three other federal elections in Canada. Let us briefly review the fate of Social Credit in Quebec in these three elections, and on the basis of this as well as of the preceding analysis, let us venture into some prognosis.[15]

---

[14] The precipitating factor in this instance was simply the call of an election.

[15] The prospects of Social Credit at the provincial level in Quebec have already been assessed in previous chapters; see in particular Chap. 4.

Table 13.1

The Results of the 1962, 1963, 1965, and 1968 Federal Elections in Quebec*

	SOCIAL CREDIT	PROG. CONSERV.	LIBERAL	N.D.P.	OTHERS
Votes (%)					
1962	26.0	29.6	39.2	4.4	0.9
1963	27.3	19.5	45.6	7.1	0.4
1965	17.5	21.3	45.6	12.0	3.7
1968	16.4	21.3	53.6	7.5	1.1
Seats (N)					
1962	26	14	35	—	—
1963	20	8	47	—	—
1965	9	8	56	—	2**
1968	14	4	56	—	—

*Data assembled from J. Murray Beck, *Pendulum of Power*, pp. 348–49, 370–71, 396–97, 418–19.
**One Independant Progressive Conservative and one Independent.

The results of the 1962, 1963, 1965, and 1968 federal elections for Quebec are presented in Table 13.1. It appears that from 1962 to 1968, that is over about six years, Mr. Caouette's party lost slightly more than a third of its popular support and of its representation. To be sure, the party gained some votes from 1962 to 1963, but this was due to a greater dispersion of its support. In fact, it generally gained votes in 1963 where it had been weak in 1962 (mainly Montreal), while it generally lost votes in its 1962 strongholds.[16] This dispersion was immediately reflected in the party's representation which dropped from twenty-six in 1962 to twenty in 1963. But after it peaked in 1963, the party's popular support declined in the following two elections. The party's representation in Parliament also declined in every election after 1962, except in 1968. In this last election, despite an overall decline in votes, the party made a net gain of five seats, reflecting its renewed concentration and slight increase of support in rural Quebec; in particular, it regained some of the rural seats it had lost since 1962.

We do not intend to engage here in a detailed analysis of the general decline of the party since 1962. We simply want to suggest some of the factors which seem to us of some importance. First and foremost, the prevailing economic recession was already coming to an end in 1962; conditions improved substantially in that year[17] as well as in the following ones.[18] Therefore, the level of

16 In 1963, Social Credit increased its proportion of the votes in 35 of the 44 districts in which it had attained less than thirty percent of the votes in 1962, while it lost votes in 24 of the remaining 31 districts; Vincent Lemieux, "Les dimensions sociologiques du vote créditiste au Québec," p. 191.

17 See Figure 6.1.

18 The unadjusted annual unemployment rate, which in Quebec was still at 7.5 percent in 1962 and 1963, dropped to 6.4 percent in 1964, 5.4 percent in 1965, and 4.7 percent in 1966; it went up again, however, in 1967, with 5.3 percent, and in 1968, with 6.5 percent. (From D.B.S., *Canadian Statistical Review* and *The Labour Force*, current issues.)

discontent reached in the years preceding the 1962 election had presumably dropped substantially. It is noteworthy, however, that with the renewed increase in unemployment in 1967 and 1968, the party made a slight comeback in 1968 in some of its previous rural strongholds.

Second, in the areas of Social Credit weakness in 1962, the party probably gained in 1963 many discontented people who had had no real chance to protest before, precisely because the party had appeared to be too weak. At the same time, however, it probably lost in its strongholds many people whom an astonishing bandwagon had brought to the movement in 1962 for no substantial reasons, or who never thought the movement would be so successful and never wanted it.[19] These opposing movements did not affect much the overall proportion of the votes, as we have seen, but the dispersion of the votes led to a drop in the number of seats from twenty-six to twenty.

Third, as soon as 1965, the party was beset by serious financial difficulties. Stein reports that in that election, the finances of the party were reduced by sixty percent, compared to 1963.[20]

Fourth, a long process of erosion, which has recurrently affected third parties at the federal level in Canada, started to set in. Though strong in Quebec, the party was at its weakest in the rest of Canada: outside of Quebec, it gained only four seats in 1962 and 1963, five seats in 1965, and none in 1968. Many voters undoubtedly realized that the chances of Social Credit's ever coming to power were very slim, and influenced by the improving conditions until 1967–68, as well as by the rejuvenation of the Liberals and the latter's strong attack on the Social Credit platform,[21] they returned to the Liberals or abstained altogether.[22]

Finally, Social Credit was beset by internal conflicts for a period, a common difficulty of new social movements. Friction existed between the national leader of the party, Mr. Robert Thompson, and his Quebec lieutenant, Mr. Caouette. For one thing, the lieutenant could boast a representation from Quebec of twenty-six M.P.'s while the leader was adding only four M.P.'s to that group: the two leaders' respective ranks were not congruent with their respective electoral achievements. Moreover, the "movement" spirit of the Quebec branch of the party and its fidelity to many of the party's most traditional planks clashed with the more matter-of-fact orientation of the older (western) branch of the party. If one realizes that these tensions ran parallel to the natural tensions of an ethnic cleavage, it is not surprising that they all finally burst into an open conflict. This happened on the eve of the September 1963 convention of the

---

[19] See, for instance, Regenstreif, *The Diefenbaker Interlude*, p. 124. We also met such people in our preliminary interviews in a strong Social Credit district a few weeks after the 1962 election.

[20] "The Structure and Function of the Finances," p. 440 and fn. 56.

[21] See Regenstreif, *The Diefenbaker Interlude*, pp. 121ff.; Lemieux, "Les dimensions sociologiques du vote créditiste au Québec," pp. 191ff. Lemieux also establishes that the federal Liberals were helped in 1963 by the November 1962 victory of the provincial Liberals; *ibid*, pp. 192–94.

[22] The turnout in Quebec dropped from 78 percent in 1962 to 76 percent in 1963, 71 percent in 1965, and 72 percent in 1968.

Quebec wing of the party, during which the rift was consummated. The convention repudiated Thompson's leadership and Caouette, together with twelve of his nineteen[23] followers in Parliament, left the party to form an autonomous Social Credit group under the party's provincial name, *Le Ralliement des Créditistes*.[24] The others, led by Dr. Guy Marcoux, remained faithful to Thompson; but the latter's group was now reduced to eleven M.P.'s (seven from Quebec and four from the rest of Canada). The Marcoux wing of seven M.P.'s, on the other hand, did not remain very cohesive: not long after the split, two of them left Social Credit to join the Progressive Conservative party, and finally, the remaining five decided to run as Independents in the 1965 election.[25]

These developments seriously harmed the Social Credit groups in that election. All five Independents were defeated (together with the two defectors), though two of their ridings returned Caouette's men. But the Ralliement also suffered serious losses: six of its thirteen M.P.'s went down to defeat and the new group, with its two gains from the Independents, was now reduced to nine M.P.'s. In terms of votes, the party's support dropped from a high of 27.3 percent in 1963 to 17.5 percent; it had lost more than a third of its support in less than three years.

One may now wonder whether this decline was only a temporary setback or whether it will continue. Our own impression is that the latter view may be closer to reality. To be sure, the party still maintains the advantages which derive from a system of one-party dominance, that is, from the lack of any real alternative to the Quebec federal Liberals. The Conservative party, with its small percentage of the votes in the last three elections (about 20 percent), and this despite serious efforts in 1968, remains a very weak political force in Quebec. Whenever this political situation is coupled with a serious economic recession again, Social Credit's fortunes could probably improve, as they did a little in 1968. Indeed, new sudden upsurges of the party under these conditions is a distinct possibility. Such upsurges could be even stronger than the 1962 one, since new followers could probably be more easily recruited. But the dates of such eruptions are like the times of volcanic eruptions. They remain almost wholly unpredictable.

Apart from these sudden eruptions, what are the chances of the party in the long run? Our feeling as stated above, is that the wholly regional character of the movement hurts it very seriously. The voters do not want to exchange their vote for nothing, and there is not much of a return if the party has no chances of forming a government.

23 Strictly speaking, eighteen, since earlier conflicts within the Quebec wing had already led a lieutenant of Caouette, Dr. Guy Marcoux, to quit the group and sit in Parliament as an Independent Social Credit.

24 On this, see the detailed analysis of Stein in his *The Dynamics of Political Protest*.

25 To these conflicts must be added the scandal which erupted after the 1963 election, and according to which six Social Credit M.P.'s would have made deals pledging their support to the Liberal minority government.

Add to this weakness our impression that the image of the party as that of a sincere, dedicated group, strongly unified behind a popular charismatic leader, has lost some of its lustre. The divisions within the party[26] may have changed that image. Moreover, the tactical moves which the parliamentary situation[27] has forced on the party until 1968 may have created the image of a leader and a party who are as ready to accept compromises and as opportunistic as any other party.

Finally, we may also mention that the party, though it has many elements of the "mass" type of party,[28] and a large number of faithful ideological followers, has also been boosted by the support of many non-ideological voters, a feature which is common to many economic protest movements. Therefore, it probably lacks the strength provided by large numbers of secondary leaders who are ideologically committed to the party, whatever its electoral fortunes. In this, it contrasts, for instance, with socialist and communist parties. It also lacks in part and again contrary to more typical mass parties, the strength provided by large numbers of followers who are strongly integrated in the party through its various activities and on whom the party may rely more surely.

To be sure, the party has of late built a provincial base by finally deciding to run in the 1970 Quebec provincial election. Despite bad economic conditions, it obtained only 11 percent of the votes; but it gained, through the concentration of these votes, 12 of the 108 seats. This should be of some help to the party since it allows faithful partisans to maintain the same allegiance at both the federal and provincial levels.

But despite this and for the reasons we have just mentioned, we fail to foresee a bright future for Social Credit in Quebec. There should be no reason, however, to be surprised by new sudden upsurges.

---

26 The last one took place in 1966; Mr. Gilles Grégoire, Caouette's latest right-arm man, became leader of the separatist *Ralliement National* party in 1966 and was forced to leave the party and sit in Parliament as an Independent. (On the Ralliement National, see Chaps. 3 and 4.)

27 From 1963 to 1968, the Liberal government was a minority government and it was in constant need of the minor parties' support to survive and prevent a new election.

28 See Stein, "The Structure and Function of the Finances."

VII

APPENDICES

Sample
Design

The individual data analysed in this study is from a sample of Quebec citizens nineteen years of age and over. The sample is a multi-stage area stratified cluster sample.

The stratification was done on a regional criterion and two political criteria.

a) The first stratification operated consisted in dividing the Province of Quebec into an urban and a rural stratum. The urban stratum is made up of the provincial electoral districts of the Island of Montreal (16) and of the capital city of Quebec (4). The rural stratum consists of all other provincial electoral districts (75). The first stratum comprised about 42 percent of the eligible voters in the 1960 provincial election, and it was decided that 400 of the intended 1000 interviews would be done in that area.

b) Within each of these two strata, the electoral districts were further subdivided according to the strength of the two provincial parties, the Liberal party and the Union Nationale party,[1] in the June 22nd, 1960 provincial election.[2] Electoral districts were divided into:[3]

[1] The Liberals obtained 51.6 percent of the vote in that election, and the Union Nationale, 46.6 percent. The rest (1.8 percent) went to independent candidates or candidates running under different labels. See H. A. Scarrow, *Canada Votes*, pp. 208ff.

[2] This criterion of stratification was introduced because the first object of the study was to assess political behavior at the provincial level, with the forthcoming provincial election primarily in view.

[3] Source: Printer to the Queen, *Report on the General Election of 1960* (Quebec 1960). One district (Joliette) was classified on the basis of a by-election which took place on Sept. 30, 1960.

Stratum 1:   Liberal victory in 1960, with a Liberal vote of 54 percent or more (7 urban districts—18 rural districts).

Stratum 2:   Liberal victory in 1960, with a Liberal vote of less than 54 percent (4 urban districts—24 rural districts).

Stratum 3:   Union Nationale victory in 1960, with a Liberal vote greater than 46 percent (4 urban districts—22 rural districts).

Stratum 4:   Union Nationale victory in 1960, with a Liberal vote of 46 percent or less (5 urban districts—11 rural districts).

c) Then, within each of the preceding strata, a further stratification was made on the basis of the Social Credit vote in the June 18th, 1962 federal election.[4] In the urban strata, the division was made between the provincial districts in which Social Credit got 8 percent of the vote or more (9), and those in which that party obtained less than that proportion of the vote (11). In the rural strata, the provincial districts were divided between those where the Social Credit candidate was elected (33), and those where he was defeated (42).

Sixteen strata were thus obtained ($2 \times 4 \times 2$), and within each of these, one district was sampled with a probability proportional to its number of eligible voters in the 1960 provincial election. The districts chosen in the urban stratum were: Bourget (Montreal), Montreal Jeanne-Mance, Montreal Mercier, Montreal St. Henry, Montreal St. Mary's, Montreal Verdun, St. Sauvenr (Quebec), and Quebec West. Those chosen in the rural stratum were: Argenteuil, Chambly, Chicoutimi, Mégantic, Montmorency, Rimouski, Rivière-du-Loup, and Three Rivers.

Each district was allocated a number of interviews proportional to the size of the stratum it represented.

Within each district, voting subdivisions (polling stations) were then stratified in "urban" and "rural" ones.[5] In order to have an average of five interviews in each subdivision, 80 subdivisions were chosen in the urban stratum and 120 in the rural one. Each district of the sample was allocated a number of subdivisions proportional to the size of the stratum it represented. Then these subdivisions were randomly chosen, within each stratum of subdivisions, with probability proportional to size.

The number of interviews to be done in each district was allocated to the voting subdivisions chosen in proportion to the size of the latter. The number of interviews to be done in a subdivision actually ranged from two in the smallest ones to eight in the largest ones.

Finally, from the electoral list of each subdivision (prepared for the 1960 election and giving the names, occupations, and addresses of all eligible voters who had accepted to be registered in a door-to-door canvass), addresses were

---

[4] To this end, the 75 federal electoral districts had to be converted into the 95 provincial electoral districts. This was done with the aid of electoral maps, and was not too difficult due to the high regional concentration of the Social Credit success.

[5] Following the classification provided in the *Report on The General Election of 1960*.

randomly chosen,[6] to which interviewers were then sent to obtain the interview. If, as often happened in very small communities, no specific addresses were given, names with the occupation of the head of the household rather than addresses were chosen. But in every case, the interviewer was instructed to go to the address or to the residence of the person indicated, whether this person was still living there or not.[7]

At each address he was visiting, the interviewer had to list in a systematic order the first names of all the people nineteen years of age and over living at that address. He was then instructed to choose a respondent on the basis of random selection tables provided.

The sample design called for completed interviews and when an interview was not obtained after two calls at a given address (for whatever reason), the interviewer had to go to a substitute address provided. When the field work was completed, 1038 interviews had been obtained (429 in the urban stratum and 609 in the rural one).

The distribution of these interviews in the sample districts was as follows:

URBAN STRATUM:

Bourget (Montreal)	51
Montreal Jeanne-Mance	40
Montreal Mercier	40
Montreal St. Henry	36
Montreal St. Mary's	27
Montreal Verdun	180
St. Sauveur (Quebec)	44
Quebec-West	11
Total urban:	429

RURAL STRATUM:

Argenteuil	41
Chambly	97
Chicoutimi	75
Mégantic	111
Montmorency	14
Rimouski	67
Rivière-du-Loup	105
Three Rivers	99
Total rural:	609
Total urban and rural:	1038

CORRECTIONS

During the course of the analysis, it was discovered that vitually all of the interviews done in one district (Rimouski) by one interviewer had apparently

6 Since the same address on the list was repeated for all the eligible voters at that address, each voter (but not each address) had an equal chance of being chosen, which is what one would want.
7 Hospitals and institutions were excluded.

been forged.[8] They were therefore excluded from the sample. Since this was reducing substantially the number of interviews from the areas of Social Credit strength, it was decided to reintroduce in the sample some additional interviews available from two relatively similar districts (Chicoutimi and Montmorency) in which too many interviews had been done. A total of 27 additional interviews were so reintroduced, respecting the actual distribution of the 1962 Social Credit—non-Social Credit vote in the stratum which the original district represented. A new sample of 998 interviews[9] was thus obtained and these are the data analysed in the present study.

[8] This was discovered on the basis of an examination of the marginals to some questions. An internal analysis of these 67 interviews gave weight to our suspicions (there was no association between such things as education, occupation, and income, for instance!) and it was decided to exclude all of them from the sample.

[9] That is, the original 1038 interviews, minus the 67 in Rimouski, plus the additional 27 (10 in Chicoutimi and 17 in Montmorency).

Relevant
Parts
of
Questionnaire

APPENDIX B

1— 8   Sex of respondent: Male . . . Female. . .

1— 9   Were you born in Canada or outside of Canada?
Born in Canada . . . Born outside of Canada . . .

1—10   (IF BORN IN CANADA) Do you consider yourself a French Canadian, an English Canadian, a Jewish Canadian, or a Canadian of another nationality?
French Canadian . . . English Canadian . . . Jewish Canadian . . . Canadian of another nationality . . .

(Answers to Questions 12-31:
Agree . . . Disagree . . . Qualified answer . . . Don't know . . .)

1—12   It is more and more difficult to trust the people with whom we deal.

1—13   It is never wise to want to change rapidly many things in a society.

1—14   Newspapers, radio, and television enjoy too much freedom in Quebec.

1—15   Generally our elected deputies soon lose touch with the people.

1—16   Intellectuals take up too large a position in our governments.

1—17   Generally governments don't care what most people think.

1—18   Nowadays, there exist too many social security measures, such as family allowances, old-age pensions, etc.

1—19   Film censorship should be less severe in the Province of Quebec.

1—20   Politicians should not introduce religion into politics.

1—21   The organization of society is so complicated that if one starts changing things, one risks much of upsetting everything.

1—23   The most important thing to teach children is strict obedience to their parents.

1—24   Labor unions are much more harmful than useful.

1—26   The State should nationalize the big private companies and thus become their owner.

1—27   A strong leader is better for a country than all the laws and talk.

1—28   If one starts changing what already exists, one usually makes things worse.

1—29   Jehovah's Witnesses should not be allowed to hold activities in the Province of Quebec.

1—30   French Canadians must often keep a watch in order that English Canadians do not take advantage of them.

1—31   (DO NOT ASK JEWISH CANADIANS) Generally Jews take up too large a position in the Province of Quebec.

1—32   In the last few years, among all the taxes you pay, are there any that have increased?
Yes . . . No . . . Don't know . . .

1—33   (IF YES) Do you feel that your taxes have increased much, too much, a little bit too much, or normally?
Much too much . . . A little bit too much . . . Normally . . . Don't know . . .

1—34   So far as your present financial situation and that of your family are concerned, would you say that you are fairly satisfied with them, more or less satisfied, or not satisfied?
Fairly satisfied . . . More or less . . . Not satisfied . . . Don't know . . .

1—35   Would you say that the financial situation in which you and your family are is better or worse than that in which you were 2 or 3 years ago?
Better . . . Worse . . . Same, neither better nor worse . . . Don't know . . .

1—36   Now thinking of the people living in this region of the province, is their financial situation, in your opinion, generally better or worse than that in which they were 2 or 3 years ago?
Better . . . Worse . . . Same, neither better nor worse . . . Don't know . . .

1—37   Do you think that in this region of the Province, people in general are much worried a little worried, or almost not worried about how they'll get along financially in the next year?
Much . . . Little . . . Almost not . . . Don't know . . .

1—38   So far as you and your family are concerned, are you much worried, a little worried or almost not worried about how you will get along financially in the next year?
Much . . . A little . . . Almost not . . . Don't know . . .

1—40   Let's now proceed to some political questions. All your answers will of course be kept secret. If there were a *provincial* election in a few months to elect a government in the province, for which candidate would you vote: that of the National Union Party, of the Liberal Party, of the Social Credit or Union of Electors, or of the New Democratic Party (C.C.F.)? (IF THE RESPONDENT HESITATES, REASSURE HIM THAT HIS ANSWERS WILL BE KEPT COMPLETELY SECRET.)

National Union . . . Liberal . . . Social Credit or Union of Electors . . . New Democratic Party . . . Would not vote . . . Too young to vote in a few months . . . Don't know . . . Won't answer . . .

A   (IF THE RESPONDENT NAMES A PARTY TO QUESTION 40)

I—41 Is this a definite decision or are you only inclined to support this party? Definite decision . . . Only inclined . . .

B   (IF THE RESPONDENT IS TOO YOUNG TO VOTE OR IF DON'T KNOW OR WON'T ANSWER TO QUESTION 40)

I—43 Maybe you are not decided (*or* you are too young to vote): But if you had to make a decision, which party would you be inclined to support presently at the provincial level? National Union . . . Liberal . . . Social Credit or Union of Electors . . . New Democratic Party . . . Would not vote . . . Don't know . . . Won't answer . . .

AA. (IF R. DID *NOT* NAME THE SOCIAL CREDIT OR UNION OF ELECTORS TO QUESTION 40 OR 43)

I—44 If Mr. Caouette's Social Credit Party were to present candidates at the provincial level, would you be very inclined, a little inclined or not inclined to vote for them? Very inclined . . . A little inclined . . . Not inclined . . . Don't know . . . Won't answer . . .

BB. (IF R. NAMED THE *SOCIAL CREDIT OR UNION ELECTORS* TO QUESTION 40 OR 43)

I—45 If the Social Credit or the Union of Electors were not to present candidates in the next *provincial* election, would you be inclined to vote for the Liberal Party, the National Union Party or the New Democratic Party (C.C.F.)? Liberal . . . National Union . . . New Democratic Party . . . Would not vote . . . Don't know . . . Won't answer . . .

I—46 At each election, many people cannot vote for one reason or another. At the last provincial election, in 1960, in which Mr. Lesage's government was elected, did you vote or not?
Yes . . . No . . . Don't know . . . Won't answer . . .

I—47 (IF R. VOTED) Did you vote for the Liberal candidate, the National Union candidate, or for another candidate?
Liberal . . . National Union . . . Other (specify) . . . Don't know . . . Won't answer . . .

I—48 If there were a *federal* election in a few months to elect a government in *Ottawa*, for which candidate would you vote: that of the Liberal Party, of the Progressive Conservative Party, of the Social Credit Party, or of the New Democratic Party (C.C.F.)?
Liberal . . . Progressive Conservative . . . Social Credit . . . New Democratic Party (C.C.F.) . . . Would not vote . . . Don't know . . . Won't answer . . .

I—49 At the last Federal election, last June, in which Mr. Diefenbaker's government was reelected, did you vote or not?
Yes . . . No . . . Don't know . . . Won't answer . . .

I—50 (IF R. VOTED) Did you vote for the Progressive Conservative candidate, the

Liberal candidate, the Social Credit candidate, or the New Democratic Party (C.C.F.) candidate?

Progressive Conservative ... Liberal ... Social Credit ... New Democratic Party ... Other (specify) ... Don't know ... Won't answer ...

1—51   Think at which point during the last federal campaign you decided for whom to vote: had you decided for whom to vote a few months before the election, about a month before, about two weeks before, or in the last week?

A few months before ... About a month before ... About two weeks before ... In the last week ... Don't know ...

1—52   At the *preceding federal* election, in 1958, when Mr. Diefenbaker was also elected, did you vote or not?

Yes ... No ... Don't know ... Won't answer ...

1—53   (IF R. VOTED) Did you vote for the Liberal candidate, the Progressive Conservative candidate, or for another one?

Liberal ... Progressive Conservative ... Other (specify) ... Don't know ... Won't answer ...

1—54   Let's return to *provincial* elections. At the last election in which Mr. Duplessis was elected, in 1956, did you vote or not?

Yes ... No ... Don't know ... Won't answer ...

1—55   (IF R. VOTED) Did you vote for the National Union candidate, the Liberal candidate, or for another one?

National Union ... Liberal ... Other (specify) ... Don't know ... Won't answer ...

1—56   Let's proceed now to more general questions. In your opinion, does the Federal Government, when it decides a question, take as much care of the interests of the French Canadians as of those of the English Canadians?

Yes, as much ... No, not as much ... Qualified answer ... Don't know ...

1—59   Has anyone in your family been unemployed at any time during the last twelve months?

Yes ... No ...

1—60   (IF YES) Have you personally been unemployed at any time during these last twelve months? (IF YES) For how long?

No ... Yes: length of time: ... months: ... weeks.

1—61   Are there any other persons in your family who have been unemployed at any time during these last twelve months? (IF YES) How many people?

No ... Yes: Number of persons ...

1—62   Has anyone in your family, though not unemployed, been working shorter hours than usual at any time in the last twelve months?

Yes ... No ...

1—63   In this community, was there an unemployment problem more serious than usual in the last 2 or 3 years?

Yes ... No ... Don't know ...

1—66   Some people suggest that the Province of Quebec separate from the rest of Canada

to form an independent country, while others are opposed to that. Are you personally for or against the separation of Quebec from the rest of Canada?
For ... Against ... Qualified answer ... Don't know ...

I—67   Some separatist organizations, which propose to separate Quebec from the rest of Canada, intend to form a provincial political party: if such a party were formed, would you personally vote for it or not?
Yes, would vote for it ... No, would not vote for it ... It depends; qualified answer ... Don't know ...

I—74   Think of provincial politics: would you say that it interests you very much, moderately, very little, or not at all?
Very much ... Moderately ... Very little ... Not at all ... Don't know ...

I—75   Do you happen to try to convince others of your own political beliefs?
Yes ... No ... Don't know ...

I—76   What about yourself: would you say you are a convinced partisan of a provincial political party?
Yes ... No ... Don't know ...

I—77   For the last three or four years, the Social Credit Party has had regular programs on television in some regions: have you personally seen these programs often, once in a while, rarely, or never?
Often ... Once in a while ... Rarely ... Never ... Don't know ...

I—78   (IF SAW PROGRAMS) Have you been seeing these programs only in recent weeks, or for about a year, or for more than a year?
Recent weeks ... About a year ... More than a year ... Don't know ...

I—79   Do you think that if the Social Credit Party were to present candidates at the *provincial* level they would have some chances of winning the next provincial election?
Would have chances ... Would not have chances ... Don't know ... Won't answer ...

I—80   People have diverging opinions on the platform and the ideas of the Social Credit Party: do you personally consider that in their platform and their ideas, there are many good points, or that there are some good and some bad points, or that there is not much good in them? Many good points ... Some good, some bad points ... Not much good ... Don't know or won't answer ...

2—19   Do you think that there are too many companies in Quebec that are owned by English Canadians or Americans?
Yes ... No ... Qualified answer ... Don't know ...

2—20   (IF YES) Do you think it is the Provincial Government's role to turn these companies into the hands of the French Canadians by nationalizing them?
Yes ... No ... Qualified answer ... Don't know ...

2—28   In your opinion, are the rights of the French Canadians in the Federal Government, in Ottawa, very well respected, fairly well respected, fairly badly respected or very badly respected?
Very well ... Fairly well ... Fairly badly ... Very badly ... Don't know ...

2—34 If the labor unions in the Province should recommend to vote for a given party in an election, could this influence you up to a point to vote for that party? Yes . . . No . . . Don't know . . .

2—35 (IF NO) Could this influence you up to a point to vote against that party? Yes . . . No . . . Don't know . . .

2—49 Could you tell me the names of the following Ministers *in Quebec:*

2—50 a) The Minister of Youth . . . . .Don't know . . .
      b) The Minister of Natural Resources: . . . . .Don't know . . .

2—51 Could you tell me the names of the following Ministers *in Ottawa*

2—52 a) The Minister of External Affairs: . . . . .Don't know . . .
      b) The Minister of Justice: . . . . .Don't know . . .

2—61 *In this district,* have you ever met personally one of more organizers of a provincial political party? Yes, one . . . Yes, more than one . . . None . . . Don't know or won't answer . . .

3—18 Comparing yourself with people living around here, would you say that your economic situation is better or worse than theirs? Better . . . Worse . . . Same . . . Don't know . . .

3—19 There is much talk these days about different social classes. Most people say they belong either to the middle class or to the working class. Do you ever think of yourself as being in one of these two classes? Yes . . . No . . .

   A (IF YES TO QUESTION 19)

3—20 To which class do you belong: the working class or the middle class? Working . . . Middle . . .

   B (IF NO TO QUESTION 19)

3—21 To which class would you say you belong, if you had to make a choice: the working class, the middle class, or another one? Working . . . Middle . . . Other (specify) . . . Don't know . . .

3—22 Are you (or is the head of the household) a member of a labor union, a trade association, or a professional association? No . . . Yes, labor union . . . Yes, trade association . . . Yes, professional association . . . Don't know . . .

3—24 Do you (or does the head of the household) attend the meetings of this union (or of this trade or professional association) rather regularly, rarely, or never? Rather regularly . . . Rarely . . . Never . . .

3—25 (IF THE RESPONDENT (OR HEAD OF HOUSEHOLD) IS A UNION MEMBER) What are your feelings towards this labor union (or the head of household's feelings); are you (is he) very interested, somewhat interested, nearly uninterested, not interested, in this union? Very interested . . . Somewhat interested . . . Nearly uninterested . . . Not interested . . . Don't know . . .

3—26 Do you also personally belong to other associations, clubs or various movements, such as social, religious, cultural, civic, or political associations?
Yes . . . No . . .

3—28 Are there other groups which you meet quite regularly, such as card clubs, golf clubs, recreation centers, or similar groups?
Yes . . . No . . .

3—29 During the last seven days, how many times have you visited other people at their homes?
Number of times: ....

3—31 During the last seven days, how many times have people visited you at your home?
Number of times: ....

3—33 During the last seven days, how many times have you been out *with other* people, to go somewhere else than to relatives' or friends' homes?
Number of times: ....

3—35 Think for a moment of your three best friends: without telling me their names,
3—36 could you tell me the type of work they have (or their husband, or father have,
3—37 if these friends are not usually working)?
1st friend . . . . 2nd friend . . . . 3rd friend . . . .

3—38 Are you a member of any religious faith?
Yes . . . No . . .

3—39 (IF YES) What is your religious faith?
Catholic (of any rites) . . . Protestant (or any denomination) . . . Jewish . . . Other specify) . . .

3—40 In general, people are not all religiously inclined to the same degree: as for yourself, do you go to church (or to a synagogue) more than once a week, once a week, not every week, rarely, or never?
More than once a week . . . Once a week . . . Not every week . . . Rarely . . . Never . . .

3—41 Apart from going to church, do you happen to pray God almost every day, a few times a week only, a few times a month only, less often, or almost never?
Almost every day . . . A few times a week only . . . A few times a month only . . . Less often . . . Almost never, or never . . .

3—42 Now, to end this interview, I still have a few general questions to ask you. Are you single, married, widowed, separated, or divorced?
Single . . . Married . . . Widowed . . . Separated . . . Divorced . . . .

3—43 (IF MARRIED, WIDOWED, SEPARATED, OR DIVORCED) How many children have you?
Number of children: . . .

3—44 In what year were you born? . . .

3—45 How many years did you attend school?
None . . . 1 year to 4 years . . . 5 years to 8 years . . . 9 years to 12 years . . . 13 or more years . . .

3—46   Are you (or is the head of the household) a tenant, a roomer, or the owner of this residence?
Tenant . . . Roomer . . . Owner . . .

3—47   a) (IF TENANT OR ROOMER) How much rent do you pay for your home?
$ _____
b) Is this a monthly or a weekly payment?
Monthly . . . . . . Weekly . . . . . .

3—48   (IF OWNER) Could you tell me at about what amount you evaluate your house?
$ _____

3—50   Concerning your occupation or work, could you tell me in which of the following groups you fall into?
A Gainfully employed . . . B-Keeping house (women) . . . C-Working without pay on a farm or in a trade or business of a relative with whom he lives . . . D-Permanently incapable of working . . . E-Student (even if working during holidays) . . . F-Unemployed . . . G-Retired or voluntarily inactive . . .

I   (IF "A," "B," "C," "D," "E" TO QUESTION 50; IF "B," ASK FOR *HUSBAND* OR *FATHER*; IF "C," "D," "E," ASK FOR *FATHER* OR *PERSON* ON WHOM R. IS DEPENDENT)

3—51   a) Are you (or your husband, or if single your father) self-employed or employed by someone else?
Self-employed . . . Employed by someone else . . . Husband or Father unemployed . . . Husband or Father retired, inactive . . .

3—52   a) What work do you perform (or your husband or your father does)? (HAVE R. SPECIFY EXACT DETAILS: Ex: A machine operator) . . . .
b) What is the main activity of the firm or the place where you work (or where your husband, or your father works)? . . . .

3—53   a) How much do you earn (or does your husband, or father earn) on the average per week (or, IF SELF-EMPLOYED, per year) after tax and other deductions?
$ . . . per week. IF SELF-EMPLOYED $ . . . per year.

II   (IF "F" OR "G" TO QUESTION 50)

3—51   b) In the last job you held, were you (or your husband or your father) self-employed or employed by someone else? Self-employed . . . Employed by someone else . . .

3—52   c) What consisted the work you (or your husband or your father) performed in that last job?
(SPECIFY: Ex: machine operator) . . . .
d) What was the main activity of the firm or the place where you (or your husband or your father) were working?
. . . .

3—53   b) In that job, how much did you (or your husband or your father) earn on the average per week, (or IF SELF-EMPLOYED, per year) after tax and other deductions?
$ . . . . . per week. IF SELF-EMPLOYED $ . . . . . per year.

(IF RESPONDENT LIVES ON A *FARM*)

3—56   How many acres does this farm have?

     .... Acres   Don't know ...

3—57   In your opinion, have the profits from your farm products increased, decreased, or remained almost the same, in the last 4 or 5 years?

     Increased ... Decreased ... Same ... Don't know ...

Indices

The indices are presented in the order of their appearance in the study.

1. SOCIAL CLASS SCALE OR OCCUPATIONAL GROUPS

The social class scale or the occupational groups used in this study are derived from the Edwards' "social-economic status" groups, as modified by the 1960 United States Census and presented as "major occupation groups."[1] These "occupation groups" were further modified in the following ways:

(a) All self-employed proprietors with an annual net income of $4,000 or less or (if the income was unknown) with eight years of education or less were considered as members of the lower-middle class and as small businessmen. All others in the professional or managerial groups were considered as members of the upper-middle class.

(b) All members of the operatives or service groups who were self-employed were classified with the craftsmen group.

These classifications were made from the data of Questions 3–50 to 3–55.[2] Note in particular that housewives and other people who were not in the labor

[1] United States Bureau of the Census, *Alphabetical Index of Occupations and Industries* (rev. ed.), 1960 Census of Population (Washington: 1960). The U.S. index rather than the Canadian one was used because it is more adapted to sociological analysis.

[2] All questions referred to in this Appendix can be found in Appendix B.

force were given the occupational group of their husband or other person of whom they were dependents.

The social classes and occupational groups obtained are as follows:

U.S. CENSUS MAJOR OCCUPATION GROUP	SOCIAL CLASSES	OCCUPATIONAL GROUPS (in this study)	
Professional, technical, and kindred	Upper-Middle	Professionals and Managers	Non-manuals or White collars
Managers, officials, and proprietors, except farm			
Clerical and kindred Sales workers	Lower-Middle	Small Businessmen Salaried L-M	
Craftsmen, foremen, and kindred	Working Class	Skilled workers Semi-skilled workers Service workers Unskilled workers	Manuals or Blue collars
Operatives and kindred			
Service workers, except private household			
Laborers (except farm), and private household workers			
Farmers, farm managers, laborers, and foremen	Farmers	Farmers	

2. EMPLOYMENT SITUATION IN THE FAMILY

This index is based on Questions 1–59 to 1–62 and 3–50. Respondents who had not been unemployed or in whose family none had been unemployed in the last twelve months, form the "full employment group"; if the respondent or someone else had been working for shorter hours at any time during this period, they are classified in the "shorter hours" group; others are classified according to the number of persons in the family unemployed at any time during these last twelve months. The "no unemployment" group in many Tables includes both the "full employment" and the "shorter hours" groups.

3. INDEX OF ECONOMIC GRIEVANCES

This index is based on Questions 1–34 and 1–35. Respondents obtained a total score ranging between 0 and 4; it is the sum of the following scores:

Q. 1–34:   Fairly satisfied: 0
             More or less: 1
             Not satisfied: 2

Q. 1–35:   Better: 0
             Same, neither
               better nor worse: 1
             Worse: 2

4. INDEX OF ECONOMIC CONDITIONS

The index of economic conditions, which ranges between 0 and 4, combines the index of economic grievances (I.E.G.) with the employment situation index in the following way:

Score on I.E.G. and full employment:	0
Score 1 on I.E.G. and full employment:	1
Score 2 on I.E.G. and full employment (or)	
score 0 on I.E.G. and not full employment:	2
Score 3 on I.E.G. and full employment (or)	
score 1 on I.E.G. and not full employment:	3
Score 4 on I.E.G. and full employment (or)	
scores 2, 3, 4 on I.E.G. and not full employment:	4

5. INDEX OF EXPOSURE TO SOCIAL CREDIT PROPAGANDA

This index is based on Questions 1–77 and 1–78. Respondents got a total score, ranging between 0 and 5, which is the sum of the following scores:

Q. 1–77:	Never:	0
	Rarely:	1
	Once in a while:	2
	Often:	3
Q. 1–78:	Recent weeks and	
	don't know:	0
	About a year:	1
	More than a year:	2

6. INCOME GROUPS

The income groups' classification takes into account the fact that the income of farmers is not comparable to that of other citizens; moreover, since many respondents refused to reveal their income, it uses the property value of their house for owners and the rent paid for renters whenever the income was not revealed. As in the occupational classification, housewives and other people not in the labor force were given the income group of their husband or other person of whom they were dependents. The classification is as follows (the data are from Questions 3–46 ff.):

Low-income group: non-farmers with annual net income of less than $3,500 or
(the poor)   (if income unknown) with a property value of less than $5,000 or a rent of less than $40 per month; farmers whose farm was less than 70 acres in size.

Middle-income group: non-farmers with income between $3,500 and $4,999 or (if income unknown) with a property value between $5,000 and $9,999 or a rent between $40 and $59; farmers whose farm was between 70 and 179 acres in size.

High-income group: non-farmers with income of $5,000 or more, or (if income unknown) with a property value of $10,000 or more, or a rent of $60 or more; farmers whose farm was 180 acres or more in size.

7. INDEX OF POLITICAL INFORMATION

This index is based on Questions 2–49 to 2–52. Each respondent was given a total score, ranging between 0 and 4, based on the number of correct names (0 to 4) which he gave in answers to these questions.

8. INDEX OF PRIMARY GROUP PARTICIPATION

This index is based on Questions 3–29, 3–31, and 3–33. Those who gave a negative answer to all three questions received a score of 0; those who gave one positive answer, a score of 1; etc. The index thus ranges between 0 and 3.

9. INDEX OF SOCIAL CREDIT ENTHUSIASM

This index is based on Questions 1–79 and 1–80. Respondents were given a total score, ranging between 0 and 4, which is the sum of the following scores:

Q. 1–79:   Would not have chances: 0
            Don't know: 1
            Would have chances: 2

Q. 1–80:   Not much good: 0
            Some good, some
              bad points: 1
            Many good points: 2

10. INDEX OF POLITICAL ALIENATION

This index is based on Questions 1–15, 1–16, and 1–17. Respondents were given a total score, ranging between 0 and 6, which is the sum of their scores on each of the three questions. Each question was scored in the following way:

Disagree: 0
Qualified answer or don't know: 1
Agree: 2

11. INDEX OF PRIMARY GROUP CLIMATE

This index is based on the occupational groups of the respondent's three best friends (Questions 3–35 to 3–37). The total possible score of each respondent ranges between 0 and 9 and was arrived at by totaling the scores of each occupation (for the substantive justification of the index, see p. 198):

Friend's occupations:	white collar:	0
	unskilled or service worker:	1
	skilled worker or farmer:	2
	semi-skilled worker:	3

(Those who gave the name of fewer than three friends received a score of 0 for each missing friend. In the case of those who mentioned at least three friends but were able to identity the occupation of only two of them, the nonclassified occupation was given the mean score of the other two occupations.)

12. INDEX OF ACTIVITY IN OCCUPATIONAL ORGANIZATIONS

This index is based on Questions 3–24 and 3–25. Those who said that they attended the meetings of their organization "rather regularly" or (if members of a labor union) that they were "very interested" in their union were classified as active members; all others were classified as nonactive members.

13. INDEX OF MEMBERSHIP IN VOLUNTARY ASSOCIATIONS

This index is based on Questions 3–26 and 3–28. Those who answered "no" to both questions received a score of 0, those who answered "yes" to only one question, a score of 1 and those who answered "yes" to both questions, a score of 2.

14. INDEX OF RELIGIOUS INVOLVEMENT

This index is based on Questions 3–40 and 3–41 and was derived as follows:

Q. 3–40	Q. 3–41	SCORES:
Go to church:	Pray God:	
More than once a week	Almost every day	1
"	Less than every day	2
Once a week	Almost every day	3
"	A few times a week only	4
"	Less than that	5
Less than once a week	Almost every day	6
"	Less than every day	7

The "lukewarms" are those who received a score between 4 and 7; the "ritualists" are those who received a score of 3; the "devouts" are those who received a score of 1 or 2.

Index